U.S. Government
for Catholic Students

by Dr. Paul Clark

Seton Press
Front Royal, VA

About the Author

Paul Clark earned his B.A. from Christendom College and both an M.A. and a Ph.D from The Catholic University of America. Clark also obtained a law degree from the University of Chicago. After Law School Clark clerked for the Supreme Court of Alaska and the Ninth Circuit Court of Appeals. He is also combat veteran of Desert Storm where he served in the U.S. Marines. He has been teaching Philosophy and Political Science at the college level for ten years.

Cover Information

Front Cover: *Lansdowne Portrait of George Washington* by Gilbert Stuart

Back Cover: St. Ignatius Church in Charles County, Maryland. This church is at the site of an original Jesuit mission dating from 1641 and is the oldest active Catholic parish in the original thirteen colonies.

© 2025 Seton Press
All rights reserved.
Printed in the United States of America.

Seton Press
1350 Progress Drive
Front Royal, VA 22630

Phone: (540) 636-9990
Email: info@setonpress.com
Web: www.setonpress.com

ISBN: 978-1-60704-221-1

Table of Contents

Introduction 1

Chapter 1: The Purpose of Government 2

Chapter 2: Roman Republic to American Independence 22

Chapter 3: Independence and Self-Government 52

Chapter 4: The Legislative Branch: Congress 80

Chapter 5: The Executive Branch: The President 116

Chapter 6: The Judicial Branch 148

Chapter 7: The Bill of Rights 176

Chapter 8: Federalism and Subsidiarity 211

Chapter 9: State and Local Government 238

Image Attributions 270

Index 271

St. Thomas More, Patron Saint of Politicians

Introduction

This textbook is unusual for a few reasons. First, it examines American government from a Catholic perspective, something that is not much done today. This means that this book evaluates government in general, and America's government specifically, in light of Catholic morality and social teachings. It heavily relies on the teachings of St. Thomas Aquinas and his philosophy of Law and Government, a rarity these days. This means that the way government functions in its laws and policies is gauged by the effect they have on the Church and society from a focus of Catholic moral and social teachings. Thus, the legalization of abortion, or the institution of slavery, or new definitions of "family" can only be seen as inherently immoral. While some may see such polices as morally neutral, the Catholic Church does not. Thus, while this is not a theology textbook, we must remember that the Church's moral and the social teachings can never be detached from good government. In other words, politicians cannot honestly claim to be "personally opposed" to evil, yet support it as much as possible.

Second, this book addresses the Framer's Intent in creating America's government. While this has been a traditional means of understanding our government, it has become somewhat less accepted by many who see the Constitution as systemically flawed, racist, and hopelessly outdated. However, in this textbook, we examine what the authors of the Constitution and the other laws that govern our nation meant when they created those laws. To that end, the book contains numerous sections of The Federalist Papers, which most people still consider the finest explanation of the U.S. Constitution ever written. Students will also read sections of Supreme Court opinions which have shaped America's government from *Marbury v. Madison* to more current decisions.

Finally, this text will trace the development and growth of government, often contrasting what the Founders intended with the way things actually are today and how they became that way. It will discuss the branches of the Federal government and their roles and duties. It will address the states and the powers and duties they possess. Also, it will discuss the Amendments and the rights that every American has. Knowing one's rights is vitally important in today's society as government on all levels becomes ever more powerful.

CHAPTER ONE
THE PURPOSE OF GOVERNMENT

GOD CREATED HUMANS TO BE SOCIAL ANIMALS

"It is not good for man to be alone." Genesis 2:18.

God created mankind as social animals.[1] As St. Thomas Aquinas (1225-1274) wrote in the 13th Century: "It is natural for man, more than for any other animal, to be a social and political animal, to live in a group."[2] Every human is born physically and mentally helpless. Even if a human infant miraculously survived in isolation from other humans and reached physical maturity, that person would not be able to speak — among other basic "human" qualities. Such a person would seem more like a beast than a human. Without speech, the ability to reason would be severely limited. Such a person would lack love, friendship, human companionship, and religion.

God created mankind to know, love, and serve Him in this world and to be with Him and the Community of Saints in Heaven.[3] Moreover, God created humans in His image and likeness, and God is a Trinity or community of persons. So physically, emotionally, intellectually, and spiritually, God designed us to exist as part of a community.

God might have designed us differently. God created angels to be self-sufficient, invulnerable, and with infused knowledge. "If men were angels,

St. Thomas Aquinas

---

[1] Aristotle, Pol. I.
[2] Aquinas, On Kingship.
[3] Catechism of the Catholic Church section 1

The Month of September, from the Grimani Breviary

Medieval workers bring in the harvest under the supervision of their lord.

no government would be necessary."[4] Humans are not angels, so we depend upon each other and upon the greater community not just to survive, but to flourish, that is, to reach our full potential as intellectual and spiritual animals made in the image and likeness of God.

As creatures made in the image and likeness of God, we have reason and free will. There are other social animals in the world. Ants and bees, for example, work together. Ants and bees do not have free will. Chemicals guide them to behave in certain ways. Ants and bees are biologically compelled to cooperate for the well-being of the hive. Humans, also, need to cooperate to survive and flourish. Yet, "reasonable minds can differ." To use a simple example: should we drive on the left side of the road or the right? Neither option is intrinsically better than the other. In a society that has roads and vehicles, we need some sort of mechanism, or "authority," for determining which side of the road to use.

In every human community there will be legitimate differences of opinion about how to cooperate, where no option is inherently better than the alternatives. In every community, even with the best of intentions, there will be accidents and injuries and disagreements about how to allocate scarce resources. Sadly, in every community, there will be people who deliberately harm others. Every society needs some sort of social organization and mechanism for making decisions to deal with these problems and allow a group of unique, rational individuals to cooperate and live in harmony with each other. As Pope St. John XXIII (1881-1963) wrote in *Pacem in Terris* quoting St. John Chrysostom (347-407):

> God has created men social by nature, and a society cannot "hold together unless someone is in command to give effective direction and unity of purpose. Hence every civilized community must have a ruling authority, and this authority, no less than society itself, has its source in nature, and consequently has God for its author."[5]

Humans form all sorts of different communities for a variety of purposes, but the two most basic and universal societies are the family and the state.

HUMAN NATURE IS EMPIRICALLY VERIFIABLE.

The above discussion assumes that humans, like ants and bees, have a basic, unchanging nature. There have been a number of ideologies that have insisted either that there is no such thing as "human nature," or if there is "human nature" it is malleable. There remain some "utopian" ideologies that insist that there is no fixed human nature. However, cultural anthropologists now accept

---
[4]James Madison & Alexander Hamilton, Federalist 51
[5]*Pacem in Terris*, sec. 46.

that all humans and human societies, since time immemorial, share a wide variety of common traits and practices.

Some of these traits are obvious and undisputed. For example, humans smile when they are happy. But the common behavior of humans goes well beyond mere physical responses such as smiling. Other than the rare sociopath, all humans have a sense of right and wrong. Again, even secular anthropologists have established that historically, virtually all human societies have shared some fundamental behavioral patterns. Some of the basic features common to all human societies from the beginning of time until the late 20th century, include marriage (the enduring union of a man and a woman), the family, the father as the recognized head of the family, and the fact that people care more for their own children than they do for strangers. Every language ever encountered has a distinct word for "mother" and "father." In other words, there is no language in the history of the human race that simply has a generic word "parent" without a sex-specific "mother" and "father." This fact strongly implies that humans have always considered the roles of mothers and fathers to be distinct, and based on natural differences. Accordingly, secular anthropologists agree that human nature is real and empirically verifiable.[6] One of the most notorious modern atheists, Steven Pinker, has argued that human nature is real, verifiable, and includes a basic sense of right and wrong.[7]

Of course, Aristotle (384-322 BC), Augustine (354-430) and Aquinas all said the same thing, but we now possess even more evidence to support this view. Theists and atheists disagree about what to make of human nature. Atheists assume that human nature is simply a result of random

Aristotle (384 B.C.-322 B.C.)

St. Augustine (354 AD-430 AD)

evolution. Christians know that human nature was designed by God. Atheists acknowledge that religiosity is a basic part of human nature but insist that religiosity is purely a result of random chance, because thousands of years ago religious people had a survival advantage over non-religious people. However, St. Augustine points out that humans are fundamentally spiritual because God made them this way. Humans care more for their own children than for strangers, and humans ought to care more for their own children, because God made humans this way.

IF HUMAN NATURE IS EMPIRICALLY VERIFIABLE, SO IS NATURAL LAW.

By observing and reflecting upon human nature, and to some extent the rest of the natural world, humans are able to discern God's plan for us. **The Natural Law is the set of moral principles that are discernible from nature and flow from human nature as created by God.** We can use the terms "Moral law," "Natural Law," and "Natural Moral Law" interchangeably, but it should be noted that some theorists refer to a "Moral Law" as a law that is not based in nature but in something else.

The Natural Law is not self-evident. We must use our reason to discern the Natural Law. However, some principles of the Natural Law are so obvious that there is rarely disagreement. For

---

[6] Donald E. Brown, *Human Universals and Their Implications* (2000).
[7] Steven Pinker, *The Blank Slate* (2002).

example, no one really disagrees that humans should not kill each other without some serious justification. Other requirements of the Natural Law require more reflection.

Some moral theories, like Utilitarianism, argue that all humans should be treated equally and humans should NOT give preference to their own children over any other human in the world. Natural Law theory rejects the view that humans are interchangeable units of utility. A Natural Lawyer would survey humans and note that giving preference to one's own children is a universally embraced practice. Humans *by nature* have a built-in desire to protect their children. We can even see this in other non-human animals. Other species of mammals also protect their offspring. If we reflect rationally on the issue, we recognize that infants rely much more on their parents than on strangers, and parents have the knowledge and emotional commitment to help their own children far more than strangers. While more can be said on this issue, the point is that the Moral Law is not self-evident. It should also be noted that this issue of giving preference to certain people will arise again in the responsibilities of government. Some people argue that governments should not prioritize their own citizens, but should treat every human as equally important. Of course, it should be obvious that the Natural Law applies to all human actions whether the person is a private citizen or a president.

We call these moral principles that govern human behavior "Law," because 1) God implanted in us a basic sense of morality; 2) God gave us reason and capacity to discern right from wrong; and 3) because God designed humans this way, it is appropriate to speak of God as The Lawgiver. Moral precepts of the Natural Law are not just good advice that humans are free to accept or reject. Violations of the Natural Law are violations of our own nature as rational, social animals, and a rejection of God's plan for our happiness and flourishing.

The most basic precepts of the Natural Law are unchanging, but applications of the Natural Law

will depend upon variables, so the Natural Law may be applied in different ways. According to the Natural Law, taking another's property with the intent to deprive the owner of the property permanently without compensation, is always wrong. However, the seriousness of theft will vary considerably depending on the circumstances. Moreover, questions regarding the punishment of theft may not have a clear answer: a fine, imprisonment, or corporal punishment might each be a reasonable response.

In other words, there are some basic commands of the Natural Law that are unchanging, such as, do not murder, do not steal. However, within the confines of the Natural Law, there is often latitude or discretion. The Natural Law governs all human actions, whether as individuals, members of a family, members of a society, or leaders of a country.

Justice is the part of the Natural Law that governs our interactions with other people. We sometimes use the word "justice" interchangeably with "morality." For example, it could be said that sloth or gluttony are "unjust" insofar as the Natural Law forbids gluttony and sloth. However, traditional philosophers, like Aristotle and Aquinas, say that we should use the term "justice" only to apply to our responsibilities towards other people. Aquinas defines *justice* simply as *giving to each person what is his due.*

THE FAMILY

The most fundamental human society is the family. God, Who is the Creator of the natural world, implanted in humans a basic desire to reproduce. In chapter 1 of Genesis, God's very first command to humans is: "Be fruitful and multiply." (Gen 1:28). Thus, the union of male and female is not only essential to the survival of the species but part of God's plan for humankind. Again, because human infants are so helpless, support of the parents is also essential to the survival of mankind. Because of this, the union of a man and woman for the purpose of procreation should be lasting. This lasting relationship is called marriage. A marriage is not the same thing as a family, but marriage is one of the building blocks of family.

Aristotle said marriage is a partnership between a man and a woman. In a partnership, it is optimal if both partners agree; however, when a husband and wife cannot agree, the husband has the final say, according to Aristotle and Aquinas. St. Paul concurs in his epistle to the Ephesians. (Eph 5:22). In every association, there must be some final means of resolving disputes or the association breaks down. In a business partnership, when two partners cannot agree, sometimes the only solution is for the partnership to dissolve; however, a marriage is too important to be dissolved when there is disagreement. The evidence is that all societies, since mankind's earliest days until quite recently, regarded the father of a family as the highest authority. Even those who attack "patriarchy" as evil, acknowledge that "patriarchy" in the family has been the historic norm. This is why some ideologies advocate that the government should intervene in the family to destroy patriarchy.

A mother alone, who has just given birth, is often not in a strong position to care for an infant by herself. This was even more true historically before the advent of labor-saving devices. Even today, children who live in a house without a father have a significantly lower life expectancy and are far more likely to suffer from physical and mental illness. It takes years to support and educate a child, so it is natural for parents to remain together to educate and raise children. God has implanted in humans a fundamental desire to protect and love their children, and grandchildren. Children have a natural "attachment mechanism" whereby they tend to "cling to" their parents. These basic drives are built into the human genetic code. This is why the relationship between parents and children is the strongest and longest lasting of human relationships. Of course, people have free will and are able to abandon their children, but this is profoundly contrary to nature.

Historically, raising a child alone was difficult and larger families were more common. Most couples had many children, who often lived with, or in close proximity to, their parents and siblings. Grandparents, aunts, uncles, and older siblings typically helped to raise children. Regardless of the size of the family, the basic idea is the same: a family is a group of people related by blood.[8]

---

[8]There are also families, or relationships, such as adoption, by which people not related by blood are brought into the family and considered natural offspring.

Marriage of the Virgin, Pietro Perugino
St. Joseph and the Blessed Virgin Mary are married.

Scene of a Farming Family, Adolf Müller-Grantzow.

THE COMMUNITY AND THE STATE

It should be noted that the English word "state" is sometimes used to apply to a political community and sometimes to the government of a political community, and sometimes to the community and the government taken together. Of course, a political community is not the same thing as the government. There can be a political revolution which results in an entirely new government, but the community itself continues. It should also be noted that there can be changes in government, short of revolution, where there is still basic continuity, for example, when a new ruler is inaugurated. So, the political community, the government, and the regime that controls the government, are different things.

Aristotle tells us that "the family is the association established by nature for the supply of men's everyday needs."[9] Nevertheless, the family is not self-sufficient, and a larger community is necessary for full human flourishing. For one thing, a community must be large enough to protect itself against criminals and invaders. Only a community composed of thousands of people will have the variety needed to allow for leisure and reflection. Therefore, if the family is natural, so too is the city or political community because both stem from human nature and serve basic human needs. The family provides the most basic everyday needs while the city provides more remote needs that are necessary for humans to reach their full potential.

A full-blown city contains a large variety of experts and artisans who are able to specialize in their craft. A city has professional lawyers, plumbers, carpenters, computer repairmen, cyber-security experts, and a thousand other professions. Specialization of this type greatly increases human prosperity, allows for leisure time, and the emergence of artists, poets, actors, historians, and philosophers. Aristotle and Aquinas agree that humans need both physical and mental periods of relaxation, such as reading, watching plays, or playing games.[10] This is why God ordained that at least one day a week be set aside for rest and relaxation.

---

[9] Aristotle. Pol. Bk 1 Ch 2.
[10] Summa Th. II-II, Q. 168.

For a large number of artisans and artists to work together in harmony, a medium of exchange is needed, that is, money. When people can enter into contracts they trust will be enforced, then prosperity and efficiency can be increased even further. Coining money and enforcing contracts are two things governments have done for thousands of years to increase prosperity. The main benefit of prosperity is not physical, but rather intellectual and spiritual. People who must spend every waking hour just trying to survive will not have time to develop their minds, pray, and contemplate God.

Basic human needs are not just physical, but emotional, intellectual, and spiritual. Aristotle says all humans by nature desire to understand the world around them and its origins.[11] It is only when humans possess enough leisure beyond mere survival that they have the opportunity to contemplate the divine. The family is imperfect and limited. A family in isolation can no more achieve perfection and fulfillment for its members than could an individual in isolation. This is why, while the family is the most basic unit of society, the state is, in a sense, even more fundamental to human success. As St. Thomas writes commenting on Aristotle:

> Man is by nature a social animal, needing many things to live which he cannot get for himself if alone, he naturally is a part of a group that furnishes him help to live well. He needs this help for two reasons. First, to have what is necessary for life, without which he cannot live the present life; and for this, man is helped by the domestic group of which he is a part. For every man is indebted to his parents for his generation and his nourishment and instruction. Likewise, individuals, who are members of the family, help one another to procure the necessities of life. In another way, man receives help from the group of which he is a part, to have a perfect sufficiency for life; namely, that man may not only live but live well, having everything sufficient for living; and in this way man is helped by the civic group, of which he is a member, not only in regard to bodily needs—as certainly in the state there are many crafts which a single household cannot provide—but also in regard to right conduct, inasmuch as public authority restrains with fear of punishment delinquent young men whom paternal admonition is not able to correct.[12]

Thus, the family is able to exist as a society with minimal coercion given the affection and convergence of interest found in small groups of people related by blood. But when we consider a civil community composed of thousands of members, a more powerful form of control is inevitable and necessary.

The purpose of both paternal authority and civil authority is to ensure virtue and justice within their proper spheres. The distinction between paternal or private authority and civil authority is that civil authority possesses the power to enforce its authority by coercion. Families have limited power and authority to enforce their demands. Private parties can only admonish and encourage, but the state can compel compliance with the law.

According to Natural Law, a legitimate government has authority to coerce and punish its citizens to achieve the Common Good. A government is legitimate when it is based on the customs, traditions, and laws of the society and exercises authority in accord with Natural Law. Because all civil authority is derived from the Natural Law, all human law must conform to the Natural Law. Any edict contrary to Natural Law, or contrary to the Common Good, is not law but a perversion of law.[13] Thus, the Natural Law gives human government authority but limits that authority.

When St. Thomas speaks of the "civic group" which allows people to live well, the specialization of labor is an important part, but the existence of a public authority is also a necessary part. Historians have never, in the history of the human race,

---

[11] Metaphysics book 1.
[12] Commentary on Nic. Ethic. Lecture 1.
[13] Catechism, sec 2242.

encountered any society of thousands of people without some form of recognizable government. To be sure, forms of government vary. In medieval Iceland there was no permanent executive, rather all the citizens would periodically gather and any citizen who had a complaint against another person would ask the community to resolve the dispute. Nevertheless, this was still a recognizable form of government.

Civil society and human law are basic supports for morality and virtue. As St. Thomas further explains in his Treatise on Law:

> As to those young people who are inclined to acts of virtue, by their good natural disposition, or by custom, or rather by the gift of God, paternal training suffices, which is by admonitions. But since some are found to be depraved, and prone to vice, and not easily amenable to words, it was necessary for such to be restrained from evil by force and fear, in order that, at least, they might desist from evil-doing, and leave others in peace, and that they themselves, by being habituated in this way, might be brought to do willingly what hitherto they did from fear, and thus become virtuous. Now this kind of training, which compels through fear of punishment, is the discipline of laws. Therefore, in order that man might have peace and virtue, it was necessary for laws to be framed.[14]

Ultimately, the purpose of the law is to encourage citizens to be virtuous. Of course, humans can only be saved through the gift of God's grace, but virtue makes us more worthy and able to accept God's grace. Aristotle wrote that the purpose of the law of a community is to lead its own citizens to virtue not to worry about whether citizens of other states are virtuous. This is because law is always made by and for a particular community. St. Thomas defines law as "an ordinance of reason for the common good, made by the community as a whole or by him who has care of the community, and promulgated."

Law is "an ordinance of reason" or an act of judgment, because human law is an attempt to use human reason to apply the unchanging principles of Natural Law to particular contingent circumstances that exist here and now. This view of law is contrary to a theory called **legal voluntarism**. Legal voluntarism is the theory that law is whatever the rulers arbitrarily decide it is. Therefore, law is not derived from Natural Law, or anything else, but the will of the sovereign.

Law and government do not exist simply to prevent negative outcomes, that is, the law is not merely to halt injustice; rather law seeks to *positively* encourage virtue and overall human success. This idea that the purpose of government is to encourage virtue and justice has been the basic theme of all traditional philosophers since Plato (c.

---

[14] Summa Theologica, I-II q. 95 art 1

427-347 B.C.). In book 1 of *The Republic*, Plato argues that a society lacking justice would collapse into anarchy. St. Augustine in his great work *The City of God* wrote that a government that lacks justice is nothing more than a band of criminals. American founding father James Madison (1751-1836) wrote that: "Justice is the end of government. It is the end of civil society."[15]

Opposed to the traditional view, that the purpose of government is to encourage virtue, is **political liberalism**. Political liberalism is an ideology that asserts that law and government should be neutral with respect to ideas about justice or virtue. According to political liberalism, law and government policy should be based on non-moral grounds, such as purely economic considerations or upon whatever the majority agree (a form of voluntarism).

According to St. Thomas, however, the Natural Law places strict limitations on the power of government, regardless of what the ruler or the population desires. The initiative and creativity of individuals adds much to prosperity and the common good. Therefore, government must not restrict liberty to such an extent that it stifles individual initiative and creativity.

One of the most important limits on civil authority is the **principle of subsidiarity**:

> A community of a higher order should not interfere in the internal life of a community of a lower order, depriving the latter of its functions, but rather [the State] should support it in case of need.[16]

The *Catechism* later adds:

> The family is the original cell of social life. … The family must be helped and defended by appropriate social measures. Where families cannot fulfill their responsibilities, other social bodies have the duty of helping them and of supporting the institution of the family. Following the principle of subsidiarity, larger communities should take care not to usurp the family's prerogatives or interfere in its life.[17]

The Natural Law requires that government support the family rather than usurp, destroy,

James Madison

or re-define it. The state is necessary for human prosperity but it is also the greatest danger to human flourishing. As George Washington (1732-1799) reputedly said, government "like fire, is a dangerous servant and a fearful master." Until quite recently, humans depended on fire to survive, and fire allowed humans to accomplish many marvelous things, such as craft metal tools and make steel. Washington's point was that just as we needed fire, we also need government; but both must be kept within strict limits. Fire in a furnace is wonderful, but if it escapes its confinement, fire can destroy the whole house or an entire city.

Throughout history, rulers have overstepped the authority granted to them by the Natural Law. This point was illustrated by the Athenian playwrite Sophocles in his play *Antigone* (c. 441 B.C.). When the ruler of the city orders that Antigone not bury her brother, she disobeys the command and explains to the ruler that:

> I deemed not that thy decrees were of such force, that a mortal could override the unwritten and unfailing statutes of heaven. For their life is not of to-day or yesterday, but from all time, and no man knows when they were first put forth.

This issue with rulers overstepping their legitimate authority can also be found in sacred

---
[15] Federalist 51.
[16] Catechism of Catholic Church para 1883.
[17] Catechism para 2207-2209.

Antigone is arrested for disobeying a tyrant's command and burying her dead brother.

scripture. In the First Book of Samuel, the Jews decided that they wanted a more powerful government to replace the decentralized system that had been in place since the death of Joshua. God, through the prophet Samuel, warns the people about the dangers of government:

> These will be the ways of the king who will reign over you: he will take your sons and appoint them to his chariots and to be his horsemen to run before his chariots; and he will appoint for himself commanders of thousands and commanders of fifties, and some to plow his ground and to reap his harvest, and make his implements of war and the equipment of his chariots. He will take your daughters to be perfumers and cooks and bakers. He will take the best of your fields and vineyards and olive orchards and give them to his courtiers. When that day comes, you will cry out for relief from the king you have chosen, but the Lord will not answer you in that day.

As the great 19th century Catholic theorist Lord Acton (1832-1902) famously said, "Power tends to corrupt, and absolute power corrupts absolutely." In *City of God*, St. Augustine says that as a result of original sin, humans are tempted to dominate others, what he called the *libido dominandi* ("the desire for dominating"). This desire to dominate applies not just to individuals but to states. Augustine said that history shows that states are constantly trying to dominate other states. So political rulers are tempted to illegitimately dominate their own citizens and even the citizens of other states. Like fire, power feeds power. The more powerful a person or group is, the easier it is to acquire more power. St. Thomas points out that the stronger a human desire is, the more checks and limitations must be placed upon it.[18]

A portrait of Hammurabi is located in the U.S. Capitol

Accordingly, one of history's great dilemmas involves structuring a government so it has power to do the good things that people need, but prevents rulers from going beyond the limits established by Natural Law. For example, one of the most ancient legal codes, the Code of Hammurabi (composed circa 1750 B.C.) provided severe penalties for judges who failed to do justice or those who made false allegations against others in court.

Because the main role of government is to encourage virtue, it might seem that government should have complete control over every aspect of people's lives. That is not the case. Aquinas explains:

> Now human law is framed for a number of human beings, the majority of whom are not perfect in virtue. Wherefore human laws do not forbid all vices, from which the virtuous abstain, but only the more grievous vices, from which it is possible for the majority to abstain; and chiefly those that are to the hurt of others, without the prohibition of which

[18] Summa Th. I-II Q.151.

human society could not be maintained: thus, human law prohibits murder, theft and such like.[19]

Government should encourage virtues such as generosity and religiosity. However, charitable giving must be voluntary. Thus, government can only nurture generosity, e.g. by giving tax credits for charitable contributions, but not mandate it. The same is true for religion. Religion must be freely chosen. Government should help people to be religious but cannot force them to practice a religion.

THE COMMON GOOD

One of the core concepts of Catholic Social teaching which stems directly from Natural Law is the common good. The Catechism states unequivocally: "It is the role of the state to defend and promote the common good of civil society, its citizens, and intermediate bodies."[20] The idea of the common good stems from the recognition that all humans share common human nature, so certain things exist which are good for all of us. Ideologies such as political Liberalism and Utilitarianism (the theory that we should maximize individual pleasure), either deny that human nature is knowable, or reduce human good to the least common denominators: pleasure and pain. For example, Utilitarianism assumes that there will be winners and losers. For the Utilitarian, the just society is one that maximizes the total aggregate amount of human happiness. In other words, the pleasure of the "winners" outweighs the pain of societies' "losers."

The common good, however, includes the basic goods that benefit every single person in the society without exception. For example, the justice of a criminal penalty does not only benefit the majority, the criminals also benefit from the opportunity to make restitution for their crime. Therefore, the common good is the collection of basic goods in **which all members of a society are able to share without diminution.**

We can speak of "The Common good" as a singular thing, but "the common good" can also be viewed under a variety of different common goods. The most basic common good is peace, "that is, the stability and security of a just order."[21] In the last quote from St. Thomas, he says that the most basic law "prohibits murder, theft, and such." Thus, protecting life and

Pope St. John Paul II

property are two of the most basic requirements of the common good.

Pope St. John Paul II (1920-2005) points out that a government's failure to protect all innocent life "is what most directly conflicts with the possibility of achieving the common good."[22] The Pope further explains:

> The State is no longer the "common home" where all can live together on the basis of principles of fundamental equality, but is transformed into a tyrant State, which arrogates to itself the right to dispose of the life of the weakest and most defenseless members,

---

[19] Summa Th. I-II, Q. 96.
[20] Catechism sec. 1910.
[21] Catechism, sec 1910.
[22] Evangelium Vitae, sec 72.

from the unborn child to the elderly, in the name of a public interest which is really nothing but the interest of one part.[23]

Pope St. John Paul goes so far as to say that a government that fails to protect its most innocent and defenseless members "would not only fail in its duty; its decrees would be wholly lacking in binding force."[24] This statement is a bit ambiguous. It might be interpreted narrowly as only saying decrees that purport to authorize killing of innocents are "lacking in binding force." However, the Pope seems to say that failure of a government to protect its most vulnerable and innocent member is such a grave dereliction of duty that all of "its decrees would be wholly lacking in binding force." That is, the government itself wholly lacks legitimacy. This conforms with the comment that follows a paragraph later that government's failure to protect all innocent life "is what most directly conflicts with the possibility of achieving the common good." [25]

Next to protection of life, the next most essential role of government is protection of property. If property is not secure, then peace and security is impossible. A society could not exist if anyone could simply take whatever they wanted. St. Thomas quoting Aristotle writes "many states have been ruined through want of regulations in the matter of possessions."[26] There is nothing wrong with some communal property. In the middle ages, common areas existed, which citizens shared, where they could plant crops or graze cattle. However, common property is dangerous. Aristotle was the first to point out what has been called **the tragedy of the commons**, when he wrote: "That which is common to the greatest number gets the least amount of care. Men pay most attention to what is their own: they care less for what is common." Accordingly, private property, and laws protecting private property, are essential to the common good.[27]

A hammer and sickle, the symbol of communism

Communism is the ideology which teaches that there should be no private property, but that all property will be owned by the government or "held in common." Doctors of the Church and a long line of Popes have consistently condemned communism as contrary to Natural Law and a doctrine that is so pernicious that it would lead to "the complete destruction of all laws, government, property, and even of human society itself."[28] Pope Leo XIII (1810-1903) in his great encyclical *Rerum novarum* wrote: "The first and most fundamental principle, therefore, if one would undertake to alleviate the condition of the masses, must be the inviolability of private property."[29]

One point that often causes confusion is that while private property, and laws protecting private property, are an essential part of the common good, *specific items of property* cannot be designated as the common good. Remember "common good" uses the word good in terms of "good and bad" never in terms of "goods and services." Do not confuse "Common Good" with "public good." The term "public good" refers to a commodity or service that is made available to all members of society. So, public property, such as a road or a park, might be conducive to the public good, but public property is not a common good in the strict sense.

---

[23]Evangelium Vitae, sec 20.
[24]Evangelium Vitae, sec 71 (quoting Pacem in Terris)
[25]Suma Th. I-II, Q 105. A 1. (citing Pol. book 2)
[26]Suma Th. I-II, Q 105. A 1. (citing Pol. book 2)
[27]The tragedy of the commons led to the Enclosure Movement in England during which fields were enclosed for the use of individual farmers.
[28]Qui Pluribus ("On Faith and Religion") Pope Bl. Pius IX – 1846 para 16.
[29]Rerum Novarum ("On the Conditions of Labor") Pope Leo XII – 1891 para 15.

Other common goods include community health and morals. All people strive to be healthy, so laws against pollution, such as protecting the community's drinking water, are ordained to the common good. Similarly, laws to prevent the spread of disease would be ordained to the common good. Recently, some Catholic scholars have argued that *health care* itself ought to be considered a "common good." However, because healthcare is a limited resource, it should probably be analyzed under the aspect of a public good not a common good. The most basic common goods that make up "The Common Good" include freedom, peace, justice, and the protection of life, property, health, and morals.

THE CHURCH

The other community ordained by God for the fulfillment of basic human needs is the Church. While the family and the state are ordained by Natural Law, the Church is established by Divine Positive Law, that is, by God's direct command. Of course, piety and worship of God are required by the Natural Law. One reason we know piety is part of the Natural Law is that throughout history, humans have been religious. Archaeological evidence from thousands of years ago shows that humans buried their dead using religious ceremonies. Pagan philosophers such as Plato, Aristotle, and Cicero (106-43 B.C.) all agree that we owe the Creator honor and worship.

Accordingly, worship of God is one of the most fundamental precepts of the Natural Law. Prior to Divine Revelation, humans had to worship God as best they could and were free to worship God in a variety of ways. However, Christ organized a Church and gave His apostles, and their successors, authority to teach, sanctify, and rule. In Matthew 28:18-20, Jesus tells His disciples:

> "All authority in heaven and on earth has been given to me. Go therefore and make disciples of all nations, baptizing them in the name of the Father and of the Son and of the Holy Spirit, teaching them to observe all that I have commanded you."

Thus, by direct divine command and authority the Church is to make disciples of all nations, teaching them to observe the divine law. By this Great Commission, the Apostles and their successors were to teach authoritatively and to "make disciples" of entire nations, not just individuals. Of course, nations are composed of individuals who are subject to divine law.

FORMS OF GOVERNMENT

St. Thomas and the other doctors of the Church agree that the Natural Law permits many different forms of government. In other words, communities are free to adopt a form of government that works for that community. While there are some forms of government the Church has condemned, there is no form upon which the Church has insisted.

Traditionally, government is divided into three basic types: rule by a single person, rule by a small group of people, and rule by a large group of people. A system where one person is empowered to make all decisions without the need for approval from anyone else, is called an **autocracy**, literally to rule by oneself. An autocracy where the sovereign rules for the common good is called a **monarchy**, but a **tyranny** or a **dictatorship** when the sovereign rules for selfish reasons. Rule of the few is called an **aristocracy**, which literally means rule of the best, and an **oligarchy**, when the few rule for their own self-interest. Oligarchy is also often called **kleptocracy**, which means rule of thieves, because those in power rule for their own personal benefit not that of the people as a whole. Rule by a large number of people is called a **democracy** (literally, rule of the people) when everyone is directly involved in the government, or a **republic**, when the people elect representatives to run the government on their behalf. Democracies and republics can be either good or bad, depending on the people or their elected representatives. Today, "democracy" generally applies to any system that relies on "majority rule." Although not strictly the opposite of democracy, **anarchy**, which literally means "without rulers," represents a lack of government. Anarchists claim to rely on the innate goodness of men and women, who according to them, do not need government and laws to attain self-fulfillment. Throughout history, anarchy has always led to chaos and misery, not fulfillment.

In addition to these forms of government, various hybrids or mixed governments exist that combine aspects of them. St. Thomas says that monarchy is the best form of government so long as the monarch is virtuous, wise, and benevolent. Monarchy is very efficient because it allows decisions to be made quickly, especially in the event of an emergency. On the other hand, tyranny is the worst form of government because there are few legal checks on the power of a tyrant.

Moreover, autocracies can take various forms. For example, one of the earliest autocracies occurred in Biblical times when the Israelites were directly ruled by God. Although this was unusual, the Israelite government was a **theocracy**, which means "God rules." Today, many Islamic nations have autocratic rulers who are religious leaders as well. These nations are theocracies, because their leaders follow God's commands. There are many Islamic "republics" which are also theocracies because they have elected religious leaders to positions in the government.

Today, most people believe that a democracy or a republic is the best form of government. However, historically, that has not been the case. Philosophers since Plato have distrusted democracy. First, large groups of people cannot actually rule, but large groups are particularly vulnerable to demagogues who claim to rule in the name of the people but are, in fact, tyrants. Second, because the number of poor people will always outnumber the rich, the constant temptation in a state that has majority rule, will be for the poor to use their

King David was a monarch who ruled in a theocracy.

vote to confiscate the wealth of the most successful members of society. This is why Aristotle argues that rule of the many (democracy) is only workable in a society that possesses a large middle class.[30] Finally, democracies tend towards mediocrity and licentiousness because popular votes tend to lower the standards of a society to achieve agreement among a large number of people.

Because the dangers of tyranny are so great, St. Thomas, following Aristotle, argues that, in practice, a mixed government is best:

> Two points are to be observed concerning the right ordering of rulers in a state or nation. One is that all should take some share in the government: for this form of constitution ensures peace among the people, commends itself to all, and is most enduring, as stated in Polit. ii, 6. The other point is to be observed in respect of the kinds of government, or the different ways in which the constitutions are established. For whereas these differ in kind, as the Philosopher states (Polit. iii, 5), nevertheless the first place is held by the "kingdom," where the power of government is vested in one; and "aristocracy," which signifies government by the best, where the power of government is vested in a few. Accordingly, the best form of government is in a state or kingdom, where one is given the power to preside over all; while under him are others having governing powers: and yet a government of this kind is shared by all, both because all are eligible to govern, and because the rules are chosen by all. For this is the best form of polity, being partly kingdom, since there is one at the head of all; partly aristocracy, in so far as a number of persons are set in authority; partly democracy, i.e. government by the people, in so far as the rulers can be chosen from the people, and the people are able to choose their rulers.[31]

Because government is so dangerous when left unchecked, all forms of government contain potential dangers. A mixed government attempts to mitigate these dangers by requiring consent from a variety of different people and groups. For example, the king, the nobility, and the common people all must agree on any new laws. No major thinker in history has ever thought that pure majority rule is a good idea. No serious political scientist thinks that law should be whatever the majority happens to approve of at any given time. Political philosophers from Plato to Madison have been concerned about the tyranny of the majority. A constitution, or a basic law, is, in a sense, *anti-democratic* because it places limits on the majority.

AUTHORITY AND LEGITIMACY

Closely related to the issue of forms of government are the issues of legitimacy and authority. Even if it is obvious that communities need some government, how does one determine *who* should govern? Perhaps even more important is the problem of *authority*. How do some people, or groups of people, possess the authority to tell the rest of their community how to behave?

The theory of government discussed in this chapter is known as the **corporate** or the **organic theory of government**. Plato wrote in *The Republic* book 2 that "The State is Man writ large." This simple phrase reflects two basic truths. First, the state and government are a basic outgrowth of human nature. Second, the state is an organic unity analogous to an individual organism. St. Paul uses this same terminology to describe the Church: "There are many parts, but one body. The eye cannot say to the hand, "I don't need you!" And the head cannot say to the feet, "I don't need you!" (I Cor. 12:21)

Robert Bellarmine developed the traditional doctrine of authority in opposition to modern ideologies that denied the existence of natural authority. He argues that a political community is more than the sum of its parts. In other words, a political community is not just a collection of individuals. For example, a pile of sand is nothing more than a collection of individual grains of sand, but a living organism is an organic unity and essentially one thing.

Imagine that 100,000 people assemble in a stadium for some sporting event, and while

---

[30] Arist. Pol. bk 4.
[31] Summa Th. I-II, Q. 105.

Charlemagne is crowned by Pope Leo III. Throughout the history of the Church, popes have often provided an important balance to the power of monarchs.

waiting for the event to begin, they take a vote and purport to pass a law. These 100,000 have no authority to make law, because they are not a true political community. This would just be an artificial group of individuals. However, 100,000 living together on an island somewhere would (presumably) be a political community, and would have a government already, so voting on a new law would probably be legitimate. Bellarmine writes that political authority "resides immediately in the whole multitude as in an organic unit."[32]

Bellarmine proclaimed that the authority of government is granted to it by the consent of the people. According to Bellarmine, "The people themselves, immediately and directly, hold political power so long as they have not transferred this power to a king or ruler."[33] Moreover, every nation and its citizens have a natural right to choose the form of government it desires. "It depends upon the consent of men to place over themselves a king, counsel, or magistrate."[34] Most importantly, *people have the right to resist the rule of a tyrant.* "For legitimate reason the people can change the government to an aristocracy or a democracy or vice versa."[35]

Bellarmine's theory of government was not new. The Church had propounded this political philosophy since the Middle Ages. The power of monarchs was balanced by the Church, which, since the time of Pope Gregory VII, had always maintained the right to judge and remove tyrants, as well as by the nobles and the people. Since the early Middle Ages, the Catholic Church maintained that mankind is naturally endowed and born free from all subjection, and free to choose what form of government the people wish.

St. Robert Bellarmine

---

[32] De Laicis, or "On Civil Government," 1579.
[33] De Clericis, Ch. VII.
[34] De Laicis, Ch. VI.
[35] De Laicis, Ch. VI.

Even if it is obvious that communities need some government, how do we figure out who should govern? After all, there are times when two people or two groups of people both claim to be the "legitimate" government of a society. There may also be times when there is only one "claimant" but even then, the lack of a rival does not necessarily mean that a self-proclaimed ruler is "legitimate."

St. Thomas explains that an apparent office holder may lack all authority if the ruler obtained office, "for example, through violence, or simony or some other illegal method." In these instances:

> … such defect prevents the establishment of any just authority: for whoever possesses himself of power by violence does not truly become lord or master. Therefore, it is permissible, when occasion offers, for a person to reject such authority; except in the case that it subsequently became legitimate, either through public consent or through the intervention of higher authority.[36]

Therefore, legitimacy, that is, authority to exercise sovereignty, must be based on the law of the community. It is important to note that law includes the traditions and customs of the community, which is a group of people united by a common set of traditions and a shared conception of justice and community. Customs are very important for St. Thomas. Customs are practices that have existed for long periods of time and have the explicit, or at least tacit, approval of the community as a whole. In fact, customs tend to reflect the collective wisdom of many generations of people; although St. Thomas acknowledges that there can be evil customs. Nevertheless, customs have the force of law and should be followed by everyone including rulers:

> Custom counts far more … than does the authority of the sovereign, who has not the power to frame laws, except as representing the people. Wherefore although each individual cannot make laws, yet the whole people can.[37]

Consequently, legitimacy depends upon conformity to long-standing customs and traditions that represent the community as a whole, over multiple generations. Legitimacy is not based upon the momentary support of a bare majority of voters at any given time.

Thomas does add that an illegitimate ruler can become legitimate "either through public consent or through the intervention of higher authority." Obviously, this is far from ideal, but there must be some means of reconstituting a legitimate government. "Intervention of higher authority," such as the Holy Father, is not the normal method of choosing rulers, so this is only for exceptional circumstances. Presumably "public consent" would mean acceptance of the whole people. Thomas, obviously, is not against "public consent," but this does not necessarily mean voting. The way the community, or the people as a whole, best expresses its agreement is through long-standing customs and traditions. Why this theory makes most sense is best illustrated by comparing alternative theories.

The most prominent theory opposed to this organic view of society is **social contract theory**, which holds that both government and human society itself are artificial and result from arbitrary agreement. Some social contract theorists posit a less radical version, that society is natural and only government is based on agreement. For example, John Locke (1632-1704) sometimes suggests that human society is natural. However, other social contract theorists such as Thomas Hobbes (1588-1679) and Jean-Jacques Rousseau (1712-1778) insist that all human associations are artificial and based only on arbitrary agreement.

The social contract theory in its pure form is based on an even more basic and pernicious concept known as **moral subjectivism**. Moral subjectivism holds that there are no objective moral truths or principles. Rather morality is limited to each person's personal subjective view of right and wrong. Moral subjectivism does not deny that humans are fundamentally moral and possess strong feelings about right and wrong. However, subjectivism posits that feelings about good and evil are no more than feelings. Thus, for subjectivism, morality is nothing more than each person following his or her own subjective feelings. Obviously if moral subjectivism were correct,

---
[36] Commentary on Sentences, book 2, dist. 44, quest. 2, art. 2
[37] Summa Th. I-II, Q. 97, A. 3.

it would make no sense to speak of justice or of society trying to establish justice.

Closely associated with moral subjectivism is the concept of **moral autonomy.** The word autonomy comes from two Greek words auto for self, and nomos for law. The term moral autonomy is used in different ways by different thinkers, but in this context, moral autonomy is the idea that no human person is ever subject to any external moral law or standard. In other words, no one can ever tell any human how to behave, not political rulers, not priests, not God Himself.

Obviously, the concepts of moral subjectivism and moral autonomy are profoundly contrary to Catholic teaching and have been constantly condemned by the Church. Notice what becomes of human community if moral subjectivism and moral autonomy were true: no human ever has any moral obligation to anyone else; no human ever has any obligation to work for the common good or to obey any law, civil or ecclesiastical. There is no "common good" at all because all goods are subjective. If a person accepts these theories, the family and the state are not based on any sort of natural obligation. Rather the state, like all other human societies, is based on nothing more than arbitrary consent of a group of autonomous individuals.

Aside from the social contract being contrary to Catholic doctrine, it contains major practical problems. One version of social contract theory, espoused by Thomas Hobbes, is that concepts like legitimacy and authority are fictions. Under this theory, no government is ever legitimate or illegitimate, people must follow "the law" simply because those in power will kill those who disobey. For Hobbes, people should just do what they need to do to survive and not worry about questions of legitimacy. The problem with this theory is that it contradicts the fundamental principle that the purpose of government is to establish justice and the common good. Under Hobbes's theory, politics devolves into constant civil war, with each party trying to murder their opponents and seize control of the government.

John Locke and many of his followers tried to articulate a more moderate version of the Social

Thomas Hobbes

Contract. At times, Locke says there is a "Natural Law" but proceeds to ignore it and writes as though Natural Law does not exist. In any event, more moderate followers of Locke advocate the limited idea that government legitimacy is always based on majority rule. Whatever regime the majority supports is the "legitimate government." However, even this more moderate view of majority rule has problems.

In his *Second Treatise on Government* (1689), Locke denied that anyone naturally has political authority at all, and therefore, each person individually must consent to be governed. But because universal consent is "next to impossible," says Locke, we must settle for what he thinks is the next best thing: the majority vote of adult, male, Protestant, English, property owners.[38] Why did women, Catholics, Irish, or American colonists not get to vote? As even secular philosopher David Hume (1711-1776) pointed out, Locke's "social contract" was logically contradictory and historically no more than a fairy tale.

In 1688, Locke's theories were used to justify the overthrow of King James II, largely because he was Catholic. Under the laws and traditions

---

[38] Locke, Second Treatise on Government, § 95

A portrait of Catholic King James II and his family

of England that had been in effect for a thousand years, James was the legitimate King of England. So, under the theory of St. Thomas, these long-standing laws and traditions of England should continue to govern, not what a bare majority happens to support, even assuming that the Protestants possessed a majority. The community as a whole can make laws, but that does not mean that 50.1% can suddenly reject long-standing traditions and create a totally new system without legitimate reason.

Of course, the principle that legitimacy is determined by long-standing customs and traditions does not guarantee a dispute will never arise. One of the recurring controversies in English law was whether a woman could succeed to the throne. *The Anarchy* (an English civil war from 1138-1153) resulted because when King Henry I died he had no male heirs and a dispute developed between Henry's daughter Matilda and Henry's nephew Stephen as to who was the legitimate monarch. In such circumstances, as when there is a usurpation, the best alternative may be seeking public consent, e.g. the English barons, or the intervention of higher authority, e.g. the Pope.

The final point about legitimacy is whether one community can rule over another. Because law is made by the community as a whole or by a person acting on behalf of the community as whole it is a usurpation for one community to invade another and impose "law." There could be some limited exceptions, for example, when society breaks down entirely it might be permissible for another society to intervene temporarily to help restore order. Generally, however, communities must be permitted to make their own laws reflecting their own interpretations and applications of the Natural Law. Thomists such as Francisco Suárez (1548-1617) argued that it was contrary to Natural Law for European countries to invade and conquer communities in the New World.

If it is contrary to Natural Law for one community to impose its law on another what happens when a community grows apart and ends up as two distinct communities? This is what happened to England and her English colonies in North America. Over time, the English colonists in North America developed their own distinct communities that were different from England. The colonies demanded the authority to make their own laws without interference from England.

The greatest American Catholic political theorist of the 19th century, Orestes Brownson (1803-1876), defended American Independence by applying a traditional Natural Law view. Brownson argued that the social contract view of government had been largely discredited and abandoned. He maintained that the various American colonies were actually several distinct sovereignties, e.g. Virginia, Maryland, etc. St. Thomas confirms that a sovereign "has not the power to frame laws, except as representing the people." If Americans or Virginians constitute a distinct people, then clearly the English sovereign has no authority to impose laws on them and, under the Natural Law, such a community should exercise self-government.

REVIEW QUESTIONS

1. What is political authority?
2. Define Natural Law.
3. What are the precepts of Natural Law?
4. According to Robert Bellarmine, where does political authority reside?
5. How did Orestes Brownson justify American Independence?
6. What was John Paul II's view of a government that fails to protect the lives of its most vulnerable members?
7. What are the various elements of the "common good?"
8. According to St. Thomas Aquinas why is God the "lawgiver" of Natural Law?
9. What does the moral theory known as Utilitarianism teach?
10. How does St. Thomas Aquinas define "law"?
11. What is political liberalism?
12. What government does Natural Law require?
13. What is the Organic Theory of Government?
14. What is the Social Contract Theory of Government?
15. What is a person's obligation to worship God?
16. What is the central teaching of legal voluntarism?
17. What is the position of St. Thomas Aquinas regarding legitimate government?
18. What is Aristotle's view of the role of virtue in law?
19. What is Moral Subjectivism?
20. Who wrote *Rerum Novarum*?
21. What elements are common to all human societies?
22. What does Communism teach?
23. How does St. Thomas Aquinas define "justice?"
24. What does St. Thomas Aquinas say about Law and Virtue?
25. What is "the tragedy of the commons?"
26. What is the difference between Monarchy, Tyranny, and Dictatorship?
27. What is the difference between Republic and Democracy?
28. How do Aristocracy, Autocracy, and Anarchy differ?
29. What is the difference between Theocracy and Kleptocracy?

CHAPTER TWO

BACKGROUND TO AMERICAN GOVERNMENT: ROMAN REPUBLIC TO AMERICAN INDEPENDENCE

ROMAN LAW

Chapter One described how a political community's most basic laws include customs and traditions embraced by generations over hundreds of years. This chapter will trace the American political tradition back to its roots in the first century—if not earlier. Today, much of contemporary American property law, contract law, and basic concepts of due process are based in Roman Law passed down through the centuries. Moreover, many of America's Founding Fathers greatly admired and sought to emulate the ancient Roman Republic (509 B.C. to 27 B.C.).

In 55 B.C. (and again in 54 B.C.), Julius Caesar raided the British Isles, which were populated by Celts. The Irish, Scots, and Welsh are the descendants of these ancient Celts. Between 43 AD and 84 AD, the Romans launched a more determined invasion of Britain, but never gained full control over the northern and western parts of the island.

St. Augustine, in his great work *City of God*, condemned Roman imperial invasions as unjust. The Romans killed or enslaved hundreds of thousands of British. While the Roman invasion of Britain was undeniably harsh and unjust, the Romans also brought with them technology and a well-developed legal system. They built bridges and a network of good roads that facilitated commerce and prosperity. Archeologists have recovered contracts from First-century London. Roman Britain was ruled by an appointed governor but assisted by a *legatus juridicus*, or legal official, who was assisted by a team of trained lawyers.

Roman courts had professional lawyers, judges, established procedures and laws. Many of the basic procedures Americans apply today came from Roman Law. For example, the law against *hearsay* was well established in Roman Law. Evidence needed to be based upon the testimony of a witness who could swear he had personally seen an event and was not repeating what someone else told him. All witnesses were subject to cross examination. Litigants were entitled to assistance of counsel and all trials were conducted in public to discourage dishonesty both from witnesses and judges.[1] The basic idea of due process is found in Roman law. In 57 B.C., Cicero could say that "that nothing concerning the life of a citizen or his goods can be taken without a judgment of the senate or of the people, or of those constituted judges concerning a particular matter."

Roman citizens also possessed the legal right to appeal to Rome, the *provocatio ad Caesarem* or "appeal to Caesar." In *Acts* Chapter 25, St. Paul exercises this right. A local judge presented with a difficult case could write to Rome for guidance. In theory, the Emperor was the highest authority; however, most emperors were too busy with other matters, so they left legal decisions to professional legal scholars.

---

[1] Frank R. Herrmann, S.J., The Establishment of a Rule Against Hearsay in RomanoCanonical Procedure, VIRGINIA JOURNAL OF INTERNATIONAL LAW, 1995.

CHAPTER 2: ROMAN REPUBLIC TO AMERICAN INDEPENDENCE

ANGLO-SAXON LAW AND THE BIRTH OF ENGLISH COMMON LAW

In the centuries after Roman occupation, the population of southeastern Britain became thoroughly Romanized. These British Romans also appear to have been largely Christian. The Council of Arles in 314 was attended by three bishops from Roman Britain. Around the year 400, Roman legions withdrew from Britain to defend the more "important" parts of the Empire. The Roman British were left on their own to defend against incursions from the non-Roman North and West.

In the early fifth century, Angles, Jutes, and Saxons (Germanic tribes) began raiding from the East. Over the next two centuries, these tribes displaced the British and created an Anglo-Saxon nation. Starting in 595, the Anglo-Saxons were converted to Christianity by St. Augustine of Canterbury. Then, in 793, the Danes began attacking Anglo-Saxon Britain.

King Egbert of Wessex, who reigned from 802 to 839, is often considered the first King of England because he united the kingdoms of Wessex and Northumbria in 829. However, it was under Egbert's grandson Alfred that all of the Anglo-Saxon kingdoms were united, so some regard Alfred as the first true King of England.

Alfred the Great (850-899, reigned 871-899) united the kingdoms of Anglia, Kent, Murcia, Wessex and Essex

Alfred the Great (850-899) became King of Wessex, or West Saxons, in 871. To fight the Danes, Alfred united all the Anglo-Saxon kingdoms into a single kingdom. He strengthened the militia requiring all able-bodied men to own weapons and help defend the community. Alfred was not only a war leader. He was a devout Catholic, a scholar, and a law-maker. As a condition of peace with the Danes, Alfred demanded that they convert to Christianity because he could not trust them to follow any agreements if they remained pagan. Thus, Alfred explicitly saw England as a Christian nation, largely defined by its religion. Alfred also promulgated an English legal code, synthesizing many of the old provisions from the earlier precursor states to the newly unified England.

One of Alfred's closest advisors was Asser, Bishop of Sherborne, who wrote *The Life of King Alfred*. Asser wrote that one of the responsibilities Alfred took most seriously was reviewing judgments to ensure they were just. Asser wrote:

> The king was a most acute investigator in executing his judgments, as he was in all other

U.S. Government for Catholic Students

things. He inquired into almost all the judgments which were given in his absence, throughout all his dominion, whether they were just or unjust. If he perceived there was iniquity in those judgments, he would, of his own accord, mildly ask those judges, either in his own person, or through others who were in trust with him, why they had judged so unjustly[.][2]

Modern trial by jury has its roots in the *volksmote* of King Alfred the Great.

This quote makes it clear that a functioning court system existed in Alfred's kingdom, although, not much is known about its day-to-day functioning. Historians believe that the system combined Roman law and Anglo-Saxon customs. There do not appear to have been any trained lawyers but, according to Bishop Asser, Alfred demanded that his judges and counselors study the liberal arts. Judgments were rendered at a **shire moot** or a **people's moot** ("*volks-mote*"). Laws promulgated by King Alfred speak of legal disputes being resolved before a volksmote. Alfred's son, King Edward, promulgated a law declaring that the volksmote should meet each month to resolve legal disputes quickly.

Amazingly, records of specific legal disputes still exist. One case from 825, for which detailed records survive, involved a dispute over pasture lands. Archbishop Wulfred supervised the trial and the verdict was rendered by vote of the people at the moot. These "people's moots" were a precursor to the **jury system**. As communities grew too large, juries acted as representatives of the community as a whole. The jury system, which relies on ordinary citizens to render decisions in both civil and criminal trials, remains a distinctive part of the Anglo-American legal tradition.

One of the great scholars of English law, Sir Frederick Pollock, describes the Anglo-Saxon court system as follows:

> The courts were open-air meetings of the freemen who were bound to attend them … there was no class of professional lawyers; there were no judges in our sense of learned persons specially appointed to preside, expound the law, and cause justice to be done; the only learning available was that of the bishops, abbots, and other great ecclesiastics.[3]

Kings such as Alfred and Edward made specific promulgations, but these written pronouncements were not comprehensive. The legal system continued to depend heavily on unwritten customs and traditions. Pollock points out that *"Anglo-Saxon written laws, though of priceless use to students of the times … It is altogether misleading to speak of them as codes, or as if they were intended to be a complete exposition of the customary law."*

Thus, in the Anglo-Saxon period, there was an established legal system in which bishops or nobles presided over moots, and the common people (presumably men only) voted on the outcome. All of this could be reviewed by the king, who had ultimate authority to revise judgments. There was no legislature as such. Both criminal and civil law was customary as interpreted by local moots. In other words, during this early period, the common people, nobles, clergy, and king all played a role in making and enforcing the law.

Finally, in the Anglo-Saxon period, the most basic division in England was the *shire*. The shire was presided over by the "shire reeve," later known as the "sheriff." After the Norman invasion, shires came to be known as "counties" but most counties in England still have "shire" in their names, e.g. Berkshire or Yorkshire. The county with a sheriff as the chief law enforcement officer remains one of the most basic units of local government found throughout the United States.

---

2 The Life of King Alfred, paragraph 106.
3   Sir Frederick Pollock, History of English Law Before the Time of Edward I (1895).

CANON LAW AND ITS INFLUENCE

In *Acts* 15, St. Peter resolved a dispute between Christians who were arguing over whether Christians should follow the Jewish dietary laws. Over the years, councils and popes made pronouncements about various issues of Church discipline. In fact, here there is a convergence of Roman Law and Church law.

In the sixth century, the Emperor Justinian (482-565) who reigned from 527 to 565, commissioned a group of legal scholars to synthesize and codify Roman Law that had accumulated over the previous thousand years. The commission compiled a large Codex, as well as Digest summarizing laws, and finally a short summary of basic principles called the *Institutes*. The *Institutes* was completed around 533, long after Roman rule had broken down in Britain, so these works did not immediately impact Anglo-Saxon law. However, the *Code of Justinian* would be very influential in the Middle Ages.

Soon after Justinian's commission completed its work, Byzantine theologians decided that they should do the same for Church pronouncements. In the late sixth century, Byzantine theologians collected Church pronouncements into "nomokanons." *Nomos* means law, *canon* means rule or guideline. This practice eventually spread to the West. The greatest of these Medieval legal scholars was **Gratian** (d. circa 1159), a Benedictine monk who collected and commented on some four thousand church statements relating to church discipline. Gratian taught law at University of Bologna which was founded in 1088. Oxford (late 11th century) and Cambridge (1209) also became centers for the study of Roman Law and Canon Law.

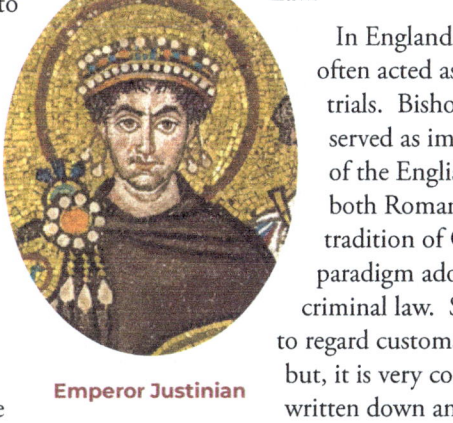

Emperor Justinian

In England, bishops and lower clergy often acted as judges in Anglo-Saxon trials. Bishops and abbots usually served as important advisers to kings of the English. Unsurprisingly then, both Roman Law and the growing tradition of Canon Law became a paradigm adopted for all civil and criminal law. St. Thomas continued to regard customs and traditions as law; but, it is very convenient to have law written down and codified to avoid any confusion. Indeed, Natural Law is not written down, although Thomas says the Natural Law is written in our hearts. However, God gave humanity the Ten Commandments written down to ensure there would be no confusion.

Accordingly, from the eleventh century onward, the paradigm was that laws should be written

Presentation of the Pandects to the Emperor Justinian, Hermann Knackfuss

U.S. Government for Catholic Students

down whenever possible. These written laws often reflected unwritten customs. Laws were also understood to reflect the unwritten Natural Law, or law of nations which are the basic laws common to all civilized societies. However, a written law is not the same thing as a constitution. Today, Americans think of a constitution as a law that is *fixed* as opposed to a written law which can evolve and change over time. English common law, despite being increasingly written down, continued to change over time as new problems arose. *Common law* is the body of customary law, primarily as interpreted and applied by judicial decisions.

THE NORMAN CONQUEST

In January 1066, England's king, Edward the Confessor, died leaving three claimants to the throne: Englishman Harold Godwinson, Dane Harald Hardrada, and William of Normandy. Godwinson defeated Hardrada at the Battle of Stamford Bridge on September 25, 1066, then marched south to face William, who decisively defeated him at Hastings on October 14. When William became King, he instituted a number of legal innovations, but also maintained continuity with the centuries long Anglo-Saxon tradition. Sir Frederick Pollock noted that:

> For most practical purposes the history of English law does not begin till after the Norman conquest .… Nevertheless, a student who does not look farther back will be puzzled by relics of archaic law which were not formally discarded until quite modern times[.][4]

The next 150 years saw a constant struggle between the French-speaking Norman rulers, who wanted to see French, Roman, and Ecclesiastical Law predominate, and the native Anglo-Saxons, who demanded that their traditional customs and liberties be preserved. When William died, his son Henry was poised to be crowned king, but a significant number of Anglo-Saxons opposed him. To reduce this opposition, in 1100, Henry agreed to a "Charter of Liberties" that included the following:

> I restore the law of King Edward and the amendments which my father introduced upon the advice of his barons. …
>
> If any of my barons commit a crime, he shall not bind himself to the crown with a payment as was done in the time of my father and brother, but shall stand for the crime as was custom and law before the time of my father, and make amends as are appropriate.

Evidently, William had shielded Norman barons from punishment when they committed offenses against Anglo-Saxons. In fact, soon after his coronation, Henry issued a writ proclaiming that shire moots and volk moots should be held as in the days of Edward the Confessor.

Much of this period can be seen as a struggle between the French-speaking kings to centralize authority and the English trying to preserve their old traditions and power of common people to participate in the administration of justice.

King Henry also struggled with the Church. Bishops and abbots performed secular functions, such as presiding over trials at shire moots. The king could review and set aside judgments he

A depiction of the Battle of Stamford Bridge, from the 13th century book *The Life of King Edward the Confessor*

---
[4]Sir Frederick Pollock, History of English Law Before the Time of Edward I (1895).

considered unjust. The king was the supervisor and superior of these clerics insofar as they carried out secular functions. Problems arose when kings thought that because they possessed authority to supervise clerics who performed secular duties, the king could choose who would be made bishop or abbot. This dispute is known as the Investiture Controversy. Rulers across Europe claimed authority to appoint or "invest" bishops, abbots, and other church officials.

St. Thomas Becket. Murdered in 1170 by knights when King Henry II supposedly cried out "Who will rid me of this troublesome prelate."

This dispute was ostensibly resolved in 1107 when Henry agreed to the Concordat of London with Pope Paschal II. Under the Concordat, Henry renounced any authority to appoint church officials while Paschal agreed that clerics, who also had purely secular duties, could be required to obey the king with respect to secular functions. As a result of the Concordat of London, English monarchs began relying more heavily on professional lawyers.

In 1154, Henry II became King of England. He also had problems with the Church. Henry issued the Constitutions of Clarendon in 1164 that tried to exert more control over the Church. Under canon law, disputes involving clerics were to be adjudicated in ecclesiastical courts, but Henry insisted that in a dispute between a cleric and a non-cleric the secular courts would have jurisdiction. Another provision granted the king the power to confiscate all revenue of a diocese if a bishop's see was vacant. The English hierarchy, led by Archbishop of Canterbury Thomas Becket, opposed these provisions. Becket was murdered in 1170 at the instigation of King Henry. Becket's murder caused such outrage that for a time Henry had to back off on some of his more radical attempts to control the Church.

THE MAGNA CARTA

The struggles between the king on one side and the Church, nobility, and common people on the other, culminated in the most famous document of the Middle Ages, the **Magna Carta**, or Great Charter, in 1215. Like the "Charter of Liberties" of 1100, Magna Carta attempted to codify the basic traditions and liberties the English had practiced for centuries. The text of Magna Carta was revised and re-issued several times over the next century. The exact text of the document was less important than the ancient traditions that stood behind it.

The driving force behind Magna Carta was **Stephen Langton** (1150-1228), Archbishop of Canterbury from 1207 to 1228. Langton was a scholar who taught theology at the University of Paris before becoming Archbishop. When Langton returned to England he found a country on the verge of civil war. King John (1166-1216, reigned 1199-1216) was unpopular for a variety of political and personal reasons. Archbishop Langton hoped to maintain peace by having King John agree to a list of basic traditional English liberties that he, and future kings, would support. On May 28, 1215, King John, along with a group of bishops and nobles, signed Magna Carta.

A 13th-century copy of the Magna Carta

Archbishop Stephen Langton

King John

The first article of Magna Carta guaranteed freedom to the Catholic Church: "by this present charter have confirmed for us and our heirs in perpetuity, that the English Church shall be free." This is not some vague affirmation of "freedom of religion" but a specific guarantee of freedom for the Catholic Church. Magna Carta restored property that King John had seized and guaranteed a variety of privileges of the nobility. Article 20 guaranteed that no one would be imprisoned "for a trivial offense" nor would fines be ruinous to a person's livelihood.[5] The most important provision was article 39 which provided:

No free man shall be seized or imprisoned, or stripped of his rights or possessions, or outlawed or exiled, or deprived of his standing in any way, nor will we proceed with force against him, or send others to do so, except by the lawful judgment of his equals or by the law of the land.

The word "or" in the phrase "except by the lawful judgment of his equals or ("vel") by the law of the land" was later changed to read "except by the lawful judgment of his equals *and* by the law of the land." The Latin word "vel" normally means "one or the other, but not both." Some scholars argue that the 1215 draft was always intended to mean that no one could be convicted of a crime unless the crime was both well-established as the law of the land, and a group of one's peers agreed that the offense should be punished. Another interpretation is that "judgment of his equals *or* by the law" was intended to preserve broad power of local moots unrestrained by written laws.

During the Anglo-Saxon period, most trials occurred at local moots that had power to render verdicts the people considered just. It is assumed that a crime or civil action would need to be based on established customs even at a moot. For example, imagine that one man demands action against his neighbor for calling him "ugly." Falsely accusing someone of a crime is "slander," and punishable in Anglo-Saxon times, but calling someone "ugly" is just an opinion and was never actionable in English law. So, a hypothetical accusation that the defendant had called the plaintiff "ugly" should be dismissed because there is no civil or criminal law against calling someone ugly.

In the definition of "law," St. Thomas Aquinas included the requirement that it be promulgated or made known. Punishing a person for doing something that was not illegal when it was done, is called an *ex post facto* law. In fact, such a thing is not a "law" at all. The purpose of law is to guide people towards acting in the future. These concerns resulted in the language of Magna Carta being clarified over the next hundred years. It soon became well-established that no one could be punished for a crime unless the crime was

King John reluctantly signs the Magna Carta.

---

[5]This can be seen as the origin of the Eighth Amendment to the U.S. Constitution which prohibits "excessive fines."

both specified in the law at the time of the alleged offense *and* an unbiased group of the accused's peers agreed to the punishment. This group of fellow citizens who had to concur in the judgment were later known as "jurors" from the Latin word "iura" (or "jura") meaning oath because these people were sworn to do justice.

THE ORIGINS OF PARLIAMENT

Article 61 of Magna Carta provided that a group of barons monitor the king to ensure he abided by Magna Carta:

> The barons shall elect twenty-five of their number to keep, and cause to be observed with all their might, the peace and liberties granted and confirmed to them by this charter. … If one of the twenty-five barons dies or leaves the country, or is prevented in any other way from discharging his duties, the rest of them shall choose another baron in his place.

This provision was the ultimate origin of the English parliament. The word "parliament" comes from the French word "parley" or "speak," and reflects the fact that initially this provided an opportunity for the barons to discuss their concerns with the king. This group of nobles, which also included bishops, has been known as "Parliament" since the 1230s.

Parliament's first and most basic power was that it agree to any new taxes. Even before Magna Carta, it had been traditional for the king to call a meeting of the kingdom's leading men to obtain their support for new revenue. Some taxes were permanent, for example, in 1275, parliament granted a permanent tax on wool exports. However, most taxes were temporary and needed to be renewed periodically. As early as 1237, King Henry III sought Parliament's approval for a new tax which was only granted when Henry agreed to reaffirm Magna Carta. In 1295, Edward I tried increasing the wool tax without Parliament's approval—which led to widespread opposition. In 1337, Edward III attempted to raise taxes without parliament's approval and again there was huge opposition. From the reign of Edward III onward, it was settled law that no new taxes could be collected without the consent of parliament.

In 1258, the barons agreed to accept representatives from the counties and towns. By 1295, it was settled that Parliament would consist of bishops, hereditary nobles, and two

A 14th-century depiction of King Edward I presiding over Parliament in 1295

representatives from each county and town. Towns and counties elected representatives according to their own local customs. Most towns appear to have followed the basic procedure of the traditional moot, where people were selected in large open-air meetings. Most areas required voters to own property worth at least 40 shillings, which was not a large amount, but very poor people could not participate in these elections. In 1341, parliament divided itself into two chambers, the House of Commons and the House of Lords, composed of bishops and nobles.

At this point, there was no concern about proportional representation. A town of a few hundred people sent two representatives to parliament just as did a county of ten thousand people. What was important was that the parliament represented the people as whole. This changed somewhat after the industrial revolution. Some of the ancient towns had almost become ghost towns as people moved away to big factory cities. These small towns, sometimes with less than a dozen voters, became known as **rotten boroughs**.

In 1284, England annexed Wales, a region that the Anglo-Saxons had not conquered. The Welsh were permitted to send representatives to parliament as were the Scots four centuries later. During the 18th century, American colonists did not understand why the Welsh and Scots could send representatives to parliament but they could not.

In 1414, King Henry V agreed that no measure could become law without the assent of both Houses of parliament. However, Parliament could not make law without the assent of the king, or queen, either. This power to reject a measure passed by the legislature is called a "veto," and is an important prerogative given to American presidents and governors.

TRIAL BY JURY

One of the best sources for understanding English law in the late medieval period is Sir John Fortesque (1394-1479), a judge and Thomistic philosopher. In his work *In Praise of the Laws of England* (1470), Fortesque argues that despite the Norman Conquest, English laws were based on customs and traditions of the ancient Britons and the later Anglo-Saxons. Fortesque writes that the main advantage of a parliament is that laws are hard to change, because it is difficult to convince the kingdom as whole to agree to a change.

Fortesque also explains the jury system that had developed in the 14th and 15th centuries. All civil suits in which the dispute involved 40 marks or more had to be tried by a jury. Jurors had to own property worth at least 40 shillings and come from the neighborhood where the issue arose. Fortesque says that it was impractical to have a jury for small cases. He notes that it is easy to bribe one judge but difficult to bribe twelve jurors. However, he thinks that when the amount in dispute is small the chances of bribery are reduced.

Every criminal case had to be tried by a jury. In both civil and criminal cases, a litigant could ask to have jurors removed "for cause" if the juror was thought to be biased and the judge agreed. In felony cases, the accused could disqualify, or "preempt," up to thirty-five jurors without having to give a reason.[6] Fortesque sees jurors, far more than parliament or judges, as the chief safeguard of liberties. He thought that these procedures would protect innocent people from wrongful conviction.

Sadly, there were always ways to subvert the jury system. One of the most notorious examples occurred in 1535 during St. Thomas More's trial, which violated nearly every section of Magna

---

[6]*In Praise of the Laws of England*, Ch 29.

Sir John Fortesque

St. Thomas More

King Henry VIII

Carta. In 1534, Henry VIII pushed the Supremacy Act through parliament which purported to make him the head of the Catholic Church in England—a clear violation of Magna Carta Article 1. Thomas More, who had been Lord Chancellor, the highest legal official in the government, refused to swear to follow the Supremacy Act. He was arrested and held without formal charges for almost a year. He was then tried before a handpicked "jury" and not permitted to challenge any of the jurors. Henry also chose the judges to ensure the proper verdict. One of the judges, William Paulet, received Thomas More's lands, which were forfeited to the crown as a result of the conviction, as a reward for doing Henry's bidding. This was basically open bribery of a "judge" of the case.

A 20th-century depiction of the Pilgrimage of Grace

Henry VIII dashed Fortesque's hope that parliament would check the king's power. As new head of the Catholic Church in England, Henry confiscated the property of the Church, including land, money, books, and sacred vessels. Between 1535 and 1539, Henry seized all of Britain's monasteries. He used the proceeds to fund his wars and bribe important people to support him.

Monasteries functioned as the "safety net" for poor people and their dissolution resulted in a massive resistance movement by the common people. In Yorkshire at least 30,000 people protested and refused to disburse unless the monasteries were restored. The Yorkshire protest was known as the **Pilgrimage of Grace**, and spread throughout much of northern England. Henry appeared to agree to the protester's demands to convince them to disband, but then executed hundreds of people he thought were the leaders. Historians estimate that between 1535 and 1547 Henry killed as many as 72,000 English men and women, out of a population of 2.5 million, making it one of the greatest reigns of terror in history. All the legal and political institutions of England not only failed to prevent this reign of terror, they were subverted to support it.

CIVIL WARS RAVAGE ENGLAND

Between Henry's Act of Supremacy in 1534 and King James II's loss at the Battle of the Boyne in 1690, England was frequently fighting large or small civil wars. The first permanent English settlement in North America, at Jamestown, occurred in 1607. The colonization of North America took place in the midst of this great upheaval and many of the colonists fled England to escape this violence.

Henry died in 1547 and was succeeded by his nine-year-old son Edward. During Edward's reign, England moved more towards Protestantism. In early 1549, the government prohibited saying Mass in Latin and mandated the use of English. A new English book of prayer was promulgated. Thousands of people took up arms to protest these "reforms." Ultimately their rebellions failed and thousands died in battle or were hanged without a trial.

Meanwhile, more radical elements favored eliminating any vestiges of Catholicism from England. Among these more radical groups were the Anabaptists and Calvinists. The government also persecuted them, as Anglicans and Lutherans viewed the Anabaptists as violent revolutionaries seeking to overthrow the government.

Edward died in July 1553, and his half-sister Mary became Queen. A devout Catholic, she was the daughter of Catherine of Aragon and the granddaughter of Isabel of Spain. Mary sought to restore the Catholic Church in England, and had she lived longer or had a child, this might have been accomplished. However, Mary reigned for only about five years and when she died in 1558, her half-sister Elizabeth (1533-1603) succeeded her.

Because Elizabeth was a Protestant and owed her throne to the support of Protestants, her forty-five-year reign was a time of great suffering and persecution for Catholics. Elizabeth revoked all Mary's attempts to restore the Church. Priests were executed for secretly administering the sacraments and torture became common. By the time of her death, being a Catholic was almost the equivalent of a death sentence.

In 1603, Elizabeth died without children so James Stuart, her closest living relative, was proclaimed King of England. James, who had been raised a Protestant, had been ruling Scotland as James VI but in 1603 was named James I of England. James advocated absolutism and a theory known as the "**Divine Right of Kings**," which holds that the king is answerable to God alone and need not seek permission from anyone to do as he wishes. Because of this belief, James tried to dissolve parliament and rule without it. James and the leaders in parliament were constantly at odds.

James was succeeded by his son Charles I (1600-1649, reigned 1625-1649). Like James, Charles espoused absolutism and also tried to rule without parliament. In 1627, Charles tried to impose a tax without parliament's approval by claiming it was not really a tax, but a "forced loan" that citizens were required to pay. Even worse, Charles insisted that he had authority to imprison without trial anyone who refused to comply with the "loan."

From 1629 to 1640 Charles I ruled without parliament ever meeting. Finally, beset with financial problems, Charles was forced to ask parliament to convene. However, the king and parliament were violently opposed to each other. To avoid Charles dissolving it, parliament passed a bill proclaiming that it could stay in session for as long as its members wished. Because Parliament stayed in session from 1640 to 1660, it is known as The Long Parliament.

In addition to his financial difficulties, Charles also had religious conflicts with Parliament. Charles tried to enforce uniformity in religion by trying to

Queen Mary I

Queen Elizabeth I

return to the 1549 *Book of Common Prayer* – the book which started the Prayerbook Rebellion. However, a group of radical protestants, called Puritans, saw this as being too Catholic. They also distrusted Charles because he was married to French Catholic princess Henrietta Maria, who was known to celebrate Catholic Mass in the palace. In 1630, Charles and Henrietta had their first son, the future Charles II; their second son, the future James II, followed in 1633. While officially practicing the religion of his father, many people assumed, correctly, that Charles II would be friendly towards Catholicism because of his mother. Charles and Henrietta's second son, the future James II, later openly embraced Catholicism.

The Battle of Marston Moor, a key battle in the English Civil War

The dispute between Charles and parliament erupted into full scale Civil War in 1642. The nobles and more conservative religious elements supported Charles. The Parliamentarian army was led by Oliver Cromwell and composed largely of Puritans. Ultimately Cromwell's army prevailed. Cromwell was declared Lord Protector and Charles was charged with treason and executed January 30, 1649. The Civil War affirmed parliamentary dominance.

Cromwell ruled England, Scotland, and Ireland until his death in 1658. At that point, leaders in parliament realized they had gone too far. Charles's son, Charles II, was brought back and declared King in 1660. Parliament required that Charles swear he would remain Protestant which he did. However, in 1672, he issued a decree stating that he would not enforce the penal laws against Catholics. Sadly, under pressure from parliament, Charles was forced to backtrack the following year. These events were repeated in 1687 when James II also declared he would not enforce penal laws against Catholics.

Several events of Charles's reign are important in the American legal background. In 1670, parliament passed "An Act for the better preservation of the Game" that completely banned the possession of firearms and/or bows by anyone who did not own land worth at least 150 pounds. The land value was so high that it likely prohibited 98.8% of all Englishmen from owning a firearm or a bow. Although allegedly passed to prevent poaching, Americans saw this law as a notorious example of an attempt to disarm the common man.

Another infamous episode was the execution of **Algernon Sydney**. Sydney composed *Discourses Concerning Government*, but did not publish it, fearing retribution if he did. Nevertheless, Charles II suspected Sydney of being disloyal and the government raided Sydney's home looking for incriminating evidence. The police found the unpublished manuscript of *Discourses Concerning Government*. In 1683, Sydney was executed for "treason."

During the reign of Charles II, the first modern political parties were created: the Whigs and the Tories. The names were actually intended as derogatory terms that each used against the other. The parties originated during the *Exclusion Crisis,* in which Parliament sought to exclude Charles' brother James from succeeding to the throne of England. James was Catholic and because Charles had no children, James was heir to the throne and Charles' legal successor. In 1679, some members of parliament proposed an Exclusion Act that would have banned James from becoming king. The party that opposed James were the **Whigs** and the party that supported him were the **Tories**. The Whigs opposed James because they tended to be Puritans, or others not in conformity with the Church of England, and resisted any Catholic on the throne. The Tories tended to be more religiously conservative and were willing to support James because he was Charles' lawful successor, even though he was a Catholic. The Exclusion Act failed to pass. Even if it had, it is clear that Charles II would have vetoed it.

THE HABEAS CORPUS ACT 1679

The Exclusion Crisis resulted in the passage of one of the most important laws in all of English history. Apparently, supporters of Exclusion were so afraid that King Charles would try to punish them that, in 1679, parliament codified *habeas corpus*. *Habeas corpus* is Latin for "you have the body." Its legal meaning is more like "produce the person." The basic idea of habeas corpus is that when someone is arrested they must be brought before a judge, thus "produce the body," so the detention of the person is shown to be legal. The central concept of habeas corpus is found in the Assize of Clarendon of 1166 and Magna Carta. Nevertheless, parliament had never formally approved habeas corpus.

The **Habeas Corpus Act 1679** provided that **a person arrested had to be brought promptly before a local judge and the arrest justified as legal; moreover, prisoners had the right to challenge the legality of their detention before a neutral judge.** Jailors who refused to comply with the provisions of the Act were subject to civil suits instituted by the prisoner whose rights were violated.

THE "GLORIOUS" REVOLUTION

Charles II died in 1685 and James II became king. In 1687 James II declared he would not enforce penal laws against Catholics, but there is more to the story.

Sir Edward Hales converted to Catholicism in 1685. James appointed Hales to the army, but Hales was ineligible for command because he refused to swear an Oath of Supremacy. The case went to trial where the court ruled that Hale was ineligible for command. Hales appealed to the Court of King's Bench. The case is *Godden v Hales* (1686).[7]

James and Hales actually designed the chain of events by which the issue was brought into court. To ensure Hales won, James dismissed and replaced several of the justices on the King's Bench. While the King had authority to dismiss judges, many people considered James' actions dishonest. Under the U.S. Constitution, judges would be appointed for life precisely to avoid this sort of mischief. At trial, Hales argued that he was eligible to serve, despite a law passed by parliament that required all officers to take the Oath of Supremacy because the king had authority to refuse to enforce penal laws on a case by case basis. Lord Chief Justice Herbert, writing for eleven of the twelve justices, sided with Hales and King James, declaring:

> We were satisfied in our judgments before and, having the concurrence of eleven out of twelve, we think we may very well declare the opinion of the court to be that the king may dispense in this case; and the judges go upon these grounds:

King James II

- that the kings of England are sovereign princes;

- that the laws of England are the king's laws;

- that therefore it is an inseparable prerogative in the kings of England to dispense with penal laws in particular cases and upon particular necessary reasons[.]

---

[7] 11 State Trials 1166.

This was the first example of what would later be called "**judicial review**," that is, the idea that courts are able to review the legality of legislation. Everything Hales and King James had done had been perfectly legal—and brilliant. Backed up by the decision of the King's Court in *Godden v Hales*, James proclaimed his intent to stop enforcing all the penal laws against Catholics. On April 4, 1687, James issued the Declaration of Indulgence, also known as the Declaration for Liberty of Conscience.

Critics argued that James' proclamation and the decision in *Godden v. Hales* amounted to an absolute monarchy, that is, if the king could refuse to comply with acts of parliament was he not putting himself above the law? Of course, James was not claiming he could make new laws or create new *crimes*, he was saying he could refuse to enforce *specific laws* when their application would be unjust.

In the midst of this ongoing constitutional crisis the Queen gave birth to a son on June 10, 1688, James (1688-1766). English Protestants now rallied behind James II's adult daughter Mary, who was a Protestant. They invited Mary and her husband, the Protestant William of Orange, to take over the government. In December 1688, William and Mary landed in England with a small force. The commander of James' army defected to the Protestant side and James fled England.

In February 1689, Parliament passed a "Declaration of Right" declaring that James had abdicated, and listing a series of grievances. The first item on the list was that James had subverted the law by "exercising a power of dispensing with and suspending of laws and the execution of laws without consent of Parliament." [This important statute will be discussed in detail later.]

James went to Ireland, which was solidly Catholic and supported him, to continue his fight. The Irish parliament confirmed James as King of Ireland. However, in 1690, an English army landed in Ireland. On July 1, 1690, the English defeated James at the Battle of the Boyne, effectively ending the dispute over the English crown.

The Battle of the Boyne, Jan Hoynck van Papendrecht

U.S. Government for Catholic Students

DECLARATION OF RIGHT AND BILL OF RIGHTS

In February 1689, Parliament passed **The Declaration of Right followed by the "Bill of Rights"** in December 1689. Both are important documents for the American legal tradition. The *Declaration of Right* began with a series of complaints about actions that King James had supposedly undertaken. [The American Declaration of Independence begins the same way.] The Declaration broadly declared parliamentary supremacy over both the king and the courts. Many of the issues would be brought up again in both the Bill of Rights and the American Constitution. The list included the following:

1. By assuming and exercising a power of dispensing with and suspending of laws and the execution of laws without consent of Parliament; …

4. By levying money … in other manner than the same was granted by Parliament;

5. By raising and keeping a standing army within this kingdom in time of peace, without consent of Parliament, and quartering soldiers contrary to law;

6. By causing several good subjects, being Protestants, to be disarmed, at the same time when papists were both armed and employed contrary to law; …

8. By prosecutions in the Court of King's Bench, for matters and causes cognizable only in Parliament; and by diverse other arbitrary and illegal courses[.]

All of these points contained some validity, but all appear to have applied more to Protestant Charles II than Catholic James II. Citizens had been disarmed in 1670. The line "papists were both armed and employed" appears to refer to Hales who was given a commission in the army. There was a tradition of no standing army, but the Royal "Household Guard" had been expanded under Charles in 1661. A later statute, the *Act of Settlement of 1701*, barred any monarch who "shall profess the popish religion, or shall marry a papist." The 1689 Declaration did not contain this clause.

The *Declaration of Right* contained no assertions of any sort of individual rights of citizens. It was a declaration that parliament had unlimited power to do whatever it wished. On the other hand, kings and judges only had those powers allowed to them by parliament.

The *Bill of Rights* addressed many of the same issues, but this time, much of the document was phrased in terms of individual rights. This emphasis on individual rights was a major change from earlier English documents, but even here the "rights" articulated were weak and apparently subject to restriction by parliament. Moreover, the document insisted that it was doing nothing more than "vindicating and asserting their ancient rights and liberties."

Once again, the first item listed was: "the pretended power of suspending the laws or the execution of laws by regal authority without consent of Parliament is illegal." The document went on to assert several important legal rights:

[5] That it is the right of the subjects to petition the king, and all commitments and prosecutions for such petitioning are illegal;

[6] That the raising or keeping of a standing army within the kingdom in time of peace, unless it be with consent of Parliament, is against law;

[7] That the subjects which are Protestants may have arms for their defense suitable to their conditions and as allowed by law; …

[9] That the freedom of speech and debates or proceedings in Parliament ought not to be impeached or questioned in any court or place out of Parliament;

[10] That excessive bail ought not to be required, nor excessive fines imposed, nor cruel and unusual punishments inflicted;

All of these provisions would later be included in the U.S. Constitution.

ADMINISTRATION OF ENGLAND IN THE 18TH CENTURY

The "Glorious" Revolution confirmed parliamentary supremacy which was reinforced by a series of weak foreign kings. William and Mary reigned as joint monarchs until Mary died in 1694 without a child. William reigned for a few years on his own. When William died in 1702, James II's next daughter, Anne, became Queen. Anne also died without a direct heir. The Whigs, who were dominant in Parliament, brought over the Duke of Brunswick, who was distantly related to the English royal family, to become King George I.[8] The Whigs dominated parliament for the next fifty years. People throughout England and Scotland rioted when George was proclaimed king and he was never popular with the English people.

George I was succeeded in 1727 by George II, who was succeeded by George III in 1760. George III was king when the American colonies won their independence. These weak, unpopular foreign kings made it easy for parliament to rule with little interference from the king. The power of the monarchs was reduced and the government was in

The Lords and Commons presenting the crown to William of Orange and Mary Stuart by Edward Matthew Ward

the hands of a group of ministers approved by the House of Commons. The leader of this group of ministers came to be known as the Prime Minister, a term first applied to Robert Walpole in 1741.

BRITAIN'S AMERICAN COLONIES

VIRGINIA

In April 1606, King James granted a "Letter Patent" to a group of men authorizing them to form a settlement on the east coast of North America somewhere between present-day North Carolina and New Hampshire. This "Letter Patent," generally called the "First Charter of Virginia," declared that one of the main purposes for permitting colonization of America was for "propagating of Christian Religion to such People, as yet live in Darkness and miserable Ignorance of the true Knowledge and Worship of God." The most important point of this Charter was that it authorized the colonists to form a council to "govern and order all Matters and Causes, which shall arise, grow, or happen, to or within the same several Colonies," subject to ultimate royal approval or veto. During this time, parliament could only pass laws subject to royal approval.

The Charter granted several other prerogatives to the colonists. Among the most important was the section which authorized the colonists to coin money "of such Metal, and in such Manner and Form" as the colony's council determined. This issue of money became a constant dispute throughout the colonial period. Although Virginia did not issue coinage until just before independence, Massachusetts and Maryland issued silver coins in the 1650s. This is important because issuing money is considered one of the main prerogatives of **sovereignty**, that is, the power to make decisions without being subject to any

A "pine tree shilling," one of the first coins issued in Massachusetts

---

[8] It is estimated that 57 people had better claims to the throne than George, but they all were disqualified for being Catholic.

A historical re-creation of a settler's house in Jamestown, Virginia

higher appeal to human authority. Thus, from the beginning, American colonies were allowed self-government and sovereignty.

In 1607, colonists established the first permanent English settlement in America at Jamestown, Virginia. This was followed by The Second Charter of Virginia signed by King James on May 23, 1609. In the Second Charter's most important section, King James named a group of people as the council to rule Virginia, and provided that when a member of the council died or resigned his replacement would be elected by majority vote of the "Adventurers." Replacements who were elected did not need the king's approval; however, they were required to take a loyalty oath to the king before they could take office. The 1609 Charter further provided that the council could appoint a governor and other officers with

> Power and Authority to correct, punish, pardon, govern, and rule all such the Subjects of Us, our Heires, and Successors as shall from Time to Time adventure themselves in any Voyage thither ... according to such Orders, Ordinances, Constitutions, Directions, and Instructions, as by our said Council as aforesaid, shall be established;

The Charter also provided that *"such principal Governor, as from Time to Time shall duly and lawfully be authorized and appointed in Manner and Form in these Presents heretofore expressed, shall have full Power and Authority, to use and exercise Martial Law in Cases of Rebellion or Mutiny."*

The Charter of 1609 concluded by declaring that *"the principal Effect which We can desire or expect of this Action, is the Conversion and Reduction of the People in those Parts unto the true Worship of God and Christian Religion,"* which forbade Catholics from traveling to Virginia.

A Third Charter, promulgated in 1612, confirmed the first two and added that any child of an English subject born in Virginia would have the same "Freedoms, Liberties, Franchises[9], Privileges, [and] Immunities" as those born in England. The 1611 Charter verified that colonists were not "second class" subjects. Yet, if Virginians enjoyed the same liberties as other English subjects, why were they not permitted to send members to parliament or participate in parliamentary elections? There seems to have been two answers to this question.

First, seats in parliament had been well-settled for centuries. Newly-established cities did not get to send a representative to parliament while old towns did, even when the old town's population was reduced. Voting for members of parliament was not a privilege possessed by individual Englishmen. Voting was certainly not a "right" either, as the word "right" is not in the charter.

A second reason Virginians could not send representatives to parliament was that Virginia was self-governing. Parliament helped the king rule England, but the Virginia council helped the king rule Virginia. In other words, in the early 17th century, parliament had little input regarding events in Virginia. So, what would be the point of Virginians sending a member to parliament?

In November 1618, Virginia Governor, George Yeardley, ordered the creation of a general assembly to address concerns of the colonists. The Virginia General Assembly met for the first time at Jamestown from July 30 to August 4, 1619. By a 1621 statute, the executive council of Virginia, not just the governor as in 1618, declared that "by Authority directed to us from his Majesty" there was to be a "General Assembly" for Virginia. According to the 1621 statute:

---

[9]The word *franchise* came from the Anglo-French word "franche" meaning "free." In 1600, *franchise* was synonymous with *freedom*, although in the 18th century "franchise" came to be associated with voting.

this General Assembly shall have free Power to treat, consult, and conclude, as well of all emergent Occasions concerning the Publick Weal of the said Colony and every Part thereof, as also to make, ordain, and enact such general Laws and Orders, for the Behoof of the said Colony, and the good Government thereof, as shall, from time to time, appear necessary or requisite[.]

The governor of Virginia, however, retained an absolute veto over any legislation the General Assembly passed. The statute further required both the General Assembly and the executive council "to imitate and follow the Policy of the Form of Government, Laws, Customs, and Manner of Trial, and other Administration of Justice, used in the Realm of England, as near as may be, even as ourselves, by his Majesty's Letters Patent, are required." This 1621 statute, often called the first Constitution of Virginia, notably proclaimed that the legislature had no authority to alter the "Laws, Customs, and Manner of Trial" that had been established in England. This seems to be nothing more than the logical implication of the 1611 Royal Charter that had already declared that American Colonists had the same liberties as every other Englishman. If this was the case, then the General Assembly had no power to destroy any of these traditional liberties. By 1688, Parliament declared that it had plenary power to alter any law, even, for example, Magna Carta. Virginia's 1621 "constitution" was much more like what today is called a "constitution" because ordinary laws passed by the legislature would be invalid if they contravened this higher law.

NEW ENGLAND

In 1620, King James issued a royal patent to allow another settlement in America north of Jamestown, but still part of Virginia, that was designated as "New England." The 1620 patent for New England was quite similar to the 1607 Virginia patent. New England was authorized to create a local council to deal with local matters. The powers granted to the New England's council were less extensive than those granted by the 1607 patent because the New England settlement was to be subordinate to Virginia.

The most notable difference between Jamestown and the New England settlement was that Puritans settled New England. "Puritanism" was a development of the "Anabaptist" movement of the 16th century. Puritans took their name because they wanted to "purify" the Anglican Church of any lingering vestiges of Catholicism. Puritans wanted to abolish the sacraments, the priesthood, and all sacred images. Politically, Puritans also held radical views. Many Puritans denied that the king possessed any political authority, just as they denied the Pope possessed religious authority. During the 16th and 17th centuries, many Puritans called for the abolition of the monarchy. They got their wish for a time when Charles I was executed in 1649.

Both Catholics and Anglicans distrusted and persecuted Puritans. In the first decade of the 17th century, several hundred English Puritans formed a community in Holland, but they were not welcome there either. So, in 1620, these Puritans sought and obtained permission to form a new

The Mayflower in Plymouth Harbor, William Halsall (1882)

colony in the northern part of Virginia. In 1620, about one hundred Puritans aboard the *Mayflower* landed at Cape Cod in present-day Massachusetts.

In November 1620, the adult males on the *Mayflower* signed an agreement called The **Mayflower Compact**. Religiously, Puritans rejected all hierarchy such as ordained priests or bishops. As a result, the political systems they established in America were more egalitarian than those established in Virginia. The *Mayflower Compact* formed a local government, but there was nothing radical about it. The *Compact* acknowledged their loyalty to King James I but did not mention any colonial governor. However, as Cape Cod was 600 miles from Jamestown, the New England settlement at Plymouth was, for all practical purposes, autonomous.

Puritans flocked to New England seeking religious freedom. About 20,000 Puritans emigrated to New England between 1620 and 1640. In 1629, Charles I granted a charter to the Massachusetts Bay Company to form a settlement in New England. The 1629 Charter provided for a governor, deputy governor, and eighteen assistants. These officials were named by the king in the 1629 Charter but replacement officers were to be chosen by popular vote in later years. The council was authorized to make laws "not contrairie to the Lawes of this our Realme of England."

As more Puritans came to New England, they began forming a number of separate settlements. Because Puritans rejected all hierarchy, and every individual believer interpreted the Bible for himself, it was difficult to settle disputes. Inevitably, Puritans saw other Puritan settlements as not pure enough.

For example, Roger Williams emigrated to Boston in 1631 and switched back and forth between Boston and Plymouth. Williams was put on trial in Massachusetts Bay for his "radical" views, convicted, and banished from the colony. He then led a small group of his supporters to form a new colony at Providence. Unlike many other English colonists, Williams believed that the land belonged to those who were living on it. Therefore, his group purchased land from the Narragansett tribe.

In 1637, the settlers signed **The Providence Agreement**, a short document in which heads of families agreed to obey any orders enacted by

The signing of the *Mayflower Compact*, painted by Jean Leon Gerome Ferris

majority vote of the heads of families in the town. This settlement was somewhat different from the others already discussed, in that Providence had no authority or charter from the king to exist. However, in 1643, Williams obtained a patent from parliament that gave the "Inhabitants of the Towns of Providence, Portsmouth, and Newport … full Power and Authority to rule themselves," by majority vote of town residents so long as the local laws were "conformable to the Laws of England." This last provision is problematic, insofar as in 1643 penal laws against Catholics were still in effect in England. Nevertheless, under the leadership of Williams, all religions were tolerated in Rhode Island. A small group of Jews even settled there in 1658.

Another early group of Puritans settled around the Connecticut River and formed their own local government. The 1639 **Fundamental Orders of Connecticut** began by explaining:

> Well knowning where a people are gathered togather the word of God requires that to mayntayne the peace and union of such a people there should be an orderly and decent Goverment established according to God, to order and dispose of the affayres … enter into Combination and Confederation together, to mayntayne and prsearve the liberty and purity of the gospell of our Lord Jesus[.]

As a Protestant document, it refers to "the word of God" rather than to "Natural Law" but the idea is much the same: government authority is ordained by God, but the community can structure government in different ways. The Fundamental Orders provided for a governor, who had to be protestant, and an assembly for Connecticut. The governor was authorized to arrest criminals and bring them before the assembly but the governor's powers were limited. For example, the governor had no authority to veto statutes passed by the assembly. The governor's term was a single year. The governor was required to take an oath swearing:

> I will mayntayne all the lawfull priviledges therof according to my understanding, as also assist in the execution of all such wholsome lawes as are made or shall be made by lawfull authority heare established[.]

Seal of the Massachusetts Bay Colony

The "lawfull priviledges" were not specified, but presumably included such things as trial by jury and habeas corpus.

Finally, in 1641, Massachusetts adopted the **Massachusetts Body of Liberties**, one of the most extensive declarations of liberties for citizens and churches. As with most other documents of this period, it speaks of liberties and privileges but does not mention any "rights." The Body of Liberties summarized many of the basic liberties found in documents like Magna Carta but it contained a few new ones, or at least, some liberties were expressed in a new way. The Body of Liberties was directed to the Massachusetts courts, to ensure that judges respected these important liberties.

The significant provisions include that no property "shall be pressed or taken for any publique use or service" without "reasonable" compensation. Everyone was allowed to present a petition to any Court, Council, or Town meeting without penalty. Other than for a capital crime, bail was required for those facing trial. Everyone was permitted to have an advocate in court to speak for him. Other provisions guaranteed trial by jury, appeal to a higher court, and a speedy trial. No one could be sentenced twice for the same offense. "Inhumane, Barbarous or cruell" punishments were prohibited. All people had liberty to search the records of any court or public body. Finally, the Body of Liberties proclaimed that *"all the people of god … shall have full libertie to gather themselves into a Church Estaite. Provided they do it in a Christian way, with due observation of*

An artist's depiction of the founding of Maryland and the first Mass celebrated in English America

the rules of Christ revealed in his word." This was far from full freedom of religion, as the government could judge whether the church was sufficiently observing the rules of Christ. Many of these basic liberties later appeared in the United States' Constitution.

MARYLAND

Maryland was the project of George Calvert (1580-1632), the first Baron Baltimore. Calvert was born to a wealthy family in the north of England. As a child, Calvert's family was required to renounce the Catholic Church, and George's father was forced to educate George as a Protestant. George attended Oxford then studied law, and became one of the highest-ranking officials in the government of James I. For his service, James elevated Calvert to the nobility, awarding him the title Baron Baltimore in 1625. Soon after, Calvert announced that he was Catholic.

In 1625, it was illegal to practice the Catholic faith in England. Calvert considered moving to Virginia, but Catholics were banned from Virginia, and the government in Jamestown forbade Calvert to settle there. In 1630, Calvert asked Charles I to grant a charter for a new colony north of the Potomac River. Calvert died in 1632, but several weeks later The Maryland Charter was approved.

The Maryland Charter declared that a main goal was "extending the Christian Religion," but unlike the Virginia Charters there was no religious restriction on who was permitted to settle in Maryland. The Charter further provided that Baron Baltimore and his successors were given *"full, and absolute Power, by the Tenor of these Presents, to Ordain, Make, and Enact Laws, of what Kind soever, according to their sound Discretions ... with the Advice, Assent, and Approbation of the Free-Men of the same Province, or the greater Part of them, or of their Delegates or Deputies[.]"*

The government of Maryland was equivalent to the government of England at this time. Maryland and England were governed by a hereditary ruler, but laws needed to have the consent of the realm. Neither Parliament nor the Maryland assembly had any authority to make law without the approval of the hereditary ruler.

The Maryland Charter also appointed Baron Baltimore Captain-General of a militia. It provided for the creation of towns, boroughs, and cities "with suitable Privileges and Immunities." Finally, because the Virginia charters had declared that all of the land around the Chesapeake Bay was part of Virginia, the Maryland Charter specified that it was not part of Virginia nor subordinate to Virginia.

Two ships brought some 200 settlers to Maryland in 1634. On March 25, 1634, the first Catholic Mass in English America was celebrated. The first capital was St. Mary's, the site of a native village inhabited by a tribe called Yaocomico. The Yaocomico agreed to trade 30 acres of land for some steel tools. Native Americans possessed no metal tools so metal tools such as axes and saws were invaluable to them. The Marylanders had friendly relations with the natives, a number of whom converted to Catholicism in the next few years. A temporary chapel was erected in 1634, and the first Catholic church in Maryland, St. Ignatius, was completed in 1641.

Maryland's first governor was George Calvert's son, **Leonard Calvert**, the Lord Baltimore. Although Maryland's founding documents made no explicit declaration of religious toleration, the Calverts practiced a policy of full religious freedom for all Christians. In the 1630s, Maryland was the only place in the entire English-speaking world where all Christians enjoyed freedom of religion.

In 1638, the Maryland Assembly met for the first time. Its most important action was passing the "Act for the Liberties of the People." This short document provided that inhabitants of Maryland:

> Shall have and enjoy all such rights liberties immunities priviledges and free customs within this Province as any natural born subject of England hath or ought to have or enjoy in the Realm of England by force or virtue of the common law or Statute Law of England (saving in such Cases as the same are or may be altered or changed by the Laws and ordinances of this Province)

The second and final paragraph added that no one could be deprived of liberty or property except "according to the Laws of this province."

It is interesting to see that the rights, liberties and privileges enjoyed by every Englishman could be "altered or changed by the Laws and ordinances of this Province." As a sovereign, self-governing "province," Maryland had authority to enact its own laws, even if contrary to English custom, common law, or Statute. Indeed, the toleration of religion practiced at this time, was actually contrary to English law.

The first Maryland Assembly also passed "An Act for Church Liberties" (1638) which stated:

> Be it enacted by the Lord Proprietary of this Province by and with the Advice and approbation of the freemen of the same that Holy Church within this Province shall have all her rights liberties and immunities safe whole and inviolable in all things.

Presumably for political reasons, the Act avoided reference to the "Catholic" Church. Some people might have understood "Holy Church" to apply to all Christian churches, but the effect was that Catholics and all Christians were, by statute, afforded freedom of worship.

Unfortunately, Catholics in Maryland would not be left in peace for long. In 1645, during the English Civil War, a group of Puritans attacked Maryland in the name of parliament and briefly seized control of the colony. The colony's leaders and two Jesuit priests were arrested. [Lord Baltimore himself was not captured.] Property of Catholics was stolen or destroyed. In December 1646, Lord Baltimore restored order with the help of troops from Virginia.

When Lord Baltimore died, a protestant, Thomas Greene, was appointed the new governor in 1649. This appointment of a Protestant was evidently a compromise. Under the governorship of Greene, the Maryland assembly passed "Act Concerning Religion" or "Toleration Act" in 1649. The Toleration Act provided that no one "professing to believe in Jesus Christ" would be molested "for or in respect of his or her religion or the free exercise thereof within this Province *other than is provided for in this Act*." In fact, the Act provided for a variety of punishments aimed at Puritans. For example, it was a crime to "use or utter any reproachful words or Speeches concerning the Blessed Virgin Mary the Mother of our Savior or the holy Apostles or Evangelists." The penalty was a fine of five pounds, but if the person did not have five pounds he was to be "publicly whipped."

The 1649 Act of Toleration was less tolerant than the 1638 Act for Church Liberties. Of course, the Act of Toleration did not punish anyone for their beliefs but it punished certain expressions Puritans often used to incite religious discord. Many people thought that allowing complete freedom of religion actually attracted some of the most radical Puritans to settle in Maryland.

The Revolution of 1688 everything changed. During the "Maryland Revolution of 1689," also known as Coode's Rebellion, several hundred protestants again overthrew the established government. In 1692, the Church of England was declared the established church of Maryland, and Maryland was declared to be a "royal colony," stripping Baron Baltimore of his rule. Henceforth, England's monarch would appoint the colonial governor.

NEW YORK AND NEW JERSEY

In the 1660s, the English defeated the Netherlands, and the Dutch surrendered their lands in North America to the English, essentially present-day New York and New Jersey. The Duke of York, the future James II, was granted all the land between Connecticut and Maryland. The English agreed to allow freedom of religion for the Dutch settlers, and because James was a Catholic, New York was more religiously tolerant than many of the other colonies.

In 1664, James granted two other nobles, Lord John Berkeley and Sir George Carteret authority to act as proprietors of the land between the Hudson and Delaware rivers, the area to become known as New Jersey. Carteret was from the Isle of Jersey, hence the name "New Jersey." Berkeley and Carteret were to pay James a yearly rent of 20 gold coins as a symbolic amount to recognize that he was the ultimate overlord of the colony. Because there were two proprietors, for a short time, New Jersey was divided into East and West Jersey.

In 1664, Berkeley and Carteret promulgated a plan of government called *Concessions and Agreements of the Proprietors of East Jersey*. This document provided for an elected assembly to make laws "agreeable to the Lawes and Customs of … England" and agreeable to the proprietors. The document also declared that:

> no person qualified as aforesaid within the said Province at any time shall be any ways molested punished disquieted or called in Question for any difference in opinion or practice in matters of Religious concernments, who does not actually disturb the civil peace of the said Province[.]

Neither Berkeley nor Carteret had shown any interest in religious liberty and both were lifelong Protestants. So, this was almost certainly the idea of James. However, allowing two Protestants to proclaim religious liberty was politically expedient.

In 1676, the people of West Jersey voted to adopt *The Charter* or *Fundamental Laws of West New Jersey* which declared that it was "to be the foundation of the government, which is not to be altered by the Legislative authority." Of course, the king or the governor appointed by the king had declared himself to be superior to the people's assembly, but this appears to be the first time that a convention of ordinary citizens declared that the legislative assembly could not change a more basic law. The Charter reaffirmed freedom of religion that had been declared in the 1664 Concessions. It also reaffirmed

A 1706 map of East and West Jersey

several of the most basic ancient liberties such as trial by jury.

In 1683, New York's assembly met for the first time and promulgated a "Charter of Liberties and Privileges." New York had taken longer to organize because of fighting between the English and the Dutch. The Charter approved a form of government based on England's. The assembly could meet and propose changes in law, but no change could be made without the approval of the governor, who, at this time, was appointed by James, Duke of York. No taxes could be assessed without the approval of the New York assembly. To protect religious liberty, the Charter provided that:

> No person or persons which profess faith in God by Jesus Christ Shall at any time be any way molested punished disquieted or called in Question for Difference in opinion or Matter of Religious Concernment, who does not actually disturb the Civil peace of the province[.]

The Charter also stated that no particular Christian church was to be afforded any privileges above any other Christian church. Every church was to "Enjoy all their former freedoms of their Religion in Divine Worship and Church Discipline."

PENNSYLVANIA

In 1666, at age 22, William Penn (1644-1718) joined the Quakers or "Society of Friends." The Quakers, like Puritans, rejected all hierarchy. Quakers were primarily known for their doctrine of absolute pacifism. In 1670, Penn was arrested for violating a statute making it a crime to attend any religious service other than the Church of England. However, the jury acquitted him. Remarkably, the judge held the jurors in contempt of court for refusing to convict Penn who clearly had attended a non-Anglican gathering. One of the jurors, Edward Bushel, refused to pay the fine and was imprisoned. Bushel brought a case under the habeas corpus act and the Chief Justice ruled that jurors could not be punished on account of their verdict. *Bushel's Case* (1670) (124 E.R. 1006), became a celebrated case on both sides of the Atlantic. It reinforced the American belief in the role of the jury in preserving freedom. The government could enact whatever laws it wished, but the final word lay with the jury who could refuse to convict. As a result of his prosecution, William Penn became an advocate of religious liberty.

When Penn's father died in 1672, he inherited a small fortune including a large debt Charles II owed to his father. In 1681, Charles II granted the land southwest of the Delaware River (present-day Pennsylvania and Delaware) to William Penn as repayment of the debt. The following year, William left England with a Royal Charter for his colony in America, Pennsylvania.

Pennsylvania's Royal Charter granted Penn power to appoint judges and other local officials. He also had authority to pardon crimes. Significantly, the Charter granted a great deal of sovereignty to the new colony. The laws of Pennsylvania:

> shall be and continue the same as shall be for the time being, by the general course of the Law in our Kingdome of England, until the said Lawes shall be altered by the said William Penn, his heirs or assigns, and by the freemen of the said Province, their Delegates or Deputies, or the greater part of them.

The king reserved the power as overall sovereign to veto any new laws passed by the new colony. However, this was a major concession of sovereignty: it said that Pennsylvania could change any law passed by parliament and make their own laws, so long as the king did not veto it. Pennsylvania's Charter was granted in the midst of the Exclusion Controversy and no doubt Charles and James were happy to try to take parliament down a peg or two. Regardless of the motives, the Royal Charter explicitly authorized Pennsylvania to alter the laws of England and make their own contrary laws. This was a crucial concession for freedom of religion, because under English laws, the only legal religion was the Church of England. Penn, or the people of the colony, were free to change that law. Indeed, this may have been the primary purpose for this striking provision.

In 1682, Pennsylvania's General Assembly met for the first time and enacted a list of provisions to govern the new colony. The first Article of what was called "The Great Law" provided that no person

> who Shall Confess and acknowledge one Almighty God to be the Creator Upholder and Ruler of the World and that professes him or herself Obliged in Conscience to Live Peaceably and Justly under the Civil Government shall in any case be Molested or Prejudiced for his or her Conscientious Persuasion or Practice[.]

Article 2 required that no person could hold office or be employed by the government of Pennsylvania except "Such as profess and Declare they Believe in Jesus Christ to be the Son of God the Savior of the World." While there was freedom of religion for anyone who believed in God, there was also no doubt that Pennsylvania was a Christian state.

CAROLINA

In 1663, King Charles II granted a royal charter to "Carolina" which was named after him. Carolina was a large territory comprising all the land south of Virginia and north of Spanish Florida. In 1712, Carolina was divided into North and South Carolina, and later into Georgia (1732). As in other colonies, Carolina was granted self-government under a group of proprietors. The most notable provision of its Charter regarded freedom of conscience. This provision recognized that *"some of the people and inhabitants of the said province, cannot in their private opinions, conform to the public exercise of religion, according to the liturgy, form and ceremonies of the church of England,"* and therefore the proprietors of Carolina were authorized to grant exemptions to the penal laws to those who had religious objections.

In 1669-1670, the proprietors of Carolina drafted (but never formally implemented) *The Fundamental Constitutions of Carolina.* The document is mainly significant because English philosopher John Locke is said to have helped draft it. The document was quite abstract and broke with English tradition in a variety of ways. For example, voting was severely restricted to those who owned at least fifty acres of property. Ultimately, it was rejected and exerted little influence on later American thought.

SUMMARY

In the 1600s, England afforded her American colonies a great deal of self-government. Most colonies allowed freedom of conscience, or freedom of religion, to varying degrees. This began to change in the late 1600s and accelerated in the 1700s.

THE NAVIGATION ACTS

During the second half of the 17th century, parliament passed a series of laws known as the **Navigation Acts** which required that the American colonies only trade with England. Americans could not trade with France or Spain or their colonies, like Canada. Technically, this was not interference in the internal affairs of the colonies, nor a direct tax on them, since goods were taxed as imports once they arrived in England. Nevertheless, colonists resented any restrictions: why could New England not trade with nearby French Canada?

The 1696 Navigation Act tightened control considerably. It declared that any colonial laws contrary to the Navigation Acts were null and void. Moreover, any violation of the Navigation Act, mainly smuggling, was to be tried in England, not in the colonies. All governors were required to swear to uphold the Navigation Act.

London moved to exert direct control over the colonies by appointing royal governors. In 1692, the Maryland Charter was revoked. The Crown appointed Sir Lionel Copley as Governor of Maryland and declared the Church of England to be Maryland's official religion. In 1695, the crown appointed Richard Coote to be royal governor of New York, New Hampshire, and Massachusetts. His attempts to enforce the Navigation Act of 1696 made him very unpopular. For example, in 1698 Coote asked the New York assembly to grant him a salary as governor and the assembly refused.

After a century of Americans largely being left to rule themselves, they resented these attempts by Parliament to exert more control over them.

For their part, the English thought that they were protecting the American colonies from attacks by the Dutch, French, and Spanish. Moreover, they felt Americans should be contributing more money to their own defense.

In 1733, Parliament passed the Molasses Act, which taxed all molasses imported into the colonies. Molasses was valuable mainly because it was used to make rum. Like the other Navigation Acts, Americans resented the Molasses Act and responded by increasing their smuggling efforts. The Molasses Act expired in 1763. In 1764, Parliament passed the Sugar Act which cracked down on smuggling and added other products to the list of those to be taxed to raise revenue from the colonies which, in 1764, England desperately needed to pay for the Seven Years' War.

THE STAMP ACT AND THE STAMP ACT CONGRESS OF 1765

From 1756 to 1763, England, France, and most other major European powers fought the Seven Years' War, known in America as The French and Indian War (1754-1763). England and France were long-time enemies and had fought off and on for the previous 700 years. In the 1750s, one of their major disputes involved competing claims to the land northwest of the Ohio River.

Under its charter, Virginia claimed all of the land between the Ohio River and the Great Lakes. In 1753, when Virginia Governor Robert Dinwiddie learned that the French had tried to set up a fort in Virginia territory, he sent George Washington to kick them out. Washington led a force of several hundred men to the area south of present-day Pittsburgh and attacked the French in May 1754. The skirmishes were inconclusive, but they launched the war and George Washington's career. England eventually prevailed in the Seven Years' War and, under the peace treaty, the French ceded the disputed territory and all of French Canada to England. However, the Seven Years' War was ruinously expensive, leaving England with a massive debt.

England looked to her American colonies to help pay the debt, because after all, England had helped defend the colonies. In the mind of Englishmen, it was only fair that the colonies pay their fair share of the war's expenses. To help pay for the war, Parliament enacted the Sugar Act of 1764. In 1765, Parliament passed The Stamp Act, which required almost every document and publication in the colonies to contain a revenue stamp. The Act also required duties to be paid in English coin rather than colonial currency.

Unlike some earlier laws, where arguably the taxes were imposed on goods before they arrived in the colonies, the Stamp Act directly regulated

Major George Washington (seated on the white horse) at the Battle of the Monongahela in 1755

actions of colonists. For example, it was illegal to distribute a newspaper or handbill unless it had the revenue stamp on it. Any person who sold a newspaper or distributed handbills in violation of the Stamp Act would be fined twenty pounds for each offense which was almost a year's wages for the average worker. Moreover, any person in the colonies who created a counterfeit stamp was subject to the death penalty. So, parliament was asserting authority to create criminal laws for the colonies. Finally, the Act allowed trials for these offenses to be tried in Admiralty Courts rather than tried by local juries

These draconian measures caused the Stamp Act to be hugely unpopular. In October 1765, delegates from nine American colonies met in New York to formulate a response. Known as the **Stamp Act Congress**, it issued a "Declaration of Rights" setting forth a series of grievances. The Declaration began with the remarkable expression that the colonists admitted "all due subordination to that august body, the Parliament of Great Britain." Of course, the degree of subordination that was "due" was not absolute subordination but nonetheless this recognized parliament's authority over the colonies. The Declaration declared that the colonists possessed all the same traditional rights and liberties that "natural born subjects" possessed. Some of these traditional privileges violated by parliament included the power to consent to new taxes and trial by a local jury of one's peers. The Declaration concluded with an explanation that it was exercising "the right of the British subjects in these colonies to petition the king or either house of Parliament" and did nothing more than call on parliament to repeal the Stamp Act.

The Stamp Act Declaration was quite tame. The handful of privileges demanded were unquestionably deeply rooted in centuries of English tradition. The Declaration claimed that the Stamp Act was "Inconsistent with the principles and spirit of the British constitution" but did not deny that Parliament possessed authority to pass the Stamp Act. The Stamp Act Declaration of Rights was not remotely "revolutionary," but it signaled an attempt of the colonies to formulate a concerted plan of opposition to British measures.

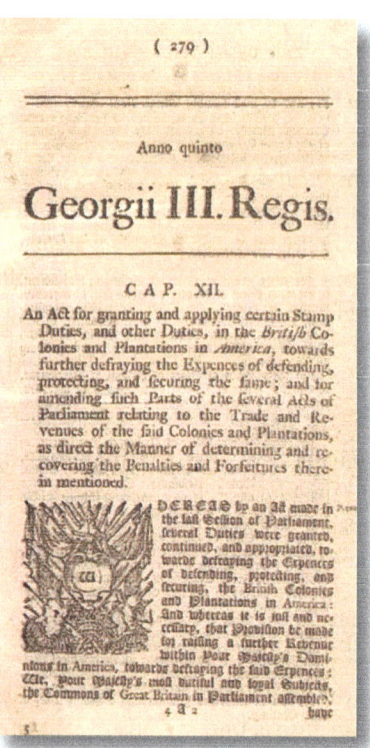

A copy of the Stamp Act

Unlike the Stamp Act Congress' rather mild petition, individual Americans took more direct, violent, approaches. One famous group in Boston was the Sons of Liberty, who attacked tax collectors and burned down warehouses full of English imports so that the Stamp Act could not be enforced. Partly as a result of this violent opposition to the Stamp Act, Parliament repealed it in 1766. However, in repealing the Stamp Act, parliament passed the **Declaratory Act** which asserted parliament's absolute authority to make any law for the American colonies. In other words, the colonies had no sovereignty at all, and whatever self-government the colonies possessed was exercised at the sufferance of parliament.

In 1767, Parliament passed the Townshend Acts, at the behest of Charles Townshend, the Chancellor of the Exchequer, England's chief tax collector. The first of the acts was The Revenue Act of 1767 which taxed a variety of products including tea, a favorite colonial beverage. To inflame matters further, the Revenue Act authorized customs officers "to enter and go into any house, shop, cellar, warehouse, or room or other place," to search for contraband. This was truly shocking. English tradition had always maintained that "A man's home is his castle." The Act reached into every home in England's North American colonies and allowed revenue agents to search those homes on the mere suspicion they might contain contraband.

In July 1767, Parliament passed The New York Restraining Act. In 1765, parliament passed the Quartering Act which demanded that New York pay to house English soldiers in the colony. The

An engraving of the Boston Massacre made by Paul Revere

Acts were illegal. Massachusetts sent a petition to the King but refused to send a petition to parliament, arguing that parliament had no authority to tax Americans. The Massachusetts Circular Letter of 1768 objected to taxation without representation, but declared that Massachusetts did not want to send representatives to parliament, which was impractical given the distance. Instead, "his Majesty's royal predecessors" gave the colonists "the unalienable right of a representation" so only the Massachusetts assembly could authorize a tax of Massachusetts.

The Massachusetts Circular ended by appealing to King George III as "our common head and father" to intervene and end the Townshend Acts. Perhaps this was just a rhetorical device, but it is clear that George had no legal authority to override parliament. Unlike the very mild Stamp Act Declaration of 1765, the Circular Letter of 1768 insisted that parliament had no authority to tax colonists without their consent and colonists had no duty to obey these statutes.

Parliament responded by dispatching 2,000 more English soldiers to Boston hoping a show of force would calm the situation. It did not. Protests and riots continued. On March 5, 1770, a group of Americans pelted some English soldiers with snowballs and stones. The English fired at the crowd killing five people in what became known as **The Boston Massacre**. On December 16, 1773, about one hundred Sons of Liberty, disguised as Native Americans, boarded three British merchant ships and threw 342 chests of tea into Boston Harbor, destroying the tea, during the Boston Tea Party.

New York assembly refused to appropriate any money, believing it did not need English soldiers for protection. The Restraining Act proclaimed that the New York Assembly could not enact any laws until it agreed to pay for the English soldiers. Essentially, this Act abolished representative government in New York! If Parliament could do this in New York it could do it elsewhere. The Restraining Act once again meant that Americans exercised self-government only at the sufferance of parliament. The New York legislature appropriated the money so the Act never became effective, but colonists everywhere were furious.

Led by Samuel Adams, the Massachusetts House of Representatives declared the Townshend

THE INTOLERABLE ACTS OF 1774 AND THE FIRST CONTINENTAL CONGRESS

Parliament responded to the Boston Tea Party by passing a series of measures known in the colonies as **The Intolerable Acts**, the most important of which was the Massachusetts Government Act. This Act said that the king could replace all of the elected representatives of the Massachusetts Assembly with people he appointed. The Act also expanded the power of the royally-appointed governor to fire sheriffs and local judges, then replace them with candidates of the royal governor's choice. Effectively, the Act declared martial law and abolished any role for elected representatives in Massachusetts' government.

Another Act of parliament that upset many American colonists was The Quebec Act, which extended the territory of Quebec to all the land northwest of the Ohio River—the disputed land over which the French and Indian War had been fought. Because many of the colonies, including Virginia, Pennsylvania, and Massachusetts had claims to this land under their royal charters, many colonists resented the Quebec Act and saw it as another slap in the face to the American colonies.

In response to the Intolerable Acts, representatives from twelve of the American colonies met in Philadelphia in September 1774. This was the **First Continental Congress**. Delegates were divided between those who just wanted to issue a petition asking parliament to repeal the Intolerable Acts and more "hardliners" who wanted to declare that all the acts of parliament were entirely null and void because parliament had no authority to make laws for the American colonies. The more cautious faction prevailed, and the First Continental Congress resolved that only "peaceable measures" would be used, including an economic boycott of English goods. The Congress issued a Declaration that began:

> That the inhabitants of the English Colonies in North America, by the immutable laws of nature, the principles of the English Constitution, and the several Charters or Compacts, have the following Rights:
>
> Resolved, 1. That they are entitled to life, liberty, and property, and they have never ceded to any sovereign power whatever a right to dispose of either without their consent.

THE FIRST CONTINENTAL CONGRESS · 1774

The Congress asserted several other fundamental liberties of Englishmen including participating in formation of new laws, trial by jury of the accused's peers, the right to assemble and petition, and that "keeping a Standing Army in these Colonies, in times of peace, without the consent of the Legislature of that Colony, in which such Army is kept, is against law." Finally, the Congress declared that "his Majesty's Colonies, are likewise entitled to all the immunities and privileges granted and confirmed to them by Royal Charters, or secured by their several codes of Provincial Laws." This was tantamount to denial of parliament's authority because it declared that "Provincial Laws" passed by local bodies were superior to acts of parliament. This was not a Declaration of Independence, but it was a declaration of autonomy, that is, the colonies were entitled to make their own laws, at least to the degree that that self-government had been authorized by their initial charters.

CONCLUSION

Ultimately, the dispute between the Americans and the English was about sovereignty. A large number of American colonists believed that they were legally and morally entitled to self-government. Massachusetts, New York, and Virginia were entitled to rule themselves. At this time, no one thought that the colonies collectively had sovereignty or a claim to collective self-government. Essentially, the colonists thought they had been promised self-government and now parliament wanted to change the rules and take it all away. Rulers in London insisted that parliament was supreme with authority to make laws for England and for all England's colonies. The two views were irreconcilable. Neither side was going to convince the other.

REVIEW QUESTIONS

1. How did St. Augustine feel about the Roman conquests?

2. What was a "moot" as used in terms like shire moot or people's moot?

3. Who supervised completion of the legal work known as The Institutes?

4. Who was St. Thomas Becket?

5. Stephen Langton, Archbishop of Canterbury, is famous for what document?

6. John Fortesque is famous for what documents?

7. What is the power of the executive to prevent a measure passed by the legislature from becoming law?

8. What is a rotten borough?

9. What was the Pilgrimage of Grace?

10. What were penal laws?

11. What was the Exclusion Controversy?

12. Why are The Fundamental Constitutions of Carolina famous?

13. What was the Stamp Act?

14. What year did the Stamp Act Congress meet?

15. What did the Americans call the conflict between England and France fought between 1754 and 1763?

16. What was the main point of the Navigation Acts?

17. What is the best definition of English Common law?

18. What was the "Charter of Liberties"?

19. What is the title of the chief law enforcement officer in a county from Anglo-Saxon times until today?

20. What was the controversy over a "forced loan" in 1627?

21. What is habeas corpus?

22. How did its Royal Charter impact government in colonial Virginia?

23. How did its Royal Charter impact government in colonial Maryland?

24. What was significant about "An Act for Church Liberties" passed by the Maryland Assembly in 1638?

25. Why was Maryland's "Act Concerning Religion" or "Toleration Act" of 1649 significant?

26. Why was the 1686 case *Godden v. Hales* important?

27. What did Parliament declare in the February 1689, The Declaration of Right?

28. What are some of the rights guaranteed in the December 1689, Bill of Rights?

29. Why did the First Continental Congress meet in 1774?

30. What did the First Continental Congress declare with respect to the authority of parliament over the American colonies?

CHAPTER THREE
INDEPENDENCE AND SELF-GOVERNMENT

By the rude bridge that arched the flood,
Their flag to April's breeze unfurled,
Here once the embattled farmers stood,
And fired the shot heard round the world.

"Concord Hymn" by Ralph Waldo Emerson

"THE SHOT HEARD ROUND THE WORLD"

The First Continental Congress adjourned on October 26, 1774, determined to reconvene the following year, the Second Continental Congress. Initially, neither the First nor the Second Continental Congress were legislative bodies with authority to make law or assert independence. The state legislative assemblies appointed delegates who were only authorized to consult with each other and report back to their home state.

However, in April 1775, English soldiers in Boston tried to seize a cache of weapons that the colonial militia had stored in Concord (about 19 miles from Boston). The citizens' militia had been a cornerstone of Anglo-American law since at least the 8th century and the citizens' militia of Massachusetts were not about to disband without a fight. On the morning of April 19, about 700 English soldiers marched out of Boston to confiscate or destroy the colonial weapons.

When the English soldiers were about halfway to Concord, they were confronted by a group of Massachusetts militia. Who fired first has been a matter of debate ever since. A few days later, the commander of the militia, Captain John Parker, swore under oath that the militia simply stood by the road in an attempt to convince the English not to continue, but the English fired first and "killed eight of our party, without receiving any Provocation."

After a series of skirmishes, the English were forced to retreat back to Boston, suffering about 300 casualties in the fighting. These skirmishes are known as The Battles of Lexington and Concord. They were the first Battles of the American War for

Stand Your Ground, Don Troiani

Independence. Years later, the opening salvo of the battle was proclaimed to be "The Shot Heard Round the World." War had started and neither side was prepared to back down. In May 1775, the English dispatched another 4,500 soldiers to Boston. The first big battle of the War was fought at Bunker Hill on June 17, 1775, where the English suffered over 1,000 casualties.

THE SECOND CONTINENTAL CONGRESS AND THE DECLARATION OF THE CAUSES AND NECESSITY OF TAKING UP ARMS

The Second Continental Congress convened on May 10, 1775. Once again, 12 of the 13 colonies participated.[1] Despite an undeclared rebellion underway in Massachusetts, Congress drafted another appeal, known as the Olive Branch Petition, asking King George III to rescind the Intolerable Acts and re-affirm self-government for the colonies. Somewhat incongruously, almost the same day Congress approved the Olive Branch Petition it also approved "A Declaration Setting Forth the Causes and Necessity of Taking Up Arms." The July 6, 1775 Declaration began by denying that parliament had any authority over the American colonies. The Declaration asserted that God never "intended a part of the human race to hold an absolute property in, and an unbounded power over others." It went on to explain:

> The legislature of Great Britain, however, stimulated by an inordinate passion for a power not only unjustifiable, but which they know to be peculiarly reprobated by the very constitution of that kingdom … have thereby rendered it necessary for us to close with their last appeal from reason to arms. Yet, however blinded that assembly may be, by their intemperate rage for unlimited domination, so to slight justice and the opinion of mankind, we esteem ourselves bound by obligations of respect to the rest of the world, to make known the justice of our cause.

---

[1] Georgia was in the middle of a fight with Native Americans and needed the protection of the British army so felt it could not afford to antagonize England by attending the Congress.

Effectively, this was a declaration of war. Nevertheless, the Declaration stated that, "We have not raised armies with ambitious designs of separating from Great Britain, and establishing independent states." Rather, the colonies simply demanded that they be allowed the self-government under the crown that the colonies had been granted in the Royal Charters of the 17th century. The Declaration concluded:

> In our own native land, in defense of the freedom that is our birthright, and which we ever enjoyed till the late violation of it—for the protection of our property, acquired solely by the honest industry of our forefathers and ourselves, against violence actually offered, we have taken up arms. We shall lay them down when hostilities shall cease on the part of the aggressors, and all danger of their being renewed shall be removed, and not before.

Thus, the colonists claimed to be defending their "own native land" against invaders and aggressors. On June 15, 1775, Congress voted to appoint George Washington as commander of the united colonial forces. From this point forward, there was war between the Americans and the English.

INDEPENDENCE

On May 4, 1776, the Rhode Island legislature enacted a statute legally severing all relations between Rhode Island and the British government. The official reason was because the king and his government had violated "the compact most solemnly entered into, ratified and confirmed to the inhabitants of the Colony by his illustrious ancestors." This was not a claim to a violation of some mythical social contract; rather, it was the literal, historical grant of self-government made to Rhode Island in the 17th century. The final provision of the Rhode Island Act stated: *PROVIDED, nevertheless, that nothing in this act contained shall render void or vitiate any commission, writ, process or instrument heretofore made or executed[.]* So this was not a revolution, it was a separation. All laws previously in effect remained in effect.

On May 6, 1776, a constitutional convention met in Virginia to create a new constitution to replace the old colonial charter. On May 15, the Convention declared that the colonial government of Virginia was "dissolved" and replaced by a Republic with a new constitution. That day the British "Union Jack" was taken down from flying over the Virginia Capital. On June 29, 1776, Patrick Henry became the first governor of the independent Commonwealth of Virginia.

Patrick Henry

Meanwhile, back in Philadelphia, the Continental Congress re-convened on May 10, this time with all thirteen colonies in attendance.[2] One of Congress' first actions was approving a resolution stating:

> That it be recommended to the respective assemblies and conventions of the United Colonies, where no government sufficient to the exigencies of their affairs have been hitherto established, to adopt such government as shall, in the opinion of the representatives of the people, best conduce to the happiness and safety of their constituents in particular, and America in general.

Congress could only "recommend" that a colony act and this resolution carefully avoided the appearance of demanding or ordering a colony to do anything. The recommendation was clear however: colonies that had not yet done so, should follow the example of Massachusetts, Rhode Island, and Virginia to form their own governments on the basis of popular sovereignty. In the spring of 1776, most of the colonies were already planning constitutional conventions but the Congressional Resolution helped encourage the rest to move forward.

As late as May 1776, several colonies still refused to vote for outright independence. For

---

[2] By this point, Loyalists were no longer in control in Georgia and the new leaders realized they needed to join the other colonies in the War of Independence.

example, on May 21, 1776, the Maryland Convention voted against full independence. This began to change in June 1776. On June 15, New Hampshire and Delaware authorized their delegations to support independence. The following week, New Jersey agreed to independence but then went a step further. On July 2, 1776, New Jersey's constitutional convention approved a new constitution declaring New Jersey to be independent and explaining:

> whereas George the third, King of Great Britain, has refused Protection to the good People of these Colonies … all civil Authority under him is necessarily at an End, and a Dissolution of Government in each Colony has consequently taken Place.

The New Jersey Constitution additionally provided:

> That the Common Law of England, as well as so much of the Statute-Law, as have been heretofore practiced in this Colony, shall still remain in Force, until they shall be altered by a future Law of the Legislature[.]

Finally, on June 28, 1776, Maryland's Constitutional Convention instructed its delegates to support a Declaration of Independence. New York was the only colony that had not agreed to independence; but New York had repeatedly abstained in all votes, so a vote now would be 12-0 with one abstention. As it turned out, the New York delegation did abstain, but the New York Constitutional Convention issued a separate Declaration of Independence for New York on July 9, 1776.

THE DECLARATION OF INDEPENDENCE

With opposition to independence having fallen away, the Second Continental Congress authorized a committee to draft a formal Resolution or Declaration of Independence. Strictly speaking, the Continental Congress had no authority to make laws, and the statements passed by the Congress were non-binding resolutions. Thus, the Declaration of Independence has no legal status. It is not a law and confers no rights or duties on anyone. Nevertheless, the Declaration of Independence is the most famous document of this period and both symbolizes and embodies many basic American principles.

The Committee assigned to craft the Resolution agreed that Thomas Jefferson should write the first draft. However, it went through a series of revisions. The Declaration begins:

> ***The unanimous Declaration of the thirteen united States of America,***
>
> When in the Course of human events, it becomes necessary for one people to dissolve the political bands which have connected them with another, and to assume among the powers of the earth, the separate and equal station to which the Laws of Nature and of Nature's God entitle them, a decent respect to the opinions of mankind requires that they should declare the causes which impel them to the separation.

First, this is the unanimous Declaration of all the States. It had to be unanimous because each State was sovereign and independent. Note that "united" is not capitalized. "United" was not a name, it was merely an adjective describing the

The Signing of the Declaration of Independence

thirteen States as united. Second, the Declaration declares that this is the separation of "one people" from another. The implication is that each distinct "people" are "entitled" under Natural Law to "separate and equal" legal status with every other "people." This is entirely in accordance with St. Thomas's view that law is made by and for the whole people or the representatives of the whole people.

The second paragraph makes the following assertions:

We hold these truths to be self-evident,

(1) that all men are created equal, that they are endowed by their Creator with certain unalienable Rights, that among these are Life, Liberty and the pursuit of Happiness.

(2) That to secure these rights, Governments are instituted among Men, deriving their just powers from the consent of the governed,

(3) That whenever any Form of Government becomes destructive of these ends, it is the Right of the People to alter or to abolish it,

The Declaration claims a number of "self-evident" truths, not all of which are "self-evident." First the Declaration claims that "all men are created equal." The use of the abstract word "created" obscures the issue, but it seems to mean that "all humans are equal." Of course, *legally* this is not true. Minors and adults are not equal before the law and, at the time, only men were permitted to vote. In fact, equality had never been a concern of English Law. On the other hand, it was true that anyone accused of a crime—man or woman, young or old, common or noble—was equally entitled to a trial by a jury of his peers. Numerous colonial charters said that colonists in America had the same privileges as people in England.

Moreover, racial slavery existed everywhere in the colonies at the time. So, *legally* blacks were not considered equal to whites. Thus, Jefferson's phrase expresses a noble sentiment, but one which was more theologically accurate than politically or socially "self-evident." Nevertheless, the idea that all humans are created equal in the sight of God

Thomas Jefferson

is a statement that should influence all societies in the same way that society should be based on the Golden Rule: "Do unto others as you would have them do unto you." Thus, the statement sets forth a fundamental truth: all people should be treated equally as much as is humanly possible.

The next line asserts a few "unalienable rights." "Unalienable" means that these rights can never be taken or given away. Interestingly, English documents had never before spoken of unalienable liberties. The use of the word "right" as a noun, that is, something a person can "have," comes from the early 17th century. Magna Carta had said that no one would be deprived of life or liberty except by judgment of his peers, but no one prior to 1776 claimed that there was a right to "liberty" or "life." Because the English government routinely executed people for felonies, the right to life is, strictly speaking, not "unalienable." Rather it is only "unalienable" insofar as a person has not been found guilty after having received a fair trial. Moreover, people routinely sacrifice their lives in the service of their country or to defend family members. Our Lord sacrificed His life for the salvation of Humanity. Certainly, the right to life is the paramount right that all people have been granted by God and should only be taken away through

CHAPTER 3: INDEPENDENCE AND SELF-GOVERNMENT

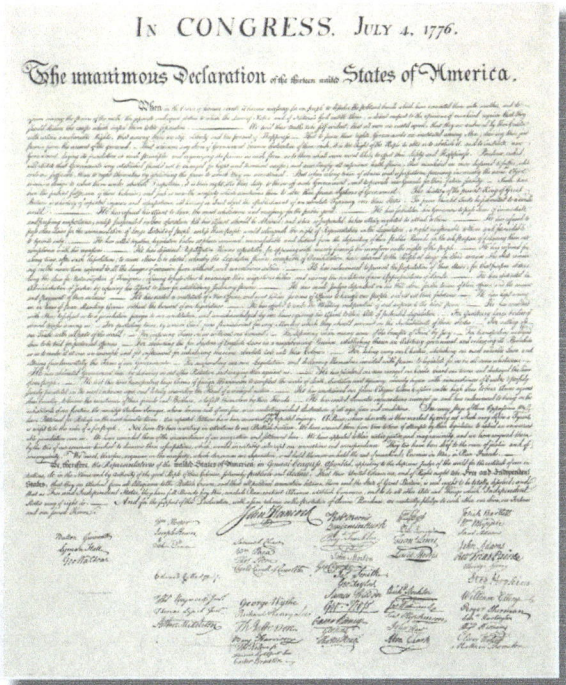

Original copy of the Declaration of Independence

due process of law.[3] Thus, *technically*, the use of the word "unalienable" in this context is inappropriate given the historical and judicial processes.

Next, the Declaration asserts that liberty is unalienable. Once again, because the government takes away liberty constantly, although it is a God-given right like the right to life, it is not an absolute right and, under certain circumstances, can be alienated to one degree or another. For example, criminals lose their liberty after they are convicted of crimes. Soldiers who are drafted lose their liberty because the government compels them to serve in the armed forces.

Finally, the "pursuit of happiness" is a rather vague term which could mean almost anything and is certainly not self-evident. Based on contemporary documents, the phrase has been interpreted to mean that everyone possesses the "right to be happy." Once again, this seems more aspirational than actual because at the time there were hundreds of thousands of black people living in an enslaved condition who certainly possessed no "right to be happy." Nevertheless, the idea is that God has created in every human being the right to live a happy life which government cannot casually alienate.

Jefferson next declares that to protect the right to life, liberty, and happiness, men institute governments. Governments do not occur by accident, people need to create them. Then the Declaration claims that governments "deriv[e] their just powers from the consent of the governed." This conforms to the teachings of Robert Bellarmine who wrote that, "The people themselves, immediately and directly, hold political power so long as they have not transferred this power to a king or ruler."[4] Jefferson, like Bellarmine goes on to declare that since government is created by "the people," the people can replace it if the government acts tyrannically. According to Bellarmine, *people have the right to resist the rule of a tyrant*. "For legitimate reason the people can change the government to an aristocracy or a democracy or vice versa."[5] Therefore, in the second paragraph of the Declaration, Jefferson asserts the justification for changing governments.

Contemporary documents provide greater insight to the meaning of and actual understanding of the document at the time. For example, just a few years later, the New Hampshire Constitution restated the principles of the Declaration more straightforwardly:

    I. All men are born equally free and independent; therefore, all government of right originates from the people, is founded in consent, and instituted for the general good.

    II. All men have certain natural, essential, and inherent rights; among which are—the enjoying and defending life and liberty—acquiring, possessing and protecting property—and in a word, of seeking and obtaining happiness.

    III. When men enter into a state of society, they surrender up some of their natural rights to that society, in order to insure the protection of others; and, without such an equivalent, the surrender is void.

    IV. Among the natural rights, some are in their very nature unalienable, because

---

[3] Although the Catholic Church has historically allowed capital punishment; recently, the Church has begun arguing against capital punishment because an individual life is so precious.
[4] De Clericis, Ch. VII.
[5] De Laicis, Ch. VI.

U.S. Government for Catholic Students 57

no equivalent can be given or received for them. Of this kind are the RIGHTS OF CONSCIENCE.

This clarified many of the ambiguities of the 1776 Declaration. The *unalienable* "right to life" and "right to liberty" has been more clearly defined as a right to defend one's life and liberty. Moreover, only a few very important rights are unalienable. The only example given here is freedom of conscience, but the rest are alienable. Even the right to life is not unalienable because the government can execute people or imprison them.

As with Bellarmine, the Declaration suggests that the decision to change government is not one that should be undertaken lightly for any reason. Bellarmine uses the phrase "legitimate reason" which implies a serious breach of the Natural Law or, and these are probably the same thing, tyrannical rule by the government. Thus, paragraph two adds: "Prudence, indeed, will dictate that Governments long established should not be changed for light and transient causes."

The Declaration then asserts twenty-seven specific "injuries and usurpations" that justify abolishing English rule. Unlike the more abstract rights found in paragraph 2, the list of grievances is based on the charters that founded the colonies, as well as objections to various legislation recently enacted by Parliament. For example, one grievance was "For Quartering large bodies of armed troops among us," a clear reference to the Quartering Act. Another complained about the king "imposing Taxes on us without our Consent," a reference to the Stamp Act and the Tea Act. On the other hand, some grievances were rather slight or apparently non-existent. The Declaration complained that the king had protected British soldiers "by a mock Trial, from punishment for any Murders which they should commit on the Inhabitants of these States." Historians are puzzled by this grievance as the only incident to which it might refer seems to be the trial of the soldiers involved in the Boston Massacre. As they were represented at the trial by John Adams, one of the members of the Declaration Committee, it seems rather implausible that he would consider his defense of these men as part of a "mock trial." It was one of the most heroic moments of his life as he was defending men most Americans wanted to hang.

John Adams

After setting forth America's grievances, the Declaration concluded by asserting the independence of each and every individual colony:

> We, therefore, the Representatives of the United States of America, in General Congress, Assembled, ... declare, That these United Colonies are, and of Right ought to be Free and Independent States; that ... they have full Power ... to do all other Acts and Things which Independent States may of right do.

This leaves no doubt that, while issuing a *joint* Declaration, Massachusetts, New York, and the rest, were each "*Independent* States." Having fought for autonomy and self-government, they were not going to surrender their sovereignty to a central government. It would take another 18 months for Congress to put together a draft plan of confederation and several more years after that until each state ratified the Articles of Confederation in 1781.

The Declaration of Independence began a war of independence which sought to separate one nation from another. It was not a revolution. Americans declared their independence but did not reject the laws, customs, and traditions that they had followed for centuries.

THE DECLARATION FROM A CATHOLIC PERSPECTIVE

From the Catholic perspective, the Declaration of Independence contains many excellent points. First, it recognizes that the power of government is limited by the higher power of God and by certain self-evident and fundamental rights that God bestows on mankind. While these rights may not be unalienable, people should not lose these rights except under extraordinary circumstances. The highest, most fundamental right, is the right to life, without which, no other rights matter.

Second, the Declaration indicates the importance of including prayer in government and important government decisions. In the final paragraph of the Declaration the representatives appeal *"to the Supreme Judge of the world for the rectitude of our intentions…"* This contradicts recent notions that the Church should be separate from the State and that all references to God should be removed from public discourse. Tragically, in the past few decades, government on all levels has become overtly hostile to religion in general and Christianity and Catholicism in particular. These anti-Christian views deny the Declaration.

Third, the Declaration further declares that a government cannot easily lose its legal authority. Only "a long train of abuses… committed by an absolute despot" merits withdrawing sworn allegiance to a government. While this might be a bit exaggerated, it reflects Catholic and Biblical teaching. In Romans 13:1-7, St. Paul says that Christians must respect and submit to authority. Section 1899 of the *Catechism of the Catholic Church* declares: The authority required by the moral order derives from God: *"Let every person be subject to the governing authorities. For there is no authority except from God, and those that exist have been instituted by God. Therefore, he who resists the authorities resists what God has appointed, and those who resist will incur judgment."* (Quoting Rom 13:1-2). However, obedience to authority does not mean absolute obedience to authority which, through its actions, has become unlawful. For example, in the last one hundred years, Catholics have rebelled against Communist governments in Spain and have opposed the Nazis in Germany. As Bellarmine notes, sometimes tyranny can be, and needs to be, overthrown.

Thus, Catholics would not have a problem of conscience signing a Declaration containing these political beliefs. Charles Carroll of Maryland, a well-known Catholic colonial leader, did sign the Declaration of Independence. He was the only Catholic signer.

THE IMPORTANCE AND INFLUENCE OF THE DECLARATION OF INDEPENDENCE

Aside from the Constitution, the Declaration of Independence is the most important and influential document in American history. However, there are a few errors involved with the Declaration. The first error is that the Declaration created a new "nation" on July 4, 1776. This inaccuracy was created by Abraham Lincoln at his 1863 *Gettysburg Address* which he began by proclaiming: "Four score and seven years ago [1776] our fathers brought forth, upon this continent, a new nation…" No "nation" was created in 1776. In 1776, there was a loose association of thirteen sovereign and independent countries. While the point may seem trivial, it is important to realize that the Declaration was not the foundation document for the United States.

Lincoln also, because of the times in which he found himself, declared in his speech that the "new nation (was) conceived in Liberty, and dedicated to the proposition that all men are created equal." It is somewhat hyperbolic to claim that the American states were dedicated to the proposition that all men are created equal. Jefferson owned slaves and women were not allowed to vote or hold office in most states for more than a century. On the other hand, John Adams hated slavery, and his son John Quincy Adams became a leading abolitionist. In fact, nearly every Northerner found slavery abhorrent and sought its abolition. People criticized Jefferson and other Founding Fathers as being hypocrites for proclaiming "all humans are equal" but denying equality in practice. However, these people also fail to explain what equality would have looked like in 1776. One might inquire whether perfect equality exists anywhere in the world, even today. The Founders were working towards equality by creating the Declaration.

Despite these issues, the Declaration of Independence should be seen as establishing *aspirational* goals which is why it is so influential even almost 250 years after it was written. Remember that the Declaration was written to *explain* and *justify* the colonists' decision to break away from England. Historically, this was the first time that any group of "rebels" had ever issued a document explaining their reasons for their rebellion. In a sense, it demonstrates how honorable these men were. This is reflected in the final line of the Declaration where they "mutually pledge to each other our Lives, our Fortunes and our sacred Honor." They were men with flaws, but they wished to act honestly and forthrightly, setting forth their grievances and the reasons that they were engaging in this momentous task.

Also, as rebels, they could be executed for treason. Every man who signed the Declaration literally was pledging his life. They were engaging in an armed insurrection against the greatest power in the world; however, they had no navy and a tiny, badly trained and equipped army. Recall that as late as 1774, some colonial legislatures prohibited their delegates even from talking about independence. Although most of the signers suffered little ill effects from signing, they all knew the risks. They were men of great courage.

Also, it is amazing that any document of the time even recognized that men were created equal. Such an idea was quite radical. Although they failed to achieve equality, they should be credited for creating a document which acknowledged that all human beings are equal before God. Sadly, it would take many decades before equality for blacks and women was achieved. Yet those seeking equality could point to the Declaration as a source to support their position.

This important paragraph has been cited by many Americans, including Dr. Martin Luther King, Jr. On July 4, 1965, he gave a sermon in his church in Atlanta in which he referenced the second paragraph of the Declaration. Of it he said, *"This is a dream. It's a great dream. The first saying we notice in this dream is an amazing universalism. It doesn't say, 'some men;' it says 'all men.' It doesn't say 'all white men;' it says 'all*

Martin Luther King admired the Declaration of Independence and referenced it in his speeches.

men,' which includes black men. It does not say 'all Gentiles;' it says 'all men,' which includes Jews. It doesn't say 'all Protestants;' it says 'all men,' which includes Catholics. It doesn't even say 'all theists and believers;' it says 'all men,' which includes humanists and agnostics."

King concluded that *"Never before in the history of the world has a sociopolitical document expressed in such profound, eloquent and unequivocal language the dignity and the worth of human personality. The American dream reminds us—and we should think about it anew on this Independence Day—that every man is an heir of the legacy of dignity and worth."*

Thus, America's great civil rights' leader expressed his admiration for the Declaration of Independence and the influence which it had upon him and the civil rights movement.

Next, although most people now accept as a given that government must be based on the consent of the governed, this was not the case in 1776. Crafting a document which specifically laid the foundations for democracy created what amounted to a new form of government in an age when all governments were forms of monarchies. Jefferson also asserts that American independence is not based on British common law, the Magna carta, or any positive law. Power comes from God. It is given to the people who consent to be governed by a king or some other form of government.

Finally, the notion that everyone is equal before the law means that, unlike most societies of the time, America will not have a king or an aristocracy. There will be no class distinction between high born nobles and low born commoners. People have rights, not rank. Whatever place they achieve in society they obtain through their hard work and how they apply themselves and their rights. This is what Dr. King meant when he said that equality was a great dream. It is the American dream and it began with the Declaration of Independence.

THE ARTICLES OF CONFEDERATION

Benjamin Franklin presented the first draft of the Articles of Confederation to the Continental Congress in July 1775. Several important provisions became part of the final draft and later became part of the Constitution of 1787.

Article 1 declared: "The Name of this Confederacy shall henceforth be The United Colonies of North America." Article 2 said "United Colonies hereby severally enter into a firm League of Friendship with each other, binding on themselves and their Posterity, for their common Defense … and their mutual and general Welfare." The term "general Welfare" appears to have been a deliberate attempt to avoid the term "common good." A number of state constitutions referred to the "common good." For example, the New Hampshire Constitution expressly says the purpose of government is the common good. However, the Articles used the term "general Welfare" to indicate that the role of the Confederate government was more limited than that of the state government. State governments were devoted to common good or their citizens but the confederate government was limited to the general welfare of the colonies.

Article 3 provided that "each Colony shall enjoy and retain as much as it may think fit of its own present Laws."

Article 5 provided:

> That the Power and Duty of the Congress shall extend to the Determining on War and Peace, to sending and receiving ambassadors, and entering into Alliances, the Settling all Disputes and Differences between Colony and Colony …
>
> The Congress shall also make such general Ordinances as thought necessary to the General Welfare, particular Assemblies cannot be competent to; viz., those that may relate to

Benjamin Franklin

our general Commerce; or general Currency; to the Establishment of Posts; and the Regulation of our common Forces.

Again, we see this important term "General Welfare;" but Congressional authority only extends to areas where state governments were incompetent such as "general Commerce."

Revenue was to be "supplied" by each colony proportionate to its population but the draft left open how this was to be collected.

Representation in Congress would be proportionate to the number of tax-paying adult males, with one representative for each 5,000. Voting in Congress would be a simple majority vote. This plan was much more democratic than either the final Articles or the Constitution of

The first page of the Articles of Confederation

1787. For example, this plan would have allowed 125 representatives, while under the Constitution initially there were only 59 representatives. Under the final Articles, states had one vote each regardless of population, which was how the Continental Congress had been operating. Moreover, the draft provided the Articles could be amended if a majority of Congress sent a proposal to the states and a mere majority of state legislatures voted to approve the proposal. Under the final Articles, a change had to be unanimously approved by all the states, and under the Constitution it would require approval by three-fourths of the States. In other words, the 1775 proposal was much less protective of state autonomy.

Article 9 proposed an executive council to run the government. This was very similar to the parliamentary system of England, where the Prime Minister and the other Ministers are members of parliament and are approved by the majority of parliament. Because there was no independent executive, or judges, all power was concentrated in the Congress.

In June 1776, Congress appointed a committee of thirteen, that is, one delegate from each colony, to revise the draft Articles. The committee recommended sticking with each state having one vote. Franklin, arguing for his plan of proportional representation, said that "if we vote equally we ought to pay equally." John Adams supported Franklin, asking whether partners who contribute unequal amounts to a partnership should have unequal votes.

Ultimately, Franklin's proposal was defeated badly with only Pennsylvania and Virginia, the two most populous states, supporting the proportional plan. The issue of proportional representation was dropped and not revisited. There does not appear to have been any serious controversy that "one man one vote" was a principle of justice. It was true that the Founders believed in "no taxation without representation" but this did not require equal representation. In fact, it was the exact opposite. Both Adams and Franklin agreed that people who paid more in taxes should have more say in how the money was spent. Franklin's plan was to base representation on the number of *taxpayers* not the number of *people*. So, neither side in the debate supported "one man one vote," nor did they view this as an affront to "equality."

The main issue that was debated by Congress for several weeks was the powers of the central government. The final version of the Articles was approved November 17, 1777 and sent to the States for ratification.

The final title of the document was *Articles of Confederation and Perpetual Union*. Article 13 declared two separate times that plan of government was to be "perpetual," that is, lasting forever. Article 1 declared the name of the new nation: "United States of America." The second article stated unambiguously:

> Each state retains its sovereignty, freedom and independence, and every Power, Jurisdiction and right, which is not by this confederation expressly delegated to the United States, in Congress assembled.

The lack of a corresponding provision in the 1787

Constitution would lead to adoption of the Tenth Amendment, which effectively said the same thing as Article II. In addition to this explicit denial of any "implied powers" of the central government, the biggest structural change was that all votes would be by state with each state having one vote. States could freely choose their delegation in any way they wished. The Articles could not be amended without the *unanimous consent* of every state. Executive powers were held by an executive committee of thirteen—one for each state—but any decision of the executive committee needed support of at least nine members of the committee. Moreover, the powers to be exercised by the executive committee were only those powers approved by the delegations of at least nine states in Congress. A commanding general of the armed forces also had to be approved by at least nine states. There was no permanent judiciary. Congress would appoint judges to temporary courts as needed. This structure granted a great deal of power to individual states and made it difficult to concentrate any power with the central government. There was no thought that the courts or the executive would restrain Congress, the states themselves and the supermajority needed for delegation of powers was the structural restraint.

The final draft added a large number of specific powers to be exercised by the central government. The most important powers involved

- exclusive power of determining peace and war
- entering into treaties and alliances
- appointing courts for the trial of piracies and felonies committed on the high seas;
- regulating the alloy and value of coin
- regulating the trade and managing all affairs with the Indians, not members of any of the states; provided that the legislative right of any state, within its own limits, be not infringed or violated
- establishing post-offices
- appointing all officers of the armed forces in the service of the United States
- making rules for the government of the land and naval forces

The Articles also made explicit a number of duties states had toward each other and towards the citizens of other states, providing:

- the free inhabitants of each of these states, paupers, vagabonds and fugitives from Justice excepted, shall be entitled to all privileges and immunities of free citizens in the several states; and the people of each state shall have free ingress and regress to and from any other state, and shall enjoy therein all the privileges of trade and commerce, subject to the same duties, impositions and restrictions as the inhabitants thereof
- If any Person guilty of, or charged with, treason, felony, or other high misdemeanor in any state, shall flee from Justice, and be found in any of the united states, he shall upon demand of the Governor or executive power of the state from which he fled, be delivered up
- Full faith and credit shall be given in each of these states to the records, acts and judicial proceedings of the courts and magistrates of every other state.

Each of these provisions were later included in the Constitution of 1787. To this day, a dispute exists as to what privileges and immunities all citizens have. Immediately after mentioning "privileges and immunities" the provision adds "and the people of each state shall have free ingress … and shall enjoy therein all the privileges of trade." Unfortunately, no debate in Congress on this provision has been recorded. One reason for the lack of debate about "privileges" of citizens was that there was no mechanism for the central government to enforce these provisions. While states pledged to protect these privileges, in practice, states were free to interpret this provision as they wished. This was true of most of the provisions of the Articles. The central government had no power to compel states to do anything if they refused to comply with a provision.

Nine states quickly ratified the Articles, but three states held out, primarily because they wanted to see conflicting land claims resolved before they would agree to ratify the Articles. Ultimately, all the states agreed. Maryland finally ratified the Articles on March 1, 1781, *technically* the birth date of the United States of America.

THE NORTHWEST ORDINANCE

The most important law passed by the United States under the Articles of Confederation was the **Northwest Ordinance.** The area between the Ohio River, the Mississippi River, and the Great Lakes was called the Northwest Territory. Thomas Jefferson penned the first draft of the Northwest Ordinance in 1784, but it took three years to obtain final passage. Everyone knew that this was an important law, so a lot of effort and deliberation went into it. Congress overwhelmingly approved it in 1787.

The Ordinance began by proclaiming it was "temporary" and only intended to last until the people of the territory formed their own state governments. Thus, local self-government was the cornerstone of the Ordinance. Until states formed, Congress would appoint a governor and judges for the territory. However, the Ordinance provided for territorial legislatures elected by the people to make laws with the agreement of the governor. Notably, no one was eligible to be elected as a territorial representative unless he owned at least 200 acres of land. Voting for a representative was restricted to men who owned at least fifty acres of land. These property qualifications were not found in Jefferson's draft but were added to the final Ordinance.

Section 13 contained two important points. First, it said that "civil and religious liberty … form the basis whereon these republics, their laws and constitutions are erected." As in many of the state charters, religious liberty was a foundational principle of American society. Second, the ordinance said that new states would be admitted "on an equal footing with the original States." This "equal footing doctrine" became a cornerstone of American policy under the Constitution as well.

Because the Ordinance was essentially a constitution for the territory, the final section of the Ordinance (section 14) was effectively a "Bill of Rights." The first article of this bill of rights proclaimed religious liberty: "No person, demeaning (conducting) himself in a peaceable and orderly manner, shall ever be molested on account of his mode of worship or religious sentiments,

The Northwest Territory in 1787

in the said territory." Notice, that freedom of religion was so important that it was listed first in a separate article.

The second article listed a series of important liberties, almost all of which were well-established and all of which would also be found in the Constitution of 1787:

- The inhabitants of the said territory shall always be entitled to the benefits of the writ of habeas corpus, and of the trial by jury;

- proportionate representation of the people in the legislature;

- All persons shall be bailable, unless for capital offenses, where the proof shall be evident or the presumption great.

- All fines shall be moderate; and no cruel or unusual punishments shall be inflicted.

- No man shall be deprived of his liberty or property, but by the judgment of his peers or the law of the land.

These were simply provisions of good government that had been recognized in Anglo-American law for centuries. The only "new" provision was "proportionate representation of the people in the legislature." In England during this period there were so-called "rotten boroughs," where only a handful of people elected a member to parliament. Congress did not want to see rotten boroughs appearing in America.

The third article proclaimed: "Religion, morality, and knowledge, being necessary to good government and the happiness of mankind, schools and the means of education shall forever be encouraged." Later theorists argued that government should be neutral with respect to religion and morality, but this was not the view of early Americans.

The fourth article proclaimed: "The said territory, and the States which may be formed therein, shall forever remain a part of this Confederacy of the United States of America, subject to the Articles of Confederation." This provision is somewhat ironic given that the following year, twelve of the original thirteen states voted to leave the Confederation and form a new federal union. More importantly, the fourth article allowed Congress to sell land in the territory to private citizens. Sale of "public land" was hugely important for two reasons. First, between 1787 and 1836, sale of "public land" to private purchasers accounted for about half the total federal revenue. Most of the rest of federal revenue came from tariffs on imports. This meant that the vast majority of Americans paid no direct taxes to the federal government. The second reason goes back to the "equal footing" doctrine. In 1787, the central government owned almost no land inside the original states. The central government operated a handful of military forts, but the state governments owned all of the public lands. For example, today the federal government only owns 0.3% of the total acreage in Connecticut. Imagine if the federal government retained ownership of most or all of the property in a new state. It could control where roads were built and how all the land in the state was used. This would give the federal government enormous control over new states and effectively deny them "equal footing" with the original states. To avoid this, Congress provided that vast tracts of land would be sold to private purchasers. Later, when these territories became states, all the public lands were transferred to the new states, e.g. Ohio, Indiana, etc. Thus, for example, even today the federal government only owns about 1% of the total land in Ohio.

The last provision of the Ordinance declared that slavery was illegal in the new states created from the Northwest Territory. Specifically, it said:

> There shall be neither slavery nor involuntary servitude in the said territory, otherwise than in the punishment of crimes whereof the party shall have been duly convicted: Provided, always, that any person escaping into the same, from whom labor or service is lawfully claimed in any one of the original States, such fugitive may be lawfully reclaimed and conveyed to the person claiming his or her labor or service as aforesaid.

This section appears to reflect the basic rule under English common law. Slavery had disappeared in England after Roman times. In a famous case in 1772, an English customs officer, Charles Stewart, brought James Somerset with him back to London. Somerset had been a slave in Boston, but when he arrived in England he filed suit against Stewart arguing that slavery was illegal under English law. (*Somerset* v *Stewart* (1772)). The English courts agreed with Somerset and ruled that slavery had always been contrary to English law. The court acknowledged that parliament could authorize slavery if it wished to modify common law, but parliament had not done so. This became the dominant view in the United States in the late 18th century. Although slavery was contrary to common law, states, as sovereign entities, had jurisdiction to depart from common law and permit slavery. Because states could permit slavery, and because states were required under the Articles of Confederation to respect each other's laws, the Ordinance provided that an escaped slave must be returned to his home state.

For the next eighty years, Congress enacted numerous laws constantly seeking a balance between slave and free states. The Northwest Ordinance makes it clear that Congress was determined to restrict slavery as much as possible until it could be abolished. Thus, from its earliest days, significant elements of the United States government were working to abolish slavery.

THE CALL FOR A NEW CONSTITUTION

The Articles of Confederation took effect in 1781, but almost immediately there were calls to replace them with something providing for a stronger central government. As we know, back in 1775 and 1776, the main legal argument of the colonies was that they had each been guaranteed self-government by their royal charters. Accordingly, the sovereignty of each colony was a crucial part of their claim for independence, and the people were distrustful of any central government whether it be in London or Philadelphia. However, under the Articles, the Continental Congress had won the War with England, and negotiated a favorable peace treaty. Congress had also been careful not to overstep its bounds and take actions that might be threatening to state sovereignty. It might be said that the Articles were a victim of their own success. Because Congress had managed the situation quite well, people's distrust of a central government was diminished.

However, the economic situation in America in the 1780s was terrible. The War had largely destroyed the American economy. Trade was disrupted. Tens of thousands of people had served in the military rather than work in private jobs or on their farms. States had borrowed heavily to finance the War and had printed paper money to fund the war as well. As a result, the States emerged from the War with horrible debt and terrible inflation. Just as the states had to borrow to get through the War, individuals did too. Many farmers had to borrow heavily. For example, a farmer would buy seed on credit to be repaid at harvest time, but if the harvest failed they were left in debt. Moreover, banks and equipment companies often demanded payment in gold or silver but most people, especially veterans, had been paid in paper money. After the War ended, Congress paid each soldier a bonus in Continental currency which was practically worthless because Congress lacked the gold or silver needed to guarantee the currency's value. The phrase "not worth a continental," meaning "worthless," became common. More and more there was discontent among the people, especially farmers, who were facing the loss of their land.

One of the most infamous events that proponents of a new constitution often cited was **Shays Rebellion**. Daniel Shays had been an officer in the militia and owned a farm in western Massachusetts. Shays and others were threatened with losing their farms due to debt. Hundreds of farmers surrounded the courthouses in western Massachusetts and forced them to stop hearing cases so that the judges were unable to issue judgments against the farmers. When several of the leaders were indicted, they could not be tried because crowds kept preventing the courts from sitting. This continued for several months in the summer and fall of 1786. In January 1787, a mob marched to the federal arsenal at Springfield and threatened to seize the arms there. The garrison fired cannon into the crowd, killing three or four people and the crowd disbursed. In May, John Hancock was elected governor. Hancock pardoned the rebels and promised to protect the property of ordinary citizens and the "rebellion" subsided.

As Shays and his fellow farmers were rebelling in Massachusetts, a group of delegates from Virginia, Delaware, Pennsylvania, New Jersey, and New York met in Annapolis in September 1786 to discuss how to improve trade and commerce among the states. These states recommended to Congress that the central government's power over commerce be expanded to prevent issues such as one state discriminating against other states. In February 1787, Congress responded to the Annapolis Convention by authorizing

> a Convention of delegates who shall have been appointed by the several states be held at Philadelphia for the sole and express purpose of revising the Articles of Confederation and reporting to Congress and the several legislatures such alterations and provisions therein as shall when agreed to in Congress and confirmed by the states render the federal constitution adequate to the exigencies of Government[.]

THE WEAKNESSES OF THE ARTICLES OF CONFEDERATION

Shays Rebellion and the Annapolis Conference demonstrated that the Articles of Confederation contained many weaknesses. First, Congress possessed no financial authority. The Articles of Confederation denied Congress the power to levy taxes on the states or to collect tariff duties on foreign trade. The national government could generate revenue only if the states chose to give it money. For example, because Georgia feared an invasion from Spanish Florida, and North Carolina faced Native American attacks, these states contributed to the national defense. On the other hand, South Carolina, which was protected from attacks by Georgia in the south and North Carolina in the north, felt no need to subsidize national defense. This led to serious disagreements among the states.

Second, because the Continental currency had no value, several states, and even local banks, began issuing their own paper currency. This paper money was honored only in the small areas where the currency issuer was known and trusted. This created almost unimaginable instability and chaos. Foreign nations and most colonial merchants refused to accept paper currency and insisted payments be made in gold or silver. Thus, intrastate commerce, interstate commerce, and international commerce were all negatively impacted as no one trusted any paper currency. It was clear that a national currency was needed to avoid a disaster. However, the Articles did not permit the federal government to issue currency.

Third, the Articles of Confederation did not allow the federal government to regulate commerce between the states or with foreign nations. Before the War, American merchants sold three-fourths of their goods either in Great Britain or the British West Indies. After the War, Britain launched a brutal trade war against the United States. After making peace, Great Britain and the West Indies only purchased 10% of American exports. At the same time, Britain flooded American markets with less expensive British products. American manufacturers could not compete with the

A Continental thirty dollar bill

very low British prices. Americans purchased the British goods which caused domestic manufacturers to suffer.

If Congress had possessed the power to regulate commerce, it could have imposed an import tax, or tariff, on the British goods, making them more expensive, which would have protected American business. Also, Congress could have negotiated a commercial treaty with England. There was no way that thirteen states, essentially thirteen nations, could regulate commerce with a foreign nation. Even if one state tried to tax imports, England would just do business in one of the other twelve states.

Basically, the Articles withheld sufficient authority for a central government to function effectively. To gain this authority, the federal government needed a number of powers, including the power to raise money through taxation, to be solely responsible for coining money, to regulate interstate commerce, and to draft troops to enforce law and order. The Articles were a noble effort which had served the United States well during the War. However, they were an utter failure during the peace. Something needed to be done before the United States fell into anarchy.

Scene at the Signing of the Constitution of the United States, Howard Chandler Christy

THE CONSTITUTIONAL CONVENTION OF 1787

Delegates from the states met in Philadelphia in May 1787. Rhode Island refused to send a delegation, which was problematic because any change in the Articles had to be unanimous – another major flaw in the document. The convention got around this legal point by positing that regardless of what the Articles said about being "perpetual," they were only a treaty among sovereign states. Under international law, sovereign states could freely repudiate treaties when they deemed it in their interest.[6]

On May 25, 1787, a group of fifty-five remarkable men, renowned for their character and ability, assembled in Independence Hall in Philadelphia. Most of the men were well known throughout the states and the nation, since they had served in significant leadership positions in their states or the Continental Congress. Yet most of the men who created the Declaration of Independence did not attend the Constitutional Convention. Only six of the fifty-five had signed the Declaration. Thomas Jefferson and John Adams could not attend as they were representing America abroad. Many of the men who led America during the War of Independence also did not attend because they opposed strong central government or felt the Articles would be discarded. Thus, John Hancock, Patrick Henry, and Sam Adams chose to be absent.

Of the various delegations, Virginia had perhaps the most important. Virginia was represented by George Washington; Virginia's governor, Edmund Randolph; and George Mason, the author of Virginia's constitution. James Madison also represented Virginia. During the War, Madison had become one of Virginia's most important political leaders. He knew more about making a government function than any other delegate at the convention. Madison's brilliance and foresight during the convention earned him the title "Father of the Constitution."

Of the fifty-five delegates, only two were Catholic: Daniel Carroll of Maryland and Thomas

[6] Madison's Notes, June 19, 1787, Speech by J. Madison.

FitzSimons of Pennsylvania. However, neither Carroll nor FitzSimons played a particularly important role at the convention. Also, worth noting is the presence of Father John Carroll, who traveled to Philadelphia where he pleaded with the convention delegates for the rights of his fellow Catholics. His efforts aided in the adoption of Article VI of the Constitution which abolished all religious tests for any public office.

The delegates' first act was to unanimously elect George Washington to preside over the convention. Washington was universally admired. Two other vital figures emerged as prominent leaders at the convention. The first was Alexander Hamilton (1755-1804). Hamilton had been General Washington's aide-de-camp during the War, and had remained Washington's most trusted advisor. After the War, Hamilton had been elected to Congress to represent New York. He had also been one of the leaders of the 1786 Annapolis Convention. The second figure was James Madison (1751-1829). Madison was a close friend of Washington, and the two were distantly related. Madison's wife, Dolly Madison, was the sister-in-law of Washington's nephew. Hamilton and Madison both fervently supported Washington, and they aimed at the convention to create a new government with Washington at the head.

After a good deal of arguing over possible amendments, changes, and compromises to the Articles of Confederation, it became clear that they would never provide a satisfactory government to solve the nation's current problems. Consequently, the delegates decided to end the useless discussion over fixing the Articles and start over. Thus, they changed the purpose of the convention from correcting the Articles to writing a new constitution.

In creating a new constitution, the delegates had three main objectives. First, they sought to create an executive who could act quickly and decisively in a crisis, but whose powers would not be a threat to liberty. Second, they wanted to reinforce free trade among the states, primarily by strengthening the power of the central government to prevent trade barriers. Finally, they needed to resolve the lingering dispute about whether representation for each state would be the same or whether states would have representation proportionate to their population.

George Washington

Alexander Hamilton

The issue of representation was resolved by adopting a plan suggested by the Connecticut delegation, and called The Connecticut Compromise or the **Great Compromise**. Congress would be composed of two chambers: The Senate and House of Representatives. The Senate would have equal representation, with each state sending two senators. In the House of Representatives, each state would have a number of representatives based on the population of the state.

The idea of a bi-cameral legislature was almost universally accepted. Only Ben Franklin wanted a

The modern-day Capitol building, where the two chambers of the legislature meet.

single chamber. Madison argued that a bi-cameral legislature was crucial. He pointed out that if one branch were elected by popular vote while the other branch was appointed by state officials it would help ensure that different perspectives were considered. Several delegates argued that both houses should be appointed rather than elected, but Madison's view prevailed.

The issue of counting people for representation in the House, and for taxation purposes, led to a second compromise, the **Three-Fifths Compromise.** Article 1, Section 2 of the Constitution provides:

> Representatives and direct Taxes shall be apportioned among the several States which may be included within this Union, according to their respective Numbers, which shall be determined by adding to the whole Number of free Persons, including those bound to Service for a Term of Years, and excluding Indians not taxed, three fifths of all other Persons.

The issue of slavery was incredibly divisive, and, in fact, almost led to a complete breakdown of the Convention. The Southern states possessed a very large population of enslaved persons, perhaps as many as 700,000, which represented about 20% of the total American population and a huge percentage of the South's population. The question arose as to how to count slaves for the purpose of representation in the House of Representatives. States with few or no slaves wanted to count only "free Persons" for representation. States with a large number of non- "free persons" wished to count everyone. Eventually, the delegates reached what came to be called the Three-Fifths Compromise. Slaves would be counted as three-fifths a person for representation making Southern representation in the House of Representatives much larger than it otherwise would have been.

There is a misconception that the drafters of the Constitution did not consider Blacks as persons, or at best three-fifths of a person. This view is false. No one in the 18th century denied that Blacks or slaves were "persons." The provision itself explicitly reads "three fifths of all other Persons," so personhood was not questioned. The Three-Fifth compromise was a practical resolution of a difficult dispute. More problematic is that while considered "persons" slaves were also considered property. Thus, while the solution is practical, it is completely illogical.

The problem, of course, was that slavery was so deeply embedded in Southern society that, in 1787, no workable resolution seemed to exist. To create a new Constitution, the Framers failed to deal with the issue of slavery in any meaningful fashion. Despite its significance, the words "slave" or "slavery" do not appear in the document. Moreover, Congress was prohibited from banning the foreign importation of slaves until after 1808. The delegates realized that the issue of slavery would need to be addressed, but they knew that the Southern states would never agree to a Constitution that banned slavery.

Finally, the delegates agreed to a third compromise which involved commerce. The industrial northern states wanted the Constitution to grant Congress the power to protect American, mostly northern, manufactured products, by levying a tariff on all foreign imports as well as taxing all exports. Northerners also sought to empower Congress to regulate the international slave trade.

Because the Southern states conducted a huge amount of export business with European countries, they opposed such an awesome delegation of taxing power to Congress. Ultimately, the states reached a compromise by which Congress could regulate interstate and international commerce, but not tax exports, nor ban the foreign importation of slaves until after 1808.

To create a more powerful central government, a majority of the delegates supported shifting from a confederate system to a federal or national system. Under the confederate system each state retained full sovereignty, which meant that even though the states had pledged to follow the Articles, each state determined *at its sole judgment* how to act and what its obligations were under the Articles. Under a federal system, each state agreed to cede some of its sovereignty to the central government, which would be supreme. This is reflected the Constitutional provision called the Supremacy Clause which reads:

> This Constitution, and the Laws of the United States which shall be made in Pursuance thereof; and all Treaties made, or which shall be made, under the Authority of the United States, **shall be the supreme Law of the Land**; and the Judges in every State shall be bound thereby, any Thing in the Constitution or Laws of any State to the Contrary notwithstanding. (emphasis added)

As to the administration of government, most delegates favored creating a single chief executive to run the government. Under the Articles, the administration of governmental departments was under an executive committee. Many delegates thought Congress should appoint the chief executive for a short period of time. James Wilson of Pennsylvania (1742-1798) was the first to argue that a powerful and independent president would not be a threat to liberty but rather "the best safeguard against tyranny."[7] The idea was that a president, who was independent of Congress, would act as a check on legislative excess. This view won. Hamilton took this point and argued that the chief executive should serve for life and have an absolute veto over all legislation enacted by Congress.[8] This would provide the surest safeguard against the tyranny of the majority or passage of popular, but ill-conceived, legislation.

The idea of a chief executive with an absolute veto over legislation had a great deal of support; although, Franklin and a few others argued it would make the president too powerful. Ultimately, the delegates compromised and agreed that Congress should be empowered to override a presidential veto by a two-thirds vote of both houses. Nevertheless, there was broad acceptance of the general principle that an executive veto was a vital check on ill-conceived laws. Many delegates feared there could be too much democracy. A popular sentiment might sweep the nation, but checks should exist against new laws being enacted too quickly and without full consideration.

Under the Constitution, the president would be a check on Congress and on popular opinion. However, making the president independent of both popular opinion and state legislatures—which appointed Senators until 1914—required some sort of special selection process. Although it seems the most "democratic" means, the Framers considered election by a majority vote of all citizens a bad idea because the president would just reflect popular opinion. A proposal for direct election of the president was overwhelmingly defeated by a vote of 9 to 1.[9] To insulate the president from popular pressure, the delegates proposed what became known as the Electoral College. Citizens of each state would select electors who would cast their state's vote for president. This would provide the president with the independence he needed to do his job.

The Framers all assumed that the president would only enforce laws passed by Congress. No one seriously considered the possibility that the president might just rule by executive decree. Nor did anyone genuinely seem to expect that a president would simply refuse to enforce laws.

The appointment of federal judges followed the same pattern as the veto debate. **James Wilson**, who later served as a Supreme Court justice, argued that the president should appoint all judges, just as the English king had done. Many

---
[7] Madison's Notes, June 1, 1787.
[8] Madison's Notes, June 14, 1787.
[9] Madison's Notes, July 17, 1787.

George Mason

delegates thought this gave the president too much power; but, most Framers agreed that judges should be insulated from popular opinion so that they would rule based on the law rather than on popular pressure or opinion. Madison proposed a compromise: judges would need to be approved by the Senate but not the House of Representatives, because Senators would be less susceptible to political pressure. The judiciary was designed in many ways to be anti-democratic. Judges were expected to interpret the law as it is written, not according to what is popular or what is "needed." If a law is "needed," it is the job of the legislature to enact it, not the role of an unelected judge.

The most intense debates at the convention involved the structure of Congress and its powers. Everyone assumed that the president and judges would simply enforce the laws which Congress passed. Thus, Congress was considered the most important branch of the government. George Mason (1725-1792) and Luther Martin of Maryland (1748-1826) led the opposition to expanding the powers of the central government. These two men were to be leading anti-federalists during the debate on ratification.

Martin and Mason argued that if the federal government were supreme, Congress would inevitably pass laws encroaching on the authority of the states. Wilson countered by pointing out that the Senate was to be composed of members appointed by the state governments; thus, the Senate would prevent the federal government from usurping the states' authority. This point was accepted, but Charles Pinckney of South Carolina (1746-1825) then said because this principle was so important both the House and Senate should be appointed by state legislatures. There was significant support for this proposal; but, it was defeated by a vote of six states to four.[10] It appears to have been universally accepted that at least one branch of Congress needed to be appointed by states and not elected.

This plan for the Senate to represent state interests was a crucial check on the powers of the central government. In 1913, the 17th Amendment, which provided for the direct popular election of Senators, was added to the Constitution, changing the way Senators were elected. This was a fundamental change in the form of government; however, it is unlikely that anyone living in the past one hundred years favors returning to the old system. It might be argued that in increasing the power of the individual voter, the 17th Amendment decreased the power of the individual states. There is no question that since the enactment of the 17th Amendment, the powers of the federal government have constantly expanded at the expense of state authority.

In fact, it was precisely because the Senate was more isolated from popular opinion that the delegates voted to give it more powers than the House. James Wilson took the lead and argued that ratification of treaties should be vested solely in the Senate. Wilson noted that governments had two basic areas of concern: internal safety and international relations. The House, which directly represented the people, must approve laws affecting the internal affairs of the country; however, the House did not need to be involved in approving treaties, an international matter.[11] The implication, of course, was that treaties would have little or no impact on the internal affairs of a country. Such an implication was clearly faulty as treaties do affect the internal workings of a nation.

---

[10] Madison's Notes, June 21, 1787.
[11] Madison's Notes, June 26, 1787.

The Framers also determined that the Senate alone would approve executive officers and judges nominated by the president. The delegates deliberately gave more power to the Senate than to the House, because the Senate was considered the body that was less democratic and would defend state sovereignty.

One of the most important debates involved defining the powers of Congress. The delegates also considered a series of formulations to try to define how power would be shared and divided between the state governments and the federal government, what is known as federalism. For example, one early proposal suggested that Congress would have power

> to make laws binding on the people of the United States in all cases which may concern the common interests of the Union; but not to interfere with the Government of the individual States in any matters of internal police which respect the Govt. of such States only, and wherein the general welfare of the U. States is not concerned.[12]

The delegates considered several different formulations of such a rule, but ultimately, they decided that a specific *enumeration* of powers would be better and clearer than trying to express the division of powers in more general terms. Everyone agreed that the internal affairs of individual states would be exclusively the province of those states. This is often called the "police power." The term "police power" means not only the actual police force, but includes all the general powers necessary to protect public safety, public health, morality, and peace and quiet.

On the final day of the convention, September 17, 1787, Franklin, Hamilton, and others gave impassioned speeches urging all delegates to sign the final draft. Franklin and Hamilton said there many things in the Constitution they did not like and had voted against, but that was now water under the bridge. Hamilton went so far as to say that "[n]o man's ideas were more remote from the plan [of the Constitution] than his" but he would support the Constitution as an improvement on the Articles.

Of the 55 delegates to the convention, 39 ultimately supported the final draft. Of New York's three delegates, only Hamilton signed. Only three of Virginia's seven delegates signed the final document. Among those who refused to sign were George Mason and Edmund Randolph, two of the most influential Virginians. The draft Constitution proclaimed that a new government would take effect if nine of the thirteen states approved it. However, Virginia and New York were two of the largest and most important states. Refusal of either state to approve the new government would likely doom the whole project. Based on the refusal of the New York and Virginia delegates to sign, it did not look good for the new Constitution … or the fledgling nation.

THE FEDERALIST PAPERS

In the weeks following the approval of the final draft of the constitution, supporters and opponents began publishing essays in newspapers to make their case. In New York, two writers publishing under the pen names "Cato" and "Brutus" began publishing essays attacking the constitution. Brutus was probably Robert Yates, who had refused to sign the final draft.

In his first essay, Brutus stated the most fundamental objection to the proposed government. Anti-federalists did not object to a military alliance of sovereign states, but they did not want to see those states consolidated. Brutus argued that the new system would create a single unified country out of the existing confederation of republics. This consolidation was a bad idea because the confederation as a whole was far too big for a single government. Brutus argued that:

> In a republic, the manners, sentiments, and interests of the people should be similar. If this be not the case, there will be a constant clashing of opinions; and the representatives of one part will be continually striving, against those of the other.[13]

Even in 1790, the United States was large enough that sectional differences existed. New England tended to be Puritan, more democratic,

---
[12] Madison's Notes, July 17, 1787.
[13] Brutus, Essay # 1, 1787.

and possessed an economy based on commerce and recently established factories. Southern states were Anglican, aristocratic, with an economy based on agriculture, especially cotton. The Middle states shared a combination of their neighbors to the north and south. The Middle states' citizens were mostly farmers, who produced most of the nation's food, as well as enough to export to Britain via New England's merchants. These differences would inevitably grow as the country increased in area and population. Ultimately, unless compromises can be reached, conflict is inevitable when people do not agree on basic first principles of Justice.

Think of the problem this way. Suppose ten people assemble to agree on a rule or principle of justice. This group is composed of ten members of the same family. They all speak the same language, share the same religion, and hold the same political views. Another group of ten consists of someone from China, another from India, another from Nigeria, an Aztec, and six other strangers. This group speaks different languages, practices a variety of religions, and comes from entirely different cultures. Clearly, there is going to be more agreement on a whole host of issues in the first group than in the second.

Thus, the larger the United States (or any nation) became, the less likely the chance that there will be agreement on issues and voluntary cooperation on matters in dispute. It becomes more likely that the government will need to rely on some form of force or coercion even if it is very minor or mild. Anti-federalists made other arguments as well, but this was their core concern: *a central government would inevitably destroy liberty and local self-government.*

Alexander Hamilton realized that he needed to answer the anti-federalists so devised a plan to respond under the pen-name "Publius." Hamilton recruited fellow New Yorker John Jay (1745-1829) to help him write these essays. Jay was one of the most important and influential men in the United States. Jay had been Secretary of Foreign Affairs under the Articles and had been responsible for negotiating treaties and alliances with various European powers. Jay had been a leading proponent of a new constitution but not a delegate to the Convention. Unfortunately, Jay

John Jay

became ill after writing only four essays. To replace Jay, Hamilton recruited James Madison.

Between October 1787 and the summer of 1788, Hamilton, Madison, and Jay published 85 essays, with Hamilton as the principal author. Many of the essays were picked up and republished in newspapers in other states. In May 1788, the essays that had, at that point, been printed in newspapers, were collected into a book and published under the title: *The Federalist: A Collection of Essays, Written in Favour of the New Constitution*. This collection of essays is now generally called *The Federalist Papers*. The Federalist Papers has become the authoritative interpretation of the United States' Constitution. So far as the United States Supreme Court is concerned, if one wants to know what the Constitution means, they should refer to *The Federalist Papers*.

The Federalist Papers sought to make two basic points to convince people to support the new Constitution. First, a stronger central government was necessary for the welfare of Americans as a whole. Second, the central government would not present a danger to freedom or local self-government.

The crucial concept in arguing that the central government would not be a danger was the idea of checks and balances. Under the Constitution, no single person or group of people could ever dominate because power was diffused throughout a series of institutions that had power to check and balance each other. *The Federalist Papers* argued that there were far more checks and balances with respect to the federal government than with respect to state governments, so states ceding some of their sovereignty to the federal government would make Americans both safer and more free.

Again, the crucial dispute was whether the new Constitution would create a consolidated country. *The Federalist Papers* said the anti-federalists were attacking a straw man. While a single unified government for North America might be a bad idea, the Constitution did not create such a government. Madison and Hamilton insisted that the individual states retained almost all of their sovereignty with just a few narrowly drawn exceptions. One of the most oft-quoted expressions of this is found in *Federalist* 45 in which Madison explains:

> The powers delegated by the proposed Constitution to the federal government are few and defined. Those which are to remain in the State governments are numerous and indefinite. The former will be exercised principally on external objects, as war, peace, negotiation, and foreign commerce; with which last the power of taxation will, for the most part, be connected.

> The powers reserved to the several States will extend to all the objects which, in the ordinary course of affairs, concern the lives, liberties, and properties of the people, and the internal order, improvement, and prosperity of the State.

Relying on the need for concrete structures not paper promises, *Federalist* 45 argues that the states had real power to protect their interests. Congress depended on State legislatures to select Senators, so there was no chance that Congress could ever hope to intrude into the province of the states. Moreover, even if the federal government wished to overrun the state governments, the federal government lacked the manpower to try. Given that the federal powers were few and defined, there would never be more than a small number of federal employees. In *Federalist* 45 Madison asserts that:

> The number of individuals employed under the Constitution of the United States will be much smaller than the number employed under the particular States. There will consequently be less of personal influence on the side of the former than of the latter. The members of the legislative, executive, and judiciary departments of thirteen and more States, the justices of peace, officers of militia … must exceed, beyond all proportion, both in number and influence, those of every description who will be employed in the administration of the federal system.

In 2024, the federal government has 3 million employees, while state and local governments, at all levels, employ about 20 million. Moreover, over 100 million Americans receive regular payments from the federal government. In 2024, over 71 million people received social security. In 2024, about 45 million Americans had federal student loans. In 2022, most adults in the United States received a Covid "stimulus check" from the federal government. Clearly, Madison's assertion that the federal government would have little or no impact on the lives of the ordinary citizen is no longer correct.

Referring to the phrase, "powers delegated by the proposed Constitution to the federal government are few and defined," anti-federalists objected that while it was true that Article I listed some powers of the federal government, the Constitution did not actually say that these were the only powers. In *Federalist* 41, Madison insisted that "the enumeration of particular powers" logically entailed that no other powers not enumerated, could be exercised. Nevertheless, Madison eventually agreed to draft what became the Tenth Amendment to make this point explicit: "The powers not delegated to the United States by the Constitution, nor prohibited by it to the states, are reserved to the states respectively, or to the people."

As to the anti-Federalists' main point about the dangers of a consolidated state, Madison and Hamilton insisted that the federal government possessed neither the legal authority nor the means to consolidate power and usurp that of the individual states. It should be noted that federalists and anti-federalists agreed on the benefits of a military alliance. After all, no single colony could have defeated the English. Small states maximized self-government, but small states were at risk of invasion. The answer was for small states to band together for mutual protection while maintaining their sovereignty. Thus, Hamilton and Madison insisted that the states retained almost all of their sovereignty while benefiting from mutual security.

Nevertheless, many anti-federalists object to the "supremacy clause," which reads:

> This Constitution, and the Laws of the United States which shall be made in Pursuance thereof; and all Treaties made, or which shall be made, under the Authority of the United States, shall be the supreme Law of the Land; and the Judges in every State shall be bound thereby, any Thing in the Constitution or Laws of any State to the Contrary notwithstanding.

The anti-federalists said that this clause effectively made sovereignty reside in the federal government, not in the states. Hamilton disagreed. In *Federalist* 33, Hamilton wrote that this merely expressed a fairly innocuous truism and explicitly recognized that States were free to oppose any law that exceeded the powers conferred under the Constitution:

> But it is said that the laws of the Union are to be the SUPREME LAW of the land. But what inference can be drawn from this, or what would they amount to, if they were not to be supreme? It is evident they would amount to nothing. A LAW, by the very meaning of the term, includes supremacy. It is a rule which those to whom it is prescribed are bound to observe. … But it will not follow from this doctrine that acts of the large society which are NOT PURSUANT to its constitutional powers, but which are invasions of the residuary authorities of the smaller societies, will become the supreme law of the land. These will be merely acts of usurpation, and will deserve to be treated as such. … It will not, I presume, have escaped observation, that it EXPRESSLY confines this supremacy to laws made PURSUANT TO THE CONSTITUTION[.]

Once again, the emphasis is on real power.

It was assumed that states would have power to stand up to the federal government. States did not meekly need to do whatever the federal government said. Acts beyond the power entrusted to the federal government are "merely acts of usurpation" and should be opposed. This reflects the basic idea that states and the federal government would check each other. Each was supreme within its own sphere of sovereignty with power to prevent encroachment or usurpation by the other. This was perhaps best expressed in Federalist 51; whose author is uncertain:

> In a single republic, all the power surrendered by the people is submitted to the administration of a single government; and the usurpations are guarded against by a division of the government into distinct and separate departments. In the compound republic of America, the power surrendered by the people is first divided between two distinct governments, and then the portion allotted to each subdivided among distinct and separate departments. Hence a double security arises to the rights of the people. The different governments will control each other, at the same time that each will be controlled by itself.

To the extent that States ceded some power the central government, Hamilton and Madison insisted this was beneficial and not a threat to liberty. Again, the States were intended to check the power of the central government if it attempts to usurp power.

There was still another advantage to this extended union. In Federalist 10, Madison begins by declaring, *"Among the numerous advantages promised by a well-constructed Union, none deserves to be more accurately developed than its tendency to break and control the violence of faction."* "Faction," or what today might be called "special interest," is simply *"a number of citizens, whether amounting to a majority or a minority of the whole, who are united and actuated by some common impulse of passion, or of interest, adverse to the … aggregate interests of the community."*

Small special interests often get their way despite their demands being contrary to the common good because they are willing to fight longer and more determinedly; whereas, if the burden on the whole is small, the average person has little incentive to oppose the measure. While "special interests" are annoying, far dangerous are majority factions who take control of a government. Throughout history, popular governments have been subject to constant turmoil because two or more factions fight each other, and when one faction gains control of the government it oppresses the other faction. In one of the most famous passages of The Federalist Papers, Madison writes:

> [A] pure democracy, by which I mean a society consisting of a small number of citizens, who assemble and administer the government in person, can admit of no cure for the mischiefs of faction. A common passion or interest will, in almost every case, be felt by a majority of the whole; a communication and concert result from the form of government itself; and there is nothing to check the inducements to sacrifice the weaker party or an obnoxious individual. Hence it is that such democracies have ever been spectacles of turbulence and contention; have ever been found incompatible with personal security or the rights of property; and have in general been as short in their lives as they have been violent in their deaths. …
>
> A republic, by which I mean a government in which the scheme of representation takes place, opens a different prospect, and promises the cure for which we are seeking. … The two great points of difference between a democracy and a republic are: first, the delegation of the government, in the latter, to a small number of citizens elected by the rest; secondly, the greater number of citizens, and greater sphere of country, over which the latter may be extended.

Madison argues that the larger a society is, the more difficult it will be for majority factions to form:

> The smaller the society, the fewer probably will be the distinct parties and interests composing it; the fewer the distinct parties and interests, the more frequently will a majority be found of the same party; and the smaller the number of individuals composing a majority, and the smaller the compass within which they are placed, the more easily will they concert and execute their plans of oppression.

James Madison

> Extend the sphere, and you take in a greater variety of parties and interests; you make it less probable that a majority of the whole will have a common motive to invade the rights of other citizens; or if such a common motive exists, it will be more difficult for all who feel it to discover their own strength, and to act in unison with each other.…
>
> Hence, it clearly appears, that the same advantage which a republic has over a democracy, in controlling the effects of faction, is enjoyed by a large over a small republic,— is enjoyed by the Union over the States composing it.

This argument directly challenged the anti-Federalists' main point. Madison did not dispute that a political community needed to share much in common; but just as a community could be too large and too diverse, it could also be too small and too similar. Madison thought the union created by the 1787 Constitution struck the proper balance.

The other overarching issue concerned a Bill of Rights. Anti-Federalists argued that because the new Constitution created a powerful central government it should contain a Bill of Rights to protect individual liberty. Hamilton and Madison argued that because the federal government was strictly circumscribed that a Bill of Rights was unnecessary or even dangerous. Ultimately, Madison agreed to amend the Constitution to include a Bill of Rights.

REVIEW QUESTIONS

1. What did Ralph Waldo Emerson call the opening salvo of the American War for Independence?

2. What action did the English Army take that led to the battles of Lexington and Concord?

3. What was the name of the Petition adopted by the Continental Congress in 1775 as a final attempt to avoid war with England?

4. What was the main point of the July 1775 document entitled: "A Declaration Setting Forth the Causes and Necessity of Taking Up Arms?"

5. What did Rhode Island do on May 4, 1776, that was unique?

6. When did Patrick Henry become governor of Virginia?

7. How did New York declare independence from England?

8. What did most Americans think about the Royal Charters that had guaranteed self-government for the English colonies?

9. Who was the main author of the Declaration of Independence?

10. Which colonies failed to approve the Declaration of Independence?

11. What are the main ideas of the first paragraph of the Declaration of Independence?

12. Who was the only Catholic to sign the Declaration of Independence?

13. How did the New Hampshire Constitution attempt to restate the principles of the Declaration of Independence in more realistic terms?

14. When were the Articles of Confederation finally ratified and begin to take effect?

15. According to the terms of the Articles of Confederation how long were they supposed to last?

16. What important powers did the central government NOT have under the Articles of Confederation?

17. What important restriction did the Northwest Ordinance place on people living in the Northwest Territory?

18. What disturbance in 1786 and 1787 caused many Americans to think that a stronger central government was needed?

19. Why did Thomas Jefferson not attend the Constitutional Convention of 1787?

20. What role did Father John Carroll play in the Constitutional Convention?

21. Who was unanimously chosen as presiding officer of the Constitutional Convention?

22. What was The Connecticut Compromise (also known as The Great Compromise)?

23. Who was the only delegate from New York to sign the final draft of the Constitution?

24. What was the goal of the Americans in 1787 who published under the names "Cato" and "Brutus"?

25. How did James Madison end up contributing to The *Federalist Papers*?

26. What view of democracy was expressed by James Madison in Federalist 10?

27. How did the writers of the *Federalist Papers* view the decision-making power of states in relation to the federal government?

28. How did Federalist 45 define the powers delegated by the Constitution to the federal government?

29. What is the common view of *The Federalist Papers* today?

30. What is the system developed by the Framers of the constitution to try to ensure that no one person or group would become too powerful?

CHAPTER FOUR
THE LEGISLATIVE BRANCH: CONGRESS

THE STRUCTURE OF CONGRESS AND THE DIVISION OF POWERS

Article 1 section 1 of the Constitution begins:

> All legislative Powers herein granted shall be vested in a Congress of the United States, which shall consist of a Senate and House of Representatives.

This simple phrase contains two important points. First, the "legislative Powers" of the federal government are not unlimited. They are limited to those specifically "herein granted." Second, the Constitution says unambiguously that "All legislative Powers" are vested in Congress. Only Congress has authority to make law. Neither the president nor the courts may legislate, that is, make law. The president was given power to veto (reject) laws passed by Congress, subject to Congress "overriding" that veto, but Article II, Section 3 says explicitly "he [the president] shall take Care that the Laws be faithfully executed."

Despite the provision that all legislative powers are vested in Congress, the president promulgates "regulations" that are not approved by Congress. For all intents and purposes "regulations" are indistinguishable from a "law." Regulations even create criminal offenses.

All the laws passed by Congress, and currently in effect, encompass 38 large volumes and thousands of pages of text. The *Code of Federal Regulations* is organized into 50 titles, published in roughly 200 physical books, totalling about 190,000 pages of text. These aggregate numbers are somewhat misleading, however. In the two years 2017 to 2018, Congress enacted 442 laws encompassing just under 8,000 pages of text, or about 4,000 pages of new laws each year.[1] In contrast, there are about 4,000 new federal regulations each year totaling about 10,000 pages.[2] We should not lose sight of the reality that much regarding how laws are made do not apply to federal regulations. Indeed, the Constitution's carefully constructed systems of "checks and balances" are largely eliminated by the president simply issuing regulations.

The Framers thought that the structure of the government was more important than paper barriers. Both Houses of Congress needed to agree on new legislation or a change in law, and

---

[1] Each "Congress" sits for two years. The "First Congress" sat from 1789 to 1790; the second from 1791 to 1792 and so forth. The Congress that sat from 2017 to 2018 is known as the 115th Congress. As of this writing figures for the 115 Congress are the most recent available.

[2] Congressional Research Service, "Counting Regulations," September 3, 2019.

the president also had an opportunity to veto new legislation. The constitution originally provided: "The Senate of the United States shall be composed of two Senators from each State, chosen by the Legislature thereof." The Senate and the House of Representatives were chosen by different methods to represent different interests while the president was chosen by electors. Requiring the agreement of different institutions responsible to different groups and interests provided one of the basic checks on power. Madison, and other Federalists, thought that simple majority rule was dangerous and required some form of institutional restraint. Under the Articles of Confederation, nine of thirteen states needed to agree to any major action. Federalists thought this was too difficult to achieve, but they also did not want to make it too easy to enact new laws.

The passage of the 17th Amendment in 1913, providing for the direct election of Senators, represented a major change. If both houses are popularly elected, they are less likely to be at odds and check each other. Nevertheless, the equal representation in the Senate continues to serve this purpose, although to a more limited extent than it once did. Rural states with low populations, like Alaska and Wyoming, possess the same vote as huge states like California and New York. The Senate still makes it difficult for regional majorities to control the legislative process.

THE HOUSE OF REPRESENTATIVES

Article 1 created the Legislative Branch of the federal government which consists of two chambers: **The Senate** and the **House of Representatives.** Madison believed that it was crucial for one chamber of Congress to represent the common people. This was similar to England's Parliament, where there was a House of Lords and a House of Commons. This system very much accords with the view of St. Thomas that the best system of government is a combination of monarchy, aristocracy, and democracy; thus, this allows participation by the one, the few, and the many. Senators serve for six years and are few in number. The House of Representatives, which is based on population, is larger and its members are elected every two years. (Federal elections are held in November of even numbered years.) For convenience, members of the House of Representatives are usually referred to as "Congressmen" or "Congresswomen." In the first Congress, there were 26 senators but 65 congressmen. The number of Congressmen was expected to grow as the population increased. Initially, there was one representative for each 30,000 people.

The Constitution requires that Representatives be elected, but leaves the process largely up to the

state. In England, members of parliament were elected from specific local areas, such as a county or town. Nothing in the constitution requires a state to divide the state into different districts. Theoretically, a state could elect all representatives in state-wide, so-called "at large," elections, but states have followed the English model and elected Congressmen on a district by district basis.

In *Federalist* 55, Madison explained his theory of representation. Some anti-federalists thought that representatives should represent fewer than 30,000 constituents. Madison agreed in principle that it is best to have a small number of voters for each representative, but the rapid growth of the United States meant that in fifty years, even at the 30,000 to 1 ratio, there would be 400 representatives.

The Constitution permitted Congress to decide on the number of representatives once the number initially prescribed by the Constitution reached 200. In the 19th century, as the population increased, Congress repeatedly adjusted the proportion and size of the House.

Since 1913, the number of House members has been set at 435. Accordingly, the size of a congressional district is the population of the United States divided by 435. This system of distributing representation among the states is known as **apportionment**. However, each state must have at least one representative, so some congressional districts are smaller, and some a bit larger. Wyoming and Vermont each have a population of about 600,000 and have one representative. Delaware, with a population of nearly one million, also has one representative.

Because the population of individual states changes, every ten years the federal government conducts a **census**, that is, counts the number of people in the state. Based upon changes in the state's population, the number of seats each state has in the House is **reapportioned**. The government has been conducting a census every ten years since 1790. As of the 2020 census, the average congressman represents 761,000 constituents. The Framers hoped that because Congressmen represented a small number of people, who came from the same general area, that they, unlike Senators who represented an entire state, would be more responsive to the needs of

435 congressmen

1-52 congressmen per state

2 year terms

their constituents. Today, because Congressmen represent so many people, with such diverse beliefs and demands, it seems that can no longer be possible.

After the census, Congress determines how many seats each state receives in the House. Each state then decides how to elect these representatives and sets the boundaries of congressional districts. Depending on the census, states may gain or lose representatives, which means that the district boundaries need to be redrawn to reflect the population change. *Technically*, state legislatures should try to redraw the boundaries to include the same number of people in each district. However, Congressional districts can be manipulated to achieve a desired outcome, usually giving Congressional seats to the party controlling the state legislature.

Suppose a state is evenly divided between Democrats and Republicans, with 50,000 of each. The Republican-controlled legislature seeks to divide these 100,000 voters into three districts, of 33,000 each. If they can somehow pack 33,000 Democrats into one district, then the other two districts each would have 25,000 Republicans and 8,500 Democrats. This would likely guarantee that Republicans win two out of three seats. This type of maneuver was made famous by an historical incident.

After the 1810 census, the Massachusetts legislature, which was controlled by the Democratic-Republican Party, redrew the districts for election to state senate. The legislature created several "safe" districts, which they were certain the Democrats would win, by stringing together different neighborhoods where Democrats lived. One of these districts looked so odd that people said it was shaped like a salamander. In 1811, Democrat **Elbridge Gerry** (1744-1814) was elected governor of Massachusetts. Gerry signed into law the redistricting plan which the Legislature passed. To criticize Gerry, and imply he was a bit unethical, Federalists newspapers throughout the country, published cartoons of this odd "salamander shaped" district that they mockingly called a "Gerrymander." Gerrymandering became the name given to redrawing electoral districts to benefit one side.

One particularly controversial type of such conduct is racial gerrymandering, which involves electoral districts being drawn based on racial demographics. Some people think that gathering a racial minority into their own district ensures that the minority will be represented. Others argue that all law should be "color-blind" and not based upon race.

Another criticism leveled against the large size of congressional districts is that it makes it difficult for "third party candidates," that is, candidates who are not Republicans or Democrats,

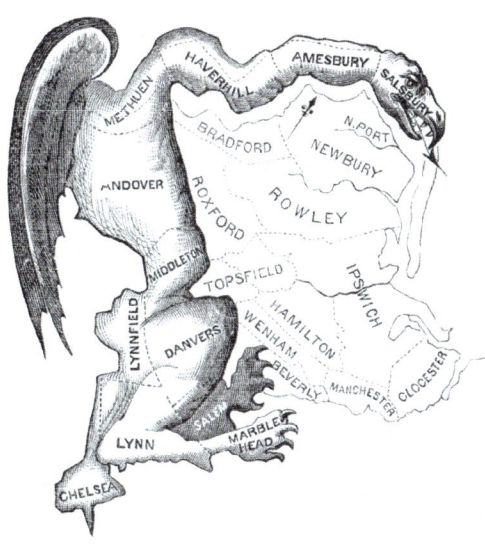

An 1812 political cartoon depicting the "gerrymander"

to win elections. In the 18th and 19th centuries, congressional districts represented 30,000 or 40,000 people, but the number of voters was much smaller. For example, when Abraham Lincoln was elected to Congress for Illinois in 1846, he received 6,340 votes. In 2020, the congressional candidate for the district Lincoln represented was elected with 249,383 votes. So, in the 19th century, a candidate did not need to be rich or famous to be elected to Congress. In 2020, the average cost of a candidate to run for congress was about $10 million. The majority of Congressmen and Congresswomen are millionaires.

Finally, under the Constitution, Congressmen need to meet certain requirements to be eligible to serve. They must be at least 25 years old, a citizen of the United States for seven years, and a resident of the state they intend to represent. In general, the eligibility requirements for Congress do not present obstacles to membership; although Congressmen and Senators are often criticized for moving to states where they have never lived to seek Congressional office. The most famous example is probably Hillary Clinton, who had been a resident of Arkansas for more than twenty-five years before moving to New York to run for the Senate in 2000.

THE SENATE

The Senate, or the upper house of Congress, consists of two members from each state. It is clear from *The Federalist Papers,* that the Framers intended that the Senate be composed of men from the upper echelons of society and not likely to be influenced by the "common man." The Senate would serve as a check against the recklessness of the members of the House. Each state is constitutionally entitled to two Senators, who serve for six years. Originally, Senators were chosen by their state's legislature, but since the enactment of the 17th amendment in 1913, they are popularly elected. To be eligible to run for the Senate, a person needs to be at least thirty years old, a U.S. citizen for at least nine years, and a resident of the state they hope to represent.

Because the Senate has fewer members than the House, it is less formal. Thus, for example, Senators can speak on the floor of the Senate almost as long as they wish, something known as the **filibuster**. A filibuster occurs when a senator, or senators, keep talking about a bill to prevent a vote. Although Senators usually speak about the bills they oppose, Senators have been known to read recipes and phone books. South Carolina Senator Strom Thurmond, who filibustered for more than 24 hours, holds the record for the longest speech. Interestingly, the most famous filibuster was a fictional one, delivered by Jimmy Stewart in Mr. Smith Goes to Washington. While it is not a constitutional requirement, the practice in the Senate for decades has been to require three-fifths of all seated Senators (currently sixty when no vacancies exist) to vote to cut off discussion, a process called **cloture**.

Unlike the House, there are fewer checks, with respect to certain powers, granted to the Senate. These powers are found in Article 2, section 2 which provides:

> [The President] shall have Power, by and with the Advice and Consent of the Senate, to make Treaties, provided two thirds of the Senators present concur; and he shall nominate, and by and with the Advice and Consent of the Senate, shall appoint Ambassadors, other public Ministers and Consuls, Judges of the supreme Court, and all other Officers of the United States, whose Appointments are not herein otherwise provided for, and which shall be established by Law: but the Congress may by Law vest the Appointment of such inferior Officers, as they think proper, in the President alone, in the Courts of Law, or in the Heads of Departments.

This means the House of Representatives does not have a say in some important decisions,

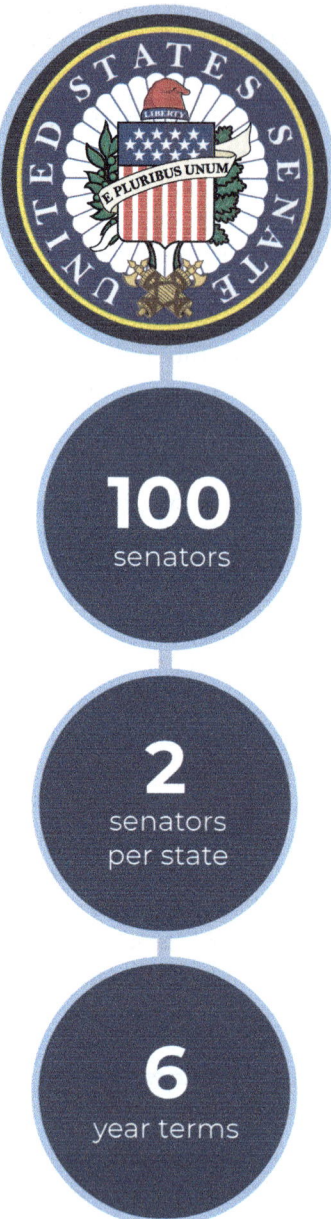

100 senators

2 senators per state

6 year terms

including approving treaties and confirming Supreme Court Justices. With respect to **treaties**, which are formal agreements between nations, while only the Senate votes, it requires the approval of a two-thirds majority. Note the clear supremacy of the legislative branch over the president. The president cannot appoint anyone to his administration unless allowed by Congress. Congress generally permits the president to hire and fire most executive officers, but this is entirely at the discretion of Congress.

The removal of officers is another important power for which the Senate holds the final authority. Article 2 section 4 provides that the president, or any other executive official, can be "removed from Office on Impeachment for, and Conviction of, Treason, Bribery, or other high Crimes and Misdemeanors." Article 1 section 2 gives the House power to "impeach," but Article 1 section 3 gives the Senate power to "try all Impeachments" and requires a two-thirds vote of the senators to remove an executive official or a judge. While both Houses of Congress are allowed to vote, it is much harder to get a two-thirds vote in the Senate than a bare majority in the House.

Historically, most members of Congress have been white, Protestant men, as they constituted the vast majority of voters until the end of the 19th century. However, as women and blacks were granted the vote, and the Catholic population increased, they also began joining Congress. The Congress elected in 2022 contains more women and ethnic minorities than any prior Congress. The vast majority identify as Christians, with 303 belonging to a Protestant denomination and 148 the Catholic Church. Additionally, this Congress also contains a small number of Jews, Mormons, and Orthodox Christians.

CONGRESSIONAL ELECTIONS

The method of electing members of Congress is mostly left to the states; although Congress has power to regulate federal elections. For example, in 1872, Congress decreed that every state should hold federal elections on the same day: the Tuesday following the first Monday in November, during even-numbered years. In 1971, the 26th amendment lowered the voting age from 21 to 18, primarily because 18-year-olds were subject to the draft and being sent to fight in Vietnam.

Throughout most of American history, congressional elections have been "winner take all," which means that the candidate who receives the most votes wins, even if they receive less than a majority. A few states have begun to change this. Georgia, for example, has a system where if no candidate receives a majority of votes, then the top two vote-getters have a run-off election. Alaska has recently adopted "ranked choice voting," which allows a voter to vote for more than one candidate in his order of preference. For example, a voter could list George Washington as first choice and John Adams as second choice. If Washington does not receive a majority he is eliminated and the second choice vote is counted. Some people prefer these options as it provides voters more choices and reduces the dominance of the two main political parties.

Finally, the states determine rules for elections, such as whether there will be paper ballots or electronic ballots; to what extent mail-in ballots are accepted; and whether identification is required to vote. Both parties have accused the other of manipulating voting rules to favor their side. For example, Democrats have argued that requiring voters to present identification before voting discriminates against Democrats because their voters are less likely to have identification. Republicans counter that *not* requiring voters to have identification allows Democrats to engage in voting fraud.

CONSTITUTIONALLY-CREATED LEADERSHIP POSITIONS IN CONGRESS

Like any organization, Congress needs people to lead it and decide what laws it will consider. The Constitution creates three positions of leadership in Congress: the Speaker of the House, the president of the Senate, and the president *pro tempore* (of the Senate). These officers are elected by the members of the House and Senate respectively.

Article 1, Section 2 establishes that the House "shall choose their Speaker." The **Speaker of the House** leads the House of Representatives. To be elected Speaker, a majority of the House needs to vote for him or her. This means that the party which controls the House elects the Speaker. The Speaker is incredibly powerful. The Speaker assigns members to House committees (discussed below) as well as determines which proposed laws, called **bills**, will be presented to the House for a full vote. The Speaker can delay action on a bill simply by refusing to allow debate. A majority of Representatives can force a vote on a Bill by signing a "**discharge petition**," but this rarely happens as most Representatives do not want to run afoul of the Speaker. Moreover, the Speaker is third in line for the presidency after the vice-president.

Section 3 names the vice-president as "**President of the Senate**." Historically, the position lacks both power and prestige. John Adams, the first president of the Senate, spent a great deal of time actually presiding over the Senate. However, the Senators generally ignored him, and even he felt that in a life filled with great accomplishments, his eight years as vice-president and president of the Senate, were a waste of time. The problem is that unless there is a tie vote, the president of the Senate possesses almost no political power. Although he or she technically presides over the Senate, unlike the Speaker, the President of the Senate can neither vote nor participate in debate. Most vice-presidents never voted to break a tie. Statistically, John Adams actually voted rather often, twenty-nine times. However, Kamala Harris holds the modern record with thirty-six tie-breaking votes.

Because the office of President of the Senate is rather dull, the vice-president normally appears only to cast a tie-breaking vote. When the President of the Senate is absent, the president *pro tempore* (or pro temp) leads the chamber. Because the president pro temp is elected by their fellow Senators, the party in the majority elects one of its own.

POLITICAL LEADERSHIP IN CONGRESS

In addition to these *constitutionally*-established Congressional leaders, there are also a number of *political* leaders, who work to enact legislation favored by their constituents. While not necessarily the intent of the Founders, the United States almost immediately developed a government centered around a "two party," or **bipartisan**, system. In the 1780s, Americans were divided into federalists and anti-federalists, but these groups were more loosely structured than today's political parties. A **political party** can be defined as a group of people organized to acquire and exercise political power, generally by electing candidates to office.

George Washington was elected president without a Party. Soon after Washington's election, Hamilton began organizing like-minded people into a coalition to support his agenda. In the 1792 election, when Washington was elected to his second term, candidates for state and federal office were openly identifying themselves as Federalists and another party known as Democratic-Republicans. Thomas Jefferson led this party, but initially from behind the scenes because he was part of the Washington Administration until the end of 1793. In the 1796 presidential election, John Adams, the Federalist candidate, defeated Jefferson.

The current division between Democrats and Republicans dates back to 1854, when the Republican Party's signature issue was opposing the expansion of slavery. Ever since, Democrats

The symbol for the modern-day Democrat party is a donkey, while the Republican party is represented by an elephant.

LEADERSHIP POSITIONS IN CONGRESS

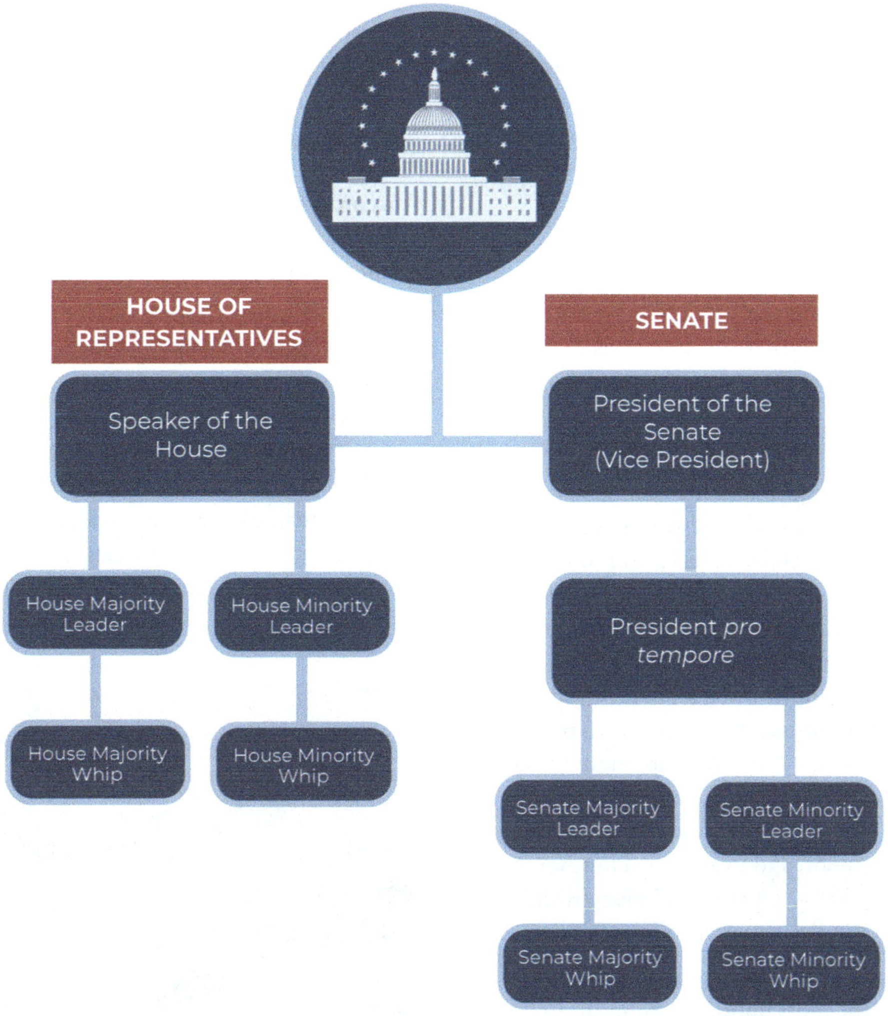

HOUSE OF REPRESENTATIVES
- Speaker of the House
  - House Majority Leader
    - House Majority Whip
  - House Minority Leader
    - House Minority Whip

SENATE
- President of the Senate (Vice President)
  - President *pro tempore*
    - Senate Majority Leader
      - Senate Majority Whip
    - Senate Minority Leader
      - Senate Minority Whip

and Republicans have dominated under a two-party system. Many countries possess multiple parties because their parliaments have proportional representation. Under these systems if a party receives only a few percentage points of a national vote that party still may obtain a seat or two in parliament. Small parties are able to gain a foothold in parliament under a proportional system. However, in the winner take all system of elections, it is difficult for new parties to elect anyone.

Because the United States has a two-party system, one can speak of the party with the most members in either chamber of Congress as the **majority party** while the party with fewer members is the **minority party**. As noted, the majority party in each chamber elects one of its own members to serve as the presiding member. The political leader of the majority party in both houses is known as the "Majority Leader." Although the Majority Leader of the Senate is a political, not Constitutional position, the Majority Leader of the Senate, in many ways, has become as powerful as the Speaker of the House. As noted, the Constitutionally-created Senate positions lack much real power. On the other hand, the Senate Majority Leader can delay bills and refuse to allow votes on bills or hearings on Supreme Court nominees.

In addition to the Majority Leader, each house

U.S. Government for Catholic Students

has a "Minority Leader," who leads the minority party. One of the most important powers of the minority and majority leaders is appointing members of their party to committees. House and Senate committees are important because a bill cannot become law without passing through a committee. Just as the Speaker can kill a bill by refusing to bring it to a vote "on the floor," a committee Chairman can kill a bill in the committee by "bottling it up."

Committees also have power to hold hearings and subpoena documents. These public hearings can play an important role in shaping public opinion. The majority party always has more members on a committee than the minority party, which means it controls the committee's agenda, another incredibly important power.

The minority leader appoints minority members to committees but also appoints the ranking minority member to each committee. Minority leaders, or ranking minority members, are more important than one might think, because minorities can cause a lot of problems for the majority. For example, when a bill is introduced, or arrives in committee, it is supposed to be read aloud on the record. Some bills are thousands of pages long, so no one wants to take time to have them read. This requirement can be waived by unanimous consent, and usually is. However, if a minority party insists on every bill being read into the Record it can delay matters quite a bit.

Both houses of Congress contain numerous committees. The most important committees include the Appropriations Committee, which approves all money spent; the Judiciary Committee, especially the Senate Judiciary, which approves federal judges; the Intelligence Committee; and the Rules Committee. The Intelligence Committee is unique because its operations are kept secret even from other members of Congress. The Intelligence Committee overseas spying and covert operations. The Rules Committee, especially in the House, determines procedures like how long debate will be on a bill and whether any amendments will be allowed. In the House, no bill can get to the floor for a vote unless approved by the Rules Committee, so the chairman of the Rules Committee wields a lot of power.

Another key political position in each party is known as the "**whip**." This rather unusual name comes from English fox hunts, in which one of the hunters was chosen to keep the hunting dogs together as they chased the fox. Today, the party whip is supposed to keep members of their party together as they chase votes to enact legislation. Through a variety of threats and promises, the whip hopes to convince the members to vote according to the party's platform. The whip also counts votes for party leadership so they are not embarrassed and schedule a vote which they lose.

Another important aspect of Congressional politics involves the party **caucus**. A caucus is simply a private meeting of the members of each party in which they decide on committee appointments, chairmanships, the party whips, and other decisions for the upcoming Congress. For the majority party in each chamber, the most important decision of the caucus is choosing the Speaker of the House and the Majority Leader in the Senate.

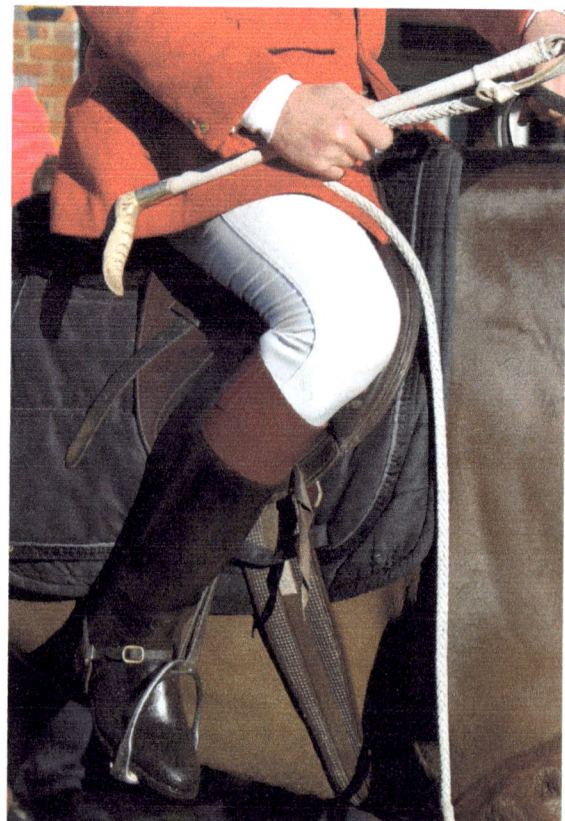

An English fox hunter holding a whip

CONGRESSIONAL RULES, PROCEDURES, AND PRIVILEGES

Article 1, Sections Four, Five, and Six establish the rules by which Congress governs itself. Although these rules have been modified by amendments, they have remained relatively unchanged since their enactment.

Under Section 4, Congress must meet at least once a year. Originally, the meeting was to occur on the first Monday in December; however, the 20th amendment moved the start date of the new Congress to January 3. Congress meets for two terms, although Congress can be called into special session in the event of an emergency, or for political expediency. Congress also can take a break, called a **recess**, during which Congressmen return home to vacation, or more often campaign for re-election.

Section 5 establishes a number of rules governing the proceedings of Congress. For example, each chamber shall judge its own elections and determine the qualifications of its own members. Once Congress meets, so long as a majority of members are present, that is, a **quorum**, Congress can conduct business. Congress can also compel absent members to attend.

Congress can also punish its members for disorderly behavior. Normally, this means that the chamber **censures** the member. Censure usually involves a public and official condemnation of a person's bad behavior. According to the House, censure is a reprimand that "registers the House's deep disapproval of member misconduct that, nevertheless, does not meet the threshold for expulsion."

While this seems dramatic, most Congressmen pay little attention to such matters and often embrace the censure as a badge of honor. Recently, Michigan's Democratic Representative Rashida Tlaib, a Muslim member of Congress, was censured for calling for the elimination of the nation of Israel. She remains a member of Congress.

If the bad behavior is serious enough, a member of Congress can be expelled. However, this is a drastic punishment, so the Constitution requires that two-thirds of the members of the chamber must vote for expulsion. To date, only six House members have ever been expelled. For example, the vote to censure Tlaib was 234 to 188, far short of a two-thirds majority.

Another rule requires Congress to keep a complete record of its proceedings. Since 1873, the official log of everything that happens in Congress has been kept in the *Congressional Record*.

The last clause in Article 1, Section 5 states that once Congress convenes, both chambers must agree to final adjournment and neither may adjourn for more than three days without the consent of the other. Moreover, neither chamber can meet somewhere else without the consent of the other. While the rules regarding meetings seem unnecessary in the Internet Age, they were absolutely necessary to ensure communications between the two chambers until quite recently. Finally, if the House and Senate are unable to agree on adjourning, the President is authorized to adjourn them. To date, no president has needed to adjourn Congress.

Under Section 6, members of Congress are to be paid for their service and are to set their own pay. In 1992, the 27th Amendment finally passed, which stated that any pay raise Congress voted on itself would not become effective until the *next* Congress. In general, members of Congress are paid well above the national average income. However, as most members are millionaires, they do not "need" the money.

One of the most important privileges granted to Congressmen is known as **congressional immunity.** Under Article 1, Section 6, Senators and Representatives "shall in all cases, except treason, felony and breach of the Peace, be privileged from Arrest during their attendance at the Session of their respective Houses, and in going to and returning from the same." The phrase "treason, felony and breach of the Peace" has been interpreted to mean *any* criminal offense. Essentially, members of Congress are free from arrest when Congress is in session. This policy follows not only the practice in England as regards Parliament, but had also been the practice under the Articles. While this seems to be a tremendous grant of protection, essentially shielding Congressmen from numerous serious crimes, the Founders were concerned that members of

Congress would be arrested on the most spurious of charges. However, members of Congress have asserted the privilege to avoid prosecution for various matters including drunk driving, e.g. Congressman Louis Stokes.

More importantly, Congressional immunity also provides an absolute protection for anything a Congressman says on the floor of Congress. The "Speech or Debate" Clause allows Congress to have a free and open debate without fear of either civil or criminal liability. This clause goes back to 1689 and the English Bill of Rights. Members of Parliament had frequently been prosecuted for comments about the monarchy. The English Bill of Rights sought to ensure free debate in Parliament, as this clause does in Congress. However, the clause is limited to speech members make in their official capacity as Congressmen. The Clause generally does not protect statements made outside of the legislative process.

Aware of the temptations faced by those in power, the Framers added a final clause to Section 6, known as the **Ineligibility Clause**, which prohibits Congressmen from being appointed to any federal job that was created, or for which the pay was increased, during the time the Congressman was in office. This clause seeks to stop Congressmen from creating high-paying jobs for themselves after they leave Congress. A second part of the clause forbids Congressmen from serving in Congress while simultaneously holding another federal office. The intent of the Framers in enacting both clauses was to prevent corruption. Unfortunately, in the last decades, following their service in government, members of Congress have enriched themselves by taking "no-show" jobs with various organizations who court them for their influence. One of the most egregious examples involved vice-president Joe Biden who was paid one million dollars to teach at the University of Pennsylvania but never taught a single class.

THE LEGISLATIVE PROCESS: HOW A BILL BECOMES LAW

As Article 1, Section 1 says, all legislative power is vested in Congress. Thus, its primary function is enacting laws for the citizens of the United States. While many people believe Congress enacts too many laws, and Americans would be better served with fewer regulations, Congress actually passes only about ten percent of the legislation that it considers.

The **legislative process**, that is, *law-making*, is not that complicated but involves a number of hurdles that must be overcome. A senator or congressman "introduces" a **bill**, the proposed new law. Often a senator and congressman will cooperate and introduce the same bill in both House and Senate. The Bill is read and referred to committee. The committee chairman then decides whether to hold hearings on a bill or schedule a vote. A bill generally must be approved by a majority of the committee to move on. In the House, the bill goes to the Rules committee. If the Speaker or the Majority leader schedules a vote, the bill must be approved by a majority of the votes cast.

Once one chamber passes a bill, it is sent to the other chamber, because both houses must approve a bill, and the two versions must be identical. Often the second house will make amendments, or changes, to a bill. When the House and Senate approve different versions of the same bill, it must go to a conference committee where the differences are resolved. Then the conference version goes back to the House and Senate for a yes or no vote where no amendments are allowed.

The President can then sign the bill into law, or **veto** (Latin for "I forbid"), it. If the president vetoes the bill, it returns to Congress which can override the veto by a 2/3 vote in each house. Finally, it should be noted that if Congress adjourns, and is not in session when the president receives the bill, the president can exercise a "pocket veto" by doing nothing. In this case, there is no veto to override. Congress often remains formally in session all year, even when members are on vacation, to ensure that no "pocket veto" takes place.

Under Article 1, Section 7 of the Constitution, only the House of Representatives may introduce "bills for raising revenue." Recall that when the Constitution was written the House was the only Federal body chosen directly by the voters (Senators were elected by state legislatures until 1913). The Framers wished to ensure that the people's money would be spent by the people's representatives, who, in the Framers' view, would be more answerable to the people than Senators.

HOW A BILL BECOMES LAW

```
Bill is introduced in the Senate        Bill is introduced in the House
            ↓                                       ↓
Bill is sent to Senate committee        Bill is sent to House committee
            ↓                                       ↓
Hearings held and vote conducted        Hearings held and vote conducted
                        ↓           ↓
                  Sent to other chamber to be approved
                              ↓
                Sent to conference committee to resolve differences
                              ↓
                House approves final bill, sends to president
                              ↓
                   President approves or vetoes bill
```

U.S. Government for Catholic Students

THE ENUMERATED POWERS (ARTICLE 1, SECTION 8)

CLAUSE 1: THE GENERAL WELFARE CLAUSE

Substantively speaking, many people regard Article 1, Section 8 as the most important part of the constitution. This section lists eighteen specific areas in which Congress can make laws, known as the **Enumerated Powers.** The section begins with the power "To lay and collect Taxes, Duties, Imposts and Excises, to pay the Debts and provide for the common Defense and general Welfare of the United States" and ends with an eighteenth power "To make all Laws which shall be necessary and proper for carrying into Execution the foregoing Powers."

Most of the sixteen powers listed between these two clauses were already found in the Articles, so the "General Welfare" and the "Necessary and Proper Clause" have always been the most controversial provisions. Anti-Federalists were concerned that the phrase "To lay and collect Taxes, … for the common Defense and general Welfare" might be used to justify spending money for things that were not among the enumerated powers of Congress. For example, creating schools is not listed among the specific enumerated areas in which Congress can make law. Anti-Federalists feared that Congress might claim authority to collect taxes and distribute it to states or private parties to pay for education. Another example involved using the taxing power to exert control over areas reserved to the states. Congress has no power to prohibit smoking tobacco, but imagine Congress placing a $10 tax on every ounce of tobacco.[3] This tax would not advance any of Congress's enumerated powers, but might be justified under the general taxing power. A worse scenario suggested by some anti-Federalists was that the taxing power could be used to destroy freedom of speech. The English Stamp Tax had placed a tax on all newspapers and handbills that were publicly posted or distributed. If Congress had an equivalent unlimited power to tax, it too could be misused.

Before addressing these objections, we should note the reason for the taxing power. Under the Articles, the states contributed to the federal budget. While states were legally required to contribute to the budget, there was no way to force a recalcitrant state to make its payments if it refused. The Federalists thought that the federal government needed a more secure source of revenue that the central government could collect itself. Even some Anti-Federalists agreed that an independent power of taxation was acceptable, but they thought that taxation should only be used for limited purposes.

In *Federalist* 41, Madison insisted that the phrase "To lay and collect Taxes, … for the common Defense and general Welfare" was not a general grant of power, but had to be understood as only allowing taxing and spending in furtherance of the enumerated powers found in the rest of section 8:

> Some, who have not denied the necessity of the power of taxation, have grounded a very fierce attack against the Constitution, on the language in which it is defined. It has been urged and echoed, that the power "to lay and collect taxes, duties, imposts, and excises, to pay the debts, and provide for the common defense and general welfare of the United

---
[3] As of 2024, the tax on tobacco is about $1 an ounce.

States,'" amounts to an unlimited commission to exercise every power which may be alleged to be necessary for the common defense or general welfare. No stronger proof could be given of the distress under which these writers labor for objections, than their stooping to such a misconstruction. … [W]hat color can the objection have, when a specification of the objects alluded to by these general terms immediately follows, and is not even separated by a longer pause than a semicolon? … For what purpose could the enumeration of particular powers be inserted, if these and all others were meant to be included in the preceding general power? Nothing is more natural nor common than first to use a general phrase, and then to explain and qualify it by a recital of particulars.

Thus, Madison assured Americans that the power to tax and spend was in fact limited by the specific enumeration of powers that followed. Madison's explanation of the taxing and spending powers prevailed for the next century, but not without controversy. When Hamilton became Secretary of the Treasury, he advocated the federal government pay for the construction of roads and canals to facilitate commerce. In his December 1791, *Report on Manufactures* to Congress asking for his plan to be funded, Hamilton argued that building harbors, roads, and canals would benefit the entire union, not just individual states. Some people have interpreted Hamilton to have suggested that Congress could spend on anything it wished so long as it was for the "general welfare," but Hamilton did not explicitly make such an argument. Supporters of "internal improvements" tended to argue that that the federal government had power to construct canals under the power to regulate commerce among the states.

Hamilton's plan for internal improvement was largely defeated by Madison, who argued that the plan was unconstitutional. This was the beginning of the falling out between Madison and Hamilton. Madison was consistent in this position for his entire life. In 1817, as president, Madison vetoed a proposal for internal improvements arguing that the federal government had no such authority, explaining:

The legislative powers vested in Congress are specified and enumerated in the eighth section of the first article of the Constitution, and it does not appear that the power proposed to be exercised by the bill is among the enumerated powers, or that it falls by any just interpretation within the power to make laws necessary and proper for carrying into execution those or other powers vested by the Constitution in the Government of the United States.

"The power to regulate commerce among the several States" can not include a power to construct roads and canals, and to improve the navigation of water courses in order to facilitate, promote, and secure such a commerce without a latitude of construction departing from the ordinary import of the terms strengthened by the known inconveniences which doubtless led to the grant of this remedial power to Congress.

To refer the power in question to the clause "to provide for the common defense and general welfare" would be contrary to the established and consistent rules of interpretation, as rendering the special and careful enumeration of powers which follow the clause nugatory and improper. Such a view of the Constitution would have the effect of giving to Congress a general power of legislation instead of the defined and limited one hitherto understood to belong to them, the terms "common defense and general welfare" embracing every object and act within the purview of a legislative trust.[4]

Madison's view dominated for the next century, but in the mid-twentieth century the Supreme Court rejected this view and declared that:

[T]he power of Congress to authorize expenditure of public moneys for public purposes is not limited by the direct grants of legislative power found in the Constitution.[5]

The interpretation feared by the Anti-Federalists and opposed by Madison throughout his life has become the dominant view of federal power: Congress can tax and spend for objects thought

---
[4]March 3, 1817: Veto Message on the Internal Improvements Bill.
[5]*U.S. v. Butler*, 297 U.S. 1, 66 (1936).

to be conducive to the "general welfare" without reference to any of the enumerated powers of Congress.

CLAUSE 18: THE NECESSARY AND PROPER CLAUSE

The other phrase that concerned Anti-Federalists was the final clause of Article 1 section 8 authorizing Congress, "To make all Laws which shall be necessary and proper for carrying into Execution the foregoing Powers." Anti-federalists feared this clause would be used to usurp powers that were properly reserved to the states. For example, Congress had power to establish post offices—power Congress had possessed under the Articles as well. Could Congress pass a law making it a federal crime to assault a postal worker? Anti-federalists thought crimes like assault were local matters, but this was the type of issue that Congress might federalize as "necessary and proper" to run a postal service.

This concern is best illustrated by comparing it to the Articles that had declared: "each state retains its sovereignty, freedom, and independence, and every power, jurisdiction, and right, which is not by this Confederation expressly delegated." (emphasis added). Compared to this language, the "necessary and proper" clause looks a lot more expansive — perhaps there are "implied powers" connected with the explicitly delegated powers of Article 1.

Hamilton addressed this objection in *Federalist* 33 arguing that the "necessary and proper" clause did not expand the powers of Congress but expressed a mere truism. If Congress is given power to establish a postal service then logically Congress must have authority to adopt measures necessary for a postal service. Even if the phrase "necessary and proper" had been omitted from the Constitution it would not matter because this power to enact necessary laws "would have resulted by necessary and unavoidable implication from the very act of constituting a federal government, and vesting it with certain specified powers." Thus, when Hamilton writes that the power to enact "necessary laws" is a "necessary and unavoidable implication" he means this conclusion is logically necessary — we cannot have one without the other.

Madison returned to this subject in *Federalist* 44, and tried to explain why the necessary and proper clause was an improvement over the "expressly delegated" language of the Articles. Following Hamilton's lead, Madison wrote even if the phrase had been omitted, logical inference dictates that Congress would still have power to enact laws necessary to accomplish each of its enumerated powers. Madison argued that the "expressly delegated" clause from the Articles had been misconstrued to unreasonably limit the powers of Congress. Madison asserted that had this "expressly delegated" language been included in the new constitution:

> it is evident that the new Congress would be continually exposed, as their predecessors have been, to the alternative of construing the term "EXPRESSLY" with so much rigor, as to disarm the government of all real authority whatever, or with so much latitude as to destroy altogether the force of the restriction.

So, the "expressly delegated" language was subject to abuse but the "necessary and proper" language was not. It was nothing but the logical implication of the enumerated powers of Congress.

However, like the "general welfare" clause, the "necessary and proper" clause has been transformed. In 1791, as Secretary of the Treasury, Alexander Hamilton recommended the creation of a national bank to facilitate commerce. Prior to this there had only been local banks. The Bank of the United States was a private company but was

The United States Postal Inspection Service is the federal law enforcement branch of the postal service established under the "necessary and proper" clause.

incorporated under federal law. Madison opposed the creation of a national bank.

In an important speech given February 2, 1791, Madison argued that in reviewing the Constitution he could not discover any Congressional power to incorporate a Bank. He suggested that the only clauses under which such a power might be "pretended" were the power to lay and collect taxes to pay the debts and provide for the common defense and general welfare; or the power to borrow money on the credit of the United States; or the necessary and proper clause. Madison immediately rejected the bill as falling under the power to tax as it imposed no tax nor provided for the general welfare. He found no argument supporting the notion that the bank was for the "common defense and general welfare" or borrowing money. This meant only the necessary and proper clause could serve as Congress' authority to create the bank. Madison argued that whatever this clause might mean, no one intended that it provide Congress unlimited discretion. Madison held that "Its meaning must, according to the natural and obvious force of the terms and the context, be limited to means necessary to the end and incident to the nature of the specified powers."

Madison then discussed each of the other enumerated powers and eliminated them because the creation of a bank was not "necessary" for the exercise of any of those powers. Despite his powerful speech, Madison was not as opposed to the creation of a bank as his words suggest. His opposition to the bank was rather tepid and the measure actually passed Congress. Years later, Madison grudgingly came to accept the bank as permissible.

In 1819, the U.S. Supreme Court heard the case *McCulloch v. Maryland* which reviewed the legality of the Bank. *McCulloch* ended up in court because the Bank claimed it could not be taxed by the State of Maryland. One of the main issues in the case was whether Congress possessed constitutional authority to incorporate a private bank. Incorporating businesses was certainly not a power specifically enumerated in Article 1, section 8. However, the Bank argued that while there was no specific power listed in the Constitution to incorporate a bank, incorporating a bank

John Marshall

was "necessary and proper" in order to exercise several of Congress's enumerated powers, such as collecting taxes.

Luther Martin, one of Maryland delegates to the Constitutional Convention who had become a leading anti-federalist, argued the case before the Supreme Court on behalf of Maryland. Martin "read several extracts from the *Federalist*, and the debates of the Virginia and New York conventions, to show that the contemporary exposition of the constitution, by its authors, and by those who supported its adoption, was wholly repugnant to that now contended for by the counsel for the [Bank]."[6] Despite these undisputed authorities, the Supreme Court decided that the word "necessary" did not mean "absolutely indispensable" but merely "suitable." Chief Justice John Marshall wrote for the Court:

> Congress is authorized to pass all laws 'necessary and proper' to carry into execution the powers conferred on it. These words, 'necessary and proper,' in such an instrument, are probably to be considered as synonymous. Necessarily, powers must here intend such powers as are suitable and fitted to the object; such as are best and most useful in relation to the end proposed. If this be not so, and if congress could use no means but such as were absolutely indispensable to the existence of a granted power, the government would hardly

---

[6] *McCulloch v. Maryland*, 17 U.S. 316, 372 (1819)

exist; at least, it would be wholly inadequate to the purposes of its formation. A bank is a proper and suitable instrument to assist the operations of the government, in the collection and disbursement of the revenue; in the occasional anticipations of taxes and imposts; and in the regulation of the actual currency, as being a part of the trade and exchange between the states.

The decision caused widespread outrage. Anti-federalists thought they had been victims of a pure lie. James Madison wrote a letter harshly criticizing the decision in which he said that the Court had adopted an interpretation of "necessary and proper" that he and other supporters of the Constitution had uniformly repudiated. Madison went further and opined that the Constitution would never have been ratified if "necessary and proper" were understood to mean "suitable." Madison stated that converting "necessary" into "suitable" was to convert a limited government into an unlimited government.

As with the General Welfare Clause, this expansive reading of the Necessary and Proper Clause became the dominant view of federal powers, but remains controversial. Today, critics of this interpretation often refer to the Necessary and Proper Clause as the "Elastic Clause," or the "Sweeping Clause," because this interpretation allows the federal government to expand into almost every area. Nevertheless, Congress now claims to have constitutional authority to pass any measure that is suitable or convenient to the exercise of an enumerated power.

CLAUSE 3: THE COMMERCE CLAUSE

While certain enumerated powers have been widely accepted and not controversial, such as Article, 1, section 8, clause 2 (**The Borrowing Clause**) which provides that Congress can "borrow Money on the credit of the United States," other powers, like the Necessary and Proper Clause are far more controversial and litigated. One of the most important and controversial powers is found in Article, 1, section 8, clause 3 (T**he Commerce Clause**) which authorizes Congress "To regulate Commerce with foreign Nations, and among the several States, and with the Indian Tribes." While the language of the Commerce Clause seems rather straightforward, over the years the Courts have managed to manipulate this language in a variety of *interesting* ways.

First, what is the meaning of "commerce." In 1755, Samuel Johnson published a *Dictionary of the English Language*, with later editions published through 1785. Johnson's dictionary is typically cited as a resource for understanding what words meant in 1785. According to Johnson, "commerce" meant, "Intercourse; exchange of one thing for another; interchange of any thing; trade; traffic." Thus, for example, a farmer growing crops or a carpenter making a table is not "commerce." **Commerce only occurs when the goods, that is, the crops or the table, are actually traded or exchanged**. Normally, commerce involves the exchange of goods and/or services for money. The farmer sells his crops for money to a grocery store. He then takes the money and buys a table from the carpenter, who takes the money to the grocer to buy food.

The other important phrase in the Commerce clause is "to regulate." Referring again to Dr. Johnson, "to regulate" means to "to adjust by rule or method" or "to direct." In other words, the clause means that Congress has the power to direct or control commerce. Recall that Madison thought the power to regulate or control commerce did not authorize the federal government to build roads or canals to *improve* commerce. Hamilton disagreed.

Regulating and encouraging commerce among the states had been a major goal of the new Constitution. In *Federalist* 11, Hamilton declared that everyone agreed that a commercial union of the states was essential. Hamilton also argued that individual states would be severely disadvantaged when negotiating treaties or regulating commerce with foreign nations as the small states lacked any real bargaining power against major commercial powers like Britain or France. However, if the States banded together and negotiated as a single entity they could press even strong commercial nations to make concessions, such as lowering tariffs on American goods.

More problems potentially lay in Congress's authority to regulate commerce "among the several States." In The Federalist Papers, Hamilton and Madison repeatedly insisted that the regulation of commerce among the states would not interfere

New York harbor is a prime example of why the Founders considered Congress needed some level of authority over interstate commerce.

with the states' broad power to regulate their internal affairs.   In Federalist 17 Hamilton writes:

> The regulation of the mere domestic police of a State appears to me to hold out slender allurements to ambition. Commerce, finance, negotiation, and war seem to comprehend all the objects which have charms for minds governed by that passion; and all the powers necessary to those objects ought, in the first instance, to be lodged in the national depository. The administration of private justice between the citizens of the same State, the supervision of agriculture and of other concerns of a similar nature, all those things, in short, which are proper to be provided for by local legislation, can never be desirable cares of a general jurisdiction.

Hamilton's remarks are particularly relevant because today there are thousands of federal criminal laws and almost all of them have been enacted to "regulate commerce." For example, under the federal "Hobbs Act," it is a federal crime to commit a robbery if the robbery "affects" interstate commerce, which, based on court decisions, covers almost every robbery.[7] Yet, Hamilton says explicitly in *Federalist* 17 that federal authority over "commerce, finance, negotiation, and war" did not interfere with reserving to the States "the ordinary administration of criminal and civil justice."

In *Federalist* 42, Madison also discussed the meaning of interstate commerce, explaining that the primary reason for giving Congress authority to regulate commerce among the states was to prevent states from imposing discriminatory taxes:

> A very material object of this power [over commerce] was the relief of the States which import and export through other States, from the improper contributions levied on them by the latter. Were these at liberty to regulate the trade between State and State, it must be foreseen that ways would be found out to load the articles of import and export, during the passage through their jurisdiction, with duties which would fall on the makers of the latter and the consumers of the former.

To illustrate this point, consider that New York City possesses one of the best harbors on the east coast and the surrounding states like New Jersey, Connecticut, and Vermont depend heavily on this port to import and export goods. Madison's point is that New York should not be able to tax goods going to or coming from these other states. That would amount to New York using its position to discriminate unfairly against these other states.

The power to regulate commerce is expressed as a grant of power to Congress; however, it also implicitly limits the states from regulating

---

[7] The Hobbs Act was passed in 1946 as an anti-racketeering measure designed to stop organized crime; however, it has grown so unwieldy that it is used very indiscriminately. The most egregious incident involved the Supreme Court case *Scheidler v. National Organization for Women* (2006) in which an abortion clinic unsuccessfully attempted to use the Hobbs Act to stop pro-life picketers from protesting outside an abortion clinic. The abortion providers claimed that the pro-lifers, members of Operation Rescue, were essentially members of organized crime.

commerce beyond their own borders or enacting laws that unduly interfere with interstate commerce. This limitation is called the "negative commerce clause" or the "dormant commerce clause." This implication derives from the underlying purpose of Article 1 authorizing Congress "To regulate Commerce ... among the several States" which was to stop individual states from erecting barriers on trade between the states.

One of the standard rules of constitutional interpretation is that states may not exercise a power that would defeat the purpose of a constitutional provision. When a state action would negate the reason for a constitutional provision, then logic dictates that the power of the federal government will be exclusively applied. For example, a state could not ban the sale of agricultural products not grown in that state. Even if no federal laws addressed this issue, this is precisely the sort of "protectionist" legislation the commerce clause was designed to prevent.

However, other local laws that are not overtly "protectionist" may also violate the negative commerce clause. One famous example illustrates the point. In the 1950s, Illinois passed a law requiring all trucks operating in the state to have *curved* mud flaps behind the wheels of trucks. Almost every other state required *straight* mudflaps. Every truck entering or leaving Illinois had to stop at the border and change its mud flaps. Congress had not enacted any "mudflap" legislation, but a shipping company sued Illinois arguing that this regulation was a pointless restriction on interstate commerce. The U.S. Supreme Court agreed. *Bibb v. Navajo Freight Lines* (1959). Consequently, even when ostensibly regulating commerce only in one state, local legislation cannot restrict interstate commerce without some extremely serious justification.

Until the 20th century, it was generally accepted that the commerce clause did not apply to purely *intrastate* commerce, that is, activities that took place strictly within one state. This view began to be challenged in the 1920s when Progressives argued that the interstate commerce clause, combined with the necessary and proper clause, gave Congress broad authority to regulate all commerce or commercial activity.

For example, in 1916, Congress passed the Keating-Owen Child Labor Act which outlawed the interstate sale of goods produced by child labor. Factories could employ children, if state law permitted, and sell the goods locally, but products could not be sold across state lines. Even so, federal courts refused to enforce the Child Labor Act which appeared to be an effort to enact social policy, not to regulate commerce.

Nevertheless, Progressives continued to push for the expansion of federal power under the commerce clause. This battle resulted in the infamous decision in *Wickard v. Filburn* (1942). In 1938, Congress passed the Agricultural Adjustment Act which limited the amount of wheat that could be grown in the United States. The idea was that this central planning would avoid both under-production and over-production and stabilize the price of wheat, thereby helping farmers hurt by the Great Depression. For 1941, Ohio farmer Roscoe Filburn was allotted 11.1 acres of his farm to grow wheat. But Filburn planted 23 acres of wheat on his farm. He only sold 11.1 acres of wheat, but used the "excess" wheat to feed his own family. The federal government fined Filburn for growing too much wheat.

It seems quite clear that Filburn was not engaging in commerce, much less interstate commerce. Recall that, historically, commerce only occurs when goods or services are exchanged. Remarkably, a unanimous Supreme Court declared that Congress had authority to regulate *any activity*—even non-commercial activities – that, in the aggregate, affect interstate commerce. It turned out that by **not buying wheat** that might have come from another state if he had bought it, Filburn was affecting interstate commerce:

> One of the primary purposes of the Act in question was to increase the market price of wheat and to that end to limit the volume thereof that could affect the market. ... But if we assume that it is never marketed, it supplies a need of the man who grew it which would otherwise be reflected by purchases in the open market. Home-grown wheat in this sense competes with wheat in commerce.

This expansive view of interstate commerce remains controversial, but has generally been embraced by the federal courts. Today, the federal government asserts authority to regulate any activity whatsoever, regardless of how local it may appear to be so long as the activity in the aggregate substantially affects interstate commerce. Under this view, there is very little the federal government may not do under the power to "regulate commerce … among the states." Indeed, the rest of the powers listed in Article I are largely superfluous because all of them could be justified as regulating commerce. It seems clear that if the Founders intended the Commerce clause to be so all-encompassing they would not have bothered including the other enumerated powers!

CLAUSE FOUR: BANKRUPTCY AND NATURALIZATION

Clause Four, sometimes called the "Uniform Clause," actually contains two powers. Congress has power:

> To establish an uniform Rule of Naturalization, and uniform Laws on the subject of Bankruptcies throughout the United States;

What is bankruptcy? Historically if a debtor was unable to pay his debt he went to prison. However, people eventually realized that locking up debtors did not really help anyone because they could not work off their debt in prison. Accordingly, the idea evolved that if a person really could not pay his debts the debts might be "discharged" or forgiven. A similar idea is found in the Old Testament. Under Mosaic law, every fifty years all debts were forgiven. (Leviticus 25:9). Bankruptcy can forgive all or part of the debt. For example, a bankruptcy court can restructure a debt and order that a debtor be given more time to repay the debt.

Recall that in the 1780s there was economic depression. Shay's Rebellion blocked local courts from foreclosing on local farms and businesses. The concern was that local courts and juries would be sympathetic to local citizens and against outside interests like banks. The Federalists were concerned that local governments would use bankruptcy laws to favor local debtors. Thus, the Federalists wanted the issue of bankruptcies to be governed by federal law. Eventually these cases were heard in federal court. Federalists were also concerned that because it was so easy to move property from one state to another it might be difficult for one state to have jurisdiction over all of a person's assets. In *Federalist* 42, Madison explained that establishing uniform laws of bankruptcy was closely connected with regulating commerce and would prevent frauds where the parties or their property were located in or taken into different states.

One of the most controversial clauses in the Constitution, both in the 18th century, and today, is Congress's power over naturalization. It must be noted that, historically, a person could become an American citizen in a few different ways. First, people were citizens if their parents were citizens. Second, in the 1860s, the 14th Amendment expanded citizenship to people born in the United States. Third, foreigners can apply to become citizens, a process known as **naturalization**, which comes from "natus" meaning "birth." Naturalized citizens are treated as if they had been born in the country.[8]

The dispute over the power of naturalization can be traced back to 1798. In the 1790s, America's relations with France deteriorated

The Uniform Clause gives Congress the power to make standardized bankruptcy laws that apply uniformly to every state.

---

[8] Notice that Article 1 section 8 only refers to a rule of naturalization. Article 1 says nothing about immigration or control of the borders. The dominant theory today is that because Congress has power to enact a uniform rule about naturalization, it has

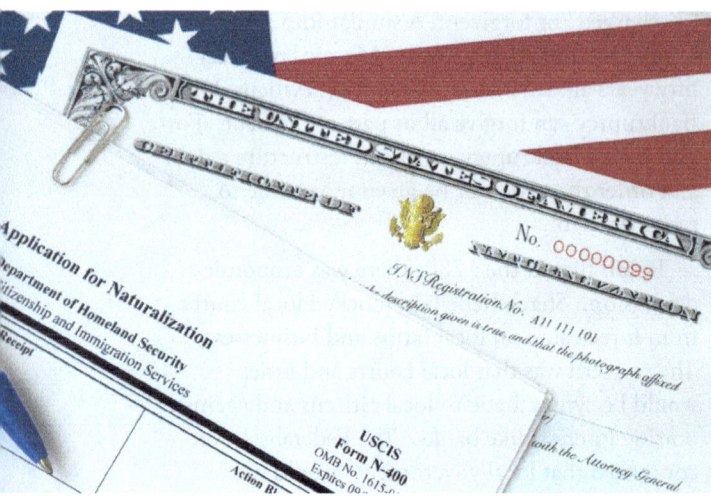

for a variety of reasons. In 1796, the French government authorized French ships to begin seizing American merchant ships. From 1798 to 1800, the United State fought an undeclared naval war with France. Largely due to the chaos of the French Revolution (1789-1799), thousands of French men and women immigrated to America. The Adams' Administration doubted the loyalty of these French people who were not American citizens. In June 1798, Federalists in Congress passed the Alien Act which authorized the president, at his sole discretion, to deport "such aliens as he shall judge dangerous to the peace and safety of the United States."

Anti-federalists disputed Congress's power to enact the Alien Act, but Federalists and Anti-federalist alike agreed that if Congress had the power, it was a result of the war powers, not the naturalization power. Federalist George Nicholas appears to have expressed the generally accepted view that the power to enact rules for naturalization was limited to rules about citizenship, and that, "each state, as a sovereign and independent state, had an unquestionable right to declare, on what terms strangers should be permitted to come into the state."[9]

Nicholas had been a delegate to the Virginia ratifying convention in 1788, where he had been a strong proponent of the new Constitution. In a speech to the convention on June 16, 1788, Nicholas assured the delegates that the Anti-federalists' concerns were exaggerated because Congress "cannot legislate in any case, but those particularly enumerated." Nicholas was also a professor of law and the first United States Attorney for Kentucky, so his opinion carries some weight.

James Madison was no longer in Congress when the Alien Act was passed. However, he authored a Resolution for the Virginia Assembly to adopt that proclaimed:

> That the General Assembly doth particularly protest against the palpable and alarming infractions of the constitution, in the two late cases of the "alien and sedition acts," passed at the last session of Congress; the first of which exercises a power no where delegated to the federal government.[10]

Interestingly, when Madison was president during the War of 1812, he thought that dangerous foreigners could be deported. However, he consistently denied that the naturalization clause allowed any such actions.

Thomas Jefferson drafted a Resolution for the Kentucky legislature that said the same thing as Madison but was perhaps even more forceful:

> Resolved, That alien friends are under the jurisdiction and protection of the laws of the State wherein they are: that no power over them has been delegated to the United States, nor prohibited to the individual States, distinct from their power over citizens. And it being true as a general principle, and one of the amendments to the Constitution having also declared, that "the powers not delegated to the United States by the Constitution, nor prohibited by it to the States, are reserved to the States respectively, or to the people," the act of the Congress of the United States, passed on the—day of July, 1798, entitled "An Act concerning aliens," which assumes powers over alien friends, not delegated by the Constitution, is not law, but is altogether void, and of no force.

Today, many people argue that the Naturalization Clause gives the federal government exclusive authority over immigration and border

---

exclusive power to regulate all immigration as convenient to regulation of naturalization.
[9] Nicholas, Letter to James Carey, 1799.
[10] Adopted by Virg. House of Delegates Dec. 21, 1798.

control. However, that was certainly not the dominant view in the 18th and early 19th century. Ironically, today's arguments, in a sense, have flipped the dispute of the 1790s. In the 1790s, Madison and others argued that the states had authority to permit aliens to remain in the state even if the federal government did not like it. Today, some people argue that federal power over immigration is so absolute that states cannot stop people from crossing the U.S. border, even when such border crossing is indisputably illegal under federal law; and that even when people criminally trespass on private or state land during border crossings, local police cannot arrest them.

CLAUSES FIVE AND SIX: MONEY (STANDARDS) AND COUNTERFEITING

Under clauses five and six, Congress has the power:

> To coin money, regulate the value thereof, and of foreign coin, and fix the standard of weights and measures;

> To provide for the punishment of counterfeiting the securities and current coin of the United States;

The Constitution talks about *coining* money not *printing* it. In February 1862, during the Civil War when the Union desperately needed money, Congress passed a statute authorizing the issuance of paper money and made it legal tender for all debts public and private. The U.S. Supreme Court initially declared that Congress had no authority to issue paper money, but, in the 1860s, Republicans expanded the size of the court from seven justices to nine, and, with the two new votes, reversed this decision. Today, it is generally acknowledged that the federal government can print as much money as it wishes, but a few people still dispute the point.

Everyone agrees that counterfeiting should be punished. Whether paper money is fake, or coins made from precious metals have been diluted so as not to contain the correct amount of gold or silver, the impact on the economy is catastrophic. First, people can not trust the "money" that they are given. Second, the value of the dollar declines as untold amounts of fake currency flood the market. Although not part of American history or government, during World War II, the Nazis launched *Operation Bernhard*, the largest counterfeiting scheme in history. The goal was to destroy England's economy by pouring millions of pounds of fake currency into Britain every month.[11]

CLAUSE SEVEN: THE POST OFFICE

The next clause authorizes Congress "To establish Post Offices and post Roads." The Articles had authorized Congress to operate post offices, but the Constitution included the power to establish "post Roads." This has always been understood to mean that Congress can designate postal routes on existing roads, not build new roads.

The clause says nothing about powers associated with post offices, but even under the Articles there were postal inspectors tasked with preventing hazardous materials being mailed. The U.S. Postal Inspection Service is by far the oldest federal law enforcement agency.

In addition to "hazardous" materials, Congress has also prevented the post office from

---
[11]The pound is the English currency.

delivering obscene and immoral items. In 1873, Congress enacted the **Comstock Act**, one of the most famous laws passed under the postal power. The Comstock Act prohibited mailing obscene or immoral materials, and also explicitly criminalized the mailing of contraceptives and abortifacients, or any written materials explaining how to obtain contraceptives or abortifacients. The Comstock Act had overwhelming support. It passed in the House of Representatives by unanimous consent. In the 19th century, no American thought there was a "right" to contraception or abortion. Most Americans considered these actions gravely immoral.

CLAUSES TEN THROUGH SIXTEEN: THE WAR POWERS

Because clauses ten through sixteen enumerate Congress's power to wage war and deal with the armed forces, they are usually grouped together and referred to as the "war powers;" although, only clause 11 specifically addresses the power to declare war.

- To define and punish Piracies and Felonies committed on the high Seas, and Offences against the Law of Nations; (Clause 10: **Maritime Crimes**)
- To declare War, grant Letters of Marque and Reprisal, and make Rules concerning Captures on Land and Water; (Clause 11: **War Powers**)
- To raise and support Armies, but no Appropriation of Money to that Use shall be for a longer Term than two Years; (Clause 12: **Army**)
- To provide and maintain a Navy; (Clause 13: **Navy**)
- To make Rules for the Government and Regulation of the land and naval Forces; (Clause 14: **Land and Naval Forces Rules**)
- To provide for calling forth the Militia to execute the Laws of the Union, suppress Insurrections and repel Invasions; (Clause 15: **Calling the Militia**)
- To provide for organizing, arming, and disciplining, the Militia, and for governing such Part of them as may be employed in the Service of the United States, reserving to the States respectively, the Appointment of the Officers, and the Authority of training the Militia according to the discipline prescribed by Congress; (Clause 16: **Organizing the Militia**)

Controversies concerning the War Powers have addressed two questions. First, to what extent can the president wage war without a Congressional declaration of war? Second, to what extent do the War Powers permit the federal government to interfere with local militias and/or the private ownership of weapons?

THE WAR POWERS ACT AND THE POWER TO WAGE WAR

Article 1 gives Congress sole power to declare war. Article 2 merely states that "The President shall be Commander in Chief of the Army and Navy of the United States." Although Congress has the power to declare war, the Framers realized that in the event of an emergency, such as a foreign attack or invasion, a single person needed to be at the head of the government who could act quickly and respond. Even if Congress completely agreed with the president's actions, it could take hours, or, in the 18th century days or weeks, before Congress could meet to declare war. During those hours, the war might be lost through inaction.

In *The Federalist Papers*, Hamilton and Madison said little about the power of the president to wage war. They suggested his power to wage war on his own was extremely limited. In *Federalist* 69 Hamilton wrote:

> The President is to be commander-in-chief of the army and navy of the United States. In this respect his authority would be nominally the same with that of the king of Great Britain, but in substance much inferior to it. It would amount to nothing more than the supreme command and direction of the military and naval forces, as first General and admiral of the Confederacy; while that of the British king extends to the DECLARING of war and to the RAISING and REGULATING of fleets and armies, all which, by the Constitution under consideration, would appertain to the legislature.

Congress alone can declare war, and has broad power to regulate the military. The president evidently is to be the commanding general who takes his orders from Congress.

While they said little about the president's war powers in the *Federalist*, both Hamilton and Madison published more extensively on the topic several years later. The French Revolutionary government declared war on Britain on February 1, 1793. Jefferson favored supporting France, but Hamilton convinced President Washington to pursue a policy of neutrality. On April 22, 1793, Washington issued a Proclamation of Neutrality.

In the middle of this controversy, Hamilton and Madison again took up their pens to hash out the issue of presidential power and neutrality in the public press. In the months that followed Washington's Proclamation, Hamilton published a series of essays under the pen name Pacificus ("Peace") while Madison published his responses under the pen name "Helvidius."

Hamilton sought to defend the neutrality policy, but also wished to defend Washington from accusations that he had exceeded his authority in issuing the Proclamation of Neutrality. Hamilton acknowledged that only Congress can declare war, but argued that the president must have authority to take measures to prevent the country from getting dragged into a war without the approval of Congress:

> If the Legislature have a right to make war on the one hand — it is on the other the duty of the Executive to preserve Peace till war is declared; and in fulfilling that duty, it must necessarily possess a right of judging what is the nature of the obligations which the treaties of the Country impose on the Government; and when in pursuance of this right it has concluded that there is nothing in them inconsistent with a state of neutrality, it becomes both its province and its duty to enforce the laws incident to that state of the Nation. ... This is the direct and proper end of the proclamation of neutrality.

Perhaps even more interestingly, some people demanded that Washington declare war on England as mandated by the treaty of friendship that had been signed with France during the American War for Independence. Hamilton argued that the treaty of friendship did not oblige the United States to aid France, but even if there were such a treaty requirement, it would still be up to Congress to declare war.

This is a crucial point because the United States currently has numerous treaties with foreign countries. Many people argue that if a member of the North Atlantic Treaty Organization (NATO) were attacked the president would not need Congressional authorization to go to war. Hamilton's position was that the ultimate decision to go to war still rests with Congress even when a treaty exists.

Jefferson recruited Madison to respond to Hamilton. However, there was not that much disagreement between Madison and Hamilton. Madison argued that the decision to go to war was entirely and exclusively the power of Congress. Accordingly, just as the president could not declare war on his own authority, neither could the president declare peace on his own authority:

> A declaration that there shall be war, is not an execution of laws: it does not suppose pre-existing laws to be executed: it is not in any respect, an act merely executive. It is, on the contrary, one of the most deliberative acts that can be performed … In like manner a conclusion of peace annuls all the laws peculiar to a state of war, and revives the general laws incident to a state of peace.

Madison's argument seems a bit strained, but the bottom line is that Madison and Hamilton agreed that the final decisions about war and peace are vested in Congress. What Madison then writes about the power of the president as commander in chief is clear and cogent. Madison explains:

> [I]t will be most satisfactory to review [presidential powers] one by one.

> "The President shall be commander in chief of the army and navy of the United States, and of the militia when called into the actual service of the United States."

President Nixon's involvement in Cambodia prompted Congress to pass the War Powers Act over his veto.

> There can be no relation worth examining between this power and the general power of making treaties. And instead of being analogous to the power of declaring war, it affords a striking illustration of the incompatibility of the two powers in the same hands. **Those who are to conduct a war cannot in the nature of things, be proper or safe judges, whether a war ought to be commenced, continued, or concluded.** They are barred from the latter functions by a great principle in free government, analogous to that which separates the sword from the purse, or the power of executing from the power of enacting laws.[12]

This is compatible with what Hamilton had written in *Federalist* 69 that the president was just the "first general." Here, Madison appeals to the idea of the separation of powers. The power of the sword and power of the purse must be kept separate because we cannot trust the person who conducts war with the power to commence war.

There is general agreement that the president can act to defend the nation when attacked and there is no time for Congress to decide one way or another. The far more controversial issue involves the situation when the president uses the military when the United States has not been directly attacked.

Over the decades, Congress and the president often clashed over commitment of American soldiers. In 1973, these disputes culminated in the enactment of the **War Powers Act**, which remains the law today. The War Powers Act resulted from the Vietnam War. Initially, Congress authorized the president to send troops to South Vietnam to oppose a communist insurgency. The communists were infiltrating Vietnam through Laos and Cambodia, the countries bordering Vietnam. To halt the infiltrations, President Nixon authorized the military to bomb communist bases in Cambodia that were being used to attack Americans in Vietnam. Many members of Congress saw this as a unilateral action by President Nixon to expand the war without

---

[12] Madison "Helvidius" Number 1, August 24, 1793.

congressional approval. In response, Congress overwhelmingly passed the War Powers Act over Nixon's veto.

The War Powers act contains two basic provisions. First, any time the president commits forces to combat he must report the fact to Congress within 48 hours. Second, if Congress does not authorize the action to continue, the forces must be withdrawn within 60 days (or 90 days if the President certifies the need for a 30-day safe-withdrawal period).

Many Constitutional scholars think the War Powers Act is unconstitutional because it allows the president to conduct wars without Congressional approval so long as they only last 90 days. For example, in 1999, President Clinton conducted a 78-day bombing campaign of Yugoslavia without Congressional approval. Clinton intervened in the Yugoslav civil war because he claimed Yugoslavia was oppressing Kosovar minorities.

Since Nixon, presidents have said they regard the War Powers Act as placing too much restraint on them. However, most presidents have avoided violating it. In 2011, President Obama bombed Libya for months without congressional authorization. The House of Representatives, in a bipartisan vote, passed a resolution condemning him for violating the War Powers Act – he simply ignored the resolution.

CLAUSES FIFTEEN AND SIXTEEN: THE MILITIA CLAUSES

The other important War Powers' clauses are those empowering Congress to call forth and regulate the militia: *To provide for calling forth the Militia to execute the Laws of the Union, suppress Insurrections and repel Invasions.* In the 19th century, Federalists and Anti-federalists alike were suspicious of any professional or "standing" army. James Madison said "a standing army is one of the greatest mischiefs that can possibly happen."[13] Edmond Randolph, another delegate to the constitutional convention assured the Virginia convention: "With respect to a standing army, I believe there was not a member in the federal

An artist's depiction of members of the Massachusetts Militia

Convention, who did not feel indignation at such an institution."[14] Anti-Federalist Yates ("Brutus") spoke for just about everyone when he wrote:

> In despotic governments, as well as in all the monarchies of Europe, standing armies are kept up to execute the commands of the prince or the magistrate, and are employed for this purpose when occasion requires: But they have always proved the destruction of liberty, and is abhorrent to the spirit of a free republic. …

A free republic will never keep a standing army to execute its laws. It must depend upon the support of its citizens.[15]

The primary concern was that professional soldiers, paid by the government, would be used as means of law enforcement. One of the best discussions of this point occurred during the debate in the Virginia Ratifying Convention between James Madison and the leading anti-federalists, Patrick Henry and George Mason. To put this debate in perspective, consider a bit of historical background.

---

[13] Madison speech in Virginia Ratifying Convention, 3 Elliot's Debates p. 380.
[14] Randolph speech in Virginia Ratifying Convention, 3 Elliot's Debates p. 401.
[15] "Brutus," Letter 1

Since at least the time of Alfred the Great, sheriffs and their constables relied on the assistance of ordinary citizens in what was called the *posse comitatus* (Latin for "power of the community"). It was also common for kings to use knights and men-at-arms to enforce the law, but this was much more common on continental Europe. The *posse comitatus* was a distinctly English system that did not exist on the continent. Indeed, in Boston in the 1770s, English soldiers were basically performing what today would be considered police functions, arresting people or breaking up demonstrations.

The first police department in the United States was formed in Boston in 1838. The Boston force was modeled on London's Metropolitan Police, which was created in 1829. So, at the time of the adoption of the Constitution, there were no professional police forces as that term is currently understood. Indeed, one of the first laws Congress passed was The Judiciary Act of 1789, which authorized federal marshals to "command all necessary assistance" to enforce federal law. Although this provision was vague as to its source and extent, Congress removed all doubt in The Militia Act of 1792, which explicitly authorized the President to call on the aid of the state militia to enforce federal laws. The Militia Act of 1792 spent more time discussing how militia would be used to enforce federal law, than how it would be used to suppress insurrections and repel invasions. This is understandable given that ordinary lawlessness is far more common than insurrections or invasions.

Thus, in 1788, when the new Constitution was being debated, the idea of a professional police force was unknown, and ordinary citizens were routinely deputized to deal with crime.

At the Virginia Convention, Patrick Henry and George Mason objected to the provision authorizing Congress to federalize state militia to enforce federal law. They believed that law enforcement was a state and local function. Therefore, allowing the federal government to use local militia to enforce federal law was at best unnecessary and at worst dangerous. Henry and Mason saw state militias as the best defense against federal usurpation of state authority. Consequently, allowing the federal government to draft local militia into federal service meant permitting the federal government to strip states of their greatest protection against the central government.

Furthermore, the Constitution places no restrictions on the length of time a state militia could be forced to remain in federal service. Without any limitation, Congress might authorize a militia to be in federal service for years; thus, converting the militia into a *de facto* standing army. George Mason did not mince words when he declared, "I abominate and detest the idea of a government, where there is a standing army." Madison basically agreed. While there was no disagreement on principles, Madison argued that allowing Congress to use the militia to enforce federal law was a protection against a standing army:

> If resistance should be made to the execution of the laws, he said, it ought to be overcome. This could be done only in two ways — either by regular forces or by the people. By one or the other it must unquestionably be done. If insurrections should arise, or invasions should take place, the people ought unquestionably to be employed, to suppress and repel them, rather than a standing army. The best way to do these things was to put the militia on a good and sure footing, and enable the government to make use of their services when necessary.

Here, Madison was referring explicitly to using the militia to enforce the law. In *Federalist* 29, Hamilton made the same argument, but lumped together all three roles of the militia, concluding that a federal "army can never be formidable to the liberties of the people while there is a large body of citizens, little, if at all, inferior to them in discipline and the use of arms, who stand ready to defend their own rights and those of their fellow-citizens." Hamilton added that a citizens' militia "appears to me the only substitute that can be devised for a standing army, and the best possible security against it, if it should exist. Hamilton cleverly grouped together the power to "repel invasions," which was not controversial, with the power to enforce federal law, which was very controversial.

In *Federalist* 29, Hamilton also discussed the relation of *posse comitatus* to the militia clause. He pointed out that the practice of *posse comitatus* was not being abolished or ignored. In fact, federal magistrates did not "want power" to invoke *posse comitatus* just because that specific phrase does not appear in the constitution. The armed citizen was not just to act as a soldier, but also played a role in law enforcement. Congress was allowed to use the militia for only three distinct purposes: to execute the Laws of the Union, suppress insurrections, and repel invasions.

As of 2024, there are approximately 137,000 full-time law-enforcement personnel working for the federal government. There are also about 1.3 million full-time active duty military personnel. Madison and the other Framers would no doubt be as shocked by these numbers.

The anti-federalists also were concerned about the provision that allowed Congress "To provide for organizing, arming, and disciplining, the Militia[.]" Many anti-federalists feared that Congress might use its "arming" power to disarm the militia. George Mason argued:

> The militia may be here destroyed by that method which has been practiced in other parts of the world before; that is, by rendering them useless — by disarming them. Under various pretenses, Congress may neglect to provide for arming and disciplining the militia; and the state governments cannot do it, for Congress has an exclusive right to arm them, &c.

Mason did not explain how this disarming would occur, but one can imagine Congress declaring that State militia could only be armed with muskets and not possess any artillery. In that case, if the federal army with artillery confronted a state militia without artillery the outcome would certainly favor the federal troops.

Madison insisted that the power "arming" the militia did not include any power to disarm. The clause existed because some states had failed to make adequate provision for their militia, and Congress needed to have some minimum requirements. Congress would establish minimal standards, but States could arm their citizens above and beyond the basic standards set by Congress.[16] Madison ultimately resolved the issue by promising

The modern day seal of the National Guard contains an image of a Minuteman, a callback to the Guard's origin as the state militias.

to enact a Bill of Rights that included the right to keep and bear arms; thus, clarifying that Congress had no power to disarm private citizens under the pretext of regulating the militia.

Finally, anti-federalists objected that Congress could use the power to call the militia into federal service to disarm a community by depriving it of its militia. Federalists insisted that the federal government would rarely call the militia into federal service, stating, for example, that the militia would never "be called forth to arrest petty offenders against the laws." In *Federalist* 29, Hamilton insisted that states should not fear Congress stripping them of their militia and marching them halfway across the continent:

> the exaggerated and improbable suggestions which have taken place respecting the power of calling for the services of the militia: That of New Hampshire is to be marched to Georgia, … and that of Massachusetts is to be transported an equal distance to subdue the refractory haughtiness of the aristocratic Virginians.

Ironically, in the 1860s, the Massachusetts militia did march to Virginia to subdue the aristocratic Virginians.

Today, for all intents and purposes, the militia has been abolished. The *posse comitatus* was effectively abolished with the rise of professional police in the mid-19th century. Then, in 1901,

---

[16] Madison, 3 Eliot's Debates, p. 382.

President Theodore Roosevelt asked Congress to pass a wholesale restructuring of the military system declaring:

> Our militia law is obsolete and worthless. The organization and armament of the National Guard of the several States, which are treated as militia in the appropriations by the Congress, should be made identical with those provided for the regular forces.

This reorganization into the "National Guard," or "organized militia," was ostensibly pursuant to Congress's power to organize the militia and not to create a national army. The Act explicitly provided that the "National Guard" could operate "only upon the soil of the United States or of its Territories." However, in 1908, Congress repealed this limitation. In 1912, during the civil war in Mexico, the President proposed deploying the National Guard in Mexico. This did not happen as the generally accepted legal opinion at the time was that the National Guard could not be deployed outside the borders of the country. To circumvent this limitation on the use of the National Guard, in 1916, Congress provided that the national guardsmen of entire units could be drafted *en masse* and simply become part of the regular army.

In 1916, this was thought to be a temporary measure in response to the World War. However, in 1933, this arrangement was made permanent and remains the legal situation today. Even in 1933, there were still a number of limitations on the use of the National Guard. One limitation was that members of a state's National Guard could not be ordered to active duty without the consent of that state's governor. This allowed states some level of protection if the federal government tried to nationalize too much of a state's National Guard.

In 1985, the Reagan Administration sought to deploy members of the California National Guard to Central America. California's Republican Governor, George Deukmejian, refused to consent to deployment. In response, Congress enacted the "Montgomery Amendment," which repealed the section of the law that allowed governors to object. Several governors challenged the Montgomery Amendment, arguing that it was unconstitutional to federalize the state National Guard without the consent of the governor. Rudy Perpich, the Governor of Minnesota, filed suit when contingents of the Minnesota National Guard were sent to Central America. Perpich lost the case. *Perpich v. Department of Defense* (1990).

In 2018, Greg Abbott was re-elected Governor of Texas by promising that he would use the Texas National Guard to safeguard Texas' border with Mexico, and prevent illegal aliens from entering the United States. On December 21, 2022, when asked why Texas had not sealed the border, Abbot answered that "thousands of our National Guard are actually deployed to other countries at this time." Even more recently, in 2024, Governor Abbott declared that he would use the national guard to protect the Mexican border; however, the Biden Administration has argued that the National Guard are federal troops and must do what the federal government commands.

Historically, the militia and the *posse comitatus* were based upon small close-knit communities where everyone may not have been a friend, but was likely a friend of a friend. There were few strangers, and people trusted each other. Those days are long gone. In 1901, President Roosevelt thought the militia was obsolete and unworkable. Today, the military and federal law enforcement are a long way from the paradigm which the Founders endorsed in the 18th century. That paradigm is probably gone forever.

Governor Greg Abbott with members of the Texas National Guard

The District of Columbia

CLAUSE 17: THE ENCLAVE CLAUSE

On June 20, 1783, a mob of about 400 veterans, who had not been paid for their service during the War, despite numerous attempts and pleas for their promised money, stormed the Pennsylvania State House, where the Articles of Confederation Congress was meeting. The veterans basically held the members hostage. The incident demonstrated another weakness of the Articles, insofar as neither the city of Philadelphia nor the state of Pennsylvania was willing to protect Congress, and Congress lacked the power to protect itself. It was clear that the new Constitution would need to include a provision creating a space where Congress could meet safely, and, if necessary, call forth a force to protect it. The result was Section 8, Clause 17, the **Enclave Clause**.

Clause Seventeen gives Congress the authority:

> To exercise exclusive Legislation in all cases whatsoever, over such district (not exceeding ten miles square) as may, by cession of particular states, and the acceptance of Congress, become the seat of the government of the United States, and to exercise like authority over all places purchased by the consent of the legislature of the State in which the same shall be, for the erection of forts, magazines, arsenals, dock-yards, and other needful buildings;

In addition to creating the District of Columbia, i.e. the Capitol, the Enclave Clause contains another section often called the "Places Purchased" Clause. The Enclave Clause and its subsection, the Places Purchased clause, should be read in light of Article 4 section 3, often called the "Property Clause," which adds:

> The Congress shall have Power to dispose of and make all needful Rules and Regulations respecting the Territory or other Property belonging to the United States

Although the Enclave Clause and Property Clause look similar, they are actually very different. The Enclave Clause applies to the "seat of government," that is, the District of Columbia, where no state government had jurisdiction. In 1800, because Congress had no general "police power" to prohibit murder or robbery, the Enclave Clause was needed to carve out an exception for "the seat of government." In the District of Columbia, Congress can pass laws against murder, robbery, or similar crimes, just as a state can within its borders

The same broad and exclusive jurisdiction is granted Congress for military bases. Under the Articles the federal government operated military bases, so in principle there was not much disagreement that there should be some federal military bases. Article 1 specifically requires that for such jurisdiction to exist the federal government needs "the consent of the legislature of the State." So, for example, if the federal government buys a building for a post office, but the state legislature does not agree to relinquish sovereignty over the building, Congress does not have exclusive jurisdiction over the building. However, if the federal government wishes to create a military base with exclusive federal jurisdiction then the state legislature must vote to permit this.

So, under the Enclave Clause, can the federal government acquire any land it wishes for any purpose whatsoever so long as the state agrees? Technically, it can not. First, there is a legal rule called "known by its associates," which says that in a list of items, the meaning of general terms is interpreted in light of the specific terms. Thus, when Clause 17 says Congress can construct "forts, magazines, arsenals, dock-yards, and other needful buildings," these "needful buildings" must be structures like forts and dock-yards.

Moreover, the phrase "other needful buildings" does not appear to permit the federal government to buy land simply to leave it empty. Suppose the federal government purchased Niagara Falls just to "preserve" it and not construct any buildings. That would not be authorized by the literal text of Clause 17.

The term "needful" is also important. The federal government cannot construct any building, only ones that are "needful." The implication is that these buildings are needed or necessary for carrying out one of the enumerated powers of Congress. Thus, it appears that Congress technically lacks the power to purchase Niagara Falls to create "Niagara Falls National Park" because Article 1 does not list running parks as a Congressional power.

Finally, it seems clear from the historical record that the Framers never intended the federal government to own vast swathes of land. The District of Columbia, the seat of government, is limited to no more than ten square miles. In *Federalist* 43, Madison commented that "the extent of this federal district is sufficiently circumscribed to satisfy every jealousy." In other words, the capital district was so small that it was not a significant source of federal power. This indicates the Framers intended for federal lands to remain rather small.

Accordingly, there are good reasons for interpreting the Enclave Clause narrowly. If the federal government could just buy land or buildings anywhere it wished, and make its own rules in those areas, this would be an enormous expansion of federal powers. However, this is the case today. As of 2024, the federal agency that manages federal civilian property, The General Services Administration, lists 8,397 federal buildings or civilian installations. The vast majority of these buildings were not purchased with the agreement of state legislatures to give the federal government exclusive jurisdiction. However, the federal government says that federal regulations take precedence over state law regardless. For example, there is a law making it a crime to bring a firearm or other dangerous object into a post office, even if the object is legal under state law or the person has a permit to carry the firearm in public.

The property clause of Article 4 section 3 gives Congress "Power to dispose of and make all needful Rules and Regulations respecting the Territory or other Property belonging to the United States." There was remarkable little debate about this clause in 1788 and Madison barely mentions it in *The Federalist* other than noting that it was "rendered absolutely necessary by jealousies and questions concerning the Western territory sufficiently known to the public." The "western

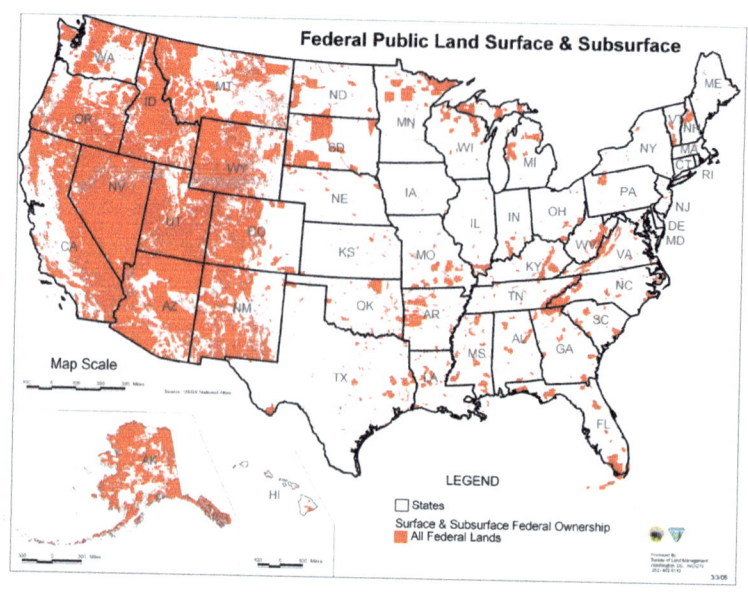

territory" was the Northwest Territory. Congress had passed the Northwest Ordinance and everyone seemed to assume that Article 4 section 3 was simply adopting the same rules as the Articles in this respect.

Article 4 only speaks of disposing of territory or other property. It says nothing about acquiring property. In 1803, when Jefferson was considering acquiring the Louisiana Purchase, he wrote a famous letter to John Dickinson expressing his concerns about the constitutionality of such an action: "*It [the Constitution] has not given it [the federal government] power of holding foreign territory, and still less of incorporating it into the Union. An amendment of the Constitution seems necessary for this.*" Ultimately, Jefferson thought that purchasing France's lands west of the Mississippi was too good an opportunity to miss and completed the Louisiana Purchase by relying on the war powers.

Today the federal government controls about 700 million acres of land and thousands of federal buildings in every state in the union. This is particularly controversial in western states where federal lands often account for most of the state. The federal government operates thousands of national parks and forests, national monuments, national wildlife preserves, and many similarly vast tracts of land, despite the fact that running parks is not one of the enumerated functions of the federal government. These vast tracts of land are usually justified as permissible under the Property Clause, although in some cases national parks have been created with the consent of the legislature pursuant to the Enclave Clause.

THE RISE OF THE "ADMINISTRATIVE STATE"

In 1790, the population of the United States was about four million people. At the beginning of 2024, it was just under 336 million, an increase of 8400%. As the nation grew, it was reasonable to expect that the federal government would grow as well. The government in 1790 could not handle the issues and problems faced by a government in 2024. Consider such agencies as the federal aviation administration or the nuclear regulatory commission. Airplanes and nuclear power did not even exist in 1790. Thus, although the government needed to grow, many Americans believe that it has grown beyond what is necessary and become a bloated bureaucracy. They agree with Ronald Reagan who said, "Government is like a baby. An alimentary canal with a big appetite at one end and no sense of responsibility at the other."

Since 1788, the powers granted to the government by the Constitution have been expanded in ways that Madison repudiated. However, as the powers of the federal government have grown, Congress has itself actually become less powerful. This was part of a change in government that occurred in the late 19th and early 20th century.

The period from about 1890 to 1920 is known as The Progressive Era. Following the Civil War, the United States experienced a period of incredible industrial growth. In 1890, the United States surpassed England as the largest economy in the world, and by 1900 possessed an economy double that of England. This amazing growth occurred partly because there were very few restrictions on business in the United States. Despite the benefits of industrialization, many people were concerned that this system of low regulation had created serious problems. For example, some people were troubled that a handful of individuals had created monopolies, or **trusts**, which allowed them immense control over the economy.[17] John D. Rockefeller, who created Standard Oil, became the richest man in the world by cornering the market on petroleum. Critics also argued that lack of regulation created unsafe work environments, endangered women and children, and allowed "big business" to oppress workers.

John D. Rockefeller

---

[17] A trust is like a monopoly in that a single person controls a number of companies in the same industry. Like a monopoly, the trust can set prices without fear of competition.

Pope Leo XIII

During the Industrial Revolution, there were undoubtedly abuses and sometimes business owners did mistreat their workers. To address these problems and gain more bargaining power, workers began banding together in unions. In the 1880s, Catholics formed the **Knights of Labor** and organized themselves into unions. In 1891, Pope Leo XIII promulgated the influential encyclical *Rerum Novarum* (On the Condition of the Working Classes).

There were also people who wanted to expand the power of government, at all levels, to address the abuses in society—real or imagined. This group of activists called themselves **Progressives**. Progressives had a broad social agenda and wished to use the power of government to advance their goals. In the 1880s, progressives began campaigning for a variety of government restrictions on business. Starting in 1890, they succeeded in convincing Congress to enact several significant changes.

One of the most important laws in American history was the **Sherman Anti-Trust Act** of 1890. The Anti-Trust Act was aimed at people like Rockefeller who managed monopolies or trusts. The Anti-Trust Act provided that:

> Every contract, combination in the form of trust or other-wise, or conspiracy, in restraint of trade or commerce among the several States, or with foreign nations, is hereby declared to be illegal.

The most remarkable part of the Act is what was absent. It did not define "restraint of trade." In fact, the entire Act was very short. Congress seemed to think that there were so many different ways to restrain trade that they could not be properly defined. Therefore, Congress would let the president and the courts decide on a case by case basis.[18]

Also, in 1890, Congress passed a law which gave the president unilateral authority to impose taxes without specific congressional approval. The Tariff Act of 1890 authorized the president to impose tariffs on any foreign country that placed tariffs on American goods. The idea was that the president could negotiate more effectively with foreign countries if he had power to impose or remove tariffs. This seems reasonable, and perhaps very efficient; however, for centuries, parliament had zealously guarded its authority to approve new taxes. Congress delegated that power to the president rather casually.

In 1897, Congress passed "An Act to Prevent the Importation of Impure and Unwholesome Tea." The Act authorized the president to establish standards of purity and quality for teas imported into the United States and to ban teas deemed unfit. This was done by the Board of Tea Experts at the Department of Treasury. It seems that Congress could have established purity standards for tea, but apparently, the Congressmen thought that determining the quality of tea was beyond their competence. Only a group of expert "tea" bureaucrats was up to the job!

While these measures may seem quite mild today, in the 19th century, they were revolutionary. Congress began setting vague general requirements and leaving it to the executive branch to implement them by promulgating regulations.

---

[18] It should be noted that any law which does not specifically define what it criminalizes is unconstitutional. Otherwise, people can be arrested for anything because the courts or the prosecutors can decide on a case by case basis whether to prosecute or convict. Moreover, people can never know whether they have violated such a law.

U.S. Government for Catholic Students

Franklin Roosevelt's New Deal created many new federal regulatory agencies, and was the birth of the administrative state.

This was an enormous shift of power to the executive branch which massively expanded by hiring an army of bureaucrats, e.g. tea experts.

Moreover, the 18th and 19th century paradigm, at least for the House of Representatives, had been for legislatures to be composed of common people. Ordinary citizens made, or at least approved, laws. As the 20th century dawned, professionals/experts increasingly made regulations, which were often highly technical, difficult for the average person to understand, and required a team of lawyers to navigate.

This trend towards bigger bureaucracy increased when Franklin Roosevelt became president in 1933. The Great Depression began in 1929 and Roosevelt tried to combat it with a plan called The New Deal. As part of the New Deal, Congress enacted a mountain of new federal legislation. Roosevelt created numerous new federal regulatory agencies which control and administer vast areas of American life previously thought to be the exclusive jurisdiction of state governments. This "administrative state" has now become generally accepted. However, many legal scholars insist that the whole idea of executive regulation violates the **non-delegation doctrine** which holds that under the Constitution only Congress can make law and Congress has no authority to delegate its law-making power to a federal bureaucracy.

THE ADMINISTRATIVE PROCEDURES ACT

In 1946, Congress enacted the Administrative Procedures Act or APA. The APA sets the basic guidelines that the president must follow when making regulations. If the president does not follow these procedures, citizens can file suit in federal court to have the regulations declared invalid.

When the president, or an executive agency, wishes to issue a new regulation, or revoke an old one, it must be published in the *Federal Register*, the official daily journal (newspaper) of the federal government. The agency must then accept public comments on the proposed regulation, as well as hold public hearings to allow interested parties to participate. The agency does not actually need to do anything with the public comments but must allow them.

On its face, the APA does not sound very onerous. In fact, it seems to streamline government, making it more efficient – something all Americans favor. However, many constitutional theorists argue that the APA allows the president to rule by decree, much like an emperor. Surprisingly often, federal courts have found that the president has failed to comply with the APA and temporarily blocked implementation of new regulations. This is only temporary because the president can always go back, comply with the APA, and re-issue the regulation.

CONCLUSION

It is clear that many, if not most, of the powers the federal government exercises today go far beyond what the Framers intended—a fact no one really disputes. Some people justify this with the idea of a "living constitution," the notion that the constitution must evolve to deal with new problems without going through the arduous process of amendment. The issue of the federal government exercising powers far beyond what the Constitution authorizes is not a minor quibble. In his Treatise on Law, St. Thomas wrote:

> Laws may be unjust in two ways: first, by being contrary to human good, through being opposed to the things mentioned above— either in respect of the end, as when an authority imposes on his subjects burdensome laws, conducive, not to the common good, but rather to his own cupidity or vainglory — or in respect of the author, as when a man makes a law that goes beyond the power committed to him — or in respect of the form, as when burdens are imposed unequally on the community, although with a view to the common good. The like are acts of violence rather than laws.[19]

Hamilton wrote something very similar in Federalist 33, referring to the Constitution's "Supremacy Clause" which states the constitution and laws passing in conformity to the Constitution will be supreme law:

> [I]t will not follow from this doctrine that acts of the larger society which are not pursuant to its constitutional powers but which are invasions of the residuary authorities of the smaller societies will become the supreme law of the land. These will be merely acts of usurpation and will deserve to be treated as such.

Furthermore, St. Thomas says that laws should reflect the values and traditions of the society as a whole. When a narrow, professional bureaucracy makes regulations, they often do not reflect the values of the community as a whole and are not for the common good. Pope St. John Paul II criticized the growth of the bureaucratic state, what he called the "social assistance state," in his encyclical *Centesimus Annus* (1991) explaining that such a system:

> By intervening directly and depriving society of its responsibility, the Social Assistance State leads to a loss of human energies and an inordinate increase of public agencies, which are dominated more by bureaucratic ways of thinking than by concern for serving their clients, and which are accompanied by an enormous increase in spending. In fact, it would appear that needs are best understood and satisfied by people who are closest to them and who act as neighbors to those in need.

In short, the growth of the centralized, inhumane administrative state, which fails to reflect the values of the entire society and acts in contravention of the common good, is antithetical to vital principles of Catholic social teaching.

---

[19] S. Th., I-II, Q. 95, Art. 2

REVIEW QUESTIONS

1. Is establishing a police force one of the enumerated powers of Congress?
2. What does the Constitution say about the power of Congress to *print* money?
3. What famous American wrote under the pen name Pacificus to defend President Washington's Declaration of Neutrality in 1791?
4. What areas are reserved to the Senate rather than the House?
5. To which political party did George Washington belong?
6. In 1941, Ohio farmer Roscoe Filburn was fined by the federal government for doing what on his own land?
7. What do critics of expansive federal power often derisively call the Necessary and Proper Clause?
8. How long is the term of a United States Senator?
9. If a state were to pass a law that excessively interferes with interstate commerce, what Constitutional provision would this violate?
10. What did Madison and Jefferson draft in response to the Alien and Sedition Acts?
11. What law did Congress pass in 1973 that limited the president's power to use military force?
12. What did the Tariff Act of 1890 authorize the president to do?
13. What was the name of Franklin Roosevelt's plan to use the federal government to fight the Depression?
14. What does the Administrative Procedures Act (APA) do?
15. What is the non-delegation doctrine?
16. How long is The Code of Federal Regulations?
17. What did the 17th Amendment do?
18. What does the Senate need to do to impeach someone?
19. What did Hamilton think about the "necessary and proper clause?"
20. What institution did Hamilton and Madison disagree about creating in 1791?
21. What was involved in the famous 1950s case regarding state interference with interstate commerce?
22. What committee holds hearings and votes on ominees to be federal judges?
23. In the House, every Bill must pass through what committee before it can be approved by the full House?
24. What might be some examples of "commerce" as that word was understood in 1800?
25. What role did Jefferson have in Washington's First Administration?
26. What role did Hamilton have in Washington's First Administration?
27. What was Hamilton's position regarding whether a president could go to war to support a country with which the United States had a mutual defense treaty?
28. As of 2024, how many representatives are there in the House of Representatives?
29. What is the technical term for distributing representation among the states in Congress?
30. What is the term for "cutting off" discussion in the Senate?
31. How long is the term for a member of the House of Representatives?

CHAPTER FIVE
THE EXECUTIVE BRANCH: THE PRESIDENT

"First in war, first in peace, and first in the hearts of his countrymen, he was second to none in the humble and endearing scenes of private life: Pious, just, humane, temperate, and sincere; uniform, dignified, and commanding, his example was as edifying to all around him as were the effects of that example lasting.... Correct throughout, vice shuddered in his presence, and virtue always felt his fostering hand; the purity of his private character gave effulgence (brilliance) to his public virtues."

Thus, did Henry Lee eulogize his close personal friend, America's first president, George Washington. While not every president has measured up to the standard set by George Washington, and some have failed miserably, most have tried to do their best and act honorably in the performance of their duties.

THE MOST POWERFUL POSITION

Article 2, Section 1 of the Constitution states, "The executive power shall be vested in a president of the United States..." With this simple phrase, the Framers created the most powerful position in America's government. Under the Constitution, the president performs five essential functions. First, he serves as the **Head of State,** that is, the leader of the nation. Second, he is the nation's **Chief Executive**, which means he is the head of the government. As chief executive, the president is primarily responsible for ensuring that the laws Congress enacts are enforced. Third, he is the **Chief Legislator**, which means that he plays the leading role in creating the agenda for the laws that Congress considers. For example, Franklin Roosevelt called upon Congress to pass an array of new laws known as the New Deal. Fourth, he serves as the nation's top **diplomat** by establishing foreign policy and interacting with other nations. Finally, the president is the **Commander-in-Chief**, or leader, of America's armed forces.

Abraham Lincoln, in his role as Commander-in-Chief of the armed forces, consulting with his generals during the Civil War

QUALIFICATIONS TO BE PRESIDENT

Article 2, Section 1 of the Constitution, often called "The Qualifications Clause," provides:

> No Person except a natural born Citizen, or a Citizen of the United States, at the time of the Adoption of this Constitution, shall be eligible to the Office of President; neither shall any Person be eligible to that Office who shall not have attained to the Age of thirty-five Years, and been fourteen Years a Resident within the United States.

Thus, *Constitutionally*, the president must be a natural-born citizen, at least thirty-five years old, who has resided in the United States for at least fourteen years. In the 21st century, where the life expectancy is about seventy-seven years, thirty-five seems rather young; however, in the 18th century people did not live quite so long, and the Framers believed that by age thirty-five, a man (women could not vote or hold office) had achieved the necessary level of maturity.

Leaders younger than thirty-five were not unusual. For example, the Prime Minister of England at this time was William Pitt ("Pitt the Younger"), who became Prime Minister at the age of 24. By all accounts, Pitt was a talented leader, but Framers thought that older men were more likely to possess the wisdom and virtue needed to govern. In *Federalist* 64, John Jay explained why there was a minimum age for senators and the president:

> As the select assemblies for choosing the President, as well as the State legislatures who appoint the senators, will in general be composed of the most enlightened and respectable citizens, there is reason to presume that their attention and their votes will be directed to those men only who have become the most distinguished by their abilities and virtue, and in whom the people perceive just grounds for confidence. ... By excluding men under thirty-five from the first office, and those under thirty from the second, it confines the electors to men of whom the people have had time to form a judgment, ... If the observation be well founded, that wise kings will always be served by able ministers, it is fair to argue,

that as an assembly of select electors possess, in a greater degree than kings, the means of extensive and accurate information relative to men and characters, so will their appointments bear at least equal marks of discretion and discernment. The inference which naturally results from these considerations is this, that the President and senators so chosen will always be of the number of those who best understand our national interests, ... who are best able to promote those interests, and whose reputation for integrity inspires and merits confidence.

Jay's article also indicates why the president is indirectly elected, but note how Jay equates age with wisdom, as well as character and virtue. With older men, the people around them have had more time to observe them and ensure that a potential president possesses a good character. After all, virtue, or character, is something that develops over time. St. Thomas, and really everyone in America in the 18th century, thought that virtues are good habits. These good habits grow through practice. People acquire the virtue of honesty by repeatedly exercising the virtue until it becomes habitual. A young man can certainly be virtuous, but his character is less set than older man's. Interestingly, two of the youngest presidents, John F. Kennedy (43-years-old) and William Clinton (46-years-old), were plagued by problems of personal immorality.

Another qualification mentions that the president needs to be a "natural born citizen" rather than a "naturalized citizen." Madison's notes of the Constitutional Convention do not record any debate on this provision, but it is assumed that the Framers were concerned that a European noble might try to run for president and set himself up as king. This seems a far-fetched idea in 1787 and even less probable today.

Currently, the main debate over the "natural born citizen" clause involves the contention that it is "un-American." In the 20th century, many people began to regard equality as one of America's core values. Some people think only allowing some citizens to be president is a pernicious kind of inequality. For example, famous American political philosopher, John Rawls (1921-2002), argued that equality demands that all elective offices must be "open to all."

Historically, with the exception of Donald Trump, who spent his life in business, and Barack Obama, a lawyer and "community organizer," most presidents have either been politicians or war heroes. George Washington, Andrew Jackson, William Henry Harrison, Zachary Taylor, Ulysses S. Grant, Theodore Roosevelt, Dwight Eisenhower, and John F. Kennedy were all war heroes. Among them, Jackson and Harrison also served in Congress before becoming president, as did Kennedy. Nearly all the other presidents have been Senators or governors, including several recent governors who became president, including Carter, Reagan, and Clinton.

THE ELECTORAL COLLEGE AND SELECTION OF THE PRESIDENT

Article 2, Section 1 sets forth the process for selecting the president:

> Each State shall appoint, in such Manner as the Legislature thereof may direct, a Number of Electors, equal to the whole Number of Senators and Representatives to which the State may be entitled in the Congress ...
>
> The Electors shall meet in their respective States, and vote by Ballot ... And they shall make a List of all the Persons voted for, and of the Number of Votes for each; which List they shall sign and certify, and transmit sealed to the Seat of the Government ...
>
> The Person having the greatest Number of Votes shall be the President... and if there be more than one who have ... an equal Number of Votes, then the House of Representatives shall immediately choose by Ballot one of them for President; and if no Person have a Majority, then from the five highest on the List the said House shall in like Manner choose the President. But in choosing the President, the Votes shall be taken by States, the Representation from each State having one Vote;

Section 1 contains two important points concerning indirect election and non-proportional voting. Furthermore, this system is quite complicated. It would have been easier to have the president elected by majority vote, but none of the Founders thought that was a good idea.

In *Federalist* 64, Jay explained the need for indirect elections. The Framers wanted each state to select a group of electors, much like delegates to the Constitutional Convention in 1787. These electors would use their judgment and experience to select a president. Hopefully, the electors would be "most enlightened and respectable citizens," who were personally familiar with the most eminent men in the country and thus could select a worthy president. Jay criticized the idea of a country-wide election, where ordinary citizens would need to rely on newspaper accounts of candidates and might be "deceived by those brilliant appearances of genius and patriotism, which, like transient meteors, sometimes mislead as well as dazzle."

The system of indirect election broke down very quickly with the rise of political parties, and necessitated a change in the way the president and vice-president were elected. In 1796, John Adams was elected President and Thomas Jefferson, who received the second highest number of electoral votes, became vice-president; although the two men were of different parties. The problem with the Electoral College was revealed during the 1800 Election in which Jefferson defeated Adams. In 1800, electors voted for the winning *party*, in this case the Republicans. However, because electors each cast two votes (technically both for president), without indicating their choice for president or vice-president, the "ticket," that is, Jefferson and his running mate Aaron Burr, each received 73 votes. Because the election resulted in a tie, it went to the House of Representatives where the members, realizing that Jefferson was the candidate for president, voted for him.

The potential for a disastrous future election caused Congress to enact the **Twelfth Amendment**. Under the Twelfth Amendment, which was ratified in time for the 1804 Election, electors cast one vote for the president and one for the vice-president. In the future, electors would vote for the party's ticket rather than the individual candidates. Thus, by the 1804 election, people were voting more for a party than for individual electors who would use their judgment to find a worthy candidate. The system has worked this way ever since, and, for better or worse, seems here to stay.

More controversial is non-proportional voting for president. The number of electors, or electoral votes, equals the number of senators and representatives. In a sense, this means that states with small populations are "over represented." For example, California, with a population of about 40 million, has 54 electoral votes. Alaska, Delaware, North Dakota, South Dakota, Vermont, and Wyoming all have small populations but each have three electoral votes. Together these six states have only one-tenth of California's population, but one-third the number of electoral votes. Moreover, if no candidate receives a majority of electoral votes, then the House elects a president with each state having only one vote. The aggregate population of the twenty-six smallest states account for just 19% of the U.S. population, less than the combined population of California and Texas. Clearly, the Framers were not concerned about "one man one vote."

In 1961, the 23rd Amendment was added to the Constitution which granted the District of Columbia three electors, the same number as the smallest state. Since then, there have been 538 members of the Electoral College. Thus, to be elected president, a person needs to win 270

US 2024 Presidential Elections
Electoral votes per state based on the 2020 census

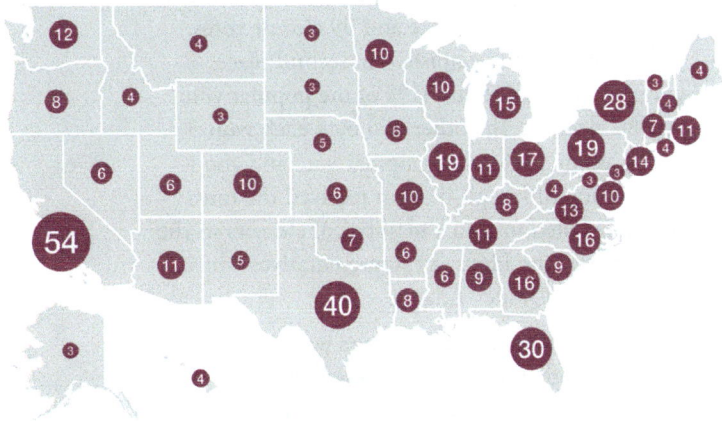

electors. Because of this, presidential candidates for at least the past thirty years have not run national campaigns but have focused on "battleground" or "swing" states to obtain the necessary 270 votes. For example, today, California, Illinois, and New York reliably vote Democrat, while Oklahoma, Texas, and Indiana, vote Republican, so neither party campaigns in these states too much. On the other hand, Arizona, Michigan, and Wisconsin are states that swing back and forth. Candidates spend more time and money in them. Because elections are so close in the Electoral College, winning the 36 votes in Arizona, Michigan, and Wisconsin might mean overall victory in the election.

More substantively, however, the Framers realized that the system of federalism is crucial to maintaining liberty. In a federal system, the states need power to represent their own perspectives. In a massive popular vote, where 150 million people elect the president, small states would become irrelevant. Small states have equal representation in the Senate, and disproportionate representation in the electoral college; so that each state retains some relevance and continues to have a say in government.

Furthermore, the common good demands that the government work for the good of everyone, not just the majority. When elections require a simple majority, it is too easy for the majority to oppress the minority. Requiring people to be elected in a variety of different ways helps ensure that everyone's voice is heard.

Also, dividing the country into different jurisdictions makes the vote of individuals more meaningful. If a person's vote is one of 150 million, it is basically meaningless. In a small town, with only a few hundred voters, each vote, especially combined with like-minded friends and family, is very meaningful. The mayor of a small town cannot take anyone's vote for granted. This principle applies, to a lesser degree, in presidential elections. Because the presidential vote is state by state, a president's election may depend on a particular state. In swing states the margin of victory may be a few thousand votes. The most famous recent case occurred in 2000, when the entire presidential election was determined by a difference of 537 votes in Florida. Accordingly, the state by state electoral system helps ensure that individuals remain relevant. Thus, the electoral college continues to serve one of the purposes of the Founders: guaranteeing that every region of the country be considered.

POPULARITY DOES NOT GUARANTEE ELECTION

Usually, the person who receives the most popular votes is elected president; however, that does not always happen. There have been a number of times when a candidate has received fewer votes than his opponents and still been elected president. For example, in 1824, four men ran for president. Andrew Jackson won eleven states, received about 41.4% of the popular vote and 99 elector votes. John Quincy Adams finished in second place, winning 7 states, about 31% of the popular vote and 84 electors. The other two men each won 3 states, about 12% of the popular vote and about 40 electors. Although Jackson received the most votes, he failed to gain a majority of electors so the race went to the House of Representatives which elected John Quincy Adams.

In 1876, Rutherford B. Hayes was elected president despite receiving only 48% of the popular vote compared to Samuel Tilden who received 52%. Harrison was

A campaign poster for Rutherford B. Hayes, who won the 1876 election by only one electoral vote

elected by one vote in the electoral college, the closest vote yet in American history. As of 2020, there have been five elections where a president has been elected without receiving a majority of the popular vote. In addition to the aforementioned elections, in 1888, Benjamin Harrison beat Grover Cleveland 233-168 in the electoral college, but won less than 49% of the popular vote. In 2000, George Bush beat Al Gore in the electoral college by five votes because he won Florida by a handful of votes, but received fewer popular votes nationally. The same thing happened in 2016, when Donald Trump decisively defeated Hillary Clinton in the electoral college but won only about 46% of the popular vote.

The disparity in the results occurs because of the **winner-take-all system** that exists in the electoral college. Thus, although George Bush won Florida by a very, very slim margin, he received all of Florida's electoral votes. In this way, candidates who receive only a *plurality* of votes can be elected. In fact, more than 25% of presidents have been elected with only a plurality. While it might seem unfair, it is the American system and will remain so until it is changed.

TERM OF OFFICE

Article 2, Section 1, Clause 1 reads that the, "… President of the United States … shall hold his Office during the Term of four Years…" While the Constitution specifies the *length* of term, it fails to address the *number* of terms a president may serve, that is, whether the president was subject to **term limits**. The Framers debated the issue with some favoring setting terms for Congress and the president and others rejecting the idea. Eventually, the Framers agreed with James Madison who believed that the longer a person served in office the better and more effective they became at their job. Madison explained his opposition to term limits in *Federalist* 53, where he wrote:

> [A] few of the members of Congress will possess superior talents; will by frequent re-elections, become members of long standing; will be thoroughly masters of the public business, and perhaps not unwilling to avail themselves of those advantages. The greater the proportion of new members of Congress, and the less the information of the bulk of the members, the more apt they be to fall into the snares that may be laid before them…

As first president, George Washington set a number of traditions, including limiting himself to two terms in office. Many of Washington's actions during his entire career were influenced by the famous Roman general Cincinnatus. In 458 BC, the Roman Senate called upon Cincinnatus to lead Rome against her enemies. Given dictatorial powers, Cincinnatus quickly defeated Rome's enemies and immediately returned to his farm rather than becoming permanent ruler of Rome. Cincinnatus stood as a model for many of the Founding Fathers, especially Washington, who returned to his home in Mount Vernon once the War of Independence had been won. Washington followed this same path by refusing to run for a third term as president, a term he surely would have won. When Thomas Jefferson also only served two terms, the tradition was enshrined in the minds of most Americans.

Until 1880, every president followed Washington's example and served only two terms.

Cincinnatus receives ambassadors calling him to lead Rome against her enemies.

However, in 1880, President Grant tried for a third term, but failed to obtain the Republican nomination, so technically did not run. The first two-term president actually to run for a third term was Theodore Roosevelt in the 1912 Election. However, he lost.

In 1940, Franklin Roosevelt had served two terms and, as late as the Spring, it appeared he would not seek a third term. However, as the war in Europe turned against the Allies, he felt that he needed to be president to save Europe and America; thus, he sought and won a third term, breaking the precedent set by Washington. In 1944, with the war going well for the Allies, Roosevelt was determined to see it through to victory. Thus, although his inner circle knew he was dying, and would never be able to serve even the first year of a fourth term, he ran again and was elected to a fourth term.

In response to Roosevelt's four terms, in 1951, the Twenty-Second Amendment was added to the Constitution which limits the president to two terms. Interestingly, the Amendment specifically excluded Harry Truman, the president at the time. However, in the spirit of Washington and Cincinnatus, Truman chose not to seek what essentially would have been a third term.

SEPARATION OF POWERS

Under the Articles of Confederation, there was no single executive, but an executive committee. The Constitution makes clear that all executive power is vested in one single person. Under the doctrine of separation of powers, Congress may not exercise "executive" powers. Moreover, Article 1, Section 6 says

> no person holding any office under the United States, shall be a member of either House during his continuance in office … and no Person holding any Office under the United States, shall be a Member of either House during his Continuance in Office.

Thus, the Framers made it explicit that no one who was a member of Congress could also be a member of the executive branch. In fact, Article 1, Section 6 really says the same thing twice to ensure no one tried to wiggle around the point.

In parliamentary systems, members of parliament, the legislature, also act as ministers who enforce the law, the executive. The head of the British government is the Prime Minister, a member of parliament who is elected by a majority of the House of Commons. Parliament can remove a Prime Minister any time a bare majority of the House of Commons wishes. The head of each department in the British system are also members of parliament. So, in the British system, the people who make the laws are the same people who enforce the laws, at least at the top. Unlike parliamentary systems, in the American system, the President, who enforces the laws, is independent of the legislative branch.

An independent executive, which is separate from the legislature, serves two purposes. First, it ensures that decisions can be made quickly and efficiently. In parliamentary systems, where the Prime Minister makes day-to-day decisions, the threat of losing the support of a majority of members of parliament can sometimes paralyze a government. The American system avoids this. The president is elected every four years, so can make controversial and unpopular decisions without fear of the government collapsing. Not everyone likes this. Many people think the president should be more responsive to the people's desires; but, that is not how the system was established. The Electoral College was created precisely to insulate the president from majority opinion.

Second, separation of powers helps maintain liberty by placing a check upon Congress. This seems counter-intuitive. On the one hand, the system is set up to allow the president independence to pursue unpopular policies. Yet, might not the president use this independence to exercise dictatorial powers? The answer lies in finding the right balance.

For example, the Framers were aware that military leaders tended to assume dictatorial powers. Presidents might be tempted to go to war to set themselves up as "conquering heroes," which is why the power to declare war and finance a war is vested in Congress. As Madison put it,

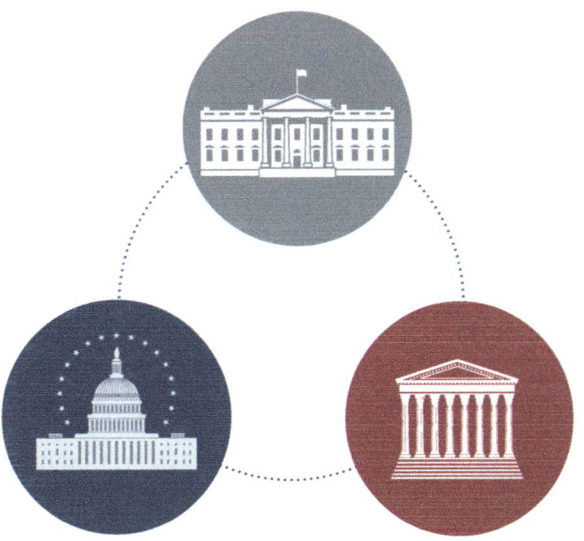

the power of the purse is separated from the power of the sword. Presidents are often remembered as great war leaders, but few remember the Congressmen who voted for war. Because Congressmen will receive little credit or blame for going to war, presumably neither pride nor vanity will motivate them to start a war.

Similarly, presidents tend to receive the praise or blame for the economy, even when economic growth or depression lies far beyond their control. Hopefully, by separating those who make policy from those who obtain the credit for enforcing the policy, less incentive exists on the part of each branch to usurp the functions of the other. That was the hope in 1787.

Article 2, Section 2 states:

> Congress may by Law vest the Appointment of such inferior Officers, as they think proper, in the President alone, in the Courts of Law, or in the Heads of Departments.

Although the president has some limitations on the appointments he makes, he is directed to "take Care that the Laws be faithfully executed." This implies that the president must ensure that all executive employees "faithfully" do their job. This further implies that there is a hierarchy, with the president at the top; so, executive employees must obey the orders of the president.

THE CABINET

No single person can run a large government by himself. Thus, the president has many people to assist him. Under President Washington, the executive branch consisted of five "Departments:" State, Treasury, Justice, War, and Postal. Washington's Secretary of State, Thomas Jefferson, was responsible for foreign policy. Henry Knox first headed the Department of War, now called the Department of Defense. Knox was a retired General, but the idea was that the Secretary of War should be a civilian. The head of the Justice Department is the Attorney General, the federal government's chief legal officer. The first attorney general was Edmund Randolph, who had been a delegate to the Constitutional convention. The first Secretary of the Treasury was Alexander Hamilton.

These four men, who headed the four principal departments, were also Washington's closest advisors, and he consulted them about all major decisions. This small group of counsellors became known as the president's **cabinet**. James Madison coined the term "cabinet" to imply that it was a small group who met in private to give advice.

The fifth executive department was the Postal Department headed by the Postmaster General. Washington's postmaster was Samuel Osgood, but he was not part of the cabinet. Today, presidents often include others in the cabinet in addition to heads of federal agencies.

The number of federal departments has grown over time. Today, there are fifteen federal departments as well as independent agencies. There were no independent agencies for the first several decades of the United States. In fact, the postal service is now an independent agency since the Postal Department was abolished in 1971.

As of 2024, in addition to the original four departments, the other eleven departments are:

An engraving of George Washington and his cabinet (from left to right, Henry Knox, Alexander Hamilton, Thomas Jefferson, and Edmund Randolph)

Agriculture, Commerce, Education, Energy, Homeland Security, Interior, Labor, Health and Human Services, Housing and Urban Development, Transportation, and Veterans Affairs. Each of these departments is subdivided into a variety of different offices.

"THE WHITE HOUSE"

In addition to the cabinet, the other organization which most directly assists the president is the **Executive Office of the President**, often informally referred to as "the White House." Strictly speaking, the White House is simply the official residence of the President of the United States in Washington DC. However, over the years, "White House" has come to mean not so much the actual building as those people who work in the building assisting the president in the fulfillment of his duties. Thus, for example, when Richard Nixon sought to deny involvement in Watergate, he gave a speech in which he sought to answer questions "about the integrity of the White House itself." He was not speaking about a leaky roof.

Until about 100 years ago, the White House, i.e. the president's personal staff, was quite small. The first several presidents had just a few assistants to help them. President Jefferson had only two assistants, who he paid out of his own salary. Presidents answered their own mail and later their own telephones. However, in 1939, President Roosevelt and Congress created the Executive Office of the President (EOP). The EOP contains about two dozen different "offices." The most important include the White House Office, the National Security Council, and the Office of Management and Budget.

The **White House Office** contains a combination of the president's closest advisors and the household staff. The White House Office is led by the president's Chief of Staff who is also the head of the EOP. In addition to managing the staff and the daily operation of the White House, the Chief of Staff is one of the president's most influential advisors. For example, George Bush's Chief of Staff, John Sununu, recommended that Bush nominate David Souter to the Supreme Court. Other staff members include the president's personal physician, who ensures his health; and a press secretary, who delivers daily briefings to the news media. The White House Office also includes a number of household staff such as chefs, housekeepers, and maintenance workers as well as secretaries and receptionists.

The **National Security Council** (NSC), which the president leads, consists of a number of cabinet officers as well as members of various intelligence agencies and the Chairman of the Joint Chiefs of Staff, the nation's highest-ranking military leader. The NSC advises the president on military and diplomatic matters impacting the United States. In recent years, in addition to traditional military and diplomatic issues, the NSC has dealt with new "modern" threats to the United States such as cyberwarfare.

The other major department within the EOP is the **Office of Management and Budget** (OMB). The OMB's main job is to assist the president in creating the federal budget and developing **fiscal policy**. Thus, the OMB is a very influential office. To quote from the White House, it "oversees the implementation of the President's vision across the Executive Branch." Consequently, it is not unusual for the Director of OMB to fight with Congress to enact the president's budget. Most members of the OMB are career civil servants; however, the top positions are political appointees. As a result, while some appointments have been economists, others seem unqualified.

In addition to these large departments in the EOP, the president also has many other counselors giving him advice regarding science,

President Lyndon B. Johnson with the Joint Chiefs of Staff

technology, and even matters dealing with outer space. Normally, the heads of these departments are professional scientists or engineers. The EOP also contains an Office of Legislative Affairs, which coordinates with Congress to pass the president's legislative agenda. Another important position is that of U.S. Trade Representative, who advises the president and helps negotiate international trade agreements. The Trade Representative is usually a business person or someone with a background in economics.

THE EXECUTIVE BUREAUCRACY

Under Article 2, Section 2, the president possesses the power to appoint judges, diplomats and "all other officers of the United States." In the last century, Congress has created a large number of independent agencies. Taken together, these government agencies comprise the federal **bureaucracy**. Originally, "bureaucracy" simply meant the structure of an organization, that is, who does what in an organization to achieve its goals. Today, "bureaucracy" possesses a double meaning. First, it refers to the "body of nonelected government officials," who run the government. There are currently about three million federal bureaucrats. Because the government's bureaucracy has become so large and unwieldy it has acquired a second meaning: a system of administration marked by inflexibility, excessively complex procedures, and unstoppable growth. In 1986, President Reagan summarized how most Americans feel about the government bureaucracy when he said, *"I think you all know that I've always felt the nine most terrifying words in the English language are: I'm from the Government, and I'm here to help."*

The closest thing to an independent agency, or bureaucracy, in the days of the Founding Fathers was the U.S. Marshall's Service, which was created by the Judiciary Act of 1789. The Marshals were part of the federal court system and their main job was to protect federal courthouses and enforce federal court orders and judgments. However, federal courts had so little to do in 1790 that Congress ordered the Marshals to perform the census. The Marshals conducted the census until 1870 when Congress transferred the Marshal's Service to the Justice Department and created a Census Office to do the counting. Today, there are dozens of independent agencies. Among the more famous are the Central Intelligence Agency (CIA), the National Aeronautics and Space Administration (NASA), the Environmental Protection Agency (EPA), and the Social Security Administration (SSA).

One of the more controversial aspects of independent agencies involves Congress's attempts to make agencies more autonomous and immune to removal by the president. These types of entities are usually called "Boards" or "Commissions." One of the most important of these is the Federal Reserve Board, or "the Fed," which Congress created in 1913. The Fed regulates the money supply, lends money to private banks, and controls the interest rate at which such money is lent. The Fed is run by a board of seven "governors" appointed by the president and confirmed by the Senate. Each governor is appointed for a 14-year term and cannot be fired by the president. Because the federal reserve board is so powerful, Congress wanted the Fed to be above political control.

Some people argue that the entire Federal Reserve is unconstitutional as the Federal Reserve Act almost seems to create a fourth branch of government beyond the supervision and control of the president. Congress can presumably impeach and remove Federal Reserve governors, but this is very difficult. Moreover, the Fed is far more powerful than the national bank that Hamilton wanted. Hamilton's national bank was not much different from every other bank, it was just chartered by the federal government. The Fed can create trillions of dollars and loan the money at whatever interest rates it likes. Some people think that an institution with that much power should be more accountable to voters and elected officials.

There are a handful of other Boards and Commissions that are independent of the President. For example, the Federal Election Commission was created to try to insulate it from political control. However, the vast majority of government officials are answerable to the president.

In fact, in 1789, Madison argued that the Constitution required that the president be able to fire executive officials. Madison contended that if the president could not dismiss federal officials then it would "abolish at once that great principle of unity and responsibility in the executive department, which was intended for the security of liberty and the public good." In explaining what he meant, Madison added that "if anything in its nature is executive, it must be that power which is employed in superintending and seeing that the laws are faithfully executed."

Accordingly, if the president feels that the Secretary of the Treasury or the Head of the CIA is not doing their job, he can fire that person and replace him—although the Senate needs to confirm a permanent replacement. It should be noted that the president can always appoint an "acting" secretary to head a department, so confirmation is not *that* important. So, having a few special offices outside the president's control is a strange exception to the rule.

Finally, there are some other Constitutional limitations on whom the president can hire or fire. Article 6 states unequivocally that "no religious Test shall ever be required as a Qualification to any Office or public Trust under the United States." Federal law makes it illegal for the federal government to discriminate on the basis of race or religion. *Theoretically*, the president may not hire, refuse to hire, or fire, any employee due to that person's race or religion. This rule is often ignored, at least at the highest levels of government, because there is usually little recourse when it happens. For example, in 2021, President Biden announced that he would not appoint anyone to the Supreme Court except a Black woman. This seems to violate the federal law requiring that the federal government not select or reject applicants for a position based on their race.

Another limitation on the president is protections for "civil servants." As a general rule, while the president may fire "political appointees" or "policy makers," low-level federal employees may only be fired for misconduct. In the nation's early days, there were few federal employees and President Adams kept almost all of them when he succeeded Washington. When Jefferson succeeded Adams, Jefferson fired about 25% of the federal

Andrew Jackson

employees, or **civil servants**, had to be hired based on non-political criteria.

To oversee these policies, in 1871, Congress created the Civil Service Commission, which was changed to the **Merit Systems Protection Board** in 1978. Presidents often clashed with these agencies. A three-member commission runs the Protection Board, another quasi-independent agency. The commissioners are selected for a seven-year term and cannot be fired by the president. Civil servants who are fired or disciplined can demand the Board review the decision. If the Board concludes that the firing was unlawful, it can order the employee reinstated.

The creation of a "civil service" has caused problems of its own. Presidents have quarreled with the Commission and Board, arguing the president must be permitted to run the administration. Civil service laws have given rise to a massive permanent bureaucracy. The number of permanent bureaucrats always greatly outnumbers the number of "political appointments" that the president can make. In 2024, there are about 1.9 million permanent federal civilian employees. The president is only able to appoint about 4,000 people to assist him in running this huge bureaucracy.

workforce who he thought would be unwilling to implement his policies. Twenty-five percent seems high, but Jefferson did not fire everyone, only those he could not trust.

The next three presidents followed the same policy and kept most low-level employees. This changed with the election of Andrew Jackson, who held the view that "to the victor go the spoils," which meant that the president could fire everyone and replace them with his supporters. Accordingly, this became known as **The Spoils System**. Jackson did not actually fire everyone, but he said that in principle he could. This seemed quite different from what Jefferson had done. Jefferson had fired people for a governmental reason, not simply to reward his supporters.

Jackson's critics complained, but the spoils system prevailed for several decades. In the late 19th century, Congress passed "civil service reform." These laws said that the president, or his subordinates, could not fire a **non-policy-making** federal employee unless he failed to do his job. These laws further required that ordinary

Civil servants are supposed to be non-political and simply implement the policies of the president and his appointees. However, presidents of both parties complain that the permanent bureaucracy often thwarts policy by dragging their feet or even sabotaging policy. This tends to be worse for presidents who advocate smaller government, because bureaucrats tend to favor large government. A number of pejorative terms have been coined for this permanent bureaucracy. One common term is **the deep state,** which refers to a network of bureaucrats who are pursuing their own agenda. Whatever one calls the permanent bureaucracy, it often stands in the way of the president accomplishing his goals—even more than Congress or voters.

LOBBYISTS

Although not part of the Constitution, nor any branch of government, **lobbying**, the process of trying to persuade members of the government to vote a certain way, is almost as old as the United States itself. The term "lobby" comes from the idea that people would wait in the "lobby," to get a chance to speak with legislators. The people doing the lobbying are known as **lobbyists**.

This political cartoon from 1889 shows uneasiness at the power that industry lobbies might have over Congress.

While the president and other executive officials lobby Congress, most lobbyists come from the private sector. These people lobby the president and Congress to convince them to adopt various policies. Lobbyists come from charitable organizations, special interest groups, unions, and business.

The authors of *The Federalist Papers* might be considered America's first lobbyists as they were lobbying the members of New York's ratification convention to vote in favor of the Constitution. However, most historians consider William Hull to be America's first professional lobbyist. In 1792, veterans of the War of Independence hired Hull, a former Continental Army colonel who had served with distinction, to lobby for additional money for their efforts during the war. Hull wrote to other veterans' groups, suggesting that they work with him during the next session of Congress to pass a compensation bill. Ever since, lobbyists have been working to enact legislation, spending billions of dollars in the process.

Because lobbyists spend such huge amounts of money to influence legislation, lobbying is quite controversial. Opponents of lobbying consider it practically bribery. They fear that people or organizations with large amounts of money will have a greater impact on legislation than the average citizen. Because of this, Congress has sought to regulate lobbying, including requiring lobbyists to register with the federal government.

Another controversial issue involving lobbying is the so-called **revolving door**. The revolving door occurs when a government official leaves his government job, then joins a lobbying group to lobby the agency for which he previously worked. Sometimes, the official-turned-lobbyist rejoins the administration. For example, a general might retire from the military, become a lobbyist for the defense industry, then after a couple of years as a lobbyist, be appointed by the president to the defense department.

Despite the controversial nature of lobbying, other people, including conservative economist Thomas Sowell, believe it is a necessary and beneficial part of government. In his book *Knowledge and Decisions*, Sowell notes that lobbyists tend to be people with a great deal of knowledge in their area of expertise and, thus, are better informed than the average voter. It is this knowledge which allows them to impact government because "reform through democratic legislation requires either 'public consensus or a powerful minority lobby.'"

The potential for corruption, bribery, and the revolving door are reasons why people view lobbying negatively; however, it is a critical part of the political process by which individuals and groups express their views to the government. For example, the United States Conference of Catholic Bishops lobbies to present the views of the bishops to Congress and the Administration. There are also numerous pro-life and pro-family lobbying organizations. Home School Legal Defense Association, the leading defender of home-schooling rights in the United States, conducts extensive lobbying on both the state and federal levels.

THE PRESIDENT AS HEAD OF STATE

One of the president's most important functions is not strictly in the Constitution: his role as *de facto* leader of the country, or the **Head of State**. In this position, the president performs various ceremonial functions and also serves as a symbol of national unity; although, in recent decades, presidents have become more divisive than in the past. Since the days of George Washington, people have looked to the president to provide moral leadership and set the tone for the country.

In 1789, Congress passed a joint resolution requesting President Washington proclaim a day of prayer and thanksgiving. It is significant that Congress asked Washington to proclaim a day of prayer, rather than simply proclaiming one itself. The majority of Congress thought that the proclamation was better coming from the leader of the country. Washington proclaimed November 26, 1789, to be a day of prayer, repentance, and thanksgiving to God, declaring:

> It is the duty of all nations to acknowledge the Providence of Almighty God, to obey His will...and humbly to implore His protection and favor; and Whereas both Houses of Congress have by their joint Committee requested me 'to recommend to the People of the United States a Day of Public Thanksgiving and Prayer to be observed by acknowledging with grateful hearts the many signal favors of Almighty God ...

This proclamation was reprinted in newspapers throughout the country, and most people obeyed Washington's request. Today, Americans still celebrate the fourth Thursday of November as a national day of prayer and thanksgiving.

Washington personally believed he needed to set a high moral standard for the country and carefully avoided any hint of scandal. Adams and Madison also proclaimed days of prayer, but Jefferson did not declare days of prayer as president. However, he did declare days of prayer as governor of Virginia. Jefferson thought this was not the proper role of a president.

Today, as immoral conduct has become widely accepted, some people argue that no one should expect politicians to be moral leaders. However, others argue that because the president inevitably sets the tone for the country, he should be held to a higher standard. One of the most notorious examples of presidential impropriety occurred in 1998, when it was shown that President Clinton had repeatedly committed adultery and then lied about it under oath. The House of Representatives voted to impeach Clinton, in part, because many people thought he had violated his most important duty as president: providing moral leadership.

Of course, the president's leadership is not just about moral guidance. In 1909, President Theodore Roosevelt famously called the presidency a "bully pulpit," that is, a powerful means to spread a message. The idea was that just as a priest uses the pulpit to speak to his parishioners, the president uses his office to spread a message to the country. Presidents use their position to advance a variety of agendas. Often these agendas are not legislative or governmental at all.

Some of the most important and enduring presidential accomplishments have been their statements which have entered the American consciousness. Washington's first proclamation of a day of fasting and his *Farewell Address,* in which he warned against foreign alliances, provide two such examples. Washington's *Farewell Address* of 1796 became the cornerstone of American foreign policy for most of the next century. Lincoln's *Gettysburg Address* and *Second Inaugural Address* are similar examples. President Eisenhower's *Farewell Address*, warning about the dangers of the "military industrial complex," is another famous oft-quoted line.

President Ronald Reagan, known as "The Great Communicator," mastered the art of communicating directly to the American people and inspiring them. As one example, in nationally televised speech on November 5, 1984, Reagan proclaimed:

> The greatness of America doesn't begin in Washington; it begins with each of you—in the mighty spirit of free people under God, in the bedrock values you live by each day in your families, neighborhoods, and workplaces. Each of you is an individual worthy of respect, unique and important to the success of America. And only by trusting you, giving

President Reagan delivers his *Farewell Address* from the Oval Office.

you opportunities to climb high and reach for the stars, can we preserve the golden dream of America as the champion of peace and freedom among the nations of the world.

Reagan's *Farewell Address*, on January 11, 1989, often called the "Shining City on a Hill" speech proclaimed:

> I've spoken of the shining city all my political life, but I don't know if I ever quite communicated what I saw when I said it. But in my mind, it was a tall, proud city built on rocks stronger than oceans, wind-swept, God-blessed, and teeming with people of all kinds living in harmony and peace; a city with free ports that hummed with commerce and creativity. And if there had to be city walls, the walls had doors and the doors were open to anyone with the will and the heart to get here.

The president, as the leader of the country, possesses enormous power by his words and actions to set the tone for the nation.

LEGISLATIVE POWER AND THE VETO

Article 2, Section 3 says that the president *"shall from time to time give to the Congress Information of the State of the Union, and recommend to their Consideration such Measures as he shall judge necessary and expedient."* In the past hundred years, presidents have appeared before Congress and given a speech called the **"State of the Union Address."** The Constitution merely says that from time to time the president will report to Congress and suggest legislation. The *Budget and Accounting Act of 1921* directs the president to propose a budget to Congress each year, but Congress must approve the budget.

In the State of the Union Address, the president is supposed to report to Congress on the condition of the country, that is, provide information on foreign and domestic issues. Often, the president uses the State of the Union to announce far-reaching policies as James Monroe did during his seventh State of the Union when he introduced the Monroe Doctrine. In one of his Addresses, President Lyndon Johnson announced a massive social welfare program that became known as the "War on Poverty." However, more recently, presidents have used the State of the Union to promote their reelections. Joe Biden's *2024 State of the Union Address* was almost entirely an attack on

Donald Trump and the Republicans. Beginning in the 20th century, presidents have delivered their State of the Union Addresses to Congress in person. Since the advent of radio and television, which carry the Address live, it presents a president with a golden opportunity to speak to the American public.

Although Congress enacts legislation, the Framers sought to check that power to prevent Congress from becoming too powerful. Thus, the president can influence legislation, and check the power of Congress, through the **veto**. The president can veto any normal legislation Congress enacts. The veto does not apply to certain specific powers of Congress, such as proposing constitutional amendments or impeaching federal officials. However, the Framers also sought to ensure that the president did not become a dictator who could simply veto all legislation. Thus, Congress can **override** a presidential veto by repassing the measure by a two-thirds majority. Because this majority is difficult to achieve, a veto threat is a powerful way to induce Congress to work with the president on legislation.

The veto has been a valuable tool for eliminating wasteful spending. Since the 19th century, Congressmen have tended to support "pet projects" for their districts. Because the president is the national leader, he is often willing to veto projects that do not benefit the entire country, but only benefit narrow interests. On the other hand, sometimes the president himself has pet projects and will "trade" with Congressmen by agreeing to their pet projects.

In 1996, Congress passed *The Line Item Veto Act*, which authorized the president to veto specific spending measures, or line items. When President Clinton vetoed a number of line items, parties who lost their budget projects brought suit in federal court arguing that the line item veto was illegal. In 1998, the Supreme Court declared that the line item veto was unconstitutional. The President must veto the entire bill or none at all. (*Clinton v. City of New York* (1998)).

President Clinton vetoing line items for a bill in 1997.

THE VICE-PRESIDENT AND THE LINE OF SUCCESSION

Although John Adams viewed his eight years as vice-president as somewhat wasted, describing it as "the most insignificant office that ever the invention of man contrived or his imagination conceived," the vice-president does play a significant role in the executive branch. First, the vice-president is the presiding officer of the Senate, with authority to vote to break ties. Historically, vice-presidents have only presided over the Senate on formal occasions. More important is their role in the line of succession to the presidency.

According to Article 2, Section 1, if the president is removed from office, dies, resigns, or is otherwise unable to continue to serve, the office of president "shall devolve" on the vice-president. Thus, following the death of William Henry Harrison in 1841, his vice-president, John Tyler, became president. Following the assassinations of Presidents Lincoln, Garfield, McKinley, and Kennedy, their vice-presidents all became president, as did Harry Truman following the death of Franklin Roosevelt. Consequently, while everyone agreed that the words "shall devolve" meant that the vice-president would become president, the Constitution did not actually say that.

In 1967, the Twenty-Fifth Amendment was added to the Constitution which specifically says that the vice-president becomes president if the president is removed from office, dies, resigns, or is otherwise unable to continue to serve. Moreover, it explains how the office of vice-president is to be filled if it becomes vacant, something which had occurred eighteen times in the past, most recently following the assassination of President Kennedy. In the event of a vacancy, any presidential appointment to the vice-presidency must be approved by a majority of both Houses of Congress. Finally, the Twenty-Fifth Amendment describes the procedure to remove the president in the event he is incapacitated either temporarily, e.g. because he is undergoing a medical procedure, or permanently e.g. because he is mentally incompetent. In the case of a temporary incapacity, the vice-president becomes acting president.

Under the Constitution, Congress creates a line of succession to the presidency following the vice-president. In 1947, Congress passed the **Presidential Succession Act** which established the line of succession. After the president and vice-president, the Speaker of the House, the President pro temp of the Senate, and the Secretary of State are next in line. They are followed by the members of the cabinet in the order they were created. Thus, because the department was created in 2006, the Secretary of Homeland Security is the last name on the succession list.

Consequently, although it seems that vice-presidents lack any real power, this is not exactly correct. As of 2024, forty-nine people have served as vice-president. Nine have become president due to the death or resignation of the president (18%). Thus, there is about one chance in five that the vice-president will become president. As older people are elected, it seems this possibility increases. Moreover, in addition to these nine, six others have been elected in their own right, the most recent being Joe Biden (32%). Therefore, there is almost one chance in three that a vice-president will somehow become president.

CHIEF DIPLOMAT: TREATIES AND FOREIGN POLICY

As Chief Diplomat, the president negotiates treaties with foreign nations. Treaties between two nations are known as **bi-lateral**, while treaties involving three or more nations are known as **multi-lateral**. While the Senate must approve treaties, most of the time it does. Because a treaty becomes the law of the land, presidents usually confer with Senators before entering into a treaty. The most famous instance of the Senate rejecting a treaty was the 1919 *Treaty of Versailles* which ended World War I. In large part, because President Wilson failed to include Republicans in discussions concerning the treaty, nor make concessions about the treaty, the Senate rejected it.

In addition to treaties, presidents enter into other sorts of executive agreements and protocols with foreign countries, often without consulting Congress. These executive agreements are considered more *informal* than treaties so presidents do not consult Congress. Nevertheless, they often bind America to certain actions or obligations which Congress might have opposed. However, Congress has tended to accept these agreements as part of the president's power as the nation's chief diplomat. As a result, the president's power to conduct foreign relations has greatly expanded.

Article 2, Section 2 provides:

> (The President) shall have Power, by and with the Advice and Consent of the Senate, to make Treaties, provided two thirds of the Senators present concur; and he shall nominate, and by and with the Advice and Consent of the Senate, shall appoint Ambassadors, other public Ministers and Consuls,

Section 3 adds that the president: "… shall receive Ambassadors and other public Ministers." So the president both appoints American ambassadors and receives foreign ambassadors. Taken together, these provisions implicitly recognize that the president is in charge of diplomacy.

President Truman signs the North Atlantic Treaty in 1949, establishing NATO.

In *Federalist* 69, Hamilton downplayed the president's power to make treaties, insisting that despite the president being head of state, his constitutional power fell well short of those of the British monarch:

> The President is to have power, with the advice and consent of the Senate, to make treaties, provided two thirds of the senators present concur. The king of Great Britain is the sole and absolute representative of the nation in all foreign transactions. He can of his own accord make treaties of peace, commerce, alliance, and of every other description. … In this respect, therefore, there is no comparison between the intended power of the President and the actual power of the British sovereign. The one can perform alone what the other can do only with the concurrence of a branch of the legislature.

This suggests that the president has no authority to make "agreements" with foreign states outside of the treaty power shared with the senate.

Thomas Jefferson, who generally took a limited view of federal power, argued that in matters of foreign affairs the president possessed broad authority. Of course, Jefferson was Secretary of State under Washington, so arguably Jefferson had a personal incentive to expand power in this area. In 1790, in his capacity as Secretary of State, Jefferson wrote that:

> The transaction of business with foreign nations is executive altogether. … The Senate is not supposed by the Constitution to be acquainted with the concerns of the Executive department. It was not intended that these should be communicated to them; nor can they therefore be qualified to judge of the necessity which calls for a mission to any particular place, or of the particular grade, more or less marked, which special and secret circumstances may call for.[1]

In other words, if the president wishes to create an embassy, consulate, or trade mission in a given city, it is entirely within his sole discretion. Similarly, if the president wishes to send "secret" envoys to foreign countries, that too is left to his discretion. If this seems like a contradiction, given Jefferson's opposition to the Washington's *Neutrality Proclamation* a few years later, the distinction seems to be that the *Neutrality Proclamation* purported to tell Americans in the United States what they could or could not do, which is a matter of domestic, not foreign, policy.

The simple phrase, "he shall receive Ambassadors" sounds trivial, but has some important implications. The significance of the power to receive ambassadors is illustrated by an incident which occurred in 1809, during James Madison's presidency. In 1808, Napoleon invaded and conquered most of Spain. He proclaimed his brother Joseph, King of Spain. For several years, two rival governments each claimed to be the legitimate Spanish government. In 1809, the real Spanish government, that is, the one opposing Napoleon, sent an ambassador to the United States. Madison refused to receive the Spaniard, Luis de Onís, as ambassador. Madison said he would not recognize Onis as ambassador because doing so meant taking sides in the Franco-Spanish conflict and Madison wanted the United States to remain neutral.

Extending diplomatic recognition to a particular government or nation can have crucial consequences. In 1778, for example, France recognized the American colonies as independent, which tremendously boosted the cause of independence. Another famous example involving the presidential use of diplomatic recognition occurred when President Carter established diplomatic relations with the People's Republic of China (Communist China) and terminated diplomatic relations with the "Republic of China" based in Taiwan. [In 1949, the anti-communist government of China relocated to the island of Taiwan when communists conquered the rest of China.] In December 1978, President Carter announced, without approval from Congress, that the United States would formally recognize the communist regime as the legitimate government of China as of January 1, 1979.

Carter's decision was quite controversial, as for decades, the United States and China (Taiwan) had had a Mutual Defense Treaty. A group of Congressmen brought suit asking the federal courts to declare that Carter had no authority to

---
[1] Jefferson, Opinion on the Powers of the Senate Respecting Diplomatic Appointments, April 24. 1790

abrogate the treaty. In *Goldwater v. Carter* (1979) the Supreme Court dismissed the suit, declaring it was a dispute between two other branches of government in which the courts should not become involved.

Thus, the Supreme Court failed to decide whether a president can *unilaterally* rescind a treaty. In 1790, Hamilton and Madison appeared to deny there was such a power. The short decision in *Goldwater v. Carter* did not offer much explanation, but the assumption is that Congress has plenty of tools to stop the president. Congress can impeach the president or any of his officers; the Senate can refuse to confirm an ambassador; Congress can refuse to appropriate money to purchase an embassy. So, Congress could check the president if it wished.

Treaties approved by the Senate are the "supreme law" of the land, and the president is tasked with ensuring that the law be faithfully enforced. Nevertheless, presidents of both parties have repeatedly repudiated treaties. In 1986, President Reagan unilaterally repudiated a treaty with Nicaragua. Once again, federal courts refused to intervene. A president's power to repudiate treaties remains controversial, but whenever they do, they have "gotten away with it." Congress has complained, but been unable to stop it.

However, Congress is far from powerless in matters of foreign policy. For example, Carter's actions regarding Communist China and Taiwan were very unpopular and Congress enacted the *Taiwan Relations Act* by veto-proof majorities. The *Taiwan Relations Act* requires the president to maintain relations with Taiwan, but neither the United States nor Taiwan can have an "embassy" or an "ambassador" for the other, which would imply that Taiwan is an independent nation. Moreover, the *Taiwan Relations Act* guarantees that the United States will continue to provide military aid to Taiwan despite its "official" status as part of the People's Republic of China.

In summary, while the president has broad powers over foreign policy, Congress also possesses tools to influence foreign policy when it wishes to do so.

In addition to sending and receiving ambassadors, Presidents also visit foreign nations and receive foreign heads of states, such as kings and other presidents. Such "state visits" are often lavish affairs where presidents can be seen looking regal and presiding over ceremonies that resemble the imperial coronations. However, these state meetings can have a serious side as well. Presidents often have **summits**, or meetings, with other foreign leaders in which they discuss very important topics. Presidents will also sometimes invite leaders of warring nations to participate in peace conferences. One of the most famous examples of this occurred in 1978 when President Carter invited the leaders of Israel and Egypt to meet with him at the presidential retreat at Camp David, Maryland. The Camp David Accords led to an important peace treaty between Israel and Egypt.

President Carter meets with the leaders of Israel and Egypt at Camp David.

EXECUTIVE AGREEMENTS

In addition to treaties, presidents often enter into various types of agreements with foreign powers. Some of these may be fairly trivial and are often called **diplomatic protocols**. For example, the president might agree to accept a certain number of foreign diplomats who have **diplomatic immunity**. According to the State Department,

"*Diplomatic immunity is a principle of international law by which certain foreign government officials are not subject to the jurisdiction of local courts and other authorities for both their official and, to a large extent, their personal activities.*" In other words, diplomatic immunity means that diplomats, and their families, are protected from nearly all civil or criminal prosecution. Diplomatic immunity has existed since ancient Greek and Roman times. It has always been necessary to protect diplomats so that nations could speak with each other without fear that their spokesmen would be arrested or killed.

However, the number of people granted diplomatic immunity is limited—for obvious reasons. No government wants millions of people to have immunity. Typically, the State Department negotiates with foreign nations and agrees upon the number of diplomats with immunity. Moreover, if a diplomat, or a member of his family, abuses their immunity by committing a crime, the immunity can be revoked and the diplomat expelled.

These minor diplomatic arrangements could be accomplished through a formal treaty. However, these day-to-day diplomatic issues tend to be handled through informal agreements. This raises the question of how to distinguish between relatively minor diplomatic protocols and more critical issues that should be the subject of a full-fledged treaty. One of the earliest and famous examples of this issue occurred in 1817 during the Monroe administration. President Monroe entered into an "agreement" with Great Britain, limiting naval armament on the Great Lakes, without consulting Congress. A number of senators objected that the agreement was illegal and needed to be presented to the Senate as a treaty. Ultimately, the Senate approved the treaty. Once again, the Senate showed it has the power to insist the president not intrude upon its prerogative to consent to treaties.

Since 1817, presidents have made dozens of executive agreements with foreign nations, often secretly. In the early 1940s, President Roosevelt began entering into large numbers of executive agreements, one of the most famous being the *Hull-Lothian Agreement* of September 2, 1940. (Cordell Hull was Secretary of State.) Under the Agreement, which Congress never approved, the Roosevelt Administration gave Britain fifty American warships in exchange for a 99-year lease on some naval bases. This was a major decision because it unambiguously placed America on England's side in the war against Nazi Germany. Thus, many people thought Congress should be consulted.

In 1942, the Supreme Court heard a challenge to the president's authority to enter into executive agreements. In *United States v. Pink* (1942), the Supreme Court said that validly made international executive agreements have the same legal status as treaties but did not require Senate approval. The issue in *Pink* involved a New York law that was contrary to an executive agreement. The Supreme Court held that executive agreements superseded state laws just as treaties did. This remains controversial.

The Constitution explicitly says that treaties are the supreme law of the land; however, when the president overrides state laws in his agreements, it pushes the boundaries of presidential power. Needless to say, this is a potentially limitless power. In recent years, the president has entered into international agreements to combat "climate change." Could the president ban automobiles or oil drilling based on an executive agreement not ratified by the Senate? Perhaps.

Despite being controversial, there has been remarkably little opposition from Congress. In 1972, Congress enacted the *Case-Zablocki Act* which said that the president must inform the Senate within 60 days of making an executive agreement. Thus, theoretically, secret agreements are no longer permitted. However, the Act implicitly acknowledges the president's authority to make executive agreements. If the treaty-making power extends to any area of national interest, and the president's power to make executive agreements is co-extensive with the treaty power, then the president's power to rule by decree is virtually unlimited.

SPIES, COVERT ACTIONS, AND PRESIDENTIAL FINDINGS

Closely related to the issues of foreign policy and diplomacy is spying on other countries. Spying, or intelligence gathering, has existed since at least Biblical times. *Joshua 2* relates how Joshua secretly sent two spies to "reconnoiter" Jericho. Both the State Department and the Defense Department engage in spying. The State Department's main intelligence service is the Bureau of Intelligence and Research, while the Defense Department relies on the Defense Intelligence Agency. Additionally, the federal government operates a host of other intelligence agencies, the most important of which are the Central Intelligence Agency (CIA), the National Security Agency (NSA), and the Federal Bureau of Investigation (FBI). Each of the uniformed military services have their own intelligence agencies, including the Coast Guard and the Space Force. The Department of Energy has an Office of Intelligence, as does the Treasury Department and Drug Enforcement Administration.

These intelligence agencies form a massive bureaucracy theoretically coordinated by the Director of National Intelligence who answers to the president. However, the intelligence agencies even spy on the president. It is well-documented that federal intelligence agencies spied on Donald Trump when he was a candidate for president in 2016. After Trump was elected president in November 2016, the spying continued at least through January 2017.

Federal bureaucracies are so large and possess so many layers of management that the president's ability to control them is limited. This problem is not confined to the national security bureaucracy, but because intelligence agencies largely operate in secret, it is difficult for the public, Congress, and even the president to keep track of their actions. Because agencies like the FBI and CIA have conducted secret surveillance operations, far outside their legal purview, some Americans now believe that they do more harm than good and should be abolished.[2]

Intelligence gathering on foreign governments and American citizens has become one of the most significant and far-reaching aspects of the federal government. Despite the documented abuses, the intelligence community argues that it protects the country from a variety of foreign and domestic threats. In an age of terrorism, no one can deny that there are people seeking to hurt the United States and individual Americans. Because by their very nature, so much of what these agencies do is secret, it is difficult to gauge whether they are preserving liberty or its greatest threat.

In addition to spying, the president also may authorize covert actions against foreign powers. The *National Security Act of 1947* authorized the creation of the CIA, and empowered the president to use the CIA to attack and undermine foreign organizations the president finds to be a threat. The CIA was the direct successor of the Office of Strategic Services (OSS), which, in addition to spying, performed acts of sabotage during World War 2.

The National Security Act says that the president may "authorize the conduct of a covert action" if he "determines such an action is necessary to support identifiable foreign policy objectives of the United States and is important to the national security of the United

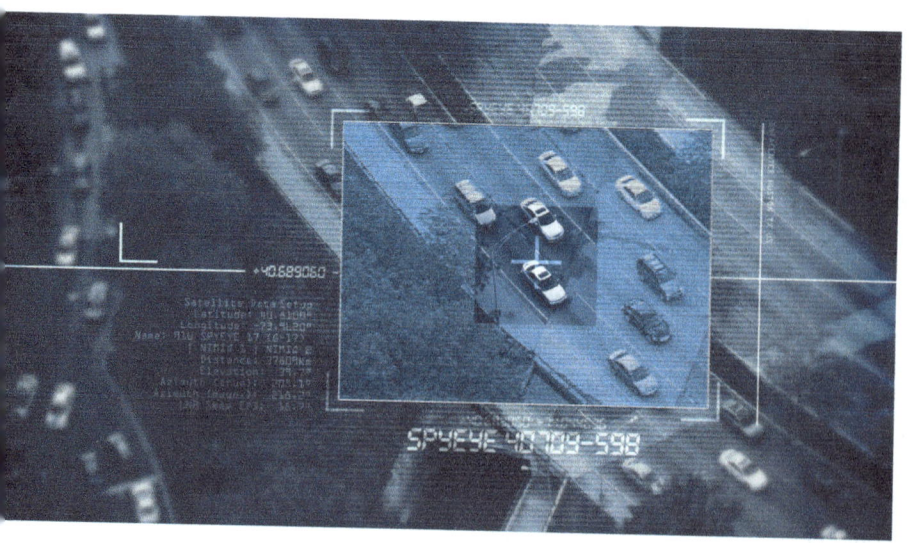

---
[2]Among the most disturbing instances of such behavior involve the FBI investigating pro-life organizations, Catholic churches and their members, and labeling parents who speak out at school board meetings as "domestic terrorists."

States." The president must make a specific "finding" in writing identifying the need for the covert action. The National Security Act further says that these findings must be shared with Congressional intelligence committees but not the entire Congress. Even then, the Act says if the president thinks secrecy is very important he is allowed to tell only the committee chairmen.

One of the most notorious attempts at covert "regime change" was the Bay of Pigs operation. In 1960, President Eisenhower authorized the CIA to train a force of Cuban exiles to invade Cuba to overthrow the communist government of Fidel Castro. President Kennedy, who was not in favor of the plan, inherited the operation. Because he failed to support the rebels, the attempt was a disastrous failure. Congress never authorized any of these actions.

Over the next 40 years, there were many operations aimed at overthrowing Communist or unfriendly foreign governments. In 1979, the Carter Administration began giving military aid to Afghan rebels fighting the Soviet occupation of Afghanistan. In the early 1980s, President Reagan authorized the CIA to train Nicaraguans to oppose the Communist government there. Although officially the United States was not involved, President Reagan openly discussed support for the rebel groups. Although the operations had been launched on presidential authority alone, in both cases Congress appropriated money for the operations.

In addition to regime-change operations, the CIA also has engaged in sabotage. The United States rarely acknowledges its efforts at sabotage, but it has on a few occasions. For example,

Cuban soldiers in the failed Bay of Pigs invasion, the result of a CIA operation

around 2010, the United States, in collaboration with Israel, developed a computer virus called *Stuxnet*. Stuxnet targeted Iran's computers and did enormous damage to Iran's economy and development of nuclear technology.

While many people believe that spying and espionage make America safer, other people think that interfering in the affairs of other nations disregards the wisdom of the Founding Fathers. In his *Farewell Address*, Washington cautioned against getting entangled in European disputes. In 1821, Secretary of State John Quincy Adams gave a famous speech in which he proclaimed

[America] goes not abroad, in search of monsters to destroy.

She is the well-wisher to the freedom and independence of all.

She is the champion and vindicator only of her own....

She well knows that by once enlisting under other banners than her own, were they even the banners of foreign independence, she would involve herself beyond the power of extrication, in all the wars of interest and intrigue, of individual avarice, envy, and ambition, which assume the colors and usurp the standard of freedom.

This accords with the view of Aquinas that law is made by and for a particular community. Thus, as a general rule, one nation should not interfere in the internal decisions of other countries. However, nations should also not abandon all morality and ignore governments which systematically murder their own citizens or persecute the Church.

EXECUTIVE ORDERS

As head of the executive department, the president has authority to issue orders to his subordinates, a practice which began with George Washington. Washington issued eight Executive

Orders, while Adams and Madison each issued only one. So, historically, Executive Orders were very limited both in scope and in number.

It is important to distinguish between *Executive Orders* and *Regulations*. Regulations are authorized by a statute passed by Congress. Executive Orders are issued by the president without any congressional authorization; rather, they are issued under a claim that the president has inherent authority to issue the Order in his own right. Moreover, when the president issues regulations, he must follow the Administrative Procedures Act, including giving prior notice and allowing a comment period prior to final approval. Executive Orders can be issued at any time without prior notice or following any procedures.

Article 2, Section 1 states that the president "may require the Opinion, in writing, of the principal Officer in each of the executive Departments, upon any Subject relating to the Duties of their respective Offices." Accordingly, the very first executive order issued by Washington to his cabinet members on June 8, 1789 stated:

> I wish to receive in writing such a clear account of the Department at the head of which you have been, as may be sufficient (without overburdening or confusing a mind which has very many objects to claim its attention at the same instant) to impress me with a full, precise & distinct general idea of the United States, so far as they are comprehended in, or connected with that Department.

This Executive Order directed Washington's subordinates to do something he clearly had authority to order. Washington's second "Executive Order" was the Thanksgiving Proclamation of November 26, 1789. Of course, this Proclamation did not actually order anyone to do anything. Thus, in the nation's early days, Executive Orders were quite limited. However, this started to change a few decades later.

President Lincoln issued forty-eight executive orders—more than the first nine presidents combined. Lincoln's most famous "Executive Order" was the Emancipation Proclamation which declared that all slaves in the Confederate states were emancipated. The Emancipation Proclamation was very different from Washington's order to his subordinates to send him a report. The Emancipation Proclamation purported to make law by presidential edict. Many later presidents issued Executive Orders that seemed to be usurpations of the legislative power entrusted to Congress.

In the 20th century, presidents began issuing hundreds of executive orders. Theodore Roosevelt issued 1,081 executive orders, while Franklin Roosevelt issued 3,721 executive orders. In the last few decades most presidents have issued about 200 to 300 executive orders.

Harry Truman issued one of the famous executive orders in 1952. In April 1952, in the middle of the Korean War, American steel workers went on strike. Truman issued an executive order seizing control of all the steel mills and forcing them to remain open and produce steel. Truman argued it was an emergency situation and therefore he had authority to address the emergency under his role as Commander-in-Chief of America's armed forces. However, this was not an order to the *military*, or even federal employees; the president was telling *private citizens* how to behave. Some of the steel mills brought suit challenging Truman's action.

A painting depicting President Lincoln reading the Emancipation Proclamation to his Cabinet

President Biden signs an executive order.

affecting hundreds of millions of private citizens. The Order did not say where Biden derived the authority to issue such an Order; it merely declared he possessed it "By the authority vested in me as President by the Constitution and the laws of the United States of America…" Biden's Order seems much less legally defensible than Truman's Steel Mill Order, as steel was at least tangentially related to the president's conduct of a war.

The Supreme Court sided with the steel mills declaring:

> we cannot with faithfulness to our constitutional system hold that the Commander in Chief of the Armed Forces has the ultimate power as such to take possession of private property in order to keep labor disputes from stopping production.

Youngstown Sheet & Tube Co. v. Sawyer (1952)

During the Covid Crisis, Presidents Trump and Biden issued a variety of executive orders. For example, on January 21, 2021, President Biden issued an executive order mandating that all passengers on any plane, train, ferry, or bus in the United States must wear a mask. This was a remarkable assertion of presidential authority

Not all Executive Orders are as broad as Biden's mask order. Most Orders direct federal employees to follow certain guidelines, but the mask Order shows how wide-ranging they can be. Moreover, the Supreme Court has held that, just like federal laws and regulations, executive orders take precedence over any state laws to the contrary.[3]

Many people think that presidents issuing executive orders, like the mask mandate, is tantamount to the president ruling by decree like an emperor. However, presidents from both parties have done this. Generally, the public accepts the orders with very little outcry.

THE PARDON POWER

Article 2, Section 2 says that the president *"shall have Power to grant Reprieves and Pardons for Offences against the United States, except in Cases of Impeachment."* Many Framers considered this one of the most important presidential powers. The Framers were concerned about a repeat of Shays' Rebellion and wanted the president to be able to counter a rebellion by promising to pardon any rebels who agreed to stop their insurrection. In Federalist 74, Hamilton explained that during an uprising, there are often critical moments when an offer of pardon to rebels may restore peace.

Just a few years after the adoption of the Constitution, President Washington personally helped suppress a small rebellion. In 1791, the federal government put a tax on liquor. Many farmers in western Pennsylvania had trouble transporting their crops to market, so they distilled much of their crop into whiskey which was easier to transport. The liquor tax threatened to bankrupt them. In July 1794, several hundred rioters burned down the home of a local tax collector. President Washington called out the militia and personally led over 10,000 militiamen to the area of the rebellion and the protesters dispersed.

---

[3] *Letter Carriers v. Austin*, 418 U.S. 264 (1974).

Washington left General Henry Lee in the region for several months to act on his behalf to ensure the rebellion did not re-ignite. On November 29, 1794, Lee declared a general pardon for most people involved in the "Whiskey Rebellion." Only a handful of leaders were arrested and charged with treason. However, President Washington even granted a presidential pardon to these men the following year. The use of the pardon power, at least with respect to the Whiskey Rebellion, worked out as Hamilton and other Framers had hoped.

Note that the president may only grant pardons "for Offences against the United States." The president has no authority to pardon state crimes. In the 18th and 19th centuries, there were only a handful of federal crimes. Today there are thousands of federal crimes. The growth of federal crimes suggests that the pardon power is more important than ever. Nevertheless, presidents in the 20th and 21st centuries have not pardoned that many people.

One famous use of the pardon, and one of its broadest applications, occurred in 1977, when President Carter issued a blanket pardon to anyone who had illegally refused to comply with the military draft. This affected tens of thousands of "draft dodgers." The pardon proved controversial, but Carter felt it was an important step to healing the divisions caused by the Vietnam War.

The biggest criticism of the pardon power is its potential for misuse. For example, the president might order a soldier to commit a war crime with the promise that he would immediately pardon him. To date, nothing this severe has occurred in American history. However, presidents have granted pardons to unsavory characters and rumors have persisted that some of these pardons may have been payoffs for campaign contributions or other favors. No such allegations have been proved. Moreover, it is not clear such payoffs would be invalid or even illegal. The Constitution places no restrictions on the president's power to pardon offenses against the United States, even when he acts for reasons that might have shocked the Founders. For example, in January 2001, President Clinton pardoned his half-brother Roger, who had been convicted of conspiracy to distribute cocaine. President Clinton certainly used his office simply to benefit his family—a form of corruption under other circumstances. Nevertheless, no one has questioned that President Clinton acted within his authority as president. Apparently, the only recourse for abuse of the pardon power would be impeachment.

FAITHFULLY ENFORCING THE LAW

Article 2, Section 3 provides that the president "shall take Care that the Laws be faithfully executed, and shall Commission all the Officers of the United States." This clause summarizes the president's job as Chief Executive: **to enforce the laws of the United States faithfully**. Thus, it encompasses a number of explicit and implicit powers and responsibilities. Technically, the provision does not say that the president *shall enforce* the laws, but emphasizes that the president shall "take care" that laws be "faithfully" enforced. This implies that the president must diligently and impartially enforce the law, must not refuse to enforce the law, nor act beyond the powers legally granted to him. Because the enforcement is connected to commissioning "all the officers of the United States," the implication is that the president must also ensure that his subordinates diligently and impartially enforce the law.

The "law," and its enforcement, can be divided into a few different areas. One part involves what is known as **administrative law,** which are the laws that govern the ways that government agencies are managed, or *administered*. In this sector of the law, the president must ensure that his subordinates do their jobs. Another area is **criminal law**, in which the president prosecutes people who have committed crimes that violate federal law, such as acts of terrorism. A third area is **civil law**. Under civil law, the president brings civil cases against private parties or local government entities who allegedly have violated a federal law but not committed a crime. For example, someone might accidentally crash their car into a mail truck. Traffic accidents are not crimes, but the government might sue the driver to collect damages.

In the 18th century, the federal government rarely brought criminal or civil prosecutions against individuals. Mainly because before the middle of the 19th century, there were only a handful of federal crimes, and very few reasons that the federal government could sue an individual. Today, criminal prosecutions and civil suits are two of the most important and far-reaching powers of the federal government.

In 1790, Congress enacted the first federal criminal statute: "An Act for the Punishment of Certain Crimes Against the United States," or simply "The Crimes Act." Because The Crimes Act was approved by many of the same people who drafted or ratified the Constitution, this first criminal code is an authoritative interpretation of constitutional authority in the area of criminal law. In fact, the main author of The Crimes Act was Oliver Ellsworth who had been a delegate to the constitutional convention.

The Crimes Act created twenty-one federal crimes. Five of these crimes applied only to acts committed in a place "under the sole and exclusive jurisdiction of the United States." These crimes were 1) murder, 2) manslaughter, 3) larceny (theft), 4) accessory to larceny, and 5) assault causing serious bodily injury. Five more crimes applied only to acts committed "upon the high seas" including murder, robbery, and similar acts considered "piracy." An eleventh crime involved concealing the commission of one of the first ten, what today might be termed "aiding and abetting." The other ten crimes applied regardless of where they were committed: treason; assisting a federal prisoner escape from jail; stealing the body of an executed convict; forgery; theft or falsification of federal records; perjury in federal court; bribing a federal judge; obstructing a federal proceeding;

assaulting a foreign ambassador; and interfering with the diplomatic immunity of an ambassador.

Obviously, there were a tiny number of federal crimes in 1790 and all were directly related to core federal functions. Over the next century, about 100 federal crimes were added, almost entirely involving interstate movement or shipment of goods or persons. For example, The Comstock Act of 1873 made it a federal crime to use the U.S. Post Office to mail abortifacients or contraceptives.

During the 20th century, the number and scope of federal crimes greatly increased. One recent study estimated that as of 2019 there were 5,199 different federal crimes. There are so many crimes, and they are constantly changing, that no one can say for certain exactly how many federal crimes there are. Recall that Madison wrote in *Federalist* 17 that "the ordinary administration of criminal and civil justice" was a power reserved for the states. That remains true—in theory. Because the federal government lacks general "police power," federal criminal statutes are often convoluted. For example, Congress presumably cannot just make robbery a federal crime, like the states do. However, the Hobbs Act makes it a federal crime to commit a robbery that "affects interstate commerce." Then there are federal laws that criminalize robbing post offices, or robbing federally insured organizations, like banks. So, while states can simply enact laws against theft, federal statutes are often highly specific, very technical, and quite obscure.

The obscurity of federal crimes raises serious issues. St. Thomas argues that promulgation of a statute is essential to all law, and punishing people for violating a statute of which they were unaware is fundamentally unjust. One of the most famous federal judges, Richard Posner, has cited St. Thomas to argue that the proliferation of thousands of obscure federal criminal statutes, of which the average person is unaware, is a denial of due process.

Because there are so many federal laws it is impossible to enforce or prosecute all of them. Thus, despite the Constitutional requirement that the president take care that the laws be faithfully executed, the president, that is, the executive branch, ends up enforcing some and not others because there are simply too many to enforce.

Even the federal government does not have infinite resources.

Thus, the president must use discretion to order his law enforcement agencies and prosecutors to disregard certain crimes, perhaps those that do not involve violence, and focus on crimes the president determines are more injurious to society. No one disputes that a president is free to set his own priorities when it comes to law enforcement. However, it is a short step from setting law enforcement priorities to selective prosecutions that single out certain people, especially the president's political opponents. Many people think this "selective prosecution" happened to Donald Trump in 2023 and 2024. State and federal prosecutors appear to have been more determined to find a crime with which to charge President Trump than to enforce the law impartially.

The flip-side of selective prosecution arises when a president refuses to enforce the law at all. While it is one thing to prioritize limited resources, it is quite another for a president simply to declare he will not enforce a law because he does not like it. Currently, under the Comstock Act, federal law forbids mailing abortifacients or contraceptives. In 2022, the Biden Administration announced it would not enforce the Comstock Act because the substances involved had been approved by Food and Drug Administration

regulations. The Administration stopped short of asserting that a regulation overrides a statute passed by Congress, but argued that the 19th century statute needed to be re-interpreted in light of 21st century regulations.

Each year the federal government prosecutes about 100,000 federal defendants and has about 150,000 convicts in prison at any given time. The power to incarcerate people, fine them, and, in rare instances, execute them, is an incredible power that can be used for good or ill. The United States has gone from twenty-one crimes in 1790 to about 5,199 federal crimes in 2019. St. Thomas argued that criminal laws should be few in number as well as easy to understand and follow. When the criminal code is extensive, complicated, and constantly changing, people will lose respect for the law, and society will be worse for it.

CIVIL PENALTIES AND ENFORCEMENT

In addition to criminal prosecutions, the federal government has a huge bureaucracy that engages in civil suits against individuals, companies, and local governments. There are tens of thousands of various regulations that can result in some sort of enforcement proceeding. For example, the U.S. Department of Health & Human Services (HHS) has more than 18,000 regulations. This is just one agency, although one of the largest, and includes the Food and Drug Administration (FDA).

The biggest difference between criminal charges and civil enforcement is that people usually do not go to jail for civil violations. However, civil enforcement can result in ruinous financial penalties. Federal regulations vary with respect to who is covered. Some regulations only apply to large companies, while other regulations apply to all companies. Some regulations apply to all private parties. Other regulations only apply to state or local government. For example, the federal Fair Housing Act makes it unlawful to discriminate against anyone because of their race or religion in selling or renting housing. Interestingly to those with large families, the Fair Housing Act makes it unlawful to refuse to rent to a family because they have children, or "too many" children.

One of the most important types of civil suits are those the federal government brings against state or local governments. For example, the federal government might receive an allegation that a local police department is discriminating against a certain racial minority. The Department of Justice will instigate a lawsuit seeking damages and an order to stop the city from doing whatever is alleged to be discriminatory.

The constitutionality of many of these laws and regulations rests on somewhat shaky ground. For example, aside from federal civil rights laws, what section of the Constitution empowers the federal government to tell a property owner to whom he can or cannot rent? The basis for this, and most regulations today, is that renting apartments, in the aggregate, affects interstate commerce. In the case of the apartment, this is even more of a stretch than a farmer growing his own wheat *not* to sell it. At least the wheat could be sold in interstate commerce. The federal government's power to enforce thousands of laws and regulations impacts everyone in the country. As with criminal statutes, there are so many possibilities for civil enforcement that the president needs to prioritize what cases to pursue.

EXECUTIVE PRIVILEGE

In the last forty years, the concept of **"executive privilege"** has become far more important than in the past. In the current context, "privilege" means an exemption from what would otherwise be a legal duty. For example, the priest-penitent privilege means that a priest cannot be legally required to reveal what a person tells him in confession. "Executive privilege" is a claim that the president and his advisers cannot be forced to testify in court or before Congress about presidential policies or provide confidential information to the other branches of government.

Presidents assert that to make decisions, they must be permitted to keep their conversations and discussions involving the formulation of policies with their advisors confidential. Otherwise, they would not be able to function efficiently, as their advisors would constantly fear having to appear before Congress to explain why and what they said. Presidents maintain the privilege allows them to have free and open dialogue with their advisors on difficult, often top-secret matters, that require honest opinions, which they would not receive, if advisors feared the discussions would be made public.

Presidential privilege is somewhat controversial. Since Congress has oversight authority over executive agencies, some people think the president should not be permitted to keep secrets from Congress. Congress has authority to make laws and must appropriate the money executive officials spend. To perform these duties, Congress has authority to hold hearings, and subpoena witnesses, which means Congress can legally order a person to testify or produce documents. Congress often holds hearings to investigate how the president is handling a particular problem to decide whether to appropriate money to address the problem. Usually, the president's agents attend these hearings willingly, but sometimes Congress needs to **subpoena** one of them. It causes problems when the adviser invokes "executive privilege" and refuses to give Congress any information.

There is no mention of executive privilege in the Constitution or *The Federalist Papers*. Yet, the doctrine is as old as the American Republic. The idea of the president keeping secrets from Congress can be traced back to President Washington. In 1796, the House of Representatives demanded Washington give them documents related to the *Jay Treaty* with Great Britain. Washington sent the House a letter refusing to comply with this demand and explaining:

> The nature of foreign negotiations requires caution, and their success must often depend on secrecy …. The necessity of such caution and secrecy was one cogent reason for vesting the power of making treaties in the President…
>
> It does not occur that the inspection of the papers asked for can be relative to any purpose under the cognizance of the House of Representatives … I have no disposition to withhold any information … and, in fact, all the papers affecting the negotiation with Great Britain were laid before the Senate when the treaty itself was communicated for their consideration and advice.

Thus, Washington refused to provide the information to the House, but provided it to the Senate. Washington argued that the House was not entitled to the information because the House is not involved in approving treaties. However, Washington appears to acknowledge that Congress has authority to demand information from the president when it acts within an area which it has power to supervise. Washington also suggested that treaty negotiations, and perhaps all diplomacy, is particularly sensitive and requires secrecy.

Washington went on to point out that he helped write the Constitution, so possessed a keen understanding of the document:

> Having been a member of the General Convention, and knowing the principles on which the Constitution was formed, I have ever entertained but one opinion on this subject; and from the first establishment of the Government to this moment my conduct has exemplified that opinion that the power of making treaties is exclusively vested in the President, by and with the advice and consent of the Senate[.] …
>
> it is perfectly clear to my understanding that the assent of the House of Representatives is not necessary to the validity of a treaty … a just regard to the Constitution and to the duty of my office, under all the circumstances of this case, forbids a compliance with your request.[4]

Thus, according to Washington, there were at least some limited circumstances in which the president could refuse to provide information to Congress.

A similar issue arose in 1807 when the Jefferson Administration prosecuted Aaron Burr for treason. Burr served as Jefferson's vice-president from 1801 to 1805. After Burr left office, he was accused of plotting to create his own empire west of the Mississippi River. Burr claimed that the charges were politically motivated and that Jefferson possessed documents proving Burr's innocence. Burr's attorneys subpoenaed President Jefferson demanding he produce the documents. Jefferson informed the federal court that the doctrine of separation of powers meant that judges had no power to compel the president to do anything. Jefferson declared that the three branches of the government are independent of each other and none can control another. The implication seems to be that the president, and perhaps the entire executive branch, need not answer to the courts nor to Congress. This assertion by Jefferson is considered the basis for the concept of Executive Privilege.

Despite Jefferson's assertion, it does not appear that any president tried to invoke Executive Privilege again for over a century. The issue really became significant when President Nixon invoked Executive Privilege during the Watergate Scandal.

On June 17, 1972, shortly before the Democrat's presidential convention, five burglars were arrested breaking into the headquarters of the Democratic National Committee (DNC) in the Watergate Hotel and Office Building in Washington DC. The suspicious items the burglars possessed made it clear they intended to photograph documents and install listening devices in DNC headquarters. Although President Nixon held a massive lead in the polls, the Republicans were suspected. This suspicion was confirmed when it was revealed that one of the burglars, James W. McCord, was working for Nixon's re-election campaign. As evidence against Nixon grew, he denied that anyone in the White House was involved with the burglary.

On January 8, 1973, the Watergate burglars went on trial. Eventually, McCord confessed and claimed that a number of leading Republicans helped plan the burglary. McCord's shocking confession caused the Senate to establish a committee to investigate his charges. One by one, members of Nixon's administration admitted they knew about the break-in. The most damaging testimony came from President Nixon's attorney, John Dean, who said he discussed the Watergate affair with Nixon many times.

On June 25, Dean started testifying before the Senate committee and claimed that President Nixon helped cover-up the break-in. For the first time, someone directly linked Nixon with the break-in. However, Nixon resolutely denied the charges. There seemed to be no way to prove who was telling the truth. On July 16, one of Nixon's former aides testified that the president had secretly recorded his Oval Office (the president's private office) conversations. These tapes of conversations between Nixon and Dean would show who

---

[4]George Washington, Message to the House Regarding Documents Relative to the Jay Treaty, March 30, 1796.

President Nixon holding transcripts of the Oval Office tapes demanded by Congress

was telling the truth. The Senate committee immediately demanded the tapes. However, President Nixon refused to comply. He claimed executive privilege, arguing that if conversations between the president and his advisors could be made public that the president would not be able to receive candid advice from his advisors and could not do his job.

The Supreme Court ultimately decided the matter. The Court said that executive privilege was real; however, it did not insulate Nixon from being required to turn over the tapes. Thus, while executive privilege is generally recognized as a real privilege, no one knows its precise extent. Executive officials have often refused to reveal to Congress details of conversations with the president. Congressmen have often complained, but unless Congress is determined to pursue the issue there has not been much it can do.

PRESIDENTIAL IMMUNITY

Closely related to presidential privilege is the idea of presidential **immunity** from civil and criminal prosecution. In 1866, Mississippi brought suit in the Supreme Court against President Johnson. Mississippi argued that the military occupation of Mississippi was unconstitutional and asked the Court to order Johnson to restore civil government. In a short and cryptic decision, the Supreme Court declared that because of separation of powers, no court could interfere with the president "in the performance of his official duties."

The Court even added that no court would have jurisdiction over suits "against Andrew Johnson as a citizen of Tennessee." That is to say, no state or federal court could entertain suits against the president for actions that are unrelated to his role as president. The Supreme Court seemed to say that even if the president personally committed a serious crime, that he would have to be impeached and removed from office before he could be criminally prosecuted. Many commentators have argued that this makes sense, otherwise any local prosecutor could charge the president with a crime and a local judge could deny bail. This would allow the smallest town in America to remove the president.

In 1997, the Supreme Court said that a sitting president could be sued for private actions he took *before being elected president*. Moreover, people can sue administration officials, like the attorney general, who carry out presidential directives. So, in almost all cases, the personal immunity of the president himself makes little difference.

As with executive privilege, the Constitution makes no reference to presidential immunity. It remains an area where people generally agree that some level of immunity exists. However, the exact limits remain disputed.

NOMINATION OF SUPREME COURT JUSTICES AND OTHER FEDERAL JUDGES

One final authority the president possesses, and one that has become more important in recent decades as the courts have become more powerful, is his power to nominate Article 3 judges, who serve for life. As the federal courts have largely taken over the formulation of social policy, many people see the president's role in selecting judges to be the most important of all presidential powers. As a result, greater and greater contention has arisen over appointment of Supreme Court Justices.

To date, the Senate has rejected fewer than forty people for membership on the Supreme Court. The first person the Senate rejected was **John Rutledge**, one of the Founding Fathers, who Washington nominated. The Senate rejected Rutledge for political reasons in 1795. Over the next nearly two hundred years, the Senate rejected a small number of nominees, nearly always for political reasons. Usually, the nominee had caused resentment among the Senators for some position he had taken. However, Senate confirmations, or rejections, which had been a rather courteous process, began turning ugly during the 1970s.

In 1969, Richard Nixon nominated Clement Haynsworth, an appellate court judge, for the Supreme Court. The Senate rejected Haynsworth, despite having confirmed him in 1957 for his appellate court position, because they claimed he favored racial segregation. The Senate's vicious opposition to pro-life candidates reached its apex in late eighties and early nineties. In 1987, President Reagan nominated Robert Bork, who was serving on an appellate court. Within minutes of the announcement, pro-abortion advocates launched a campaign to smear him. Eventually the Senate rejected his nomination. The viciousness reached a crescendo in 1991, when George Bush nominated Clarence Thomas to the Court. Although Thomas was confirmed, he described his Senate hearings as a "high tech lynching."

THE "IMPERIAL" PRESIDENCY

The growth of the president's power has been one of the most notable changes over the past century. His power in his basic functions of Chief of State, Chief Executive, Chief Legislator, Chief Diplomat, and Commander-in-Chief has expanded far beyond what the Framers intended, and likely would consider appropriate. Presidents can issue regulations and executive orders, and attack other countries without Congressional approval. They can enter into agreements, just short of treaties, with other nations. Presidents have also asserted a wide variety of presidential privileges, such as insisting that presidential advisors need not testify before Congress or insisting that presidents can make secret policies and not inform Congress. Today, some people believe that the United States has an Imperial Presidency, more akin to the rule of Roman emperors than what the Framers intended.

CONCLUSION

The president possesses very broad powers with respect to both domestic and foreign policy which far exceed what the Framers intended. This raises some serious problems from a Thomistic perspective. Thomas argues that it is an injustice for rulers to act beyond the powers granted to them. He maintains that even as it would be unjust for a private party to force another to observe a "law" or command not approved by public authority, so too, it is unjust for a ruler to compel citizens to submit to a "law" or command not sanctioned by public authority.[5] In both cases this is an act of violence. Thomas even calls this a "perversion." Rulers are often tempted to go beyond their authority to do "justice," but in the long run it only creates injustice. There is an ancient principle of morality that "the ends do not justify the means."

[5] Summa Th. II-II q. 60, art 6.

REVIEW QUESTIONS

1. According to the Constitution what is the minimum age the president must be?
2. Which article of the Constitution deals primarily with the powers of the executive branch?
3. In Federalist 64, what did John Jay say about the character of the president?
4. Which presidents were "war heroes?"
5. What president was notorious for personal immorality in office?
6. What did the Twelfth Amendment do?
7. Why is the "electoral college" important?
8. How many electors does each state have?
9. In 2000, which state decided the entire presidential election by 537 official votes?
10. Who is the only president ever to serve more than two terms in office?
11. What are some of the main differences between the parliamentary system and the presidential system?
12. Who was Samuel Osgood?
13. Who coined the term the "president's cabinet"?
14. What activity did the U.S. Marshals Service perform in the early 19th Century in addition to law enforcement?
15. What is scheme attributed to President Jackson, stating the president can hire and fire anyone he wishes to work in the federal bureaucracy?
16. As of 2024, approximately how many people can the president appoint at his discretion to help him run the government?
17. What is the meaning of the "revolving door" as applied to politics?
18. What is the common name given to the organization that controls the money supply in the United States?
19. Which president gave a famous speech often called the "Shining City on a Hill" speech?
20. What does it take for Congress to "override" a presidential veto?
21. What controversial action did President Carter take in December 1978 that led to Congress passing the Taiwan Relations Act?
22. What controversial action did President Monroe take in 1817 that Congress thought exceeded the president's authority?
23. What does the Case-Zablocki Act of 1972 require?
24. What procedure did President Biden use to make everyone in America riding on any form of public transportation wear a face mask?
25. What did General Henry Lee do in the name of President Washington in November 1794 in order to prevent further conflict?
26. How many federal crimes were defined under the Crimes Act of 1790?
27. What action did Washington take in 1796 which is sometimes considered support for "executive privilege"?
28. Why did President Nixon assert executive privilege?
29. What is generally considered the best argument for presidential immunity from criminal prosecution?
30. Who summarized the feelings of many Americans about the government bureaucracy when he said, "I think you all know that I've always felt the nine most terrifying words in the English language are: I'm from the Government, and I'm here to help."

U.S. Government for Catholic Students

CHAPTER SIX
THE JUDICIAL BRANCH

INTRODUCTION

As with both Congress and the President, the role of the courts has changed enormously over the past century. Under *The Crimes Act of 1790*, there were only twenty-three federal crimes, and federal prosecution of crime was exceedingly rare. In 1790, there were only a handful of federal civil cases each year. Today, federal courts hear about 500,000 cases each year.[1] Moreover, federal courts have expanded into almost every area of life. Many people think federal courts are out of control and exercise powers that would shock the Founders. Today, judges make most important decisions about social policy. One of the most notorious examples involves abortion. In 1973, the Supreme Court ordered all fifty states and the federal government to stop enforcing laws against abortion. Another infamous example is school prayer. In 1962, the Supreme Court ordered all prayer in public schools to stop. Even moments of silence were banned.

From about 1960 to 2020, federal courts largely dictated social policy in the United States, much more than Congress or state legislatures. Additionally, the social policy the federal courts decreed was generally anti-religious and usually anti-Christian. For decades, courts told state and local governments that they must discriminate *against* Christians in the name of a fictitious "wall of separation between Church and State." Only recently has the Supreme Court announced a change in policy to "back off" and leave more issues of social policy to the democratic process. Only in the last few years has the Supreme Court declared that states cannot discriminate against Christians.

THE FEDERAL JUDICIARY

Article 3, Section 1 of the Constitution created the federal judiciary, that is, the Judicial Branch of government: "*The judicial power of the United States shall be vested in one Supreme Court, and in such inferior courts as the Congress may from time to time establish….*" Thus, although there are now many federal courts, the Constitution only *necessitated* the creation of the Supreme Court. The Constitution empowered Congress to create "such inferior courts" as it deemed necessary. In 1789, Congress enacted the Judiciary Act by which Congress began forming the lower federal court system. The Judiciary Act created three circuit, or appellate courts, and thirteen federal courts. In the years since the **Judiciary Act**, as the United States has grown larger, Congress has created more circuit and federal courts.

The federal judiciary consists of two types of courts: constitutional and legislative. **Constitutional courts** are those Congress has created under its Article 3, that is, constitutional authority. Constitutional courts include the federal district and circuit courts.

---

[1] 2023 Year-End Report on the Federal Judiciary.

Although not created by Congress, the Supreme Court, because it is an Article 3 court, is also considered a "constitutional court." **Legislative courts** have been created by Congress to deal with specific judicial matters arising from Congress's enumerated powers. These courts are somewhat complicated in nature but handle matters involving taxes (Tax Court), military trials (Court of Military Appeals), and cases involving veterans (Court of Veterans Appeals).

The highest court in the United States is the Supreme Court. All judicial matters, whether they come from an Article 3 court or a legislative court can be appealed to the Supreme Court. Decisions of the Supreme Court are final. However, Supreme Court decisions often lead to Congress enacting new laws which address the decision.

FEDERAL JUDGES AND JUSTICES

Federal judges, or in the case of the Supreme Court, *Justices*, preside over federal courts. Federal judges, also known as Article 3 judges, are incredibly powerful. First, they are appointed for life and can only be removed, or *impeached*, if they act very badly. Second, because their salaries are protected by the Constitution, they can not be forced to retire by cutting their wages. Thus, unless a federal judge retires, they have a lifetime, permanent job. For this reason, federal judges are nominated by the president and confirmed by the Senate. The Founders hoped that only people of high moral character who were dedicated to upholding the law would become federal judges.

Although judges are supposed to be impartial and unbiased, like referees or umpires in football and baseball games, presidents historically have nominated members of their party to become judges. Presidents realize that judges will try and be impartial, but in certain instances, they will tend to support the political philosophy of their party rather than an opposing philosophy. Thus, as early as John Adams' presidency, he appointed a number of Federalists to the Judiciary, literally as he was leaving the White House, so that incoming president Thomas Jefferson could not appoint Democratic-Republicans.

Traditionally, the Senate has tended to defer to the President in matters of judicial appointments, but the Senate even rejected one of George Washington's Supreme Court nominees. In more recent years, as the nation has become more polarized over social issues, the Senate has become less likely to confirm socially conservative nominees. What was once a very respectful process has become a ruthless attack intended to destroy the character of conservative, especially pro-life, nominees. The process has become even more bitter and contentious when the person is a nominee for the Supreme Court. All deference the Senate once gave to the president is long gone.

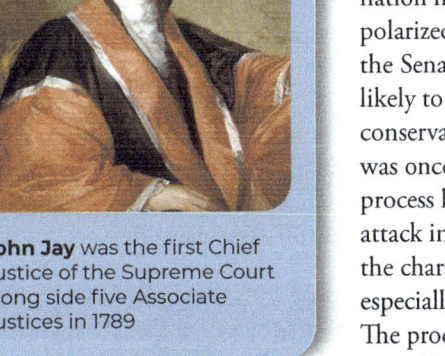

John Jay was the first Chief Justice of the Supreme Court along side five Associate Justices in 1789

THE ROLE OF JUDGES IN CRIMINAL AND CIVIL CASES

Historically, a judge's most important role was performed during **criminal** cases. Consider a system where a single person makes the law, investigates the crime, makes arrests, tries the case, serves as the main witness in the case, and sentences the party convicted of the crime. That is a lot of power even for the best and most honest individual. To prevent mistakes and deliberate oppression, it is good to have many people involved in the legal process who will spot a mistake or expose corruption. Often innocent people have mistakenly been tried and convicted while others, such as St. Thomas More, have been convicted through a perverted process.

So, during the investigation of a crime, if the investigators wish to conduct a search they must apply to a judge for a search warrant. This protects suspects from unnecessary intrusion into their lives and potential loss of their property. If investigators think they have proof that a suspect committed a crime, normally they must apply to a judge for an arrest warrant. If there is an emergency, police are permitted to arrest without an arrest warrant, but the suspect must promptly be brought before a judge.

Once a suspect has been charged with a crime, the judge must decide whether to allow the suspect to be released on **bail**. Bail is money which guarantees that a suspect shows up for trial. Today, defendants who cannot afford an attorney can ask the judge to appoint an attorney at public expense. This attorney is known as a **public defender**. As another protection, the government must tell a person charged with a crime what evidence there is against them. This revelation of evidence is called **discovery**.

Thus, even before a criminal trial begins, judges play a crucial role in protecting citizens from false or overzealous prosecution which is why judges need to be independent and not "rubber stamp" what the government does.

In addition to criminal cases, judges also resolve **civil cases**. Civil cases usually involve a dispute between two private citizens, but can sometimes involve civil suits against a private person by the state or federal government. Civil cases normally concern disagreements arising from personal injuries, property damage, or failure to complete a contract. In a civil suit the person, or "party," who begins the suit is called the **plaintiff**. The plaintiff goes to court and files a formal document, or "pleading," called a **complaint** to initiate a lawsuit. The party being sued is the **defendant**.

Civil suits almost always involve money. The plaintiff, who believes the defendant has injured him, seeks financial compensation for the damages done to him. In a few instances, the plaintiff seeks a specific item or action rather than money. For example, if a defendant promised to sell a painting to a plaintiff, the plaintiff wants the painting, not money. On the other hand, if a defendant promised to paint a plaintiff's house, the plaintiff could sue for the cost of having another painter do the job.

Despite the enormous number of lawsuits filed every year, people cannot sue someone for anything. The complaint must be based on a recognized issue, called **a cause of action**. If a plaintiff files a suit claiming the defendant did something not recognized as a cause of action, then the suit should be dismissed for **failure to state claim**.

Today, there are hundreds of different causes of action—far more than at common law. Some causes of action are recognized under state law and some under federal law. For example, one of the most common causes of action is negligence. When a person fails to exercise reasonable caution and hurts someone, then the negligent party can be sued for damages. Car accidents are a typical kind of negligence suit.

TRIALS AND JURIES

Although judges play a critical role in trials, they are only one player in an often complex drama. **Under Article 3, Section 2 every American citizen is guaranteed a trial by jury**. This is an incredibly important right for a few reasons. First, it means that a person is tried by their neighbors, not a faceless government. Trials generally take place in the **venue**, that is, location, where the crime or civil wrong occurred. This means jurors are familiar with the situation, if not the specific facts. For example, a cattle farmer in Wyoming has little in common with a man living in a tiny apartment in New York City. Other farmers should hear his case. Second, because other people are on the jury, the case is public. The United States, for the most part, does not conduct secret trials like despotic regimes such as Russia or Communist China. People cannot simply be taken off the street, given a secret trial, and then sentenced to a concentration camp – or worse.

Federal courts have two types of juries: grand juries and trial juries. A **grand jury** usually consists of 16 to 23 people who hear evidence in a criminal matter to determine whether enough evidence exists to bring an accused person to trial. If the grand jury decides there is enough evidence to support a trial, it issues an **indictment** against the accused person. If the jury feels that there is insufficient evidence to move forward with a trial, it will not indict the accused.

Grand juries have been criticized for a few issues. First, unlike most proceedings, the grand jury is conducted in secret. However, the purpose of the grand jury is not to convict a person, but to determine whether there is enough evidence that a person *might be convicted* at trial. This leads to another problem. Only the prosecutor presents evidence. The accused has limited opportunities to present a defense. As a result, nearly all accused people are indicted. There is a famous saying that a grand jury will indict a ham sandwich. This means that because they hear only one side of the argument, the jurors really have no choice but to indict unless the prosecution's case is very weak.

Because grand juries only hear part of the case, trial juries are more important. Trial juries consist of 6 to 12 people who actually hear the facts of the case from both the prosecution and the defense. At the trial, the judge rules on matters of law, usually technical items regarding whether the jury can hear or see something. The jury decides matters of fact, such as whether they believe a witness is telling the truth. Once the jury hears all the facts, they render a verdict of either "guilty" or "not guilty." Sometimes, if a jury is unable to decide on an outcome, it is known as a "hung jury." The Fifth and Sixth Amendments guarantee the right to a jury trial in a criminal case while the right to a jury trial in a civil case is protected by the Seventh Amendment.

The jury's main role in a trial is weighing the **evidence** that the two sides provide. Evidence is defined as "any item or information offered to make the existence of a fact more or less probable."

A nineteenth-century painting of a jury

Evidence can take many forms and comes in three varieties: direct, circumstantial, or demonstrative. Direct evidence generally involves evidence directly related to the event in question. For example, a witness might testify to seeing a federal crime, e.g. a bank robbery, committed in their presence. Circumstantial evidence requires the jury to draw a conclusion from *indirect* evidence that does not directly prove the fact in question. For example, in a case of racial discrimination, the plaintiff, a black man working for a taxi company, shows that the defendant always assigned black men the worst taxis to drive and sent them to areas with few customers. These facts do not necessarily prove discrimination, but along with others they present a circumstantial case. Finally, demonstrative evidence involves objects that are presented to the jury to demonstrate something about the case. In the bank robbery case, demonstrative evidence would include the gun with the robber's fingerprints or photos of him robbing the bank. With all these types of evidence, it is the jury's job to evaluate the strength or weakness of the evidence to determine if they make the fact they are intended to prove more or less likely.

As evidence is submitted, it is subject to certain rules. The courts have determined that some evidence is by its nature, unreliable, and thus inadmissible. The judge has the final decision whether to admit evidence or not and he relies on a set of instructions known as the **Rules of Evidence**. Thus, for example, the courts will not accept evidence that has been obtained illegally. Most people feel that illegally obtained evidence should be excluded, for example, when government agents break into a person's home, but courts often apply the so-called **Exclusionary Rule** to reject evidence that seemingly has been legally discovered. This excessive application of the Exclusionary Rule has caused some people to question whether juries are really being allowed to hear and see all the facts of a case, or are they finding guilty people "not guilty" because judges are not doing their jobs.

STATE AND FEDERAL COURTS WORK IN PARALLEL

Article 3, Section 1 established the Supreme Court and lower courts that Congress may create. The main role of this "Supreme Court" is to review the decisions of "lower courts," that is, the federal courts that Congress creates, and decisions of state courts insofar as they depend on federal law. Although state courts are not mentioned in Article 3, during the debates in the Constitutional Convention, Madison and others made it clear that the Supreme Court was to have authority to review state court decisions with respect to issues of federal law. In *Federalist 82*, Hamilton explicitly states that the Supreme Court could hear appeals from state courts on matters of federal law. Moreover, the *Judiciary Act of 1789* authorized the Supreme Court to hear appeals from state courts on matters of federal law, but only on matters of federal law.

The Supreme Court does not hear appeals from state courts regarding interpretations of state statutes. The authoritative interpretation and application of state law is left to state courts.

Article 6, the Supremacy Clause, assumes that state judges will decide matters of federal law, and provides that "*This Constitution, and the Laws of the United States which shall be made in Pursuance thereof… shall be the supreme Law of the Land; and the Judges in every State shall be bound thereby…*" Prior to the adoption of the Constitution, each state had its own functioning court system based upon English common law. After the adoption of the Constitution, these state courts continued to operate largely as they had previously. In *Federalist 82*, Hamilton clearly writes that state courts will have "jurisdiction in all cases" unless "expressly prohibited" by the Constitution. Thus, the federal courts were not intended to replace the state courts, but work side by side with state courts in certain limited areas. Just as the powers of Congress are limited to those areas specifically enumerated in the Constitution, so too, federal courts only have constitutional authority to decide cases in specific areas. This is called **federal jurisdiction**. The word "jurisdiction" literally means "to speak the law." A court has jurisdiction when the court has constitutional authority to decide the case. State courts are courts of "general jurisdiction," which means they can decide, or "hear," any case except in very few areas prohibited by the constitution. Federal courts are courts of "limited jurisdiction," which means they may only hear cases specifically permitted by the Constitution and also authorized by Congress.

FEDERAL COURT JURISDICTION

Article 3, Section 2 creates two types of federal jurisdiction. The first is based on the **nature of the case**, or the subject matter; while the second is based on the **nature of the parties**. Federal courts have jurisdiction when the case involves

the Constitution;

federal laws and treaties;

and matters involving admiralty and maritime jurisdiction.

In the second instance, federal courts have jurisdiction when the parties involved include

Ambassadors, foreign ministers, and consuls;

the United States;

two or more States;

a State and citizens of another State;

citizens of different States;

and between a State, or its citizens thereof, and a foreign government.

In other words, federal courts can hear cases based on federal law as well as certain disputes involving *interstate* or *international* parties even if there is no federal statute authorizing the specific cause of action. Cases arising under federal law are called **federal question jurisdiction**. Federal question jurisdiction means that the plaintiff alleges that the defendant has violated some federal law. Federal cases that are heard based on the international or interstate nature of the parties is called **diversity jurisdiction**. [Under the Eleventh Amendment (1795), a state can not be sued in federal court either by its own citizens, citizens of another state, or foreign citizens.]

Federal question jurisdiction relies on Congress's lawmaking power. Depending on how one reads Congress's power to make law under Article 1, this could be a very broad power. This point is best illustrated by the case of *Morrison v. United States* (2000). In 1994, Congress enacted a statute that allowed citizens claiming to be victims of some sort of "violence motivated by gender" to file civil suit in federal court. In other words, if a woman claimed to have been attacked because the attacker hated women, a suit could be brought in federal court. This suit would be a federal question suit because the case arises under federal law. Ultimately, the federal courts dismissed the suit explaining that assault involving two citizens of the same state was a local matter that Congress could not federalize. The Supreme Court said that disputes between two citizens of the same state were areas of law reserved to the state and had to be adjudicated in state court. Thus, cases arising under the Constitution, federal law, and treaties depend upon how broadly one interprets the powers of Congress and the Constitution.

Article 3 section 2 sets the outer limits of federal court jurisdiction. No federal court can hear any case that does not fall within one of the enumerated areas, that is, "arises under" federal question or diversity jurisdiction. For example, suppose a person signs a contract to buy 500 rifles from a factory in his own state but the factory fails to deliver them. Suppose also that the factory claims it cannot deliver the rifles because a federal law makes that type of rifle illegal. Can the purchaser sue the factory in federal court? No. First, there is no diversity jurisdiction because the parties, the factory and the customer, come from the same state. Second, because breach of contract violates state, not federal law, there is no federal question jurisdiction. Thus, it is not the type of case a federal court can hear. The dispute arises under state law, even though the defense might argue an issue of federal law.

In theory, Congress could authorize all suits between citizens of different states to take place in federal court. However, Congress has always restricted such suits to issues involving a substantial amount of money. Today, suits based on diversity of citizenship must involve more than $75,000.

FEDERAL DISTRICT COURTS

The judicial process begins when someone who believes that they have suffered an injury seeks legal compensation from the injurer. The plaintiff must determine that they have a cause of action and, if they do, whether it arises under state law or federal law. For example, a negligence suit, such as a driver hitting a pedestrian, will almost always be adjudicated in state court. The federal government can be sued if one of its agents is negligent, e.g. the driver is a federal employee, but this type of suit must be brought in federal court. If the cause of action arises under state law, then the case must be brought in a state court, unless the parties are citizens of different states, where diversity jurisdiction may exist. If the cause of action arises under federal law, then the action can be brought in federal court, and, usually, also state court.

Imagine that Smith sues Jones claiming that Jones illegally discriminated against him on the basis of his race. Although Smith could file in either state or federal court, he decides to file a discrimination suit in federal court. The filing of the lawsuit begins the trial process.

Most federal trials are heard in the **federal district courts**, the lowest level of courts in the federal system. These are also called "trial courts" to distinguish them from appellate courts which review the decisions of the trial courts. There are ninety-four different federal districts. Each state has at least one federal district, but larger states may have more than one. The federal district courts possess **original jurisdiction** which means they resolve the case in the first instance. As a result, district courts hear about 80% of all federal cases.

The judges in the district court are called district court judges. Only Congress can remove a district court judge. District court judges are Article 3 judges because they are appointed and confirmed pursuant to Article 3 of the Constitution.

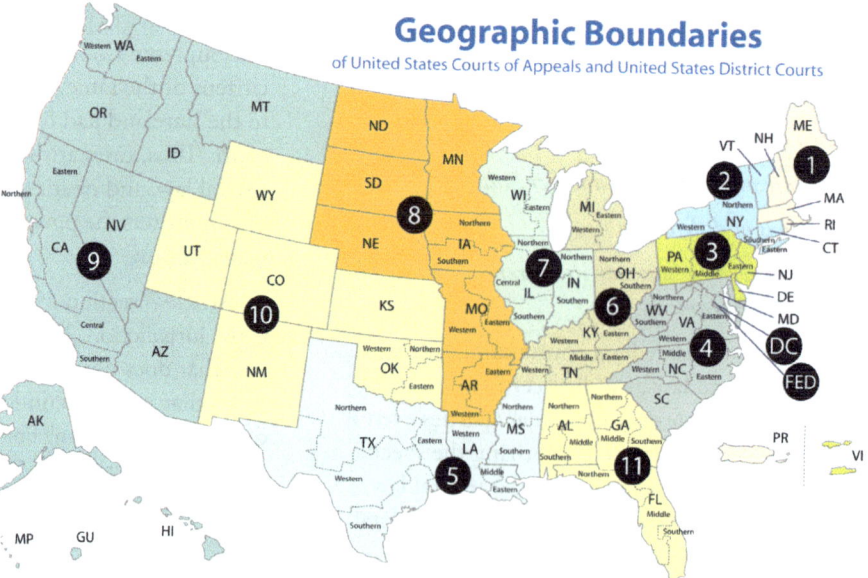

Geographic Boundaries of United States Courts of Appeals and United States District Courts

THE APPEALS COURTS

Once the trial court has rendered a decision, the losing party has a right to appeal to the **U.S. Court of Appeals**. The Appeals Court reviews the decision and the procedure of the district court to ensure there were no legal errors. Appeals courts do not hear facts and possess no original jurisdiction. They only have appellate jurisdiction which means that they can review appeals from lower courts and from administrative agencies. Because they are not finding facts, appellate courts do not conduct trials or even examine evidence. Instead, attorneys submit legal arguments known as **briefs** to a panel of judges. The briefs of the losing party point out the legal errors the attorney believes the lower court committed in rendering its decision. The winning party also submits briefs, but theirs support the lower court decision. Usually the briefs contain arguments citing **precedents**, which are earlier similar cases that support or oppose the decision of the lower court.

Once the judges have read the briefs, the court will hold **oral argument** in which the parties can explain their briefs. The judges can ask the attorneys questions about their legal positions or to provide a greater explanation of some point made in the brief. Appellate judges will render their decisions based on the briefs, oral arguments, the record of the trial court, and any applicable precedents. The judges can either affirm the decision of the lower court or reverse it if they believe that some legal mistake occurred at the trial. In the event a decision is reversed, a new trial may be ordered.

Congress created the federal Appellate Court system a little over 130 years ago as the number of cases being appealed to the Supreme Court became rather high. Today, there are thirteen Appellate Courts, including one for the District of Columbia. The U.S. Court of Appeals for the District of Columbia Circuit is considered the second highest court in the nation as it handles administrative law cases that arise from federal government agencies based in D.C. Because it makes so many important decisions, Supreme Court nominees are often selected from this Court. As of June 2024, four current Supreme Court Justices previously served on the D.C. Circuit: John Roberts, Clarence Thomas, Brett Kavanaugh, and Ketanji Brown Jackson.

THE SUPREME COURT

A person who loses in the Court of Appeals, or a state's supreme court, has no *right* to an additional appeal; however, they may ask the U.S. Supreme Court to review their case. The losing party may file a petition for **certiorari** ("to make certain"). In the 19th century, the Supreme Court heard every appeal, but in the early 20th century, Congress established the current system allowing the Supreme Court to accept only those cases it wishes.

The Supreme Court possesses original jurisdiction in matters involving foreign diplomats and states, and appellate jurisdiction in cases from state supreme courts and federal appeals courts. Nearly all cases the Court hears are appeals, not questions of original jurisdiction. The Supreme Court only takes about sixty cases each year. Usually, these are only the most important cases and often involve differences of opinion between federal circuits.

Although in recent decades, the Supreme Court has become the most powerful branch of government, this was not always the case. Until the 1950s and the *Warren* Court, Congress and the President exercised a great deal of control over the Court. For example, Congress allocated the number of Justices to sit on the Court. In 1869, Congress determined that there would be one Chief Justice and eight Associate Justices. Many people believe that Franklin Roosevelt's "court packing plan" was an attempt to bully the Court into deciding cases in favor of the New Deal. More recently, and far less successfully, Joe Biden talked about adding more Justices to the Court. Most legal scholars believe that nine is the perfect number of Justices as it allows for discussion without becoming unwieldy.

Nearly all states have a three-level judiciary reflective of the federal system. Every state has at least one level of appellate court. Most states have an intermediate level of appeal and the state supreme court. Once a **litigant** (the party involved in the lawsuit) has exhausted all his state appeals, he may ask the U.S. Supreme Court to review issues of *federal* law.

Criminal cases follow the same structure as civil

The Warren Court

cases. The primary difference is the role of the jury. Once a jury **acquits**, that is, finds the accused "not guilty," the state may not appeal. Criminal defendants may always appeal a "guilty" verdict. As in civil cases, a state criminal conviction must exhaust state appeals, after which the criminal defendant can seek review by the U.S. Supreme Court with respect to issues of federal law.

Unlike Congress, which is quite open to the public and televised, until rather recently, the Supreme Court has been cloaked in mystery. Few people are privy to its secrets. In 1979, *The Brethren*, one of the first non-fiction accounts of the Court, became a bestseller. Although the Court began recording oral arguments in 1955, the recordings were not made available until nearly a year later. Starting in 2010, audio recordings of all oral arguments heard by the Court began to be posted on the Court's website on the day they were made, thus making access to the Court much easier.

The Supreme Court convenes the first Monday in October and sits for approximately nine months during which it hears about sixty cases. During the 2022-2023 term, the Court heard exactly sixty cases. Of these cases, two were issues of original jurisdiction involving states and six were appeals from state or district courts. Traditionally, the Court delivers opinions on Tuesdays and Wednesdays.

Four of the nine justices must vote to hear a case. If that occurs, the case is set on the docket. Next, the **petitioner**, the one who has petitioned the Court to hear his case, files a brief setting forth the legal arguments which support their position. After the petitioner files their brief, their opponent, the **respondent**, also files a brief explaining their legal position. Usually, because Supreme Court cases are so important, additional briefs, known as **amicus curiae**, or "friend of the court" briefs, are filed by parties who are not parties to the case but who wish the Court to consider other issues not addressed by the main parties. For example, in an abortion case, the United States Conference of Catholic Bishops might submit a brief detailing the history of pro-life legislation from the time of the passage of the Constitution until the present-day. Once the briefs have been submitted, the Justices read them and verify that the cases cited in them are good precedents.

Next, the Court hears oral arguments. Oral arguments are heard for two weeks each month from October through April on Mondays, Tuesdays, and Wednesdays. Oral arguments are open to the public – although seating is very limited. Oral arguments last one hour with each side receiving exactly half an hour to make its case. Although attorneys practice making a half-hour speech, almost no attorney speaks for more than a few seconds before the Justices interrupt with questions they have regarding the legal points

The first photograph of the U.S. Supreme Court

in the briefs the attorneys have submitted. Often, the Justices ask the attorneys hypothetical questions based on how a decision would impact society. Attorneys need to be prepared to answer very difficult questions and most attorneys practice this as well.

After hearing the oral arguments, the Justices meet each Friday in what is known as the **Justices' Conference**, during which they will decide the case. Since the late 19th century, the Justices have begun their meeting with the "conference handshake," in which each justice shakes hands with the others as a sign of respect and friendship to remind them that although they may share differences of opinions they can work together. Because they discuss extremely important matters which massively impact society, as well as their need to communicate openly and honestly with each other, only the Justices can attend the conference.

Historically, the Justices' Conference begins with the Chief Justice giving his views on the case followed by the other justices in order of seniority. At this point, it becomes clear how the justices are going to vote, at least on the outcome, if not the actual legal reasoning of the case. Today, the Justices are generally set in their positions and not swayed by arguments presented by other justices. However, to reach a stronger opinion, justices might be willing to compromise slightly.

Once the discussion has ended, the Justices vote on the case. Five Justices need to agree on the outcome and the reasons which support the outcome to render a decision. In a case where a majority of the Court agrees, the decision of the Court is known as the **majority opinion**, while the decision of the "losing" side is known as the **dissenting opinion**. Often, a justice agrees with the decision of the majority, but has a slight disagreement with the reason they reached their decision. In such a case, the justice might write a **concurring opinion**. It is not unusual in a difficult or controversial case for there to be several concurring and dissenting opinions. Finally, and of greatest precedential value, are **unanimous decisions**, in which all the justices agree. Amazingly, while one would expect unanimous decisions to be quite rare, especially given the Court's *apparent* 6-3 "conservative" membership, during the 2022 term, 48% of decisions were unanimous, which is consistent with the Court over the last thirty years.

Since its earliest days, the Court has issued written opinions. The choice of the author of the opinion is based upon who is in the majority or the minority.

Because he is the head Justice, whether he is in the majority or minority, the Chief Justice decides who writes that opinion. He can write it himself or assign it to another Justice. The most senior Justice on the other side decides who writes that opinion.

Because so much research needs to be done checking briefs and precedents, Justices rely heavily upon their clerks. Many clerks eventually become Supreme Court Justices themselves. Of the nine current members, only Clarence Thomas and Samuel Alito did *not* clerk for a former Supreme Court Justice.

Once the opinion has been assigned, the Justice must write an opinion that the other Justices in the majority will sign. Technically, a Justice can change their vote until the opinion has been published, and there have been a few instances where Justices have changed their votes when they did not like an opinion. The Court releases its decisions on "Opinion Day," which usually occurs on Monday. With very few exceptions, the Court releases its opinions by the end of the term. Unanimous decisions and non-controversial decisions are usually issued more quickly. Controversial decisions might not be handed down until the last day of the term. Once the decision has been publicly issued, the case is ended. The Court has created a precedent which other courts must follow unless they can distinguish it.

PRECEDENT AND STARE DECISIS

The job of most courts is to resolve disputes between a particular plaintiff and defendant. However, court decisions can affect other people unrelated to the plaintiff or defendant. In the above example, when Smith sues Jones for illegal racial discrimination, Smith claims that Jones fired him because he was Canadian. The Court might dismiss the suit, ruling that as a matter of law, "Canadian" is not a racial classification; so, firing a Canadian does not violate a statute making it illegal to fire someone on the basis of race. The losing party may decide to appeal that decision to a higher court, which has additional consequences.

Suppose that a new, but similar, situation arises. Abel fires Baker because Baker is Canadian. How does the court decision between Smith and Jones affect Abel and Baker? Under English common law, precedent was followed in later cases. As previously noted, precedent means applying the law established by an earlier similar case. When Abel fires Baker because he is Canadian, Baker sues Abel. The case goes before the same judge who now rules that Canadian *is* a racial classification and *does not* dismiss the suit. Abel rightly complains that this a fundamental injustice because the judge had said that Canadian was not a racial classification and he relied on the ruling (precedent) to fire Baker.

For one judge to rule on different sides of the same issue over a very short period of time violates the principle "treat like cases alike." Acting contrary to this principle is not just unjust but illogical. It is so illogical and so unjust that litigants will suspect the judge is ruling based on improper criteria, such as personal animus or bribery. This injustice is obvious when one judge rules on opposite sides of the same issue; but suppose *Abel v. Baker* came before a different judge. Judge Two disagrees with Judge One and rules that Canadian is a racial classification. This is not an obvious logical or legal contradiction, but still presents a problem. If a court told Smith that he could fire Canadians, should Abel not be allowed to rely on that ruling whether he is in front of Judge One or Judge Two?

In the United States, because there are so many federal and state courts, the situation is quite complicated as many different judges render decisions. Suppose Smith sues Jones in California, either in state or federal court, on the basis of a federal statute making it illegal to fire someone on account of race. The California court dismisses the suit because Canadian is not a race. Baker sues Abel in New York a month later on the same basis. The New York court is *not required* to follow the California court. The California court decision may be considered **persuasive authority**, and some judges may think they should follow earlier court rulings to be consistent, unless there is a good reason to depart from them. However, the California decision is not **binding precedent**. Binding precedent means that later judges *are required* to follow the earlier ruling.

In matters involving conflicting case decisions from the same state or the same circuit, appellate courts become involved. One of the most important roles of appellate courts is resolving disputes between lower courts. Suppose that a federal court in California rules that Canadian is not a race, but a federal court in Nevada rules that Canadian is a race. The Court of Appeals for the states west of the Rockies, the Ninth Circuit, can resolve this issue. Once the Ninth Circuit Court of Appeals has ruled on the issue in a **published case** that Canadian is or is not a race, that published decision is binding precedent on district courts in the Ninth Circuit.

If the legal issue being appealed to the Court of Appeals has not been decided before, then the issue is called one of **first impression**. In matters of first impression, the Court is free to decide the case any way it wishes. If there is existing precedent from the circuit, or the Supreme Court, then the court must follow the precedent. Once a federal court of appeals decides something and issues a published decision, then the district courts in that circuit and the judges of the circuit court must follow that precedent until it is reversed.

There are a few ways that a Circuit Court precedent can be overturned. One involves Congress repealing or amending the law at issue. Also, the president may amend the regulation at issue. If the law changes, then the precedent is said to have been "superseded" and is no longer "good law." The most common way for a circuit precedent to be overturned is that the U.S. Supreme Court overrules it.

While various federal and state courts might take different views on a legal question, once the Supreme Court decides that legal issue, all state and federal courts are required to follow that precedent—at least in theory. In fact, it is surprising how often lower courts fail, or refuse, to apply precedent from the Supreme Court or the Court of Appeals. When a lower court says that a precedent is not applicable to a given case then the court is said to **distinguish** the two cases. For example, lower courts have been notoriously unwilling to follow Supreme Court precedent on gun ownership. In 2008, the Supreme Court declared that there was a constitutional right for Americans to own firearms for personal protection.[2] In 2015, two Supreme Court justices openly accused lower court judges of simply ignoring and flouting Supreme Court precedent when it came to gun control.[3] Because the Supreme Court takes so few cases each year, lower courts estimate, correctly, that if they ignore Supreme Court precedent that the Court will be unable to do much about it.

Generally, courts follow a rule called **stare decisis** which means "to stand" (*stare*) with decisions (*decisis*) or "to stand with what has been decided" or "let the decision stand." This is actually a very ancient maxim which holds that changes in law are normally to be avoided. In his treatise on law, Aquinas wrote that "… human law should never be changed, unless, in some way or another, the common weal be compensated… or from the extreme urgency of the case, due to the fact that either the existing law is clearly unjust, or its observance extremely harmful."

Moreover, people rely upon existing laws to plan their lives and businesses. Imagine someone moving to a state because of its very parent-friendly home-schooling laws. If one day a court decides to require all teachers, including home educators, to be certified by the state, that impacts the family. Frequent changes in law, or changes in the

---

[2] *District of Columbia v. Heller*, 554 U.S. 570 (2008).
[3] *Friedman v. City of Highland Park, Ill.*, 577 U.S. 1039 (2015).

interpretation of law, negatively impact society.

In the last few decades, presidents have nominated judges to the Supreme Court based upon how they are expected to vote, especially regarding social issues like abortion, euthanasia, or parental-rights. The idea is that these judges will either uphold or overturn precedent depending on their political persuasion. For example, consider a situation in which the Supreme Court was narrowly divided on the issue of Free Speech and decides a case by a five to four vote. Suppose the next year one of the justices in the majority dies and is replaced by a judge who sides with the previous minority. Now there is a new decision which reverses the previous one. The next year one of the judges in the new majority dies and is replaced with someone who swings the Court back to its original decision.[4] Everyone agrees this would be chaotic and ought to be avoided. *Stare decisis* means that previous decisions should be followed unless there is some compelling reason to reverse or overrule them.

The doctrine of *stare decisis* possesses some dangers. Just as lower courts may ignore a precedent and distinguish a case, the Supreme Court sometimes does the same thing. For example, in 1984, the Supreme Court held that it did *not* violate the Constitution for a local government to pay for and erect a nativity display on privately owned land. *Lynch v. Donnelly* (1984). Just five years later, the Supreme Court voted that a nativity display on public land, but privately owned, was unconstitutional. *County of Allegheny v. Am. Civ. Liberties Union Greater Pittsburgh Chapter*, 492 U.S. 573, 667 (1989). The dissenting justices did not understand why "placement of a government-owned crèche on private land is lawful while placement of a privately-owned crèche on public land is not." The dissent felt the two cases were not distinguishable.

Even worse than a frequent change in law or precedent are arbitrary decisions based on trivial differences. In this situation, no one even knows what the law is because there are conflicting precedents.

Thus, while frequent change in law is not a good idea, when there are conflicting precedents or a prior precedent is clearly wrong, then precedents can and should be changed. The Supreme Court has reversed itself dozens of times, and no one thinks that Supreme Court precedent should *never* change. The most famous recent example of this occurred in 2022 when the Supreme Court reversed itself in overturning decades of precedent holding abortion to be a constitutional right.

THE "LEAST DANGEROUS" BRANCH

Under the American system of government, Congress makes the laws, the president enforces them, and the federal courts interpret them. Thus, it seems that the Courts are the least powerful branch of government having no power either to enact or enforce laws. While the Founders may have believed this, over time, the Courts have become the most powerful branch of government, even, in the minds of many, usurping the authority of the other two branches to make and enforce laws.

In 1686, in the decision of *Godden v Hales*, England's highest court said that King James could appoint Sir Edward Hales to be a royal officer despite a law saying no Catholics could be military officers. James's opponents in Parliament argued that Parliament made laws and it was the responsibility of judges to *enforce the law as written*, not to find some legal technicality to override Parliament. People then, as now, argued that the proper role of

Sir Edward Hales

---

[4] Historically, Justices serve on the Supreme Court for an average of nine years, so this hypothetical is extremely unlikely in real life.

judges is to settle specific disputes between litigants, and not set national policy. In the United States, people were even more democratic and egalitarian than in England. Both then and now, many people fear that unelected federal judges could impose an agenda contrary to popular opinion.

The Articles of Confederation had no separate judicial branch of government. However, Article 3 Section 1 of the new Constitution created the Supreme Court which was made independent of Congress and the president. The president appoints judges with the concurrence of the Senate but once appointed Article 3 judges serve during "good behavior." This means judges serve for life unless they are impeached which is *very* difficult.[5] Moreover, the Constitution provides that the compensation for judges "shall not be diminished during their Continuance in Office." In other words, Congress cannot cut off the salary of judges to make them retire.

In *Federalist* 78, Hamilton explains that lifetime appointment is crucial to ensure that judges are not subject to undue pressure from the president:

> Periodical appointments, however regulated, or by whomsoever made, would, in some way or other, be fatal to their necessary independence. If the power of making them was committed either to the Executive or legislature, there would be danger of an improper complaisance to the branch which possessed it[.]

Imagine if someone were brought into court on a criminal charge and the president not only appointed the prosecutor but also appointed the judge who he could fire if the judge ruled in ways the president did not like. This is why judges are supposed to be independent and not answerable to the president. Judges need to be unbiased and not influenced by the prospect of losing their position.

As with the separation of powers between the Executive and Legislative branches, an independent Judiciary is intended to be a check on the other branches. The Framers thought that separating the power to make law and the power to execute the law should be divided. This principle applies to the courts, because the courts are often the institution that enforces law. For example, Congress makes counterfeiting money a crime, but people charged with counterfeiting must be tried by an independent and impartial court. There are a variety of problems that might result from a system where the same people who wrote the law also enforced the law or tried cases enforcing the law.

For example, suppose Congressman Tom Jones wrote a criminal law: "The Jones Law." If Congressman Jones became Judge Jones and tried a case prosecuting a "Jones Law" violation, Judge Jones might have a personal bias to ensure that his law is "effective." Judge Jones also might refuse to admit that there is any ambiguity in the law. St. Thomas tells us that laws must give a person adequate notice as to what the law requires. The basic idea is that judges must bring a fresh, unbiased perspective to enforcing the law, which is more difficult when a judge helps write the law.

While courts are part of the system of "checks and balances" that keep the government within proper bounds, the courts themselves need to be subject to checks and balances. For example, the anti-Federalist "Brutus" argued that the new federal judges would be too independent and abuse their power. Hamilton was well aware that if judges are too independent they might usurp authority not given to them and use their power for evil. He tried to convince early Americans that anti-Federalist concerns about the courts were exaggerated. In *Federalist* 78, Hamilton famously wrote:

> Whoever attentively considers the different departments of power must perceive, that, in a government in which they are separated from each other, the judiciary, from the nature of its functions, will always be the least dangerous to the political rights of the Constitution; because it will be least in a capacity to annoy or injure them. The Executive not only dispenses the honors, but holds the sword of the community. The legislature not only commands the purse, but prescribes the rules by which the duties and rights of every citizen are to be regulated. The judiciary, on the contrary, has no influence over either the sword or the purse; no direction either of the strength or of the wealth of the society; and can take no active resolution whatever. It may truly be said to have neither FORCE nor WILL, but merely judgment; and must ultimately depend

---

[5] Historically, only about 15 federal judges have been impeached.

upon the aid of the executive arm even for the efficacy of its judgments.

Aquinas took largely the same view as Hamilton about the role of judges. Aquinas argued that judges do not make law. Their job is simply to apply the law to a particular case.[6] Judges must apply the law as written, not as they think it should have been written. The exception to this is that no one may ever cooperate in evil, so an unjust statute is not a law at all and may not be followed by anyone. Even in a case of a clearly unjust statute, it would still not be proper for a judge to rewrite the law. The judge would need to refuse to participate in its implementation.

Hamilton's comment that the judiciary will be "the least dangerous to the political rights of the Constitution" has become an oft cited aphorism by critics of the courts. The comment that courts "must ultimately depend upon the aid of the executive" raises a particular difficulty. The last chapter addressed the requirement that the president ensure the laws are faithfully enforced. Some people argue that legal judgments are a kind of "law" that the president must enforce. Yet, Hamilton's comment that must "ultimately depend upon the aid of the executive" suggests that the president may refuse to enforce judgments when judicial rulings are beyond the proper sphere of the courts. This is part of "checks and balances." Just as the judiciary should be to some degree independent of the executive, that independence must go both ways. Hamilton indicates that the president is not required to slavishly obey every command of federal judges, especially if he reasonably believes a judgment to be beyond the power of the judge who issued it. St. Thomas says that for any public official to issue a command beyond the power entrusted to him is not law, but a perversion of law.[7]

One of the most infamous examples of this occurred in 1832 when President Andrew Jackson refused to comply with a Supreme Court decision. The United States had a treaty with the Cherokee Indians that guaranteed them certain lands. However, in the early 1830s, the United States decided to forcibly remove the Cherokee from their land in Georgia and then move west of the Mississippi River. The Cherokee brought suit in federal court demanding that the court enforce the treaty. The Supreme Court sided with the Cherokee, saying that evicting them was a violation of the treaty. President Jackson reportedly said "John Marshall [Chief Justice of the Supreme Court] has made his decision; now let him enforce it." Jackson sent federal troops to remove the Cherokees, thousands of whom died during this removal. The route from Georgia to Oklahoma is called the *Trail of Tears*.

Aside from the government's brutally unjust treatment of the Cherokees, Jackson's actions clearly violated the Constitution. Adjudication of treaties was something federal courts were explicitly empowered to do under the Constitution which says that "the judicial Power shall extend to all Cases … arising under this Constitution, the Laws of the United States, and Treaties made." Accordingly, there does not seem to have been any serious argument that adjudicating a treaty was improper for the Supreme Court.

Jackson's actions have been used to argue that presidents must enforce court decisions otherwise the president is acting like a king or the discredited Jackson. However, the misapplication of a principle does not mean the principle is wrong. Hamilton

St. Thomas Aquinas

---

[6] Summa Th. II-II, Q. 60.
[7] Summa Th. II-II q. 60, art 6.

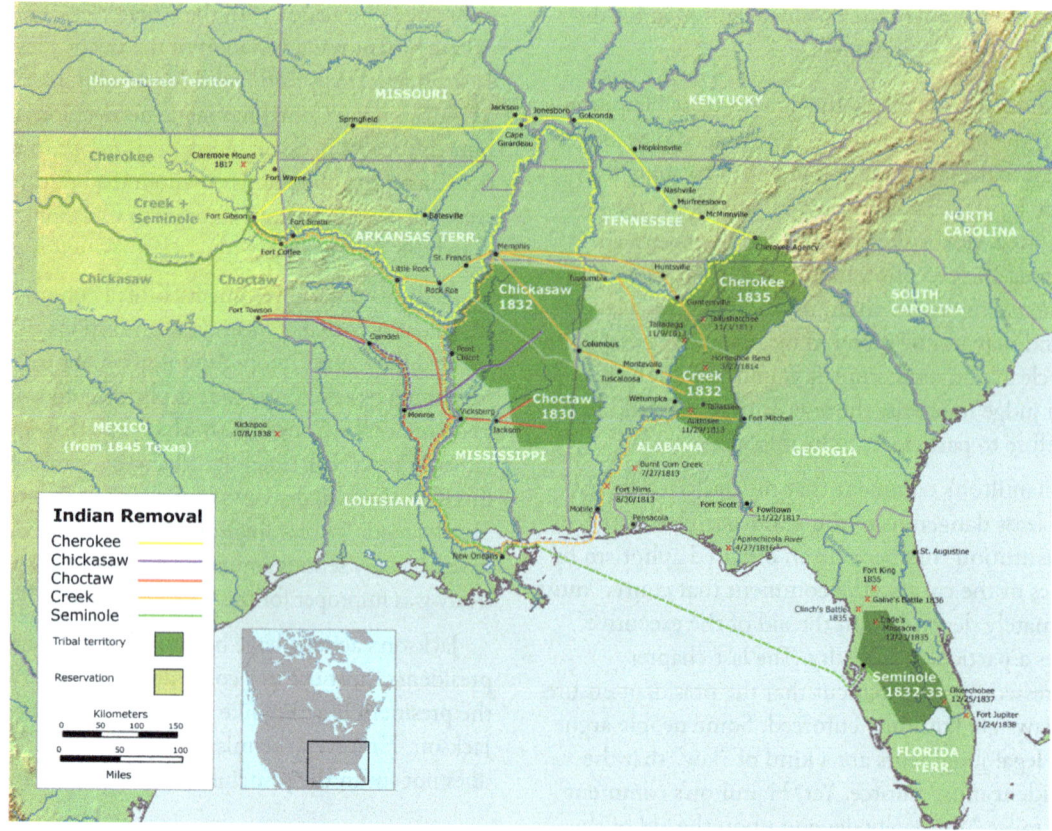

and other Founders clearly thought there would be legitimate situations in which courts exceeded their authority and ought to be opposed. For example, in *Federalist* 33, Hamilton states that actions of the federal government "which are *not pursuant* to its constitutional powers, but which are invasions of the residuary authorities of the smaller societies … will be merely acts of usurpation, and will deserve to be treated as such."

Hamilton also makes the point in *Federalist* 78 that Congress "commands the purse," and "the judiciary, on the contrary, has no influence over either the sword or the purse; no direction either of the strength or of the wealth of the society." Only Congress has authority to authorize spending. So, for example, the Supreme Court could not order the federal government to create a national healthcare system, because that would require expenditure of money.

In addition to control of "the purse," the Constitution gives Congress enormous power over the court system itself. First, Congress need not establish any "inferior" federal courts. Second, if Congress does establish lower courts it can invest them with as little jurisdiction as Congress chooses. Moreover, Article 3 provides that:

> In all Cases affecting Ambassadors, other public Ministers and Consuls, and those in which a State shall be Party, the supreme Court shall have original Jurisdiction. In all the other Cases … the supreme Court shall have appellate Jurisdiction, both as to Law and Fact, with such Exceptions, and under such Regulations as the Congress shall make.

Thus, Congress has broad authority to make exceptions and regulations to the Supreme Court's appellate jurisdiction.

"JUDICIAL REVIEW"

In the first decades after ratification of the Constitution, the Supreme Court was deferential to Congress. For example, in November 1794, the United States signed the *Jay Treaty* with Britain that increased trade between the two countries. France viewed the *Jay Treaty* as a "stab in the back," because

France helped the United States win its war of independence against the British. In 1796, France's revolutionary government authorized French ships to begin seizing American merchant ships, which was an act of war. In 1798, Congress passed the *Sedition Act* because it was concerned about getting dragged into France and Britain's war.

The *Sedition Act* was an attempt by the Federalists to tamp down debate about war. The Act formed part of a series of laws known collectively as the "Alien and Sedition Acts." Under the Sedition Act, it was a crime to falsely and maliciously criticize the government. Many people, including Jefferson and Madison, thought that the Sedition Act was unconstitutional; but, the federal courts unhesitatingly enforced it.

The Supreme Court never issued an opinion on the Sedition Act; however, it upheld convictions on appeal without substantive discussion of the merits. Moreover, individual Justices presided over trials for sedition, and they enforced the Act. Justice Samuel Chase, presided over two famous prosecutions under the Sedition Act. Samuel Chase was one of the most important leaders of the early United States. He was a member of the Continental Congress from Maryland, a signer of the Declaration of Independence, and a member of the Maryland state convention that ratified the Constitution. In fact, as an anti-Federalist, he served on a committee at the Maryland ratifying convention that was established to recommend amendments for a Bill of Rights. Chase's background shows that he possessed an excellent understanding of the Constitutional role of the federal courts.

The first important Sedition case Justice Chase heard was the trial of James Thompson Callender. In 1799, Callender attacked President Adams' policy regarding the conflict with France and England, but his publication also called Adams a liar and a coward. He was prosecuted under the Sedition Act. Callender argued that the Sedition Act was unconstitutional. Justice Chase responded that any act of Congress carried a strong presumption of constitutionality and he convicted Callender.

The other famous case involved the prosecution of Thomas Cooper who also published a pamphlet criticizing President Adams. In his ruling, Justice Chase seemed to say that even if a law were unconstitutional, Congress or the people needed to correct it, not judges. Chase said that because the

Samuel Chase

people chose the Congress and the president, "… if any improper law is enacted, the people have it in their power to obtain the repeal of such law, or even of the constitution itself, if found defective, since provision is made for its amendment." Chase's point is that in a Republic, unelected judges should not second guess the people's elected representatives but apply the law as written unless there was an indisputable violation of the explicit provisions of the Constitution.

Just a few years later, however, the Supreme Court seemed to take a more expansive view of its powers. The celebrated case of *Marbury v. Madison* involved the appointment of William Marbury to be a Justice of the Peace in the District of Columbia. In 1800, John Adams lost the presidential election to Thomas Jefferson. Knowing that Jefferson would put members of the Democratic-Republican Party on the federal judiciary, Adams sought to "pack the courts" with members of his party, the Federalists. As part of the plan, Congress created several new judicial positions. Adams signed these commissions which authorized the men to take office and gave the commissions to his Secretary of State, **John Marshall**, who delivered all but seventeen of the commissions before Adams' term of office expired. Because this procedure occurred at the last minute, these appointments became known as "midnight judges." One of the midnight judges who failed to receive his commission was William Marbury.

When Thomas Jefferson became president, he wanted to appoint his own people to the various judicial offices, not midnight judges. Consequently, Jefferson argued that the appointment of Marbury was not final. Although President Adams had signed a commission appointing Marbury, the action was not final until the Secretary of State delivered it; and Jefferson ordered James Madison, the new Secretary of State, *not* to deliver the commissions. In response, Marbury filed suit against James Madison asking the federal court to order Madison to deliver the commission so that Marbury could begin his job. Marbury asked the court to issue a "writ of mandamus," a court order directing that a party to the suit take some action.

The crux of the case revolved around the original jurisdiction of the Supreme Court and the *Judiciary Act of 1789*. Marbury argued that the *Judiciary Act* allowed him to bring suit in the Supreme Court as an original matter, regardless of what the Constitution said about original jurisdiction. Under Article 3, the Supreme Court only has original jurisdiction in cases "affecting Ambassadors, other public Ministers and Consuls, and those in which a State shall be Party…" The *Judiciary Act of 1789* appeared to expand the Supreme Court's original jurisdiction beyond those involving ambassadors and states, particularly to include granting writs of mandamus. However, the Judiciary Act did not *explicitly* say that the Supreme Court had original jurisdiction to issue writs of mandamus. Nevertheless, Marbury claimed the Act meant that the Court did have the authority, and filed suit in the Supreme Court as an exercise of original jurisdiction. At this point, the case took a decidedly political turn.

In 1801, John Marshall, Adams' former Secretary of State, became Chief Justice of the Supreme Court. As Chief Justice, he possessed enormous power and he wrote the decision in *Marbury v. Madison*. In Marshall's decision, the Supreme Court agreed with Marbury's interpretation of the *Judiciary Act*, saying it had indeed attempted to expand the original jurisdiction of the Supreme Court beyond what the Constitution permitted. However, the Court explained that Congress lacked the power to "give this court appellate jurisdiction, where the

John Marshall

constitution has declared their jurisdiction shall be original; and original jurisdiction where the constitution has declared it shall be appellate…."

Such a ruling caused a problem because the Constitution said the Supreme Court lacked original jurisdiction over Marbury's suit, but Congress *supposedly* had authorized the suit. What happens when a conflict arises between the Constitution and a law passed by Congress? In a unanimous decision, the Court said that when a court was asked to enforce a statute that was contrary to the Constitution, then the Constitution must take precedence. Marshall pointed out that judges had sworn to uphold the Constitution and it was "immoral" to demand that judges violate "what they swear to support!" Marshall recited the words of the judicial oath and asked rhetorically: Why does a judge swear to uphold the Constitution if judges are expected to ignore it when Congress says so? Of course, Saint Thomas and Catholic teaching agree. No government can demand that citizens violate the moral law, and if ordered to act immorally then citizens and officials must refuse to obey.

All *Marbury v. Madison* actually *said* was that the Supreme Court could not exercise original jurisdiction in Marbury's case because under the

Constitution, original jurisdiction only applies to cases involving ambassadors or states. However, the case *implied* much more than this and has been understood to stand for even more expansive principles. First, Marshall went out of his way to insist that Congress had violated the Constitution. The Court might simply have said that it did not read the Judiciary Act as authorizing original jurisdiction in the case and left it at that. Second, not only did the Court criticize Congress, it purposely poked a stick in the eyes of Jefferson and Madison. Despite not having jurisdiction, the Court ruled on the merits of the case anyway writing:

> To withhold the commission [of Marbury], therefore, is an act deemed by the Court not warranted by law, but violative of a vested legal right.

Thus, Madison and Jefferson were wrong to refuse to give Marbury his job, but the Court had no jurisdiction to order Madison to deliver the commission. Normally, a court considers the issue of jurisdiction, but if it lacks jurisdiction, it dismisses the case without addressing the merits. Sometimes, when there is not an actual controversy, a court will issue an **advisory opinion**. Although many state courts issue advisory opinions, the Supreme Court says it will not issue advisory opinions, even though it seemed to do exactly that in *Marbury*.

The real importance of *Marbury* stands for its creation of a very broad principle. *Marbury* involved a statute that purportedly authorized the Court to exercise power beyond those granted by the Constitution. Does it follow from this that the Court has authority to tell other officials how they should do their job? For example, what if someone took offense at George Washington's proclamation of a National Day of Prayer and Thanksgiving and files suit in federal court asking a judge to order President Washington to revoke the day of prayer because his proclamation is unconstitutional. This takes the issue to a whole new level. It is one thing for judges to refuse to enforce a law that violates their oath to enforce the constitution, but it is quite another to tell the president, or a state governor, what he is permitted to do.

The far-reaching principle which emerged from the Marbury case, **that the courts can assess every act of Congress and determine if it is constitutional**, is called **judicial review**. *Marbury* did not post such broad authority for the Court. In fact, one could argue that *Marbury* is contrary to such a reading. Chief Justice Marshall said no human institution had authority to order a person to violate his sacred oath of office and simply obey Congress. How then, can a court order a president, or anyone else, to violate his sacred oath of office and just obey the Court's orders? That would seem to make the president a mere servant of the courts who cannot exercise his own judgment. That is no better than making judges mere servants of Congress.

The idea that *Marbury* was meant to create the power of judicial review is also undermined by the fact that it was several decades before the Supreme Court declared another act of Congress unconstitutional. In the early 19th century, the Supreme Court repeatedly declared state statutes to be unconstitutional. By 1850, the Supreme Court had declared twenty-four state laws to be unconstitutional, but no other federal law was declared unconstitutional until 1856. In 1856, the Supreme Court declared that the Missouri Compromise was unconstitutional in one of the most notorious cases in American history: *Dred Scott v. Sandford*.

In 1820, Congress enacted the Missouri Compromise by which slavery was "forever prohibited" in the Louisiana Territory, and in states formed within that territory, north and west of the borders of Missouri. The Compromise was necessary to maintain the balance of power in the Senate between "slave states" and "free states." At the time, many people regarded the Missouri Compromise as one of the most important laws ever passed because it allowed these two blocks of states to continue to exist in a union rather than break apart.

The facts of *Dred Scott v. Sanford* are not disputed. Dred Scott, an enslaved person, and his "owner," Dr. John Emerson, an army physician, resided for three years in Illinois where slavery was illegal under the Missouri Compromise. Emerson and Scott moved around a bit, and Scott eventually married and had a daughter. Dr. Emerson died at the end of 1843, and Mrs. Irene Emerson "inherited" the Scott family. On April 6, 1846, Dred Scott and his wife filed suit in Missouri state court seeking to obtain their freedom based on the time spent in "free states." The case worked its way through the state court system before finally ending up before the U.S. Supreme Court. By this time, Irene Emerson's brother **John Sanford**, claimed to "own" the Scott family, so he was the party opposing Scott's freedom.

The Supreme Court decided that it lacked jurisdiction because the case did not present a federal question for appeal. It was essentially a question of state property law. Yet, as in *Marbury v. Madison*, the Court decided to resolve the substantive issue despite lacking jurisdiction. Through a very convoluted series of arguments, the majority said that Scott could not have become free by residing in Illinois because the Missouri Compromise was unconstitutional. It was the first time in more than fifty years that the Supreme Court declared an act of Congress unconstitutional. However, *Dred Scott* went much further than *Marbury*.

Marbury only said the Court itself would not exercise jurisdiction beyond its legitimate authority. The Court in *Dred Scott* seemed to say that the Court could review any act of Congress and reject it if contrary to the Constitution. Moreover, *Marbury* involved a minor dispute that impacted almost no one other than Marbury himself. *Dred Scott* involved the most significant issue of the time and impacted millions of Americans.

Dred Scott was incredibly controversial both in what was decided and how the Court reached its decision. People, then, as now, argue that the Constitution did not create the Supreme Court as a "super legislature" to sit in judgment of Congress. They asked, "Who are these few unelected justices who think they have more authority than the rest of the country combined?" In 1861, President Lincoln in his first inaugural address seemed to reject the whole idea of judicial review, explaining: "if the policy of the Government upon vital questions affecting the whole people is to be irrevocably fixed by decisions of the Supreme Court . . . the people will have ceased to be their own rulers."

Ultimately, *Dred Scott* was superseded by the 13th, 14th, and 15th Amendments. However, the legal community and the nation accepted the idea of "judicial review." By the end of the 19th century, the Supreme Court declared another twenty federal statutes unconstitutional. The rate has only increased. In the last decade the Supreme Court has declared twenty federal statutes unconstitutional.

Dred Scott

Because the Supreme Court only hears about sixty cases per year, lower courts resolve the vast majority of cases. Lower courts have declared hundreds of state and federal laws to be unconstitutional. Thus, Congress and state legislatures are often overridden by a few obscure judges that the average citizen has never heard of.

The idea of judicial review is not an absolute necessity. For most of English history the courts had to answer to the King or Parliament. Some countries, such as the Netherlands and Switzerland, require that courts enforce the law as written. Many countries, including most European nations, have a dedicated Constitutional Court which alone can declare a statute to be unconstitutional. Other courts must enforce the law as written or refer the issue to the Constitutional Court for a decision.

Article 3 of the Constitution gives Congress broad power to establish "inferior Courts" and determine their jurisdiction. Congress certainly could establish a Constitutional Court and give it exclusive jurisdiction to rule on constitutional challenges or restrict the appellate jurisdiction of the Supreme Court; however, neither is likely to happen. Sadly, most members of Congress are happy to let the courts determine social policy. This allows Congress to ignore important moral issues like abortion.

Consequently, in the 21st century, Judicial Review is well-entrenched and accepted. At this point, almost no one challenges the right of the Supreme Court to act as the final arbiter of questions of constitutional law. Whether the Court intended to create such a power by its decision in *Marbury v. Madison*, that was the result.

STATE SOVEREIGNTY, THE COURTS, AND THE ELEVENTH AMENDMENT

Among the issues that concerned anti-Federalists was *potential judgments against states in federal court*. If states could be held liable in federal court then states could be bankrupted or forced to adopt policies under threat of financial sanction. Two specific constitutional provisions in Article 3 apply to states.

First, Article 3 provides that "*In all Cases affecting Ambassadors, other public Ministers and Consuls, and those in which a State shall be Party, the supreme Court shall have original Jurisdiction.*" Congress was permitted to create lower federal courts, but the Constitution requires that any federal suit involving a state would "originate" in the Supreme Court. In *Federalist* 81, Hamilton assured his readers that people did not need to worry that some rogue federal judge could sanction a state because any suit involving a state could only be heard either in the state's own courts or in the Supreme Court. This principle was also included in the *Judiciary Act of 1789* which provided that "the Supreme Court shall have exclusive jurisdiction of all controversies of a civil nature, where a state is a party." *Marbury v. Madison* declared unequivocally that the Court's original and appellate jurisdictions were mutually exclusive. In other words, the Court cannot exercise appellate jurisdiction over areas where the Constitution says the jurisdiction is original. Even Congress could not change that because the original jurisdiction of some special cases is constitutionally required. Consequently, federal suits involving states must originate in the Supreme Court; thus, ensuring that a state could not be forced to answer to some lower court judge.

Amazingly, today, thousands of suits are brought against states every year in federal district courts. What happened? First, the federal courts decided that the provision for original jurisdiction over states in the Supreme Court was *optional* for states. Trial in the Supreme Court was a privilege states could exercise if they chose, or waive if they chose. In other words, states might voluntarily agree to be litigants in federal district courts. A state might agree to this to have a case resolved quickly, for example. However, once states allowed themselves to be sued in federal courts, the floodgates opened and today states are routinely sued in federal district court. Despite the decision in *Marbury v. Madison*, Congress has authorized such suits against states in federal court. To make matters worse, the vast majority of suits against states are never reviewed by the Supreme Court at all. Despite Hamilton's assurances, 99% of suits against states begin and end in "inferior tribunals."

The second concern that anti-Federalists had involved *lawsuits against states*. To address this, Article 3 provides that lawsuits between two or more states had to be heard in a federal forum, and while anti-Federalists might have liked Congress to retain appellate power, everyone agreed this was appropriate. There were only 13 states at the time, so the number of suits between states would be small.

Far more controversial was the apparent authorization for federal courts to hear suits against states by private citizens. Anti-Federalists feared that if foreigners could sue a state in federal court, then federal courts would effectively dictate state policy. However, Hamilton assured the anti-Federalists that they were misreading this section. In *Federalist* 81, Hamilton explained that the clause extending federal jurisdiction of suits "between a State and Citizens of another State" only meant that a state could bring suit against a private citizen in federal court. However, a private citizen could never sue a state in federal court. Hamilton explains in *Federalist* 81:

> It is inherent in the nature of sovereignty not to be amenable to the suit of an individual WITHOUT ITS CONSENT. This is the general sense, and the general practice of mankind; and the exemption, as one of the attributes of sovereignty, is now enjoyed by the government of every State in the Union. Unless, therefore, there is a surrender of this immunity in the plan of the convention, it will remain with the States, and the danger intimated must be merely ideal. …

Thus, Hamilton explicitly said that states may never be subjected to monetary suits in federal court. The related implication is that states may not be sued at all in federal court, even for some non-monetary cause of action. This seems to follow from Hamilton's general statement that "it is inherent in the nature of sovereignty not to be amenable to the suit of an individual."

Despite Hamilton's apparently iron-clad guarantee, one of the very first cases to be brought in federal court occurred in 1792 when Alexander Chisholm sued the State of Georgia. Chisholm, a citizen of South Carolina, brought suit in federal circuit court (the trial court at that time) against Georgia, claiming that Georgia owed him money for supplies he had sold to the State.

Initially, Chisolm's case was dismissed because all suits involving states had to be brought in the Supreme Court. Chisholm then refiled in the Supreme Court under its original jurisdiction. In 1793, the Supreme Court did exactly what the anti-Federalists had feared, and exactly what Hamilton had assured them could not happen. The Supreme Court sided with Chisholm ruling:

> The judicial power, then, is expressly extended to "controversies between a State and citizens of another State." When a citizen makes a demand against a State of which he is not a citizen, it is as really a controversy between a State and a citizen of another State as if such State made a demand against such citizen. The case, then, seems clearly to fall within the letter of the Constitution.

The decision caused outrage across the county. The Constitution had been adopted largely because of assurances by the Federalists that this would not happen. When the next Congress met in 1794, it overwhelmingly approved a new amendment: the Eleventh. In less than a year, three fourths of the then fifteen states ratified it. The Eleventh Amendment states:

> The Judicial power of the United States shall not be construed to extend to any suit in law or equity, commenced or prosecuted against one of the United States by Citizens of another State, or by Citizens or Subjects of any Foreign State.

Notice that the Amendment did not purport to change Article 3 section 2, it states that Article 3 section 2 shall not be "construed," that is, interpreted, to permit suits against states by plaintiffs who are not citizens of the state. By implication, as well as Hamilton's explanation in *Federalist* 81, citizens certainly may not sue their own state in federal court.

Despite the principle that states may not be sued in federal court, over the years several exceptions have developed. The oldest "exception" is that state civil or criminal cases involving federal law may be appealed from a state court to the U.S. Supreme Court. An appeal has never been considered a suit against a state. A second exception is that since the early 20th century federal courts have allowed suits against state officials that are really suits against states. The Supreme Court itself has said this is a legal fiction but with that fiction state officials may be sued for non-monetary relief. A third exception involves the 14th Amendment, which says no state may violate anyone's civil rights. The federal courts have held that Congress can authorize suits against states if a state violates the 14th Amendment. A final exception is that political subdivisions of a state, such as cities, towns, and counties, are generally not entitled to Eleventh Amendment immunity. Because local officials, like county sheriffs, often enforce state laws, this is another way to have federal courts review a state law or policy.

Unfortunately, these exceptions have swallowed the rule. Undoubtedly, the Framers who overwhelmingly supported the Eleventh Amendment would be shocked at the ease with which states can be sued in federal court. The Founding generation tried carefully to craft language to protect states from excessive interference by federal courts, but these protections are now long gone. Federal courts today are involved in the minutest decisions of state and local government.

To summarize, the Framers placed two important structural limitations on federal court jurisdiction over states. First, individuals could not sue states. Second, all suits involving states started and ended in the Supreme Court. Individuals who were prosecuted by a state could appeal a federal issue to the Supreme Court but only the Supreme Court. The federal government could sue a state in the Supreme Court if a state did something illegal. However, today, the Supreme Court does not have time to get into the minutiae of the day-to-day operation of local government the way hundreds of district judges do.

THE LIVING CONSTITUTION AND FICTITIOUS RIGHTS

Protecting personal liberty is a vital role of the courts. In *Federalist* 78, Hamilton says that provisions against bills of attainder, and ex-post-facto laws must be enforced by "courts of justice, whose duty it must be to declare all acts contrary to the manifest tenor of the Constitution void." Everyone agrees that judges should dismiss changes based on bills of attainder or ex-post-facto laws. However, what happens when judges do not merely protect personal liberty, but create "rights" where none exist? The most notorious example of this occurred when the Court created the "right" to abortion.

In 1973, in *Roe v. Wade*, the Supreme Court said that the Constitution gave women the right to kill their unborn children. This was an absolute right for the first six months of pregnancy (first two trimesters) and a limited right for the last three months (third trimester). The Court ordered the federal government and all fifty states to stop enforcing laws against abortion for the first six months of fetal life. The Constitution does not mention abortion, but intentionally killing children in the womb had been a crime in every state in the country, and in the District of Columbia, for over a century. The majority of the Court declared this new right to abortion based on a series of illogical inferences.

In 1965, the Supreme Court declared that there was a "right to privacy" *implicit* in the Constitution. Justice Hugo Black exposed the danger of creating such a right in his dissenting opinion:

> 'Privacy' is a broad, abstract and ambiguous concept which can easily be shrunken in meaning but which can also, on the other hand, easily be interpreted as a constitutional ban against many things other than searches and seizures....

Hugo Black

> The adoption of such a loose, flexible, uncontrolled standard for holding laws unconstitutional, if ever it is finally achieved, will amount to a great unconstitutional shift of power to the courts which I believe and am constrained to say will be bad for the courts and worse for the country.

Griswold v Connecticut (Justice Black, dissenting).

This new "right to privacy" included the right to purchase and use contraceptives. *Roe* expanded the right to privacy to include the right to an abortion. In 1992, this culminated in the Supreme Court declaring that privacy entailed "the right to define one's own concept of existence, of meaning, of the universe, and of the mystery of human life." *Planned Parenthood of Southeastern Pennsylvania v Casey* (1992). As Justice Scalia later commented on this passage:

> I have never heard of a law that attempted to restrict one's "right to define" certain concepts; and if the passage calls into question the government's power to regulate actions based on one's self-defined "concept of existence, etc.," it is the passage that ate the rule of law.[8]

Of course, Justice Scalia was correct. If a judge can order that a law not be enforced because it interferes with someone's "concept of existence" then every state and federal law is subject to the caprice and whim of federal judges. Even worse, these newly created rights were "positive rights" that the court ordered federal and local officials to actively enforce. For example, the Supreme Court ordered state officials to support the right of a 14-year-old girl to have an abortion; ordered that states must prevent the 14-year-old's parents from trying to prevent the death of their grandchild; and from trying to prevent their immature daughter from making a mistake she would regret for the rest of her life.[9]

In *Griswold*, the Court claimed that "privacy" meant protecting married couples from the state *interfering* in their important decisions; now it turned out that privacy *demanded* the state interfere in a married couple's most important decisions. The Right to Privacy, or "the right to define one's own concept of existence," had no objective meaning. It meant judges could reinterpret the constitution to mean whatever they wanted it to mean.

This notion that judges can create rights based on "implications" or "penumbras," that is, concepts not specifically found in the legal document is called **judicial activism**. Judicial activism occurs when judges do not interpret the Constitution as *written* but "interpret" it the way they think it *should have been written*. The opposite view is known as **judicial restraint**, which holds that judges ought to interpret the Constitution as written and its Framers intended.

Until about 1950, most judges, on both state and federal courts, practiced judicial restraint. John Marshall set the tone early when he wrote that the government of the United States is a government of laws, not of men. Judges who practice judicial restraint

Antonin Scalia

seek to interpret the law as written, or, if the law is unclear, to understand the intent of the lawgivers. They do not create new laws or new rights.

Starting in 1953, when **Earl Warren**, the former Republican governor of California, became Chief Justice, the Supreme Court began shifting from a philosophy of judicial restraint to one of judicial activism. Judicial activists hold a philosophy almost diametrically to judicial restraint. They believe the Constitution has no fixed meaning because judges always will and *should* interpret the Constitution in light of present-day concerns. Under this view, the Constitution is a **living document** which is constantly evolving and changing so judges should interpret the Constitution to suit contemporary social problems. Consequently, even if a right of privacy exists, the right to life supersedes all other rights; however, for an activist judge, the right to life might be less important than the right to an abortion if that is what the country "needs" at a particular time. If judges think that abortion ought to be a constitutional right then it is.

---

[8] *Lawrence v. Texas*, 539 U.S. 558, 588 (2003) (Scalia, dissenting).
[9] *City of Akron v. Akron Ctr. for Reprod. Health, Inc.*, 462 U.S. 416 (1983).

Once the Supreme Court moves away from interpreting law to creating rights, the system of checks and balances begins to erode. The president becomes little more than the person who nominates one of America's true rulers. The Senate then votes for that ruler. Five members of the Supreme Court decide the course of the nation, not the people, the president, or any elected representative. Moreover, other than impeaching a Justice, something that has never been done, they serve for life, even when they are no longer intellectually or physically able to do so.

Ironically, activist judges who insist that the Constitution should be a living document, fail to admit that, in fact, it is, but not the way they wish it to be. The Framers allowed for amendments. Article V details the process by which the Constitution can be amended. However, this is a difficult process which requires a great consensus, not five people. Yet, as the country grows and changes, the people can change the Constitution. Thus, if the people wish to allow women to vote (19th) or limit the terms a president can serve (22cd), the Constitution can be amended. Changing the Constitution based on the decision of a handful of judges, rather than the American people, means that the government of the United States is a government of *men*, not of *laws*.

Historically, allowing the Supreme Court this near omnipotence has resulted in terrible outcomes. The Court allowed abortion in *Roe*. It sanctioned slavery in *Dred Scott*. It declared that black Americans were second-class citizens in *Plessy v. Ferguson*. It allowed Japanese-Americans to be held without trials in internment camps during World War II in *Korematsu v. United States*. The list is long and infamous.

THE SUPREME COURT AS A POLITICAL INSTITUTION

The Framers hoped that judges would be insulated from public opinion so that they could apply the law in an unbiased manner. This is why judges were confirmed by the Senate alone, which until the early 20th century was not popularly elected. Judicial activists maintained the fiction that judges could apply the law in a mechanical way so their own personal views did not matter. Everyone knew this was a fiction, but it was a useful fiction because judges had to do their best to stay above politics and apply the law without bias.

Nevertheless, even in our nation's first years, the Senate rejected one of Washington's nominees for the Supreme Court based on his controversial political views. **John Rutledge** of South Carolina was one of the most illustrious Founding Fathers. He was one of the few people who signed both the Declaration of Independence and the Constitution. John Jay served as the first Chief Justice of the Supreme Court from October 1789 until June 1795. In those days, the Court heard so few cases that Jay had time to negotiate a new treaty with England. The *Jay Treaty* was signed in November 1794 and ratified by the Senate on June 24, 1795. Five days later, John Jay resigned as Chief Justice.

To replace Jay, Washington nominated Rutledge as Chief Justice. Unfortunately, in July, Rutledge publicly criticized the Jay Treaty. This alienated enough Senators that the Senate rejected his nomination despite his eminent qualifications. This was not the last time the Senate would reject a Supreme Court nominee due to his controversial views, but, generally, for the next 150 years, most judicial nominees were uncontroversial.

Of course, presidents criticized the Supreme Court for its decisions. Lincoln suggested that *Dred Scott* was illegitimate. Theodore Roosevelt frequently criticized judicial review as undemocratic. During Franklin Roosevelt's early administration, Justices repeatedly declared expansion of federal power to be unconstitutional and Roosevelt attacked the Court in radio addresses known as "fireside chats." In 1937, Roosevelt asked Congress to increase the size of the Supreme Court from nine justices to fifteen which would have allowed him to control the court. Roosevelt insisted that he only wanted to add new justices to ease the workload of the nine justices on the court, but no one

John Rutledge

believed him, and Congress refused to adopt his "court packing" plan. However, Justices retired and he was able to appoint men who supported government expansion and began approving his new legislation.

In 1962, the Supreme Court issued one of its most far-reaching decisions when it ordered that all prayer in public schools must stop. In *Engel v. Vitale*, the Court declared the prayer "*Almighty God, we acknowledge our dependence upon Thee, and we beg Thy blessings upon us, our parents, our teachers and our country. Amen.*" was unconstitutional. The day the Court issued the *Engle* decision is often considered the birthday of the private-Christian school and homeschool movements in the United States because it meant that the public schools, which to that time were Christian, were going to become secular and atheistic—which they did.

The *Engel* decision proved hugely controversial. The Catholic hierarchy harshly condemned the decision. Cardinal McIntyre of Los Angeles, Cardinal Cushing of Boston, and Cardinal Spellman of New York, all issued statements criticizing the decision. Billy Graham, the leading Protestant minister in the country, condemned *Engel* and explained where the Court went wrong noting "the framers of our Constitution meant we were to have freedom of religion, not freedom *from* religion." Congress proposed adopting a school prayer constitutional amendment. A constitutional amendment was never adopted but from this point onward the Court was deeply enmeshed in social disputes. Christians began closely monitoring everything the Supreme Court did.

Catholic concern for the Court's embrace of an anti-Christian social agenda reached a new level with the 1973 decision on abortion. In the 1976 presidential election, abortion was a major issue in the campaign. The Democrat candidate was Jimmy Carter and the Republican candidate was President Gerald Ford. Carter condemned abortion as wrong, but opposed a constitutional amendment to protect life. Ford actively courted Catholic voters by writing an open letter to the National Council of Catholic Bishops condemning abortion and touting his support for a constitutional amendment to protect life. However, President Ford's opposition to abortion was lukewarm at best. Ford's one appointment to the Supreme Court was John Paul Stevens who was extremely pro-abortion.

Tragically, even most "pro-life" presidents have a mixed record on appointing pro-life Justices to the Court. In 1980, Ronald Reagan ran for president and made opposition to abortion one of his core commitments. On Reagan's first day as President, he met with pro-life leaders in the White House and promised to do all he could to make abortion illegal. Reagan's first appointment to the Supreme Court was Sandra Day O'Connor, the first woman Supreme Court Justice. At her confirmation hearing before the Senate Judiciary Committee, she said abortion was always wrong. She later added she had "an abhorrence for abortion," and described abortion as "repugnant to me." In her first years on the Court, O'Connor sided with the pro-life justices, but later in her career, her position changed and she sided more and more with the so-called "pro-choice" justices.

As abortion became the "litmus test" for judges, the Senate and the president began to consider

Gerald Ford

Jimmy Carter

Sandra Day O'Connor

who a new justice was replacing. When a socially conservative president nominates a new justice to replace a retiring justice who is socially conservative, people often see this as simply maintaining the "status quo." However, people became very worked up when it appeared that a president would have an opportunity to "shift the balance" on the Court. For example, O'Connor replaced Potter Stewart, who wrote a withering dissent in *Griswold v. Connecticut*, was considered a conservative. Thus, when Reagan replaced a "conservative" justice with another conservative justice there was less opposition than there might have been. Moreover, because O'Connor was the first female Justice, it guaranteed she would not face much opposition.

When Chief Justice Warren Burger retired, Reagan had a chance to appoint a second justice. Burger was generally a social liberal. He had voted for the "right to abortion" in Roe. However, in 1986, at the end of his career, Burger sided with O'Connor and voted that states could restrict abortion after a child was capable of surviving outside the womb. Reagan nominated **Antonin Scalia** to replace Burger. Because Burger had been against abortion in the end, and because Scalia's nomination posed no threat to overturning *Roe*, it was not as controversial as it might have been.

The situation changed the following year when Justice Lewis Powell retired. Powell had provided the crucial fifth vote on several 5-4 abortion cases. A pro-life Justice would threaten *Roe*. Reagan nominated **Robert Bork**, a judge on the District of Columbia Court of Appeals. Bork's opinions as an appeals court judge showed he did not think a "right to privacy" made any sense. Everyone thought that Bork replacing Powell would flip the crucial fifth vote on abortion.

Pro-abortion groups immediately launched an orchestrated campaign to defeat Bork. In the Senate, two nominally Catholic Senators led the opposition to Bork: Edward Kennedy (D-MA) and Joseph Biden (D-DE). Many people think that the Reagan Administration and the pro-life side were caught unprepared. Supporters of Bork wanted to act like the approval process should be above politics and did little to support Bork. Meanwhile Bork's opponents protested and flooded the offices of their senators with angry calls and letters. Ultimately the Senate voted against Bork 58 to 42. The word "Bork" even

Robert Bork with President Ronald Reagan in the White House

entered the political lexicon as a verb: "to Bork" someone meant to stop them from being confirmed.

Reagan ultimately named Anthony Kennedy to the Court. Kennedy was not nearly as conservative as Bork and voted to continue the "right to abortion."

President George H. Bush made two appointments to the Supreme Court. The first appointment was David Souter, a liberal Republican who supported abortion. The following year, Thurgood Marshall, the first African-American Justice, retired. Marshall had been one of the most liberal Justices. Bush nominated Clarence Thomas, a socially and religiously conservative appeals court judge. This was another case where the replacement of a liberal with a conservative would swing the court towards a more traditional view of morality. Unsurprisingly, advocates of abortion announced that they were going to "Bork" Thomas. Despite a vicious smear campaign and the efforts of the

Chairman of the Senate Judiciary Committee, Joe Biden, Thomas was ultimately confirmed by a vote of 52-48.

Democrat nominees have faced far less scrutiny or opposition. The most controversial tactic Republicans have used occurred when Justice Scalia died during the Obama Administration and the Republican-controlled Senate refused to confirm anyone until after the next election. The tactic worked. Many traditionalists voted for Donald Trump hoping he would keep his promise to appoint pro-life Justices.

A replay of the Clarence Thomas hearings took place in 2018 when Trump nominated Brett Kavanaugh to replace Anthony Kennedy. Kavanaugh was not particularly conservative, but more than Kennedy. Once again, a brutal smear campaign failed to defeat Kavanaugh who was confirmed by a vote of 50-48.

In 2020, Trump nominated Amy Coney Barret to the Supreme Court to replace Ruth Bader Ginsberg, one of the all-time most liberal and pro-abortion Justices. Barret is a Catholic who has seven children, two of them adopted. Because she is a woman, the Democrats on the Judiciary Committee had to treat her better than Kavanaugh or Thomas, although they were as unfriendly and vicious as they thought they could be. The Senate confirmed her 52 to 48 along party lines, with all Democrats and one Republican voting against her.

As of 2024, there are six Catholic Justices on the Supreme Court: Chief Justice Roberts and Justices Thomas, Alito, Kavanaugh, Sotomayor, and Barrett. Sotomayor is quite liberal and, while she is a baptized Catholic, it seems that she no longer actively practices the Faith. Neil Gorsuch was raised Catholic but appears to be an Episcopalian. Elena Kagan is Jewish and Ketanji Brown Jackson is a "nondenominational Protestant."

Under the leadership of Clarence Thomas, and with the support of the other Catholic justices, the Court has begun rejecting abstract rights and adopting a policy of allowing social questions to be handled by the democratic process at the state level. The abortion controversy provides the best example. In 2022, the Court held that the constitution is silent on the issue of abortion and states are free to adopt whatever policies the citizens think appropriate. Thomas has signaled that the Court is going to follow this policy with the rest of the rights found under the banner of the right to privacy. Perhaps one day, if judges return to interpreting the constitution in an unbiased manner, the Court will start to lose its character as a political institution.

The Supreme Court (2025)

REVIEW QUESTIONS

1. Which Article of the U.S. Constitution is devoted to the federal courts?
2. How many federal courts are required to exist according to the U.S. Constitution?
3. For which of the federal courts do judges basically serve for life?
4. How has the Senate generally treated presidential nominees to the Supreme Court?
5. How many federal crimes were there under the Crimes Act of 1790?
6. Why are criminal defendants required to post bail?
7. Under what types of cases does a federal court have jurisdiction according to the U.S. Constitution?
8. What is the term for the practice of federal courts adjudicating suits between citizens of different states that have to do with disputes arising under state law?
9. Under what conditions does the U.S. Supreme Court hear an appeal from a lower court?
10. What type of opinions will the Supreme Court not issue?
11. What is the party called who initiates a civil suit?
12. Why is a "cause of action" important in civil suits?
13. Once a jury returns a unanimous verdict of "not guilty" what is the process the state must follow to retry the defendant?
14. What courts can hear cases involving a federal law like a federal law against discrimination?
15. What is the technical term courts used when an earlier precedent does not dictate the outcome of a later case?
16. What did Hamilton say about judges in Federalist 78?
17. What evidence supports the contention that the Framers intended the U.S. Supreme Court to hear appeals from state courts?
18. Which of the following did Hamilton say about suits against states Federalist 81?
19. What is the Trail of Tears?
20. What is Judicial Review?
21. What is "original jurisdiction"?
22. What does the 11th Amendment say?
23. What did Justice Samuel Chase do when he was required to preside over prosecutions under the Sedition Act?
24. What did the Supreme Court say in *Marbury v. Madison* about the original jurisdiction of the Supreme Court?
25. Following *Marbury v. Madison* how many federal laws were declared unconstitutional by the Supreme Court over the next fifty years?
26. How did President Lincoln feel about *Dred Scott v. Sandford*?
27. What is the name of the famous book about the U.S Supreme Court published in 1979 that revealed many of the previously secret ways the Court operates?
28. What does "to Bork someone" mean?
29. What is the "court packing plan?"
30. As of 2024, how many U.S. Supreme Court justices identify themselves as Catholics?

CHAPTER SEVEN
THE BILL OF RIGHTS

INTRODUCTION

The first ten amendments to the Constitution are known as **The Bill of Rights**. James Madison drafted these amendments, which the states ratified in 1791. The Bill of Rights contains a variety of provisions intended to protect specific liberties such as freedom of religion, freedom of speech, freedom from arbitrary search and arrest, protection of property rights, right to counsel, and the right to a jury trial. Today, many people regard The Bill of Rights as the most important part of the Constitution. Surprisingly, many Founders opposed The Bill of Rights and only agreed to include it as a political compromise with anti-Federalists. Many Federalists, like Alexander Hamilton, thought a list of constitutional rights was unnecessary at best, and dangerous at worst.

It was not that Federalists opposed freedoms like trial by jury or the right to counsel; in fact, before there was a Bill of Rights, the Judiciary Act of 1789 guaranteed the right to bail, the right to counsel, the right to a jury trial, and basic due process rights, such as the rights to compel witnesses to testify and to cross examine witnesses. Actually, the Judiciary Act went further, and guaranteed freedoms that would not be found in the Bill of Rights. For example, the Judiciary Act guaranteed that all trials must be in "open court," including civil trials. (The Sixth Amendment only prohibits secret trials in *criminal* cases.)

So, why did Federalists support a statutory right to counsel or the right to jury trial, but object to

James Madison

these same freedoms as constitutional rights? Firstly, the Framers wanted to see ultimate power and control in Congress as the elected representatives of the people. For the Framers, a *list of rights* was not nearly as important as *who* enforces those rights and the system of checks and balances that protect freedom without turning into anarchy. If the right to bail is statutory, then Congress is able to modify the right to bail by statute. Of course, some people do not want Congress to be able to restrict bail, that is the point of a constitutional provision, to limit the power of Congress. Although it seems making bail a constitutional right provides it a greater protection, it really only shifts power from Congress to courts; however, there is no guarantee that the courts are better suited than Congress for this job.

One of the arguments Federalists made against a bill of rights was that it was impossible to list every important liberty to be protected in the Constitution. Such a "Bill of Rights" would be 100 pages long, and even if such a detailed bill of rights could be created, it might make it very difficult to deal with new and unforeseen problems that might arise. So, a very detailed bill of rights would be unwise. Secondly, if some freedom is not listed in a bill of rights, someone could argue that the right does not legally exist. Consider the requirement that all trials be conducted in open court. Someone could argue that public trial in civil cases is not in The Bill of Rights therefore such secret trials must be acceptable. Madison tried to answer this concern with the Ninth Amendment that declares: "*The enumeration in the Constitution, of certain rights, shall not be construed to deny or disparage others retained by the people.*" Yet the Ninth Amendment raises its own concerns: What are these "un-enumerated rights?" Can judges simply create new rights, like the right to abortion or suicide, and argue that these are some of the un-enumerated rights of the Ninth Amendment? That is exactly what happened in the 20th century.

So, a bill of rights presented an insoluble dilemma. There is a problem if the rights set forth are either too vague or too specific! Far better, thought many of the Framers, to avoid a bill of rights altogether and leave the matter up to Congress which would amend and modify these rights as necessary.

Many of the Framers thought that what would preserve freedom was not a bill of rights, but checks

First page of the original Bill of Rights

and balances. Justice Scalia best expressed this view in a famous talk he gave to the Senate Judiciary Committee on October 5, 2011. Scalia said:

> [I]f you think that a bill of rights is what sets us apart, you're crazy. Every banana republic in the world has a bill of rights. Every President for life has a bill of rights. The bill of rights of the former "Evil Empire," the Union of Soviet Socialist Republics, was much better than ours. …
>
> Of course—just words on paper, what our Framers would have called a parchment guarantee. … The Constitution of the Soviet Union did not prevent the centralization of power, in one person or in one party. And when that happens the game is over; the Bill of Rights is just what our Framers would call a parchment guarantee.
>
> So, the real key to the distinctiveness of America is the structure of our government.

THE BILL OF RIGHTS AND THE RATIFICATION OF THE NEW CONSTITUTION

Throughout English history, kings issued various proclamations guaranteeing a variety of traditional liberties. The colonial charters had also guaranteed many traditional liberties, especially freedom of religion. Unsurprisingly then, many of the new American states wished to enshrine a variety of liberties in their new Constitutions. For example, on June 12, 1776, the Constitutional Convention of the newly independent Commonwealth of Virginia adopted a Declaration of Rights. Most other states followed suit. For example, John Adams was principal author of a Declaration of Rights that became part of the Massachusetts Constitution in 1780. Most of these "rights" were basic liberties that had been recognized in English law for centuries. Yet, when the Framers finalized the draft constitution and sent it to the states for approval in 1787, there was no "bill of rights." Of course, Article 1, section 9 did provide a handful of restrictions on the power of Congress including:

> The Privilege of the Writ of Habeas Corpus shall not be suspended, unless when in Cases of Rebellion or Invasion the public Safety may require it. No Bill of Attainder or ex post facto Law shall be passed.

Article 1, section 10 contained several similar provisions forbidding states from doing many of the same things, and a few others. For example, Article 1, section 10 guarantees freedom of contract. However, these few provisions of Article 1 failed to mention many of the freedoms that early Americans cherished most, such as freedom of religion, freedom of speech, and the right to keep and bear arms. Accordingly, many of the anti-Federalists during the ratification debates objected to the lack of a bill of rights.

Hamilton responded in *Federalist* 84 arguing that a bill of rights made sense for a government of general jurisdiction, like the states, but the federal government had very limited powers so a bill of rights was unnecessary. Hamilton did not stop there, however, he added:

> Bills of rights, in the sense and to the extent in which they are contended for, are not only unnecessary in the proposed Constitution, but would even be dangerous. They would contain various exceptions to powers not granted; and, on this very account, would afford a colorable pretext to claim more than were granted. For why declare that things shall not be done which there is no power to do? Why, for instance, should it be said that the liberty of the press

Alexander Hamilton

> shall not be restrained, when no power is given by which restrictions may be imposed?

Hamilton was saying that liberty of the press is protected because regulating speech is not among the enumerated powers of Congress. Hamilton thought this lack of power was a much stronger protection than simply listing "freedom of the press" in a bill of rights. In fact, Hamilton's prediction came true. In a famous case from 1919 (*Schenck v. United States*), the Supreme Court reasoned that the First Amendment right to free speech could not be absolute; therefore, the government must have power to restrict *some* speech.

In the Virginia ratifying convention of 1788, Madison and other Federalists continued to argue that a bill of rights was unnecessary. Madison contended that there was no need for a federal guarantee for freedom of religion, explaining:

> Is a bill of rights a security for religion? … If there were a majority of one sect, a bill of rights would be a poor protection for liberty. Happily, for the states, they enjoy the utmost freedom of religion. This freedom arises from that multiplicity of sects which pervades America, and which is the best and only security for religious liberty in any society … There is not a shadow of right in the general government to

intermeddle with religion. Its least interference with it would be a most flagrant usurpation.[1]

Like Hamilton, Madison was saying there is no need for a provision declaring that the federal government cannot restrict freedom of religion when Congress has no "shadow" of authority to interfere with religion anyway.

Edmund Randolph, the first attorney general of the United States, argued forcefully, and at length, that a bill of rights would undermine the authority of the government and therefore "A bill of rights, therefore, accurately speaking, is quite useless, if not dangerous to a republic." George Nicholas, another member of Washington's Department of Justice, insisted that a bill of rights is "no security. It is but a paper check."

Despite the efforts of Madison, Randolph, and others, it looked like Virginia would refuse to ratify the new Constitution. Patrick Henry led the opposition to ratification. Henry had been principal author of the Declaration of Rights, so the omission of a bill of rights was one of his main complaints. With ratification in doubt, Madison promised that if Virginia ratified the proposed constitution, he would ensure that a bill of rights was adopted. With this assurance, Virginia ratified the new constitution by a vote of 89 to 79.

In the First Congress, James Madison drafted a bill of rights. Madison's proposal was more extensive than what was ultimately adopted. Perhaps most notably, one of the proposed amendments he drafted read, "*No State shall violate the equal rights of conscience, or the freedom of the press, or the trial by jury in criminal cases.*" These three rights were the only ones Madison suggested should apply to the States. In his speech introducing his proposed bill of rights, Madison argued that these three rights were so important that "it is proper that every Government should be disarmed of powers which trench upon those particular rights." The rest of Congress disagreed, however, and this proposed amendment was rejected. The Bill of Rights would only restrict the federal government—at least until the 20th century.

The House of Representatives ultimately approved seventeen proposed amendments from Madison's list. This draft was sent to the Senate, which reorganized and finalized the draft. Ultimately, Congress agreed on twelve proposed amendments that were sent to the states for ratification. The first two amendments, having to do with the organization and pay for Congress, were not ratified by the states—at least at that time. The second of these twelve proposed amendments was finally ratified in 1992 and became the 27th Amendment.[2]

The current First Amendment, guaranteeing freedom of religion and speech, was actually third on the list. It is a common misconception that the First Amendment is "first" because it is the most important. The fact that the amendment guaranteeing freedom of religion comes first is simply an historical accident.

A WEAK BILL OF RIGHTS

Given that the Federalists generally agreed that a bill of rights was "quite useless," to quote Edmund Randolph, it is perhaps not surprising that for the first few decades of the United States, The Bill of Rights was almost ignored. In 1798, Congress passed The Sedition Act which made it a crime to falsely and maliciously criticize the government. Although Madison and Jefferson criticized the Act as a violation of the First Amendment, Federalist judges enforced the Act with no concern for the First Amendment.

Another reason that the Bill of Rights played little role in the early 19th century was because Hamilton and Madison were correct that the federal government's powers were very limited. Aside from the Sedition Act, Congress took almost no interest in trying to restrict freedom of religion, the press, speech, or ownership of weapons. Prior to the Civil War, almost all governmental powers were exercised at the state and local level, so The Bill of Rights, which applied to the federal government, was not that important.

---

[1] Madison Speech, Virginia Ratifying Convention, June 14, 1788, in Elliot's Debates vol. 3.
[2] The 27th Amendment says that any law to raise congressional salary does not take effect until after the next election.

This point is illustrated by the famous Supreme Court case *Barron v. Baltimore*. After the War of 1812, the city of Baltimore began a series of street improvements which resulted in a lot of silt (sand and gravel) running into the Patapsco River. The buildup of this silt in the Patapsco started interfering with the operation of Barron's shipyard. Consequently, Barron brought suit against the City of Baltimore for damages.

Barron argued that the Fifth Amendment of the United States Constitution was binding on Maryland and on Baltimore. The Fifth Amendment provides in part that "… nor shall private property be taken for public use, without just compensation." The Amendment does not say precisely *who* shall not take property. Nevertheless, Barron convinced a trial court in Baltimore that he was entitled to recover damages based on the Fifth Amendment. On appeal, the U.S. Supreme Court wrote:

> The question thus presented is, we think, of great importance, but not of much difficulty. The Constitution was ordained and established by the people of the United States for themselves, for their own government, and not for the government of the individual States. … [T]he fifth amendment must be understood as restraining the power of the General Government, not as applicable to the States.

It remains a point that is often misunderstood, but the Bill of Rights was not originally intended to be applied directly to the states – as the ruling in *Barron* makes clear. Rather, the Fourteenth Amendment guarantee that no state shall deprive any person of liberty without due process has been interpreted *implicitly* to contain many of the same provisions that are found in The Bill of Rights. It was not until some of the provisions of The Bill of Rights were applied to the states in the 20th century that The Bill of Rights began to play a significant role in American law.

Moreover, as the power of the federal government expanded in the 20th century, federal actions were far more likely to affect a person's exercise of religion, speech, or the right to keep and bear arms. For

Bennett Baltimore from Federal Hill

example, beginning in the 1960s, Congress began passing a variety of laws prohibiting certain types of discrimination. Generally, an organization cannot fire an employee due to their religious beliefs. However, what if the organization is a Church which discovers that a school teacher is openly hostile to the Church's teaching? If the church is not permitted to fire such an employee that would severely restrict the religious freedom of the church. Accordingly, anti-discrimination laws can have a very serious impact on freedom of speech and freedom of religion. In the 19th century this was not an issue, because no one imagined that the federal government possessed any constitutional authority to tell a private party who it could hire or fire. Yet, once it is accepted that the federal government has broad power to tell organizations who they can hire and fire, then the First Amendment becomes very important.

In a sense, both the Federalists and the anti-Federalists were correct. The Federalists were right that if the federal government were limited to a few well-defined powers then a bill of rights makes little difference. Yet the anti-Federalists were also correct that if the power of the federal government expands then a bill of rights is crucial.

THE FOURTEENTH AMENDMENT INCORPORATES PARTS OF THE BILL OF RIGHTS

The Bill of Rights, or parts of it, became much more important in the early 20th century when the Supreme Court declared that some of the rights found in The Bill of Rights were implicit in the Fourteenth Amendment. The Fourteenth Amendment, ratified in 1868, provides:

> No State shall make or enforce any law which shall abridge the privileges or immunities of citizens of the United States; nor shall any State deprive any person of life, liberty, or property, without due process of law; nor deny to any person within its jurisdiction the equal protection of the laws.

The most important provision of the amendment is the "due process" clause. The Supreme Court has adopted the theory that certain rights are so fundamental that they are implicit in the concept of due process. This has always been a controversial idea. Historically, the concept of "due process" means the procedures used. For example, a person accused of a crime is entitled to trial by jury and to be assisted by counsel. These are called "procedural rights." Yet, in addition to these procedural rights, the theory is that the concept of "due process" implicitly contains a variety of "substantive rights" such as freedom of speech or the right to abortion. Because these substantive rights are implicit in "due process" how do courts determine what rights are implicit? That has been the overarching controversy of the last hundred years in American constitutional law. The generally accepted formulation today is that the Fourteenth Amendment protects only those rights "deeply rooted" in American history and "implicit in the concept of ordered liberty."

A right included in The Bill of Rights, such as freedom of religion, is evidence that right is both "deeply rooted" in American history and "implicit in the concept of ordered liberty." However, not all of the freedoms in the Bill of Rights have been found to be implicit in the concept of "due process." For example, the Seventh Amendment guarantees the right to jury trial in civil cases, but this has never been applied to the States. Moreover, a number of "rights" *not* found in The Bill of Rights were thought to be fundamental, such as the right to abortion.

What may seem odd is that once some of the provisions of The Bill of Rights were applied to the States, these rights were interpreted much more broadly than ever before. For example, during the 19th century, federal courts rarely discussed the First Amendment's free speech clause and no federal law was found to violate the First Amendment's guarantee of free speech until 1965. In 1925, for the first time, the Supreme Court decided that freedom of speech was implicit in the Fourteenth Amendment due process clauses. (*Gitlow v. New York*.) Over the following decades, the Supreme Court declared that dozens of state and local laws violated the constitutional guarantee of free speech. In 1964, in *Lamont v. Postmaster General of the United States*, the Court declared for the first time that a federal law was a violation of free speech. The law at issue authorized the federal government to restrict the importation of newspapers and periodicals designated as Communist propaganda.

Old Salem County Courthouse, the Oldest Active Courthouse in New Jersey (1735)

Thus, for several decades, it appeared the guarantee of free speech that was implicit in the Fourteenth Amendment, and applicable to the States, was much stronger than the First Amendment guarantee of free speech applicable to the federal government. However, since the 1960s, the Supreme Court has held that fundamental rights, like freedom of speech, are applied identically to both state and federal government. This equal treatment of state and federal laws does not mean that fundamental rights cannot be limited. Rather, the Supreme Court has decided that fundamental rights can only be restricted if the law or policy at issue is "narrowly tailored" to a compelling interest. Being narrowly tailored means that the government is using the method that restricts individual freedom as little as possible yet still accomplishes the government's compelling interest. Although the meaning of "compelling" can be unclear and somewhat subjective, "compelling" generally means very important. Any time the federal government or a local government interferes with a fundamental right the court applies the **strict scrutiny** test to determine that the state is using the least restrictive means to achieve its compelling interest.

Thus, prior to the 1920s, The Bill of Rights placed few restrictions on the federal government and none on the States. From the 1920s to the 1960s, The Bill of Rights was applied primarily to state and local laws and the rights were interpreted broadly. Today, The Bill of Rights is interpreted broadly and applied to both local and federal actions.

THE FIRST AMENDMENT: FREEDOM OF RELIGION

The First Amendment says, "*Congress shall make no law respecting an establishment of religion, or prohibiting the free exercise thereof; or abridging the freedom of speech, or of the press; or the right of the people peaceably to assemble, and to petition the Government for a redress of grievances.*" Madison's first draft divided these issues into three separate amendments, but they were combined in the final draft. There are really four distinct freedoms listed: religion, speech, the press, and association. Freedom of religion is also generally divided into two different provisions: the **establishment clause** and the **free exercise clause**.

Notice that the First Amendment specifically says "*Congress* shall make no law …" In 1789, no one imagined that the president could simply issue executive orders. It was assumed that any federal policies would need to be based on a law passed by Congress. Nevertheless, it is now accepted that just as the First Amendment limits Congress, it also limits the executive branch. However, in 1789, the First Amendment did not apply to state or local government.

Observe also that the First Amendment is expressed in *absolute* terms: "Congress shall make *no law* …" There is every reason to believe that Madison meant this literally. After all, Madison had explained to the Virginia ratifying convention that, "There is not a shadow of right in the general government to intermeddle with religion." Moreover, that same Virginia Ratifying Convention approved a list of proposed amendments that formed the basis for The Bill of Rights. The draft approved by the Convention contained the assertion that, "among other essential rights, the liberty of conscience and of the press cannot be cancelled, abridged, restrained, or modified, by any authority of the United States." Thus, the term "no law" in the First Amendment meant that the federal government could not restrict freedom of religion *in any way*.

Sadly, in the 20th and 21st centuries, "no law" no longer means "no law." According to the Supreme Court, no right is absolute, so the federal government can restrict, or "intermeddle," with religion so long as the government has a "compelling reason" for the restriction. This is certainly not what Madison intended, but that is the accepted understanding today.

Freedom of religion, sometimes called freedom of conscience, was understood to be quite broad in 1789. The federal government could never sanction someone for mere belief or opinion. This did not mean that people could do whatever they wished so long as they claimed to be following a religious practice. This point was expressed more clearly

The Constitutional Convention in 1787, Philadelphia

in many of the state bills of rights, and was the commonly accepted view at the time. For example, the Virginia Declaration of Rights stated:

> That Religion, or the Duty which We owe to our Creator, and the Manner of discharging it, can be directed only by Reason & Conviction, not by Force or Violence, and therefore that all men should enjoy the fullest Toleration in the Exercise of Religion, according to the Dictates of Conscience unpunished, & unrestrained by the Magistrate; unless under Color of Religion, any Man disturb the Peace, the Happiness, or the Safety of Society.

Similarly, the 1777 Constitution of New York stated

> [T]he free exercise and enjoyment of religious profession and worship, without discrimination or preference, shall forever hereafter be allowed, within this State, to all mankind: Provided, That the liberty of conscience, hereby granted, shall not be so construed as to excuse acts of licentiousness, or justify practices inconsistent with the peace or safety of this State.

The Maryland Constitution of 1776, South Carolina Constitution of 1778, the Massachusetts Bill of Rights of 1780, and Northwest Ordinance all contained almost identical language. Accordingly, freedom of religion extended to opinions and sentiments about the worship of God, but did not allow people to *act* however they wished. These state constitutions made clear that freedom of religion was about worshiping God. The view that the government should not punish people for their beliefs fully accords with St. Thomas who wrote in his Treatise on Law:

> Man can make laws only in those areas where he is competent to judge. His judgment does not extend to interior acts which lie hidden, however, but only to exterior acts which are apparent.

Government can only legitimately sanction people for what they do, not for what they *think*.

The Supreme Court did not decide a major freedom of religion case until 1878, when it ruled on the issue of polygamy. Congress made polygamy a crime in federal territories but a Mormon, George Reynolds, argued that his religion encouraged polygamy, therefore he should not be prosecuted under the federal law. The Supreme Court held that while Mormons were free to believe whatever they wished, they could not violate a criminal law against polygamy. (*Reynolds v. U.S.* (1878)). Unfortunately, the distinction between religious beliefs and the external expression of those beliefs is not always simple.

Until 1940, the First Amendment's free exercise clause only protected people from interference by the federal government. However, in 1940, the Supreme Court declared very abruptly, and without much argument, that the Constitution also protects individuals from having a state or local government interfere with religion. In *Cantwell v. Connecticut* (1940), the Supreme Court said that the Constitution protected the right of a Jehovah's Witness to publicly try to convert people. Although application of the free exercise clause to the states was a radical step, it is generally accepted today even by judges who believe in judicial restraint, like Justice Thomas.

A few recent cases help to illustrate the current understanding of the free exercise clause. In *Masterpiece Cakeshop v. Colorado Civil Rights Commission* (2018), the Court held that actions by government officials that are motivated by anti-religious animosity are *per se* a violation of freedom of religion. In other words, the Court does not apply the strict scrutiny test in such a case, but any government action motivated by anti-religious animosity is illegal. In *Masterpiece Cake* the State singled out a Christian business for supposedly discriminating, but the State allowed secular businesses to "discriminate" against Christians without penalty. This amounted to the state punishing Christians for their religious beliefs.

In *Our Lady of Guadalupe School v. Morrissey-Berru* (2020), the Court said Churches, in this case the Catholic Church, are free to hire and fire whomever they wish, in this case Catholic school teachers, without interference from the state or federal government. This is called the **Ministerial Exception** to anti-discrimination laws. This applies to important employees of a religious organization who have some role in teaching or formulating religious policy.

In *Kennedy v. Bremerton School District* (2022), a public school fired the football coach, Joseph Kennedy, for silently praying after football games. The Supreme Court held that a state or local government could not fire someone for praying silently. In *Groff v. DeJoy* (2023), Gerald Groff lost his job as a mailman because he asked not to be scheduled to work on Sunday. The Court held that the Post Office was required to make a reasonable accommodation to allow Groff to exercise his religion.

Thus, the current state of the free exercise clause might be summarized as follows. First, the free exercise clause requires that neither the states nor the federal government discriminate against any person or group on account of their religious beliefs. Second, government at all levels cannot interfere in the policymaking function of religious organizations. Third, government at all levels must try to accommodate a person's religious practices when possible.

The other clause of the First Amendment concerning religion is the establishment clause which reads that "Congress shall make no law respecting an establishment of religion." For the first hundred years of American government, this clause was understood to mean that the federal government could not adopt an official national religion nor interfere with states adopting an official state religion or states giving preference to Christianity. However, in 1947, the Supreme Court suddenly declared that the establishment clause meant neither the states nor the federal government could aid or encourage religion. This idea was largely based on a line from a letter Thomas Jefferson wrote to the Danbury Baptist church, in which he stated:

> I contemplate with sovereign reverence that act of the whole American people which declared that their legislature should 'make no law respecting an establishment of religion, or prohibiting the free exercise thereof,' thus building a wall of separation between Church & State.

For several decades the Supreme Court treated the phrase "wall of separation between Church & State" as though it were a constitutional imperative and repeatedly insisted that the establishment clause required states and the federal government to discriminate *against* religion. In 1962, the Supreme Court declared that the First Amendment enacted an absolute "prohibition against … governmentally sponsored religious activity." *Engel v. Vitale* (1962). In *Wallace v. Jaffree* (1985), the Supreme Court ruled that an Alabama law permitting one minute of silence for individual prayer or reflection was unconstitutional. This line of cases on "separation of church and state" was hugely controversial for many decades; however, in the last ten years, the Supreme Court has entirely reversed itself and repudiated most of the earlier "separation of church and state" cases.

Around 2010, the Court began backing off from the most radical interpretation of the establishment clause. The definitive turning point came in a case called *Trinity Lutheran Church v. Comer* (2017). In 2012, Missouri had a program which provided grants to non-profit organizations to make children's playgrounds safer. Specifically, they would replace hard concrete or gravel playgrounds with soft rubber. Trinity Lutheran Church had a children's playground they wanted to make safer, so Trinity Lutheran applied for an upgrade to their playground. The playground would have qualified for the program except that the State refused to give any aid to churches. In fact, Missouri had a provision in the State Constitution which read, "That no money shall ever be taken from the public treasury, directly or indirectly, in aid of any church, sect or denomination of religion[.]" Missouri defended this practice based on "separation of church and state."

Trinity Lutheran brought suit in federal court arguing that it was a violation of freedom of religion to offer benefits to everyone except churches. The Supreme Court agreed. Not only did the establishment clause not require the state to avoid supporting religion, but the free exercise clause forbad states from denying anyone or any group generally available benefits on the basis of religion.

The Court went even further a few years later in *Espinoza v. Montana Dept. of Revenue* (2020). In 2015, Montana enacted a system of tax credits for education. If a person contributed up to $150 to a scholarship fund, he got a tax credit for that amount. The scholarship program and tax credit applied to all private schools except religious schools. *Trinity Lutheran* held that a state cannot discriminate against people on the basis of religion; however, *Trinity Lutheran* involved a *secular* activity, improving playground safety. The Montana program, if extended to *Christian* schools, would have directly aided Christian education. The Court held that this distinction did not matter. If a state chooses to give aid to private schools then the state cannot discriminate against some schools because they are religious:

> To be eligible for government aid under the Montana Constitution, a school must divorce itself from any religious control or affiliation. Placing such a condition on benefits or privileges inevitably deters or discourages the exercise of First Amendment rights.

Moreover, the majority opinion rejected the false reading of American history that the establishment clause was intended to create a wall of separation between Church and state. In fact, the Court said overwhelming evidence exists that for most of the 19th century states and the federal government routinely supported religious and sectarian education:

> In the founding era and the early 19th century, governments provided financial support to private schools, including denominational ones. Far from prohibiting such support, the early state constitutions and statutes actively encouraged this policy.

The Court said the "wall of separation" was a myth propagated to justify anti-Christian bigotry. Many earlier cases, such as the moment of silence case, have not been officially overruled, but the Supreme Court has repudiated the reasoning that supported those cases. At least one federal Appeals Court has decided that moments of silence in public schools to allow for private prayer do *not* violate the establishment clause.[3] As of 2024, this remains a developing area of the law, but the Court seems to interpret the establishment clause as meaning essentially what it meant in 1789: there cannot be an "official state religion," but states and the federal government can support religion. What is well-established at this point is that freedom of religion cannot be restricted in the name of "separation of church and state." Basically, in the last decade, the Supreme Court has returned to the fundamental notion that the Constitution guarantees freedom *of* religion not freedom *from* religion.

---

[3] *Sherman ex rel. Sherman v. Koch*, 623 F.3d 501 (7th Cir. 2010).

THE FIRST AMENDMENT: FREEDOM OF SPEECH

In addition to freedom of religion, the First Amendment also provides that, "Congress shall make no law … abridging the freedom of speech, or of the press." This originally meant the federal government would be prevented from regulating all speech and the issue would be left entirely to the states. This idea was expressed by Hamilton in *Federalist* 84, and by Madison and others in the Virginia ratifying convention of 1788. This position was articulated again by Madison and Jefferson in the Virginia and Kentucky Resolutions they wrote to oppose the Sedition Act. The Kentucky Resolution, written by Jefferson and adopted by the Kentucky legislature in December 1798, stated:

> [N]o power over the freedom of religion, freedom of speech, or freedom of the press being delegated to the United States by the Constitution, nor prohibited by it to the States, all lawful powers respecting the same did of right remain, and were reserved to the … libels, falsehood, and defamation, equally with heresy and false religion, are withheld from the cognizance of federal tribunals.

In short, states had authority to regulate speech but the federal government had no such authority. The Sedition Act punished defamatory (false and damaging) statements made about federal officials. Federalists defended the Sedition Act by arguing that free speech did not cover certain kinds of speech, like defamation, that had long been punishable under English Common Law. Madison and Jefferson acknowledged that defamation, obscenity, and blasphemy could never be considered speech, but it was the role of states to punish these things.

This view of Madison and Jefferson, that the First Amendment was a strong restraint on the federal government, was the dominant view for the next century. Congress passed virtually no laws restricting freedom of speech. However, in 1917, when the United States declared war on Germany, Congress passed *The Espionage Act* making it a crime to convey information that "obstructed" the war effort. The law seemed to be intended to protect military secrets, but the language was broad enough that the Wilson Administration prosecuted people who

Oliver Wendell Holmes, Jr.

simply criticized the war. This went farther than the Sedition Act, which was limited to people who made false statements that qualified as defamatory under common law. In 1917, people were sent to jail for making truthful statements or expressing an opinion such as "I believe war is unjust."

The Supreme Court upheld the conviction and imprisonment of war critics. The Court, in a famous opinion by Justice Oliver Wendell Holmes, Jr., held that criticizing the government in time of war was *not* protected by the First Amendment, reasoning "*The most stringent protection of free speech would not protect a man in falsely shouting fire in a theatre and causing a panic.*" [4]

This decision was later overturned, but it was a crucial move. By interpreting the First Amendment as an individual right, Holmes actually *expanded* the power of the federal government. Instead of regarding regulation of speech as an area of law reserved to the states, free speech was an individual right asserted against the federal government. Yet no individual right is absolute. No one has a right to *falsely* shout fire in a theatre. Accordingly, the federal government can regulate speech that it deems dangerous.

---

[4] *Schenck v. United States* (1919).

Remarkably, this was precisely what Hamilton predicted would happen in *Federalist* 84. Hamilton argued that a bill of rights "would contain various exceptions to powers not granted; and, on this very account, would afford a colorable pretext to claim more than were granted." By insisting that the First Amendment did not protect dangerous speech, this created a pretext to claim that Congress had power to regulate such speech.

Once the phrase "Congress shall make no law … abridging the freedom of speech" became essentially about individual rights, the stage was set to apply this individual right to state and local government. In 1925, the Supreme Court suddenly declared without any explanation:

> For present purposes we may and do assume that freedom of speech and of the press—which are protected by the First Amendment from abridgment by Congress—are among the fundamental personal rights and 'liberties' protected by the due process clause of the Fourteenth Amendment from impairment by the States.[5]

The Supreme Court began routinely striking down state laws thought to interfere with freedom of speech. However, it was not until 1964 that the very first federal law was declared to be a violation of free speech.[6] Today, courts apply the same test to state or federal laws that restrict freedom of speech: Any content-based restriction on speech that is not outside the confines of the First Amendment must be narrowly tailored to a compelling interest.

First, and perhaps most importantly, some "speech" is entirely outside the protection of the First Amendment. For one thing, freedom of speech is generally only applicable to government restrictions on speech. Accordingly, a private school can restrict student speech as much as it wants because the First Amendment does not apply to *private* schools. However, the First Amendment does apply to *public* schools. Second, there are four classes of unprotected "speech:" obscenity, defamation, true threats, and incitement.

At common law obscenity was defined as any publication "calculated to produce a pernicious effect in depraving and debauching the minds of the persons into whose hands it might come." More recently the Supreme Court has defined obscenity as anything intended to appeal to a "prurient interest" and "the work taken as a whole, lacks serious literary, artistic, political, or scientific value." *Miller v. California* (1973). So, pornography and other forms of obscenity are entirely unprotected and can be banned by the states or the federal government. Sadly, it should be noted that lower courts tend to have a remarkably lax view of "obscenity" when state and local governments try to control it.

Outside of these four areas, neither the states nor the federal government may restrict the content of speech unless it is narrowly tailored to a compelling interest. A **content-based restriction** is any restriction on *what* a person or organization can say. Restrictions that are not based on content but on the time, place, or manner of the speech are subject to much less rigorous constraints. A typical example of a time, place, or manner restriction is noise ordinances. A local ordinance that said sound trucks cannot broadcast messages between 10 pm and 8 am would be *non-content* based. However, a local ordinance that said sound trucks cannot broadcast *political* messages between 10 pm and 8 am would be a *content-based* restriction.

Time, place, and manner restrictions are permissible so long as they are not a pretext for suppressing content, and allow alternative opportunities for a person to express his views. For example, a law banning *all* protests within 36 feet of abortion facilities was deemed to be content neutral. Moreover, the 36-foot limitation meant that protestors could be across the street from the facility where they could still be seen and heard by people going to the clinic. *Madsen v. Women's Health Center*, 512 U.S. 753 (1994). However, a law that pushed protesters so far away that they could no longer effectively protest such a facility would be unconstitutional even if it were truly content neutral.

Finally, it should be noted that freedom of "speech" involves much more than just oral, or spoken, language. Freedom of speech also includes various forms of *expressive* conduct. For example, burning a flag is a form of expressive protest that is constitutionally protected. Even silent protests, such as picketing, are protected. So long as the "speech" conveys a message, it is likely protected.

---

[5] *Gitlow v. People of State of New York* (1925).
[6] *Lamont v. Postmaster General.*

CHAPTER 7: THE BILL OF RIGHTS

THE FIRST AMENDMENT: FREEDOM OF THE PRESS

Freedom of the press is much older than freedom of speech. In 17th century England, there was a strong tradition of newspapers publishing criticisms of the government. Today, freedom of speech and freedom of the press are effectively the same thing. The Supreme Court has said that reporters have no special privileges. A majority of states recognize a privilege of reporters not to reveal their sources, but this has never been recognized as a federal constitutional right.

Today, when anyone with a cell phone camera and Facebook page can be a "reporter," there is less distinction than ever between reporters and ordinary citizens. Federal courts have widely held that ordinary citizens have a constitutional right to audio or video record government officials, as long as the citizen is not trespassing on government property. For example, any citizen has a First Amendment right to record police officers on the street.

One important case affecting publishers was the *Pentagon Papers* case. In 1971, Daniel Ellsberg stole top secret documents from the Pentagon which showed that military officials had lied to the public

about the Vietnam War. Ellsberg gave copies of the stolen documents to the *New York Times* and *Washington Post*. The Nixon Administration tried to prevent the publication of the stolen papers. However, the Supreme Court held that while a person who actually steals information can be prosecuted, a publisher who obtains such papers has a First Amendment right to publish them.

THE SECOND AMENDMENT

The Second Amendment states that, "*A well regulated Militia being necessary to the security of a free State, the right of the people to keep and bear Arms shall not be infringed.*" Many anti-Federalists thought that the federal government might use its power to regulate the militia as a pretext for disarming the people. Ironically, for several decades of the 20th century, opponents of the Second Amendment argued that this amendment did not apply to "the people" but only to members of the military. Opponents of the Second Amendment argued that because of the introductory clause, "A well regulated Militia," only members of the military had a right to keep and bear arms. It is now almost universally acknowledged that this limitation to the military was a misreading. It is now accepted that all of "the people" have an individual right to self-defense and therefore also the right to "keep and bear arms" to defend themselves and their families.

For a surprisingly long time, the Supreme Court did not decide whether the Second Amendment protected an individual right or not. In fact, it was not until 2008 that the Supreme Court definitively ruled on this issue. Part of the reason for the scarcity of judicial interpretation was that for almost all of American history there were almost no state or federal restrictions on private ownership of weapons. The first federal attempt to restrict a "weapon" was the Explosives Act of 1917, which prohibited the possession of a large volume of explosives without a license as a temporary wartime measure.

In 1934, Congress passed the *National Firearms Act* which imposed a high tax on the purchase of certain weapons such as fully automatic weapons, that is, machine guns, as well as short-barreled shotguns, and firearm suppressors, so-called "silencers." The Supreme Court upheld this tax in an opinion which assumed that the Second Amendment conferred an individual's right to keep arms. *Miller v. United States* (1939).

A few decades later, Congress passed the *Gun Control Act of 1968*. Even then, the original Act

U.S. Government for Catholic Students

was quite limited. It placed restrictions on the sale of firearms across state lines and prohibited the importation of military surplus firearms. The main individual restriction in the Act was the prohibition on convicted felons possessing firearms. Over the past 40 years, however, many other groups have been added to those who may not possess a firearm. This list now includes illegal immigrants, drug addicts, people with mental illness, and people who have been convicted of certain misdemeanors.

Between 1970 and 2008, these federal laws were often challenged as a violation of the Second Amendment. However, lower federal courts almost always upheld these laws and the Supreme Court declined to review any of these cases. Lower courts upheld federal laws by asserting that the Second Amendment *only* extended to people who were formally enrolled in the military and *only* during periods of actual military service. In the 1970s, 1980s, and 1990s, advocates of the Second Amendment thought this reasoning of the lower courts was nonsensical and consistently petitioned the Supreme Court to become involved.

In 2008, the Supreme Court finally agreed to hear an appeal from the District of Columbia which effectively banned all handguns. Justice Scalia, writing for the majority, showed that the historical record was unambiguous: all the Founders wanted common people to keep and bear arms. Moreover, Scalia pointed out that it made no sense to imagine that an article in The Bill of Rights which referred to "the right of the people to keep and bear Arms shall not be infringed" only applied to government agents. *Heller v. District of Columbia* (2008).

Congress directly governs the District of Columbia so the Second Amendment applies directly to the District. *Heller* left open the question whether the right to keep and bear arms was implicit in the Fourteenth Amendment. In 2010, the Court declared that self-defense in general, and the right to possess arms in particular, was so deeply rooted in the Anglo-American legal tradition that the Fourteenth Amendment made these rights applicable to the states. *McDonald v. City of Chicago* (2010).

Self-defense is fully in accord with the Natural Law and Catholic teaching. The legitimacy of defending one's self and one's family was firmly established in Jewish law. Ex. 22:2. In the *Summa of Theology* (II-II, q. 64, a. 7), St. Thomas wrote "it is natural to everything to keep itself in being, as far as possible." Even though all human life is sacred and worthy of protection, people have a Natural Law obligation to preserve innocent life against attack.

First Muster, Spring 1637, Massachusetts Bay Colony

Despite the Supreme Court declaring that the right to keep and bear arms was fundamental, lower courts continued to uphold and enforce virtually every state and federal restriction on weapons. Recall that for most fundamental rights courts apply the strict scrutiny test: is the restriction narrowly tailored to implement a compelling state interest. From 2011 to 2022, lower courts consistently held that "combating crime" was so important that no restriction on possession of weapons was too much. In fact, several times between 2011 and 2022, Supreme Court justices complained that lower court judges were just rubber stamping state and federal gun control laws.

In 2022, the Supreme Court took a different approach. When it came to the right to keep and bear arms there was to be no more balancing of fundamental rights with compelling interests. Instead, federal and state restrictions on possession of weapons is only permissible if it was the type of restriction common in the 18th century. *New York State Rifle & Pistol Assn. v. Bruen* (2022). Because there were almost no restrictions on weapons' possession in the 18th century, this seemed to make virtually all restrictions on possession of weapons unconstitutional. The only restrictions that seem permissible now are restricting gun possession by people who have been convicted of violent felonies, like murder, and some restrictions as to those places guns may not be carried, such as no firearms in a courthouse. Although lower courts continue to rubber stamp gun control laws, the federal appellate courts have begun applying *Bruen* and declaring a large number of federal and state gun control laws to be unconstitutional.

Today, the test for possession of any article that might be used for self-defense, even such items as body-armor, is the state or federal government must show the regulation is closely analogous to a law that was generally accepted in 1792.

THE THIRD AMENDMENT

The Third Amendment reads: "*No soldier shall, in time of peace be quartered in any house, without the consent of the owner, nor in time of war, but in a manner to be prescribed by law.*" Notice that the Amendment says nothing about "rights." It is phrased in terms of a prohibition on what the government can do. The specific language was modeled on the Anti-Quartering Act that Parliament passed in 1679.

The Third Amendment is almost completely irrelevant today. It's only significance lies in its role as part of those Amendments which the Court used to fashion the right to privacy. In fact, the Amendment was more about property rights than privacy. The *Quartering* Act of 1774, one of "The Intolerable Acts," allowed the English army to requisition *unoccupied* homes to house soldiers, but only unoccupied homes or commercial buildings. Colonists objected to this as the English commandeered property without paying for it. This is further seen by the fact that the Third Amendment refers to "the owner" not the residents.

THE FOURTH AMENDMENT

Unlike the generally irrelevant Third Amendment, the Fourth Amendment, which also involves the right of privacy, is one of the most important and *relevant* Amendments – and one every American should understand and never hesitate to invoke! The Fourth Amendment states:

> The right of the people to be secure in their persons, houses, papers, and effects, against unreasonable searches and seizures, shall not be violated, and no Warrants shall issue, but upon probable cause, supported by Oath or affirmation, and particularly describing the place to be searched, and the persons or things to be seized.

Once again, this Amendment grew out of the colonial experience in which English soldiers and tax collectors would invade colonists' homes and businesses without a search warrant, or sometimes, with a "general warrant." A general warrant was an authorization to search anywhere and thus was really no protection at all. This is why the Amendment requires the warrant to describe "*particularly*" the places to be searched and things to be seized.

In Anglo-American tradition there is an old aphorism that "A man's home is his castle." This principle has been traced back at least as far as a statute enacted in 1275. It was splendidly expressed in 1604 in *Semayne's Case* by English Attorney General Edward Coke who, referring to the 1275 statute, proclaimed that "the house of every one is to him as his castle and fortress, as well for his defense against injury and violence, as for his repose." *Semayne's Case* proclaimed that the sanctity of the home could not be violated on mere suspicion of illegal activity. Rather, a person's home could only be invaded when agents of the king could prove to a neutral judge that such a home invasion was "necessary." *Semayne's Case* further proclaimed that the maxim of man's house being his castle extends not only to a person's house but "to him and his family, and to his own proper goods." Similar language appears in the Fourth Amendment which applies the protection to "their persons, houses, papers, and effects." The word "effects" is understood to apply in its broadest sense to all a person's property. Thus, for example, a person's bank records, medical records, and emails are protected from government intrusion.

Accordingly, if the government wants to search a person's property or effects, it needs to obtain a warrant from a judge. The agency seeking the warrant must present evidence to the judge that there is "probable cause" to think that the search will uncover evidence of a crime. Historically, "probable cause" simply meant "more likely than not." However, recently courts have said "probable cause" does not mean "more likely than not." The Supreme Court has defined "probable cause" as a "substantial chance" or "fair probability" of criminal activity, but less than "more likely than not." *Illinois v. Gates* (1983).

Like other provisions of The Bill of Rights, the Fourth Amendment initially only applied to the federal government. However, in 1961, the Court decided that the provisions of the Fourth Amendment were applicable to the states by reason of the Fourteenth Amendment. *Mapp v. Ohio* (1961). A crucial point to note is that the Fourth Amendment, as applied to the states, provides a minimum level of protection. States can place greater restrictions on police than the Fourth Amendment requires. For example, even if the Fourth Amendment does not prohibit

Edward Coke

the warrantless search of cars, a state may pass a law prohibiting police to search a car without a warrant. This is true for most of the provisions of The Bill of Rights. Those parts of the Bill of Rights that apply to the states provide minimum protections for liberty, not the outer limits. They are the floor, not the ceiling. Almost all states in one way or another provided additional restrictions on police beyond what the U.S. Constitution requires.

One of the most controversial aspects of the Fourth Amendment is the **exclusionary rule** which states that in a criminal prosecution the state cannot use evidence that was obtained in violation of the Fourth Amendment. For example, if police illegally enter a home and find a dead body, that evidence cannot be used against the murderer. To allow a person literally to get away with murder certainly is wrong, but proponents of the exclusionary rule fear that as the government becomes more powerful, government agents will illegally enter homes with little or no evidence of wrong-doing, merely hoping to find evidence. Imagine a person is home schooling and the government forces its way into the home. The police decide that the house is not clean enough or there is not enough food in the house. These do not seem to be crimes, but the government may decide that there is a "child endangerment" statute that the family has violated. The exclusionary rule protects criminals but it also protects innocent people. Moreover, the courts have reasoned that the government cannot be allowed to benefit from illegal action.

Another controversial aspect of the Fourth Amendment is the number of exceptions that have been created. Indeed, many people think that the exceptions have swallowed the rule. One exception to the exclusionary rule is known as the "good faith" exception. This allows police to obtain evidence even if a mistake was made so long as the police acted in good faith. For example, they raid 209 Maple Ave and find drugs, but the warrant was for 209 Maple *Street*. This is a good faith exception so the drugs they found at Maple Ave can be used as evidence.

Oftentimes the issue before the court involves the question whether the government conducted a search at all, that is, what is and is not a "search" for Fourth Amendment purposes. For example, what if something is in **plain view**? If a person is driving around with an illegal weapon in the back window of their pick-up truck and police can see it "in plain view" there is no search. The courts have relied on "physical intrusion" to determine whether something is a search. Thus, when a police officer shines a flashlight into a dark car, it is generally not considered a "search" under the Fourth Amendment. If an officer uses a flashlight to better see into a car's interior through a window, they are only enhancing their ability to observe what is already exposed to public view. Shining a flashlight does not involve physical intrusion into a private space, such as entering the car. The observation is made from a lawful vantage point, such as standing outside the vehicle in a public area. This principle was affirmed in cases like *Texas v. Brown* (1983), where the Supreme Court ruled that using artificial means like a flashlight to aid an officer's vision does not transform lawful observation into an illegal search. The court said the flashlight was like glasses or contact lens. It only allows the police officer to see *better*, not see what is hidden.

One of the most important searches is called a "Terry Search," named after the Supreme Court case *Terry v. Ohio* (1968) that gave rise to the

doctrine. In *Terry v. Ohio* the Supreme Court held that police could "stop and frisk" a person if the police have "reasonable suspicion" that a person might be armed and dangerous. "Reasonable suspicion" is far less than "probable cause." Nevertheless, police must have specific, articulable facts amounting to reasonable suspicion; an unparticularized "hunch" is insufficient. In some cases, these suspicions might be that a person was acting "suspiciously" or had a "bulge in the pocket" that might be a weapon. Critics argue that this amorphous standard allows police to stop any pedestrian at any time on the flimsiest pretext. Supporters argue that Terry Stops are a crucial law enforcement tool, because police, based on their knowledge and experience, often have a sense of when a person is "up to no good." Although Terry Stops are supposed to be limited to searching for weapons, police may find illegal drugs when they frisk the suspect.

Even when there is a "search," there are many exceptions to the Fourth Amendment warrant requirement. One such exception occurs when a search is performed with consent of the owner of the property to be searched. The courts have even permitted the police to obtain consent by trickery – with some limits. For example, a police officer has not gained true consent if he lies to a homeowner by falsely claiming to possess a search warrant. This is not consent, it is mere acquiescence to authority. However, police are allowed to lie about their ability to obtain a search warrant. So, courts have said police can tell a homeowner that, "You should let me in, I can get a search warrant if you refuse," even though the officer knows he has no basis for a warrant. This is considered acceptable because the person theoretically could reply, "ok, come back when you have a warrant."

Additionally, police are allowed to lie about who they are. Before cell phones became omni-present, police might check out a home by knocking on the door and falsely telling the resident that the plain clothes officer's car broke down and ask to be permitted to use the telephone. If the homeowner asked, "You're not a cop are you," the officer is permitted to lie and say, "No." The amount of deception permitted is, unfortunately, ambiguous.

The line between consent and acquiescence to authority is also ambiguous. When several police officers with badges and guns show up at a person's home and tell him: "We need to search your garage," it is difficult for an ordinary person to refuse. This demonstrates the importance of knowing one's Constitutional rights.

Another exception to the warrant requirement is called **exigent circumstances**, which means there is an immediate need for a search and it would be difficult, or inconvenient, to obtain a warrant. There are actually a variety of searches that fall under this category. One is **the automobile exception**. The Supreme Court has said that because cars are so mobile they can be searched without a warrant. Most states have refused to follow the automobile exception as a matter of state law.

Another exigent circumstance is **search incident to arrest**. The reasoning here was that when a person is arrested, then police need to be able to search that person for weapons. Over the years, police pushed this to extremes. For example, police would deliberately wait to arrest a person until he got home, then when arrested in his living room, police would search the house from basement to attic calling it a search incident to arrest. The Supreme Court held that search incident to arrest only includes the immediate area of the arrest. The Court more recently also held that search incident to arrest only applies at the exact time of the arrest. So, if a suspect is arrested in his living room, police cannot return to the living room the next day to search it in case they missed something. To do that police must apply for a warrant.

For good or ill, so many exceptions have been created to the warrant requirement that police rarely need to obtain a search warrant to conduct a search. A warrant has become the exception rather than the rule.

A final point to note regarding the Fourth Amendment is that it also covers arrests or "seizures" of people: "no Warrants shall issue, but upon probable cause, supported by Oath or affirmation, and particularly describing ... the *persons* ... to be seized." However, as with searches, the Supreme Court has permitted arrest warrants to become the exception rather than the rule. Today, about 99% of arrests are made without a warrant. This is illustrated by the case of *Atwater v. City of Lago Vista* (2001). Gail Atwater was arrested, taken to jail, and locked up for failing to wear a seatbelt – a misdemeanor punishable by a $50 fine. Atwater argued that a person should not be subject to warrantless arrest for such a minor violation. The Supreme Court held that a warrantless arrest, even for the most minor crimes, is permissible so long as there was "probable cause" that there was a violation of some law. The *Atwater* decision has been criticized, but the Court has not reversed it. However, the decision is so controversial that most state courts have ruled that arrests for minor offenses violate state law.

Most states have reasoned that arresting a person, when issuing a ticket would be sufficient,

constitutes an indignity if not an outright act of violence. This accords with Catholic teaching about justice. Use of force should always be a last resort, not a first response. Moreover, no more force should be used than is necessary to accomplish the objective. Imagine a person is trespassing on private land. The person might not even realize he is trespassing. If the property owner can safely inform the trespasser that he is trespassing and ask him to leave, that is the path justice requires. The property owner cannot instantly shoot trespassers, or throw them to the ground and handcuff them. That would violate the basic principle of justice to use force only as a last resort.

Many legal experts think it is only a matter of time before the Supreme Court overrules *Atwater*. In 2019, however, the court held if a person is singled out for arrest for an offense that would normally simply result in a citation, then the person arrested can sue the police for discriminatory treatment. *Nieves v. Bartlett* (2019). Prior to 2019, the Court said that a person could not sue for false arrest so long as there was an "arrestable offense," even if an officer acted out of animosity or vindictiveness. In fact, in *Atwater*, the Court seemed to say that it did not matter why Atwater had been singled out for arrest when most people stopped for not wearing a seatbelt would merely be given a traffic ticket.

Currently, the Fourth Amendment provides greater protection to property than to people. It is easier for police to arrest a person than obtain a warrant to seize that person's laptop. This seems upside down, but it is the status today.

THE FIFTH AMENDMENT

The Fifth Amendment is another of the incredibly important provisions of the Constitution that every American should know, understand, and rely upon when dealing with the government. As anyone who has watched a movie or television show in the last fifty years knows, criminals always claim their Fifth Amendment rights. They "take the Fifth." The language of the Fifth Amendment is somewhat complex, and contains many elements, but its effects are rather simple. The Amendment provides:

> No person shall be held to answer for a capital, or otherwise infamous crime, unless on a presentment or indictment of a grand jury, except in cases arising in the land or naval forces, or in the militia, when in actual service in time of war or public danger; nor shall any person be subject for the same offense to be twice put in jeopardy of life or limb; nor shall be compelled in any criminal case to be a witness against himself, nor be deprived of life, liberty, or property, without due process of law; nor shall private property be taken for public use, without just compensation.

Notice that this Amendment is not framed in terms of "rights," but as prohibitions on what the government can do. All of these provisions were ideas already found in English common law for centuries. Under the Fifth Amendment, Americans possess five basic "rights" or protections.

INDICTMENT BY GRAND JURY

The first right is one that has already been discussed in an early chapter: the right to be indicted by a grand jury for felony charges. This right serves to protect people from out of control government prosecutions. A prosecutor needs to present evidence to the grand jury that there is evidence to move forward with a trial. As previously noted, the grand jury system contains problems, but the Founders hoped it would limit unjust prosecutions.

DOUBLE JEOPARDY

One of the most important Fifth Amendment provisions is the protection against "**double jeopardy**." This means that once a person is acquitted of a crime they can never be tried for that same offense again. We can see why such a rule is essential. If the government could just keep trying a defendant over and over then conviction would be inevitable and the person could be kept in jail forever pending the new trial. However, if the jury cannot reach a unanimous decision then the state can try the defendant again, but this is considered a new trial, not a retrial.

SELF-INCRIMINATION

The Fifth Amendment says that no one "shall be compelled in any criminal case to be a witness against himself." This principle has been traced back to the Middle Ages in England and includes several different aspects.

One implication is that suspects cannot be tortured and forced to confess to a crime. In fact, at the Virginia Ratifying Convention, George Mason insisted there be an amendment prohibiting self-incrimination to prevent the government torturing confessions out of suspects.[7] In Elizabethan times, Catholics were tortured and forced to confess their "crimes." However, in 1696, Parliament passed a statute prohibiting coerced confessions from being used in evidence in criminal trials. The Eighth Amendment prohibits torture as *punishment* for crime, but the Fifth Amendment prohibits torture as means of *coercing* a confession.

Physical torture is only one aspect of this principle. Many people thought that forcing a person to testify against himself was a form of *psychological* torture. Imagine being accused of a capital offense but the state had a very weak case; perhaps the state had no witnesses to testify the accused was even at the scene of the crime. Now imagine that the state could call the accused as a witness and force him to admit he was at the scene of the crime, or hold the accused in prison until he agreed to answer the question. Most people think this is an intolerable situation in which to place any accused person. For centuries, the common law avoided this by preventing the prosecution calling a criminal defendant as a witness at trial. The privilege extends to non-defendants as well. The privilege would not be worth much if the state could call a suspect as a witness in another trial and force the suspect to "confess" just because he had not yet been charged with a crime. Accordingly, people "have a right to remain silent" and not give statements that might be used against them.

In 1848, Parliament passed an act requiring an arresting officer to warn the suspect that he need not answer questions. The idea was that the right to remain silent was worthless if the suspect was unaware of it, and, more importantly, the police could pressure the suspect to talk. The main purpose of the warning seems to have been to prevent police using pressure tactics. It is difficult for an officer to tell a suspect he has a right to remain silent but then punish him for doing what the officer just said, that is, remaining silent.

In 1966, in *Miranda v. Arizona*, the Supreme Court declared that before police question a suspect who was under arrest, the suspect had to be warned that he had a right to remain silent and to consult with counsel. This is called a **Miranda Warning**. If a suspect is under arrest, then any statements the suspect makes cannot be used against him in a criminal trial. However, this right is much narrower than many people think. The

---
[7] Eliot's Debates, Vol. 3, pp. 451–452.

requirement for a *Miranda* warning only applies to *custodial* interrogation. In other words, police can approach a suspect on the street and ask questions without giving a *Miranda* warning. When a suspect is "in custody" is not always clear; although, if a person is not free to leave a police station they are certainly in custody. Moreover, what constitutes an "interrogation" is also ambiguous. Police will often make comments intended to elicit an incriminating response like, "That was pretty clever the way you broke into that store."

Finally, a suspect's refusal to speak to authorities or to testify in court cannot be used against them in a trial. The right to remain silent would be worthless if a prosecutor could say to a jury, "The defendant refused to answer the questions the police asked them, but an innocent person would want to tell them his story."

A police officer reading the *Miranda* warning

DUE PROCESS

Neither the federal government nor the states may take away a person's "life, liberty, or property, without due process." What process is "due" is often somewhat uncertain. The Supreme Court has said that in the case of a criminal trial, "due process" requires that the state must prove every element of a criminal offense beyond a reasonable doubt. For example, if a statute makes it a crime to enter a dwelling place at night with intent to steal, then the state must prove beyond a reasonable doubt not just the intent, but also that it was a dwelling, that there was entry, and that it happened at night.

For civil matters, the process which is "due" depends upon the nature of the interest involved. For loss of custody of children, the state must prove abuse or neglect by "clear and convincing evidence." For relatively insignificant property interests the process due may be minimal. However, neither the federal government nor the state may take away a person's liberty or property without notice and opportunity to contest the taking.

THE TAKINGS CLAUSE

Neither the federal government nor a state may take private property for public use without just compensation. The most obvious example occurs when the government takes the land for some public project like an airport. This is called the power of **eminent domain**. Sometimes the common good requires certain things, but it would be inequitable if just a few people had to bear the total cost. So, if an airport is necessary for the common good, the state can take property, but the property owner should be compensated.

THE SIXTH AMENDMENT

The Sixth Amendment provides that

In all criminal prosecutions, the accused shall enjoy the right to a speedy and public trial, by an impartial jury of the state and district wherein the crime shall have been committed, which district shall have been previously ascertained by law, and to be informed of the nature and cause of the accusation; to be confronted with the witnesses against him; to have compulsory process for obtaining witnesses in his favor, and to have the assistance of counsel for his defense.

All of these provisions were well established at common law for centuries and many were also included in the Judiciary Act of 1789. The Sixth Amendment provides a number of guarantees to criminal defendants: a speedy and public trial, a jury trial, the right to confront their accusers, and the right to effective counsel. While some of these seem self-explanatory, a couple are worthy of further comment.

First, the Amendment guarantees a speedy and public trial. As noted, it is important that trials are not conducted in secret. Also, because a defendant might be in jail, it is important that he be tried as quickly as possible. Innocent people should be released as soon as possible and those found "guilty" should be sentenced and allowed to appeal in a timely manner.

The *confrontation clause* generally means that a criminal defendant has a constitutional right to challenge and cross examine any witness against him. This principle was part of Roman law and was well-established for the entire period of English common law. However, there were some famous examples from the 16th and 17th centuries where this concept was ignored. In 1603, Walter Raleigh was tried and convicted for treason based on the affidavit of a witness who never appeared in court and was not subject to cross examination. (Luckily for Raleigh, he was pardoned by James I.) Moreover, in the 1760s and 1770s, English courts often tried colonists for alleged violations of the Stamp Act by using affidavits rather than live testimony subject to cross examination.

As always, the court has allowed some exceptions to the confrontation clause. For example, the Supreme Court has allowed prosecutions to play "9-1-1 calls" in which a person who is not present or available for cross examination explains to police what is actually happening at the time of the call. Thus, a caller might tell police: "Come quickly my neighbor is beating up his son," which would be admissible.

Walter Raleigh

King James I

The other important aspect of the Sixth Amendment is the *right to counsel*. As with the Fifth Amendment right to remain silent, the Supreme Court in *Miranda* said that police must inform a suspect of his right to counsel. If a suspect invokes his right to counsel, police must immediately cease all interrogation or attempts to elicit information and may not attempt to dissuade the suspect from speaking to a lawyer. For example, police cannot ask a suspect, "If you are innocent why do you need a lawyer?" The Supreme Court has held that such a question violates the Sixth Amendment.

At common law, and for most of American history, the right to counsel simply meant that the government could not stop a person from obtaining counsel if he could afford it. In 1963, the Supreme Court declared that the Sixth Amendment required that people who could not afford a lawyer had to be provided one at government expense and that this right was applicable to the states. It is generally accepted today that this is a good idea since the resources of the government are enormous while those of most defendants, especially poor defendants, place them at a huge disadvantage.

The attorney appointed by the government to defend people who cannot afford counsel is known as the **public defender**. In the federal system, the federal public defender is part of the judicial branch. State public defenders are notoriously underpaid and overworked. State public defenders often have hundreds of defendants to represent at any given time. In most states, public defenders work for the governor who is often more interested in getting convictions than in defending the accused.

The right to court appointed counsel only applies when a defendant actually is facing a jail sentence. Therefore, for example, if a person is charged with a misdemeanor and is facing a fine but not jail, there is no right to appointed counsel.

Oral arguments being made before the New York Court of Appeals

THE SEVENTH AMENDMENT

The Seventh Amendment provides:

> In Suits at common law, where the value in controversy shall exceed twenty dollars, the right of trial by jury shall be preserved, and no fact tried by a jury, shall be otherwise re-examined in any Court of the United States, than according to the rules of the common law.

This Amendment has not been applied to the states, and the right to jury in a civil case has not been considered fundamental. Historically, it has not been one of the more important amendments.

THE EIGHTH AMENDMENT

The Eighth Amendment states:

> Excessive bail shall not be required, nor excessive fines imposed, nor cruel and unusual punishments inflicted.

The Eighth Amendment has become one of the most litigated amendments in recent history and one over which Catholics have begun to disagree.

This Amendment contains three different elements: 1) excessive bail, 2) excessive fines, and 3) cruel and unusual punishment. Each of these three aspects presents a different but important liberty. Note again, that the issues are not expressed as individual rights, but as absolute prohibitions on what the government can do.

EXCESSIVE BAIL

The Supreme Court first declared the excessive bail clause to be applicable to the states in 1971. *Schilb v. Kuebel* (1971). The Court made no attempt to explain why this provision applied to the states, merely declaring that the Court "assumed" that it does. It is now established that criminal defendants are presumptively entitled to bail, and that the conditions of pretrial release cannot be excessive or more than absolutely necessary. Although "bail" often is understood to mean money, the court often applies "bail conditions" or "conditions of release" either *instead* of money or *in addition* to money. For example, a condition of release might be "do not leave the state." Bail conditions can be quite onerous. For example, a court might order as a bail condition that a person remain under house arrest, that is, not leave his home, indefinitely. Such a condition might be "excessive," especially for a minor offense where jail time is not even applicable to a conviction. The burden is on the prosecution to justify that the condition or amount of bail is necessary.

The right to bail is based on the fundamental principle that a defendant is innocent until proven guilty beyond a reasonable doubt. Again, arrest only requires "probable cause," which is a far lower standard than beyond a reasonable doubt. People often wonder why, "That person is a murderer, why is he let out on bail?" Just being accused of a crime does not make a person guilty.

At common law, bail was for only one purpose: to ensure that the accused showed up for trial. A person might be required to give the court an amount of money to hold which would be forfeit if they failed to show up for trial. In some circumstances, it might be the case that no money or condition is necessary. For instance, if the defendant had "strong ties to the community," such as owning a business in the community, he was unlikely to run away and would be released on his promise to appear for trial. This is known as a person's **own recognizance**.

EXCESSIVE FINES

Amazingly, it was not until 2019 that the Supreme Court declared that the excessive fines clause was applicable to the states. *Timbs v. Indiana* (2019). Timbs was convicted of a fairly minor drug offense and sentenced to a fine of $1000 and probation. (Probation is a form of supervised release where a person is subject to specific rules and supervised by a probation officer.) In addition to the $1000 fine, Indiana also seized the $42,000 car Timbs had been driving. The car was not the proceeds of any illegal activity. The state law simply allowed the state to confiscate any property involved in illegal activity. Moreover, the crime for which Timbs was convicted carried a maximum penalty of $10,000.

The Supreme Court unanimously declared that the excessive fines clause was applicable to the states. It noted that this idea went all the way back to Magna Carta which required that economic sanctions "be proportioned to the wrong." The English Bill of Rights of 1689 condemned excessive fines. Thus, the Court said the prohibition on excessive fines was "deeply rooted" in the Anglo-American tradition and should be recognized as a fundamental right.

The Court then went on to hold that confiscating a $42,000 vehicle for a fairly trivial offense was "excessive" in terms of the 8th Amendment. This issue of **asset forfeiture** has been controversial for years. In the 1970s, both the states and the federal government decided that seizing assets involved in a crime might be a good idea to deter crime and to add to the coffers of the state. Many people argued that asset forfeiture violated the 8th Amendment, but until the *Timbs* case, courts had generally ignored this argument. It remains to be seen how states will adapt

to *Timbs*. States might increase criminal fines, rather than calling it a forfeiture of goods involved in criminal activity. *Timbs* only explicitly applied to forfeited goods, but the reasoning of the case suggests that a $50,000 fine for a trivial offense would violate the 8th Amendment.

CRUEL AND UNUSUAL PUNISHMENT

The 8th Amendment prohibition against cruel and unusual punishments was applied to the states in 1962. *Robinson v. California* (1962). This issue particularly interests Catholics as it involves capital punishment.

The Framers created the 8th Amendment as a result of early modern English law, under which, there were a variety of crimes punishable by death. However, treason was considered so heinous a crime that a person was viciously tortured to death. Thus, if a person were convicted of murder, the murderer would be hanged or beheaded as these were considered painless and humane ways to execute someone. However, a person convicted of treason would be slowly and terribly tortured to death.

In 1640, Parliament passed a law that abolished torture as a punishment for treason. The English Bill of Rights of 1689 also condemned "cruel and unusual punishment," again chiefly concerned with cruel executions for people accused of treason. Of course, the colonial patriots in the 1770s were accused of treason by the English. Although torture had not been used as a punishment for treason for over a century, no one was entirely sure that if the English won the war, they might not employ such penalties in the colonies. Accordingly, this was an issue of particular interest to many of the Founders.

One of the earliest cases that invoked the 8th Amendment was *Wilkerson v. Utah* (1878). In 1878, Utah was a federal territory so the 8th Amendment was applicable. Wilkerson was found guilty of murder and sentenced to death by firing squad. He appealed his conviction to the Supreme Court, arguing that death by firing squad was cruel and unusual. The Supreme Court affirmed the punishment and explained that the 8th Amendment was intended to prohibit particularly painful death for treason. Therefore, a death sentence must be carried out in ways that would not deliberately inflict additional suffering on the convict. The Court reasoned that death by firing squad was not much different from death by hanging or decapitation; thus, such a method of execution was not cruel and unusual.

The *Wilkerson* case remained the main precedent until the Supreme Court took up the case of a military deserter in 1958. Albert Trop was drafted in 1944 but refused to fight. He was convicted of desertion and, as part of his sentence, was stripped of all of his "rights of citizenship." The Supreme Court declared that this sentence was "cruel and unusual punishment" in violation of the 8th Amendment. *Trop v. Dulles* (1958). The Court acknowledged that loss of citizenship was not tantamount to torture, however, "[t]he Amendment must draw its meaning from the *evolving standards of decency*." From 1958 onward, "cruel and unusual punishment" was untethered from its historical understanding and tied to a subjective "evolving standard of decency."

In the 1960s, many people began arguing that all executions were cruel and unusual punishment. In 1972, the Court declared that the execution of an African-American for murder violated the 8th Amendment. *Furman v. Georgia*. By 1972, execution had become less common. Many crimes that had previously resulted in mandatory death sentences were now punishable by life in prison. The Court reasoned that execution had become "unusual" because it was no longer the most common penalty. Even worse, the Court said that the discretionary nature of capital punishment had seen it applied disproportionately to minorities and poor people. More controversially, the Court said that while the mode of execution was not cruel by historical standards, the Court had to apply an evolving standard of morality. Accordingly, execution in this case was both cruel and unusual.

Additionally, the *Furman* decision was a very short opinion that offered little explanation and no guidance. Following the decision, there was a lot of uncertainty about whether all capital punishment was unconstitutional. All executions ceased for several years as lower courts tried to determine what *Furman* meant. Executions resumed in the late 1970s, but at a much lower rate. As of 2024, there are twenty-three states that have abolished the death penalty, but the federal government has not. One of the most controversial aspects of the death penalty is that even in states that have abolished the death penalty, those defendants can be convicted in federal court and executed.

From an originalist standpoint, the idea that the 8th Amendment bans execution is highly problematic as this view is based explicitly on "evolving standards of decency." If judges can rewrite the Constitution based on their own personal concept of "decency," what prevents them from applying this to other issues like abortion, suicide, and drug use? The law must be rooted in a legal document, not a judge's whim that can change based on his personal preferences.

Catholic moralists are currently divided on the issue of capital punishment. Historically, the dominant view was that the severity of punishment must be proportionate to the crime. Suppose a person convicted of murder was fined $1. This would not be justice because the punishment would be so disproportionate to the offense. Thomas Aquinas and other Catholic theorists have argued that the most serious offenses, like murder, require the most serious penalty.[8]

Some recent Catholic theorists, including Pope Francis, have argued that all human life is sacred and should never be destroyed intentionally unless there is absolutely no other alternative. This school of thought reasons that in modern, rich societies, life imprisonment is not onerous to society and therefore life imprisonment is a better alternative than execution. Others respond that without the possibility of execution, criminals in prison will murder guards and their fellow inmates with impunity, making imprisonment of such criminals virtually impossible. Regardless of how one views the moral issue, it is very unlikely that the Supreme Court will declare capital punishment to be unconstitutional.

---

[8] Some proponents of capital punishment argue that executing criminals serves as an example to others as a deterrent to stop them from committing crime. However, if executing someone is unjust it does not become acceptable because society hopes it might produce a beneficial effect. This would be the error that the end justifies the means.

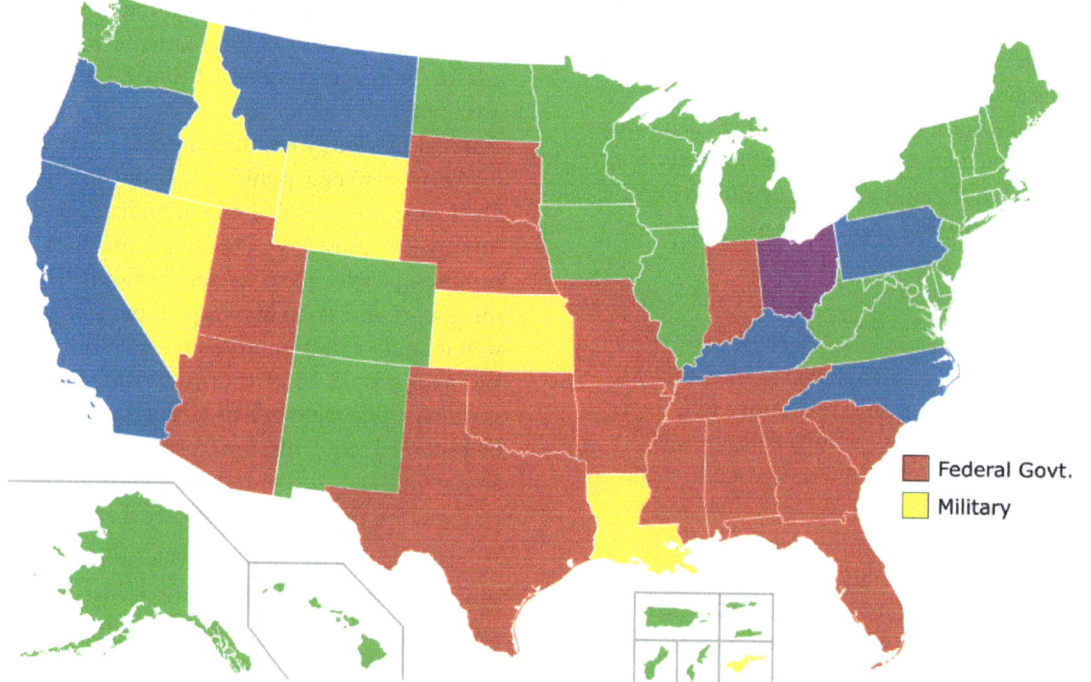

Green: Capital punishment repealed, never instituted, or struck down as unconstitutional (23 states, 5 territories)
With the death penalty:
Blue: Capital punishment in statute, but executions formally suspended (6 states)
Yellow: Capital punishment in statute, but no executions within the last 10 years (5 states, 1 territory)
Purple: Capital punishment in statute, but executions informally suspended (1 state)
Red: Capital punishment in statute and executions carried out within the last 10 years (15 states)

THE NINTH AND TENTH AMENDMENTS

The Ninth Amendment reads: *The enumeration in the Constitution, of certain rights, shall not be construed to deny or disparage others retained by the people.*

The Tenth Amendment states: *The powers not delegated to the United States by the Constitution, nor prohibited by it to the states, are reserved to the states respectively, or to the people.*

As previously noted, Madison wrote the Ninth Amendment to make it clear that the Bill of Rights was not a comprehensive list of rights. The American people possessed other rights which were not listed in the Bill of Rights. The absence of those rights did not mean that they did not exist. The Ninth Amendment played a critical role in developing the right of privacy, especially in the *Griswold* case. The Justices relied on the Ninth Amendment to conclude that the "right of privacy" was an "un-enumerated" right "retained by the people" but not specifically listed in the Bill of Rights.

The Tenth Amendment deals with the issue of Federalism which is discussed in depth in the next chapter.

THE FOURTEENTH AMENDMENT: EQUAL PROTECTION

While not part of the Bill of Rights, because the Bill of Rights has been applied to the States through the 14th Amendment, it seems appropriate to consider the 14th Amendment. Much has already been said about this amendment, but it is worth focusing specifically on the provision that no state may "deny to any person within its jurisdiction the equal protection of the laws." There are several aspects of the equal protection clause that are particularly important.

First, the Fourteenth Amendment says no state shall deny equal protection. There is no provision in the Constitution saying that the federal government cannot deny equal protection. However, just as some "fundamental rights" are applied to the states, in 1954, the Supreme Court said that the 14th Amendment guarantee of equal protection was applicable to the federal government. Accordingly, today, neither the states nor the federal government may deny any person "equal protection."

"Equal protection" and "equality" are not the same thing. During Congressional debates on the language of the 14th Amendment, proponents insisted explicitly that "Equal protection" did not mean "equality." For example, the guarantee of equal protection did not mean that states would be required to permit women to vote. In fact, this point was made absolutely clear because after the 14th Amendment guarantee of "equal protection" was passed, Congress enacted the 15th Amendment which said no state could refuse to let a person vote due to their race. Moreover, in 1919, Congress passed the 19th Amendment which said no state could refuse to allow a person to vote based upon their sex.

Equal protection meant that a state could not refuse to enforce laws against some people and not others. Thus, laws against murder had to protect everyone. There could not be murder laws that applied to white people but not black people. For decades after passage of the 14th Amendment this was universally accepted. Various groups, including racial minorities and women, repeatedly asked the Court to overrule state laws that treated groups differently, but these challenges were constantly rejected.

The equal protection clause was explicitly designed to stop a two-tier system of treatment. During the period when slavery was legal, it was always a crime to kill a slave, but in some states, it was a less serious crime to kill a slave than a free person. The 14th Amendment ended that practice. Yet, some states made killing a pre-born human a less serious offense than killing a human who had been born. That a two-tier system was permitted for abortion indicates that the Framers of the 14th Amendment understood that regulation of abortion was a state issue.

For decades, the Supreme Court said that the "separate but equal" doctrine it espoused in *Plessy v Ferguson* did not violate equal protection. All across the country public schools were *segregated*, that is, there were different schools for white and black students. The Court repeatedly said that education was not a matter of *protection*, so states and the federal government were allowed to segregate. This changed in 1954 with the case of *Brown v. Board of Education of Topeka Kansas*.

The Court in *Brown* reasoned that "equal protection" would never be fully attainable unless there was real equality. Therefore, no state or the federal government could ever treat two people differently based on their race or national origin unless the disparate treatment was (somehow) narrowly tailored to a compelling state interest. (The "strict scrutiny" test.)

The Court later expanded this "illegal discrimination" to a few other "suspect classes." The Supreme Court has said that a state cannot discriminate between men and women or between legitimate and illegitimate children without an exceedingly important reason for doing so. So, any time a state or the federal government treats people differently based on race, national origin, sex, legitimacy, or religion, the discrimination is presumptively unconstitutional. Essentially, since the 1950s, equal protection has evolved into equal treatment, but this is applied in a variety of ways.

The Catholic Church has long condemned discrimination based on racial animus. In 1971, Pope St. Paul VI wrote, "Men rightly consider unjustifiable and reject as inadmissible the tendency to maintain or introduce legislation or behavior systematically inspired by racialist prejudice." *Octogesima Adveniens, #16*. St. Thomas says that laws must always be for the common good, so states can never legitimately ostracize a whole group of people. At the same time, bear in mind that "immoral" does not necessarily equate to unconstitutional.

Finally, the 14th Amendment only applies to *government* action. Laws against private discrimination have been justified as a regulation of interstate commerce. As noted earlier, the Catholic Church has frequently been attacked for "discrimination." For example, some people have argued that the Church should be fined for failing to ordain women as priests. As always, people must distinguish between legitimate and illegitimate differences in treatments. There is no legitimate reason to treat people differently based on the color

Pope St. Paul VI

of their skin, but there are biological differences between men and women that must be considered. One of the most basic principles of justice is *to treat like cases alike but different cases differently*. Not all disparate treatment is necessarily unjust if it is based on a legitimate difference. Even the Supreme Court has recognized this and absolute equality is not justice.

The Catholic Church has condemned radical egalitarianism that seeks to deny all distinctions between male and female, young and old, married and unmarried, theist and atheist; in short to reduce humans to interchangeable units of utility. As recently as April 8, 2024, the Vatican reaffirmed that theories which "claim to make everyone equal" by denying all differences are "extremely dangerous." The Vatican goes on to affirm that "all attempts to obscure reference to the ineliminable sexual difference between man and woman are to be rejected." [9]

In fact, many courts supported a "right to abortion" based on the claim that men and women had to be absolutely equal. Supposedly, because men did not have to bear children, women must be allowed to have abortions so they could be just like men. This is an extreme form of egalitarianism contrary to nature and Catholic teaching.

---

[9] Declaration of the Dicastery for the Doctrine of the Faith "Dignitas Infinita," 08.04.2024, ¶ 59.

THE ELEVENTH THROUGH THE TWENTY-SEVENTH AMENDMENTS

ELEVENTH AMENDMENT (RATIFIED JANUARY 8, 1798)

The Judicial power of the United States shall not be construed to extend to any suit in law or equity, commenced or prosecuted against one of the United States by Citizens of another State, or by Citizens or Subjects of any Foreign State.

TWELFTH AMENDMENT (RATIFIED SEPTEMBER 25, 1804)

The Electors shall meet in their respective states and vote by ballot for President and Vice-President, one of whom, at least, shall not be an inhabitant of the same state with themselves; they shall name in their ballots the person voted for as President, and in distinct ballots the person voted for as Vice-President, and they shall make distinct lists of all persons voted for as President, and of all persons voted for as Vice-President, and of the number of votes for each, which lists they shall sign and certify, and transmit sealed to the seat of the government of the United States, directed to the President of the Senate; — the President of the Senate shall, in the presence of the Senate and House of Representatives, open all the certificates and the votes shall then be counted; — The person having the greatest number of votes for President, shall be the President, if such number be a majority of the whole number of Electors appointed; and if no person have such majority, then from the persons having the highest numbers not exceeding three on the list of those voted for as President, the House of Representatives shall choose immediately, by ballot, the President. But in choosing the President, the votes shall be taken by states, the representation from each state having one vote; a quorum for this purpose shall consist of a member or members from two-thirds of the states, and a majority of all the states shall be necessary to a choice. And if the House of Representatives shall not choose a President whenever the right of choice shall devolve upon them, before the fourth day of March next following, then the Vice-President shall act as President, as in case of the death or other constitutional disability of the President. — The person having the greatest number of votes as Vice-President, shall be the Vice-President, if such number be a majority of the whole number of Electors appointed, and if no person have a majority, then from the two highest numbers on

The Supreme Court Building

the list, the Senate shall choose the Vice-President; a quorum for the purpose shall consist of two-thirds of the whole number of Senators, and a majority of the whole number shall be necessary to a choice. But no person constitutionally ineligible to the office of President shall be eligible to that of Vice-President of the United States.

THIRTEENTH AMENDMENT (RATIFIED DECEMBER 18, 1865)

Section 1

Neither slavery nor involuntary servitude, except as a punishment for crime whereof the party shall have been duly convicted, shall exist within the United States, or any place subject to their jurisdiction.

Section 2

Congress shall have power to enforce this article by appropriate legislation.

FOURTEENTH AMENDMENT (RATIFIED JULY 28, 1868)

Section 1

All persons born or naturalized in the United States, and subject to the jurisdiction thereof, are citizens of the United States and of the State wherein they reside. No State shall make or enforce any law which shall abridge the privileges or immunities of citizens of the United States; nor shall any State deprive any person of life, liberty, or property, without due process of law; nor deny to any person within its jurisdiction the equal protection of the laws.

Section 2

Representatives shall be apportioned among the several States according to their respective numbers, counting the whole number of persons in each State, excluding Indians not taxed. But when the right to vote at any election for the choice of electors for President and Vice-President of the United States, Representatives in Congress, the Executive and Judicial officers of a State, or the members of the Legislature thereof, is denied to any of the male inhabitants of such State, being twenty-one years of age, and citizens of the United States, or in any way abridged, except for participation in rebellion, or other crime, the basis of representation therein shall be reduced in the proportion which the number of such male citizens shall bear to the whole number of male citizens twenty-one years of age in such State.

Section 3

No person shall be a Senator or Representative in Congress, or elector of President and Vice-President, or hold any office, civil or military, under the United States, or under any State, who, having previously taken an oath, as a member of Congress, or as an officer of the United States, or as a member of any State legislature, or as an executive or judicial officer of any State, to support the Constitution of the United States, shall have engaged in insurrection or rebellion against the same, or given aid or comfort to the enemies thereof. But Congress may by a vote of two-thirds of each House, remove such disability.

Section 4

The validity of the public debt of the United States, authorized by law, including debts incurred for payment of pensions and bounties for services in suppressing insurrection or rebellion, shall not be questioned. But neither the United States nor any State shall assume or pay any debt or obligation incurred in aid of insurrection or rebellion against the United States, or any claim for the loss or emancipation of any slave; but all such debts, obligations and claims shall be held illegal and void.

Section 5

The Congress shall have the power to enforce, by appropriate legislation, the provisions of this article.

FIFTEENTH AMENDMENT (RATIFIED MARCH 30, 1870)

Section 1

The right of citizens of the United States to vote shall not be denied or abridged by the United States or by any State on account of race, color, or previous condition of servitude —

Section 2

The Congress shall have the power to enforce this article by appropriate legislation.

SIXTEENTH AMENDMENT (RATIFIED FEBRUARY 25, 1913)

The Congress shall have power to lay and collect taxes on incomes, from whatever source derived, without apportionment among the several States, and without regard to any census or enumeration.

SEVENTEENTH AMENDMENT (RATIFIED MAY 31, 1913)

The Senate of the United States shall be composed of two Senators from each State, elected by the people thereof, for six years; and each Senator shall have one vote. The electors in each State shall have the qualifications requisite for electors of the most numerous branch of the State legislatures.

When vacancies happen in the representation of any State in the Senate, the executive authority of such State shall issue writs of election to fill such vacancies: Provided, That the legislature of any State may empower the executive thereof to make temporary appointments until the people fill the vacancies by election as the legislature may direct.

This amendment shall not be so construed as to affect the election or term of any Senator chosen before it becomes valid as part of the Constitution.

EIGHTEENTH AMENDMENT (RATIFIED JANUARY 29, 1919; REPEALED DECEMBER 5, 1933 BY THE 21ST AMENDMENT)

~~Section 1~~

~~After one year from the ratification of this article the manufacture, sale, or transportation of intoxicating liquors within, the importation thereof into, or the exportation thereof from the United States and all territory subject to the jurisdiction thereof for beverage purposes is hereby prohibited.~~

~~Section 2~~

~~The Congress and the several States shall have concurrent power to enforce this article by appropriate legislation.~~

~~Section 3~~

~~This article shall be inoperative unless it shall have been ratified as an amendment to the Constitution by the legislatures of the several States, as provided in the Constitution, within seven years from the date of the submission hereof to the States by the Congress.~~

NINETEENTH AMENDMENT (RATIFIED AUGUST 26, 1920)

The right of citizens of the United States to vote shall not be denied or abridged by the United States or by any State on account of sex.

Congress shall have power to enforce this article by appropriate legislation.

TWENTIETH AMENDMENT (RATIFIED FEBRUARY 6, 1933)

Section 1

The terms of the President and the Vice President shall end at noon on the 20th day of January, and the terms of Senators and Representatives at noon on the 3d day of January, of the years in which such terms would have ended if this article had not been ratified; and the terms of their successors shall then begin.

Section 2

The Congress shall assemble at least once in every year, and such meeting shall begin at noon on the 3d day of January, unless they shall by law appoint a different day.

Section 3

If, at the time fixed for the beginning of the term of the President, the President elect shall have died, the Vice President elect shall become President. If a President shall not have been chosen before the time fixed for the beginning of his term, or if the President elect shall have failed to qualify, then the Vice President elect shall act as President until a President shall have qualified; and the Congress may by law provide for the case wherein neither a President elect nor a Vice President shall have qualified, declaring who shall then act as President, or the manner in which one who is to act shall be selected, and such person shall act accordingly until a President or Vice President shall have qualified.

Section 4

The Congress may by law provide for the case of the death of any of the persons from whom the House of Representatives may choose a President whenever the right of choice shall have devolved upon them, and for the case of the death of any of the persons from whom the Senate may choose a Vice President whenever the right of choice shall have devolved upon them.

Section 5

Sections 1 and 2 shall take effect on the 15th day of October following the ratification of this article.

Section 6

This article shall be inoperative unless it shall have been ratified as an amendment to the Constitution by the legislatures of three-fourths of the several States within seven years from the date of its submission.

TWENTY-FIRST AMENDMENT (RATIFIED DECEMBER 5, 1933)

Section 1

The eighteenth article of amendment to the Constitution of the United States is hereby repealed.

Section 2

The transportation or importation into any State, Territory, or Possession of the United States for delivery or use therein of intoxicating liquors, in violation of the laws thereof, is hereby prohibited.

Section 3

This article shall be inoperative unless it shall have been ratified as an amendment to the Constitution by conventions in the several States, as provided in the Constitution, within seven years from the date of the submission hereof to the States by the Congress.

TWENTY-SECOND AMENDMENT (RATIFIED MARCH 1, 1951)

Section 1

No person shall be elected to the office of the President more than twice, and no person who has held the office of President, or acted as President, for more than two years of a term to which some other person was elected President shall be elected to the office of President more than once. But this Article shall not apply to any person holding the office of President when this Article was proposed by Congress, and shall not prevent any person who may be holding the office of President, or acting as President, during the term within which this Article becomes operative from holding the office of President or acting as President during the remainder of such term.

Section 2

This article shall be inoperative unless it shall have been ratified as an amendment to the Constitution by the legislatures of three-fourths of the several States within seven years from the date of its submission to the States by the Congress.

TWENTY-THIRD AMENDMENT (RATIFIED APRIL 3, 1961)

Section 1

The District constituting the seat of Government of the United States shall appoint in such manner as Congress may direct:

A number of electors of President and Vice President equal to the whole number of Senators and Representatives in Congress to which the District would be entitled if it were a State, but in no event more than the least populous State; they shall be in addition to those appointed by the States, but they shall be considered, for the purposes of the election of President and Vice President, to be electors appointed by a State; and they shall meet in the District and perform such duties as provided by the twelfth article of amendment.

Section 2

The Congress shall have power to enforce this article by appropriate legislation.

TWENTY-FOURTH AMENDMENT (RATIFIED FEBRUARY 4, 1964)

Section 1

The right of citizens of the United States to

vote in any primary or other election for President or Vice President, for electors for President or Vice President, or for Senator or Representative in Congress, shall not be denied or abridged by the United States or any State by reason of failure to pay poll tax or other tax.

Section 2

The Congress shall have power to enforce this article by appropriate legislation.

TWENTY-FIFTH AMENDMENT (RATIFIED FEBRUARY 23, 1967)

Section 1

In case of the removal of the President from office or of his death or resignation, the Vice President shall become President.

Section 2

Whenever there is a vacancy in the office of the Vice President, the President shall nominate a Vice President who shall take office upon confirmation by a majority vote of both Houses of Congress.

Section 3

Whenever the President transmits to the President pro tempore of the Senate and the Speaker of the House of Representatives his written declaration that he is unable to discharge the powers and duties of his office, and until he transmits to them a written declaration to the contrary, such powers and duties shall be discharged by the Vice President as Acting President.

Section 4

Whenever the Vice President and a majority of either the principal officers of the executive departments or of such other body as Congress may by law provide, transmit to the President pro tempore of the Senate and the Speaker of the House of Representatives their written declaration that the President is unable to discharge the powers and duties of his office, the Vice President shall immediately assume the powers and duties of the office as Acting President.

Thereafter, when the President transmits to the President pro tempore of the Senate and the Speaker of the House of Representatives his written declaration that no inability exists, he shall resume the powers and duties of his office unless the Vice President and a majority of either the principal officers of the executive department or of such other body as Congress may by law provide, transmit within four days to the President pro tempore of the Senate and the Speaker of the House of Representatives their written declaration that the President is unable to discharge the powers and duties of his office. Thereupon Congress shall decide the issue, assembling within forty-eight hours for that purpose if not in session. If the Congress, within twenty-one days after receipt of the latter written declaration, or, if Congress is not in session, within twenty-one days after Congress is required to assemble, determines by two-thirds vote of both Houses that the President is unable to discharge the powers and duties of his office, the Vice President shall continue to discharge the same as Acting President; otherwise, the President shall resume the powers and duties of his office.

TWENTY-SIXTH AMENDMENT (RATIFIED JULY 5, 1971)

Section 1

The right of citizens of the United States, who are eighteen years of age or older, to vote shall not be denied or abridged by the United States or by any State on account of age.

Section 2

The Congress shall have power to enforce this article by appropriate legislation.

TWENTY-SEVENTH AMENDMENT (RATIFIED ON MAY 7, 1992)

No law, varying the compensation for the services of the Senators and Representatives, shall take effect, until an election of representatives shall have intervened.

REVIEW QUESTIONS

1. What year was The Bill of Rights ratified?
2. What did Hamilton say in Federalist 84 regarding a bill of rights?
3. How did Edmund Randolph, the first attorney general of the United States, feel about a bill of rights?
4. What role did the First Amendment play in adjudicating the constitutionality of the 1797 Sedition Act in the U.S. Supreme Court?
5. What did James Madison believe about the federal government dealing with religion?
6. Why is *Barron v. Baltimore* (1833) famous?
7. Why is *Lamont v. Postmaster General of the United States* (1964) significant?
8. What is the basic holding of The Pentagon Papers case (1971)?
9. Who is famous for saying "the house of every one to him as his castle and fortress?"
10. What, historically, has been the dominant Catholic argument about capital punishment as exemplified by St. Thomas Aquinas?
11. If a suspect is being questioned by police and the suspect says he wishes to consult with a lawyer, what are police required to do?
12. In 2024, what did the Vatican say regarding the nature of men and women?
13. What amendment guarantees against excessive bail, excessive fines, and cruel and unusual punishment?
14. What amendment gave 18-year-olds the right to vote?
15. What amendment gave women the right to vote?
16. What amendment gave Black men the right to vote?
17. What amendment prohibits anyone from serving more than two terms as president?
18. Which amendment protects against double jeopardy?
19. The Miranda Warning is most associated with which amendment?
20. What test did the Supreme Court establish for reviewing restrictions on the right to keep and bear arms in *New York State Rifle & Pistol Assn. v. Bruen* (2022)?
21. What happens if police fail to give an arrested suspect a Miranda Warning?
22. Which amendment abolished slavery?
23. What amendment protects people from incriminating themselves?
24. What amendment says that anyone born in the United States is a citizen?
25. What is necessary for a law to be considered a content-neutral, time, place and manner restriction on speech?
26. Under what circumstances were 18-year-olds given the right to vote?
27. When are police required to provide a Miranda Warning?
28. How did *Wilkerson v. Utah* (1878) impact 8th amendment law?
29. Which amendment was added to the Bill of Rights to make it clear that it was not a comprehensive list of rights?
30. The only amendment to have been repealed involved what?

CHAPTER EIGHT
FEDERALISM AND SUBSIDIARITY

In a small [state], the interest of the public is more obvious, better understood, and more within the reach of every citizen; abuses have less extent, and of course are less protected.

Charles-Louis de Secondat, Baron de Montesquieu
The Spirit of the Laws, 1748

Charles-Louis de Secondat, Baron de Montesquieu

INTRODUCTION: TWO THEORIES OF SOCIETY

In September 1789, Congress passed what became the Tenth Amendment: *The powers not delegated to the United States by the Constitution, nor prohibited by it to the States, are reserved to the States respectively, or to the people.* At almost exactly the same time, France's Revolutionary government passed the *Declaration of the Rights of Man and Citizen* which proclaimed: *The principle of all sovereignty resides essentially in the nation. No body nor individual may exercise any authority which does not proceed directly from the nation.* These statements reflect two diametrically opposed theories of government, and indeed, two utterly opposed philosophies of human nature and human freedom.

Sovereignty can generally be defined as supreme authority. By declaring that "sovereignty resides essentially in the nation" the revolutionaries affirmed that the national government is absolute and there could be no authority, public or private, that was not derived from the nation. They meant this literally. The Catholic Church in France was nationalized and all clergy were ordered to take a loyalty oath recognizing the French government as having full control of the Church. In the Revolutionary model, the national government not only had a monopoly on the use of force, but a monopoly on any form of coercion or authority. In the Revolutionary view, the Church was "coercing" people through its moral teachings, and this was an exercise of "authority" not sanctioned by the state.

The American system is the complete opposite. It might be called a "bottom-up" approach to government. The American system prefers private action and local control with the central government only possessing a few delegated powers. The French system is "top-down." The French Revolutionary government possessed absolute power and private associations or families only exercise powers that the central government allows.

The choice between centralization or decentralization is not a simple selection of two equally good forms of government, such as a Republic or a Democracy. The choice has real-world applications which, as history has shown, lead to the deaths of hundreds of millions of people as centralized governments cause unimaginable hardships. Moreover, centralized governments tend to remain in power through force and coercion, as did the Revolutionary government in 19th century France and Communist governments in 20th century China and the Soviet Union. Historically, politically, morally, and economically, centralization has proven an abject failure. Even if it were not so, the Catholic doctrine of subsidiarity would mandate decentralization.

SUBSIDIARITY

Subsidiarity has been a cornerstone of Catholic moral teaching for centuries. Pope Pius XI provided the classic summary of subsidiarity in *Quadragesimo Anno*:

> Just as it is gravely wrong to take from individuals what they can accomplish by their own initiative and industry and give it to the community, so also it is an injustice and at the same time a great evil and disturbance of right order to assign to a greater or higher association what lesser and subordinate organizations can do.

More recently, *The Compendium of the Social Doctrine of the Church*, which John Paul II promulgated in 2004, explained:

> The principle of subsidiarity is opposed to certain forms of centralization, bureaucratization, and welfare assistance and to the unjustified and excessive presence of the State in public mechanisms. "By intervening directly and depriving society of its responsibility, the Social Assistance State leads to a loss of human energies and an inordinate increase of public agencies, which are dominated more by bureaucratic ways of thinking than by concern for serving their clients, and which are accompanied by an enormous increase in spending"[1]

Federalism, a principle of local self-government, is the political manifestation of the moral principle of Subsidiarity. Federalism, in which local and national governments share power, has been the cornerstone of the American political system for centuries. Regardless of what this principle is called, it is based on a series of basic truths, including:

Pope Pius XI

1) Force must always be a last resort, and voluntary cooperation is always the paradigm for addressing social issues;

2) One size does not fit all, so strict uniformity is unjust;

3) Centralization is inefficient, wasteful, and breeds corruption;

Pope John Paul II

4) By usurping the function of families, churches, and voluntary organizations, these groups, which are essential to human flourishing, are weakened.

THE NON-AGGRESSION PRINCIPLE

Christians have never been *absolute* pacifists, in the sense of condemning any use of force. St. Augustine, St. Thomas, and the rest of Catholic tradition have been uniform on this point. There may be times when a person must use force to defend himself, his family, or his community against unjust aggression. However, force must always be a last resort, when all other options have been exhausted. In 2017, the U.S.

---

[1] Compendium, sec. 187 (quoting John Paul II's encyclical Centesimus Annus, (1991)).

Conference of Catholic Bishops aptly summarized this Catholic teaching as follows:

> In situations of conflict, our constant commitment ought to be, as far as possible, to strive for justice through nonviolent means.
>
> But, when sustained attempts at nonviolent action fail to protect the innocent against fundamental injustice, then legitimate political authorities are permitted as a last resort to employ limited force to rescue the innocent and establish justice.[2]

Natural Law applies as much to government as to individuals and private associations. Governments, like individuals, may only use limited force as a last resort. Moreover, force must be "limited" to what is absolutely necessary "to rescue the innocent and establish justice." This is often called *the principle of non-aggression* or *the principle of non-violence*. As a basic principle of Natural Law, the principle of non-violence is found in Aristotle, the Old Testament, ancient legal codes, and most of the world's major religions.

Accordingly, it is gravely wrong, and an act of violence, to take from individuals what they can accomplish by their own initiative and substitute governmental coercion for voluntary cooperation. *The Compendium of the Social Doctrine of the Church*, in section 357, emphasizes that private non-profit organizations based on voluntary agreement must be "respected and promoted" by civil authorities. Insofar as government is the organized use of force, the use of the police power is a last resort to be used only in emergencies. The use of government force to achieve what could be accomplished through voluntary means is like immediately rushing out and beating a trespasser unconscious with a baseball bat rather than first asking them to leave your property. Because the use of force must be minimized, or avoided if possible, the most just social system is one in which no force is needed to attain social goals. St. Thomas wrote that legal compulsion is only used when paternal correction is ineffective.

This preference for persuasion over force is also found in the Gospel of Matthew Chapter 18:

> Jesus said to his disciples: "If your brother sins against you, go and tell him his fault

Saint Augustine

between you and him alone. If he listens to you, you have won over your brother. If he does not listen, take one or two others along with you. . . . If he refuses to listen to them, tell the church. If he refuses to listen even to the church, then treat him as you would a Gentile or a tax collector."

Numerous philosophers have emphasized this point. French philosopher Charles Secondat, Baron de Montesquieu, was one of the most important influences on early Americans. Montesquieu repeatedly stressed the idea that in small communities social pressure often makes government coercion unnecessary. He writes that "shame, and the fear of blame, are restraining motives, capable of preventing a multitude of crimes."[3] In larger communities, where there is greater anonymity and less social pressure, governments rely far more on physical force. This point was restated by the modern Austrian economist Friedrich von Hayek who wrote in *Road to Serfdom*:

> In a small community, common views on the relative importance of the main tasks, agreed standards of value, will exist on a great many subjects. But their number will become less and less the wider we throw the net; and as there is less community of views, the necessity to rely on force and coercion increases.

---

[2] The Harvest of Justice is Sown in Peace, U.S.C.C.B., 2017.
[3] Spirit of the Laws, book 6, chapter 9.

The principle of non-violence demands that social pressure or moral persuasion is preferable to violence. Of course, social pressure, like any form of power, can be misused, but government force is far more dangerous.

The principle of non-violence is also based on the understanding that humans are social animals with natural affection towards family members. People, especially families, tend to cooperate for the common good, and the state should only intervene when there is a grave breakdown of social cooperation. However, some modern ideologies deny the social nature of humans. Liberalism and moral subjectivism insist that humans are autonomous, that is, not subject to any moral law, and have no natural inclination to cooperate. Utilitarianism views humans as radically individual, interchangeable units of utility, like cogs in a giant machine. These ideologies deny the basic nature of humans as social animals. For these ideologies the family, the Church, and social organizations are not only artificial, but evil, because they place restrictions on individuals' conduct. Under these ideologies, all intermediate institutions are rejected and all that remains is isolated individuals and an all-powerful state.

Government interference with the family, the Church, and voluntary associations invariably results in negative outcomes or what might be termed a "negative feedback loop." As St. John Paul II often said, "As the family goes, so goes the nation." In other words, strong and healthy families are essential for a just and healthy society.[4] *The Compendium of the Social Doctrine of the Church* (section 186) proclaims that subsidiarity "require[s] the State to refrain from anything that would de facto restrict the existential space of the smaller essential cells of society. Their initiative, freedom and responsibility must not be supplanted." As the state usurps the role of the family, society begins to break down. The breakdown of society is used to justify even greater state control and additional usurpation of the role of the family and the Church, but this only makes the situation worse.

For example, today most parents do not educate their children and, tragically, have little control over how their children are educated. The government has taken over education. A century ago, public schools were more localized so parents could exert a lot of control over their local schools. Until after World War II, most public schools were small, and there were many more school districts. In 1957, there were 50,446 school districts in the United States. Today, there are only 12,546 school districts, although the population has doubled. Moreover, "local" school boards are forced to take their direction from state departments of education and the federal Department of Education. This results in a reduction in parental control over education and an increase in control by distant bureaucracies. The more that families, and social cohesion itself breaks down, the more the government tries to fill the void. The point John Paul II made, was the same idea John Adams expressed in 1798:

> We have no Government armed with Power capable of contending with human Passions unbridled by morality and Religion. ... Our Constitution was made only for a moral and religious People. It is wholly inadequate to the government of any other.

Ben Franklin echoed Adams when he wrote:

> [O]nly a virtuous people are capable of freedom. As nations become corrupt and vicious, they have more need of masters.[5]

Freedom and self-government can only exist among a moral people capable of exercising virtue and self-restraint. Without virtue, freedom turns to license, and self-government becomes oppression. The most basic institutions that teach virtue are the family and the Church. When these institutions are weakened the only alternatives are chaos or a police state.

TWO THEORIES OF LIBERTY

The principle of non-aggression corresponds to the early American understanding of freedom. For the Founders, and almost all early Americans, *political freedom* meant freedom from government coercion. Freedom meant getting the government out of the way so that families, churches, and civic

---
[4] Homily of John Paul II (Perth, Australia), November 30, 1986.
[5] Letter To Abbés Chalut and Arnoux, April 17, 1787.

organizations could perform their tasks. For the French Revolutionaries, families and Churches were oppressive and had to be strictly regulated by the national government. The Revolutionaries saw families and Churches as hierarchical organizations which used social pressure to limit human freedom.

In the American model, families, Churches, and civic organizations are called **intermediate institutions**. These intermediate bodies stand between the individual and the state to protect people from the all-powerful state. In the French model, the all-powerful state claims to protect individuals from the insidious control of the family, the Church, and other traditional groups.

In the American view, freedom and government are diametrically opposed. When government expands, political freedom shrinks, and vice versa. Accordingly, Jefferson commented that, "The natural progress of things is for liberty to yield, & government to gain ground."[6] George Washington shared the same feelings in a famous quote when he said, *"Government is not reason, it is not eloquence—it is force! Like fire it is a dangerous servant and a fearful master[.]"*

Although the Founders were concerned about government becoming too powerful, they were not anarchists. They recognized the need for political authority. However, they realized that government was to be the servant of the people, not the other way around. None of the Founders, including Jefferson who was the most radical Founder, thought that the power of government should be used to try to change society. Jefferson was often critical of organized religion, and thought Churches had too much influence; but, he never suggested using the power of government to interfere with the work of Churches or other voluntary associations.

The paradox is that political freedom must be sacrificed to have freedom in a more meaningful sense. Thomas Hobbes's famous thought experiment illustrates the point. Imagine living in a place without laws and everyone was free to do whatever they wished. In such a circumstance, running a business or raising a family would be almost impossible. What sounds like perfect freedom is actually absolute chaos that limits opportunities.

Consequently, America's Founders universally espoused the view that some limited government was necessary. As Washington said, government is like fire. When properly contained it is a great benefit, but if it gets out of control it becomes destructive. The early American view of limited government fully accords with the bottoms-up approach to sovereignty, and the principle of non-violence. Because government is so potentially dangerous, it should only be used to the extent that is necessary.

LOCAL SELF-GOVERNMENT

St. Isidore gave three basic requirements for any edict to qualify as law. First, it must be just. Second, it must be practical. Third, it must be "according to the customs of the country, and adapted to place and time." In his Treatise on Law (Question 95 Art 2), St. Thomas, commenting on St. Isidore, writes:

> The general principles of the natural law cannot be applied to all men in the same way on account of the great variety of human affairs; and hence arises the diversity of positive laws among various peoples.

St. Isidore

---
[6] Letter to Edward Carrington, May 27, 1788.

The great modern Catholic theorist Russell Kirk makes this point writing:

> Historical origin, character of the population, physical configuration, and a variety of other circumstances naturally distinguish one region from another. The means of protecting and perfecting those societies must vary accordingly.[7]

Imposing a one-size-fits-all "solution" on everyone on an entire continent—or the entire world—is a bad idea. There is a saying, "One law for the lion and the lamb is unjust." More fundamentally, this can be expressed by the principle "treat like cases alike but different cases differently," that is, forcing everyone to live the same way regardless of their particular needs is inherently unjust. There may be legitimate differences of condition that make particular policies impractical or unnecessary.

The natural law requirement that human law should reflect "the customs of the country, and adapted to place and time" applies to the United States in every possible way. First, local self-government was the basic "custom of the country" even prior to independence. Recall, for example, that under English law Catholic Mass was illegal in the 17th century. However, colonial Maryland possessed self-government to such a degree that it granted religious liberty to its citizens regardless of what Parliament ordained in England. Another example occurred in 1774 when Parliament passed the Intolerable Acts. The colonists responded by insisting on local self-government. Some colonists complained about lack of representation in Parliament, but most colonists were not interested in merely sending a few representatives to Parliament. Most colonists believed, correctly, that if they sent a few representatives to Parliament, it would still dictate how Americans ran their local communities.

In the late 18th century, most Americans saw local self-government as a bulwark against oppression by a distant central government, whether in London or Philadelphia. This explains why the newly-independent colonies had such a weak central government under the Articles of

Russell Kirk

Confederation. Under the Constitution, many Americans remained highly skeptical of a powerful central government, which is why the Federalists went to great lengths to assure early Americans that the federal government would not interfere with local self-government. In *The Federalist Papers*, Hamilton and Madison insisted over and over that the Constitution would only limit local self-government in a few limited areas. Hamilton, Madison, and other Federalists acknowledged that small local government was the most just, most conducive to liberty, and generally most efficient.

Early Americans agreed that self-government, on the most local level possible, was most conducive to freedom. A small town with a small government will have difficulty effectively oppressing its citizens. However, a small town with a small government has limited resources to defend itself against attack from external enemies or to defend against internal insurrection. The Federalists were not the first to point out that the answer to this problem was that several small states band together for mutual support. This federation of small communities could pool their resources in

---

[7] Kirk, The Conservative Mind (1953). Kirk, a devout Catholic layman, was one of the most influential American theorists of the 20th century.

case of invasion or local insurrection. Accordingly, a federation offered the freedom found in small states with the security from external enemies found in large states.

The most influential theorist to explain this view was Montesquieu. In *Federalist* 9, Hamilton extolls the philosophy of Montesquieu and applies it to the United States. Just as subsidiarity always counsels action on the smallest level possible, so do Montesquieu and the authors of the *Federalist*. As Montesquieu argued:

> In a small [state], the interest of the public is more obvious, better understood, and more within the reach of every citizen; abuses have less extent, and of course are less protected.[8]

Hamilton explains in Federalist 9 that many American states were too large:

> When Montesquieu recommends a small extent for republics, the standards he had in view were of dimensions far short of the limits of almost every one of these States. Neither Virginia, Massachusetts, Pennsylvania, New York, North Carolina, nor Georgia can by any means be compared with the models from which he reasoned[.]

Hamilton says that, strictly speaking, these larger states are too large and, if one faithfully followed Montesquieu, they should be broken into smaller states. While smaller states were to be preferred to larger ones, the government of the United States neither should, nor could, force the larger states to divide into smaller states. In fact, Article 4, Section 3 guarantees the territorial integrity of the states: "*New States may be admitted by the Congress into this Union; but no new State shall be formed or erected within the Jurisdiction of any other State; nor any State be formed by the Junction of two or more States, or Parts of States, without the Consent of the Legislatures of the States concerned as well as of the Congress.*"

The principle of subsidiarity favors small states. However, it would violate the principle of subsidiarity for the central government to force states to subdivide or grant autonomy to political subdivisions. This is why the organization of states into counties, cities, and towns remains entirely an issue of state law.

THE BIRTH OF FEDERALISM AND THE DOCTRINE OF INTERPOSITION

Until the 20th century, it was almost universally accepted that the powers of the federal government were few and defined, while the powers of the states were numerous and indefinite and that states retained a great deal of sovereignty. After the federal government began to operate in 1789, Rhode Island refused to ratify the Constitution. Some people suggested that Rhode Island should be forced to become part of the United States. However, Washington and other leaders insisted that Rhode Island was free to join the United States or not.

When Congress passed the Alien and Sedition Acts, Jefferson and Madison responded with the *Kentucky and Virginia Resolutions* asserting the doctrine of **interposition**. Interposition is the idea that when the federal government exceeds its authority the state should "interpose" itself between the federal government and citizens of the state. Unfortunately, few Americans today are even aware of the doctrine of interposition.

Interposition has been misconstrued, and at times, ill-applied, by states who oppose federal action. The doctrine has become somewhat lost in history, being replaced by the term "**states' rights**," a closely related concept. Although it is a very broad concept, in general, the doctrine of "states' rights" asserts that each state possesses sovereign rights that can be exercised in case of need. Historically, some have argued that states have the right to **nullify**, that is, cancel, federal laws that exceed Congressional authority. More recently, states have maintained that they possess the right to enforce state and federal laws when the federal government steadfastly refuses to do so. This sharing, or balance, of power between the states and the federal government is the philosophy which underlies Federalism. Many scholars argue that it is guaranteed by the Tenth Amendment to the Constitution.

The idea of interposition was *implicitly* contained in the Federalist Papers but *explicitly* set

---
[8] Spirit of the Law, book 8, chapter 16.

forth in the Virginia Resolution of 1798 written by James Madison and adopted by Virginia:

> ... this Assembly doth explicitly and peremptorily declare, that it views the powers of the federal government as resulting from the compact to which the states are parties, as limited by the plain sense and intention of the instrument constituting that compact, as no further valid than they are authorized by the grants enumerated in that compact; and that, in case of a deliberate, palpable, and dangerous exercise of other powers, not granted by the said compact, **the states, who are parties thereto, have the right, and are in duty bound, to interpose, for arresting the progress of the evil**, and for maintaining, within their respective limits, the authorities, rights and liberties, appertaining to them. (emphasis added)

The crucial phrase is that states "have the right, and are in duty bound, to *interpose*, for arresting the progress of the evil," when the federal government attempts to exercise powers "not granted" by the Constitution. This formulation says that states "have the right ... to interpose" themselves to protect their citizens from federal excesses. As noted, this idea is often called "states' rights,"[9] but *interposition* is the technical and specific term when a state protects its citizens from federal actions that are unconstitutional and oppressive.

Madison's expression of the principle of interposition in 1798 tracks closely with what Hamilton wrote in *Federalist* 33. In responding to those who argued that the "supremacy clause" of Article 6 would mean that states were powerless to oppose federal actions, Hamilton explained:

> But it will not follow from this [supremacy] doctrine that acts of the large society which are NOT PURSUANT to its constitutional powers, but which are invasions of the residuary authorities of the smaller societies, will become the supreme law of the land. These will be merely acts of usurpation, and will deserve to be treated as such.

Madison wrote much the same thing in *Federalist* 51. Speaking of the importance of checks and balances, Madison wrote that the division of power between the states and the federal government was crucial to liberty because "the different governments will control each other." This is a constant theme of the *Federalist*, power and interest much check power and interest. Nations cannot rely on "parchment barriers" to prevent the accumulation of power in one place. Madison and Jefferson in the Virginian and Kentucky Resolutions made this exact same point. Jefferson's *draft* of the Kentucky Resolutions of 1799 read:

> [T]he principle and construction contended for by sundry of the state legislatures, that the general government is the exclusive judge of the extent of the powers delegated to it, stop nothing short of despotism; since the discretion of those who administer the government, and not the constitution, would be the measure of their powers[.]

If "the general government is the exclusive judge of the extent of the powers delegated to it" then liberty would be dependent on a mere "parchment barrier" without the means to enforce the guarantee. Thus, Hamilton, Madison, and Jefferson all agree that states play a crucial role in the federal system of checks and balances. The reasons seemed obvious at the time, and are even more important today.

First, state legislatures, and *legislators*, represent the people of the state on a local level and tend to be more responsive to the needs and concerns of their constituents than national representatives who often lose sight of local politics. Second, state legislatures are in a position to identify and oppose any infringements on their authority or the rights of their citizens by the federal government. State legislatures act as "guardians" who can "sound the alarm" if the national government exceeds its Constitutional authority. Finally, state legislatures can shine a light on federal government overreach and, with other states, work to change the law or reduce federal power. The idea was that if enough states worked together, they could produce the necessary political pressure either to compel the Congress or the president to change course, or in the case of a Supreme Court decision, convince Congress to pass a law which effectively overturned

---

[9] "States' rights" is not a technical term and is used in a variety of ways. It has been stretched to cover some conduct that the Framers would probably find unacceptable. Remember, the Tenth Amendment speaks of the states having "reserved powers," not rights.

the decision. The first opportunity for states to implement the doctrine of interposition occurred during the War of 1812.

The War of 1812 was in many ways unnecessary. It was extremely unpopular in New England, where people felt it would destroy their economy. Several governors of New England states refused to send their state militias to participate in the War. New Englanders openly spoke of their states seceding from the Union. This opposition culminated in the **Hartford Convention of 1814**.

The president of the Hartford Convention was George Cabot. Cabot had been one of the leading Federalists at the Massachusetts ratification convention of 1788. Along with Hamilton, Cabot is considered a founder of the Federalist Party. The delegates to the Hartford Convention were a "who's who" of prominent New England Federalists. For example, Timothy Pickering had been a delegate to Pennsylvania's ratification convention of 1788 and the first Postmaster General under Washington. Ironically, Pickering was Secretary of State under President Adams when the Alien and Sedition Acts were enacted. Another delegate, Daniel Lyman, was then Chief Justice of the Rhode Island Supreme Court. A third delegate was Timothy Bigelow, Speaker of the House for Massachusetts.

The convention produced a report, signed by all the delegates, which contained some notable points. The report said that "a severance of the union, by one or more states, against the will of the rest" was to be a last resort only justified by "extreme necessity." Given this, the convention did not wish to take "precipitate action to disunite the states." The report complained about several actions taken by the federal government which the delegates thought were unconstitutional. Basically, the report concluded that it was not up to the president to determine the extent of his own powers, rather the Convention declared, "It is as much the duty of the State authorities to watch over the rights *reserved* as of the United States to watch over the powers which are *delegated*." This was another way to formulate the basic principle that in the American system of government, with its checks and balances, states must defend against federal usurpation just as much as the federal government should prevent

George Cabot

state encroachments. This was the doctrine of interposition all over again.

It is important that Madison and the Hartford convention limited state interposition to instances where the federal government exceeded its authority. Thus, a state cannot interfere with the federal government simply because a state thinks the policy is unwise. In his draft of the 1799 Kentucky Resolution, Jefferson included stronger language:

> That the several states who formed [the Constitution], being sovereign and independent, have the unquestionable right to judge of its infraction; and that a nullification, by those sovereignties, of all unauthorized acts done under color of that instrument, is the rightful remedy[.] (emphasis added)

Again, Jefferson was only saying that "unauthorized acts" could be nullified. States could not nullify mere differences of opinion about the wisest policy. Jefferson apparently

John C. Calhoun

asked Madison to use this same language for the Virginia Resolution, but Madison refused. Despite being Jefferson's protégé, Madison was far more conservative than Jefferson, and perhaps better understood the potential damage that could be done by the term "nullification" as opposed to "interpose." This is notable because in 1832 Vice President John C. Calhoun developed a doctrine of nullification that should not be confused with interposition.

What became known as "The Nullification Crisis" began in 1828, when Congress passed a very high tariff, called the *Tariff of Abominations* by most Southerners. South Carolina thought that the tariff would ruin its economy. In 1828, Calhoun, who was from South Carolina, published an "Exposition and Protest" arguing that the Tariff was unconstitutional; therefore, South Carolina could stop the tax from being collected in the state. Calhoun claimed to be following in the footsteps of Madison's *Virginia Resolution* and much of what he wrote sounded like Madison. Yet, Calhoun spent little time arguing that the Tariff was unconstitutional. Congress was authorized to enact tariffs and had done so since George Washington's administration. Calhoun simply asserted that the tax was unconstitutional and then argued that a state could stop unconstitutional actions. Many people then, and since, have maintained that Calhoun's doctrine of nullification allowed states to interfere in federal action any time a state claimed an action was unconstitutional—regardless of the weakness of the claim of unconstitutionality – and Calhoun was on terribly weak ground. The issue becomes more problematic if the federal government seeks to impose morally impermissible requirements on states or their citizens. If interposition fails, is nullification justified?

When asked about the doctrine of nullification, Madison absolutely rejected it and clearly stated he had never supported the idea, nor written anything in support of it. In a long letter to Edward Everett in August 1830, Madison said he saw no basis for thinking the tariff was unconstitutional. Madison explained: "it is understood that the nullifying doctrine imports that the decision of the State is to be presumed valid, and that it overrules the law of the United States." Madison then asked rhetorically: "How many [objections to the Constitution] might be ingeniously created, if entitled to the privilege of a decision in the mode proposed?" For the next eight years he lived, Madison worked to affirm that interposition was different from nullification.

As South Carolina began speaking of seceding, Madison also spoke against secession which he decried as a "twin" to the "heresy" of nullification. He believed that "a severance of the union, by one or more states, against the will of the rest" was to be a last resort. Perhaps more importantly, Madison seemed to be saying, if a state truly thought that disunion was essential to its survival, a state could withdraw from the union, but unless and until that "last resort" was invoked, a state could not pick and choose what parts of the Constitution would apply to it.

THE GROWTH OF FEDERALISM

In the 1830s, a young French nobleman named **Alexis de Tocqueville** visited the United States and published a summary of his findings. De Tocqueville's *Democracy in America* is universally recognized as the most authoritative description of American culture in the early 19th century. One of de Tocqueville's most oft-cited observations was that there was less freedom of opinion in the United States than in France. However, this was not a result of government control but of social pressure. He explained:

> Whenever social conditions are equal, public opinion presses with enormous weight upon the mind of each individual; it surrounds, directs, and oppresses him; and this arises from the very constitution of society, much more than from its political laws. ... The majority do not need to constrain him—they convince him.

Of course, this presents dangers, as well as benefits. Social pressure can be used to enforce bad attitudes as well as good. This is very similar to what Montesquieu had argued: in small communities, social pressure takes the place of criminal sanction. In 19th century America, there were few criminal laws; instead, society relied chiefly on social pressure. Sometimes this pressure can be oppressive; nevertheless, most Americans thought it was better to "convince" people to behave rightly, than to "constrain" them by governmental force.

In fact, de Tocqueville wrote that Americans generally did not look to government to solve problems. Individual Americans were reluctant to call upon the government for assistance in times of poverty or distress. When people encountered social problems, they preferred to use private cooperation rather than a government program. Americans were willing to help their fellow citizens; they just did not think government was the means for doing so.

Finally, de Tocqueville noted that Americans had no desire to centralize power in a national government. This was striking for de Tocqueville because in France all power was concentrated in the national government in the name of "democracy"

Alexis de Tocqueville

because the nation was the embodiment of "the people." In France, institutions such as the nobility and the Church were so strong that only a powerful national government could challenge them. However, in America there was never a powerful nobility or Church, so Americans saw no need for a powerful central government. Because America was *de facto* quite egalitarian, there was no need to impose equality at the point of a bayonet.[10]

During the 1840s and 1850s, as the debate over slavery grew, even opponents of slavery generally took the position that the federal government had no power to abolish slavery in states that already allowed it. A few of the leading abolitionists suggested that the *northern* states secede from the union, or at least threaten to secede, if the slave states continued practicing slavery. In 1845, the Massachusetts Anti-Slavery Society called for secession or "disunion." The society's motto was "No Union with Slaveholders!" Abolitionists also embraced interposition or even nullification. They argued that northern states should

---
[10] Democracy in America, Volume 2, Bk 4, Ch 4.

not permit the federal Fugitive Slave Act, which required escaped slaves to be returned, to be enforced in the North. Unfortunately, Article 4, Section 2, Clause 3 of the Constitution, the "Fugitive Slave Clause," explicitly provided for escaped slaves to be returned to the state from which they had fled.[11] The Virginia and Kentucky resolutions only asserted that States could interpose themselves when the federal government exceeded its Constitutional authority.

The *Dred Scott* decision held that Congress could not prohibit states from enacting laws with respect to slavery. While there is much to criticize about *Dred Scott*, the central holding remains valid: Congress has no authority to tell states what laws they may or may adopt beyond the explicit limitations found in the Constitution. That is exactly what the Tenth Amendment says: "*The powers not delegated to the United States by the Constitution, nor prohibited by it to the States, are reserved to the States respectively, or to the people.*"

For example, Congress cannot forbid a state from authorizing sports gambling. This was the holding of *Murphy v. National Collegiate Athletic Association* (2018). Unless the Constitution forbids a state from taking a certain action, a state can take that action. Because the Constitution—prior to the 13th Amendment—did not forbid slavery, states could permit it. In fact, the same argument was made about "disunion." Because the Constitution did not forbid leaving the union, states were (apparently) allowed to leave if they wished. In fact, the omission from the Constitution of the "perpetual union" language found in the Articles of Confederation seemed implicitly to acknowledge this.

Consequently, prior to the Civil War, Americans had a strong belief in state sovereignty. Even in the five decades after the Civil War, this understanding of state sovereignty changed very little. Until the 20th century, the federal government did very little; local government performed most government tasks. The loss of a strong sense of state sovereignty, or state's rights, began about 1913.

THE DEATH OF FEDERALISM?

Starting in 1913, the federal government began to grow and increase its spending. The primary mechanism for the increase in spending was the federal income tax. Prior to 1913, the Constitution prohibited a federal income tax. However, in 1913, the 16th Amendment was passed that permitted an income tax. That same year, the 17th Amendment, which required the direct election of senators, was also ratified. These two Amendments consolidated economic and political power in the national government.

Of course, the income tax was a mechanism, not the cause of the increase in the size of the federal government. The cause was the rise of a new theory of government called **Progressivism**. In the early 20th century, Progressives began advocating the use of government power to address social problems, real or imagined. Progressives had some successes in various states; then decided to employ the federal government to address problems on a broader scale.

Initially, Progressives failed to make much progress on the federal level. Attempts to enact federal legislation were stymied by the Supreme Court which declared a variety of Progressive measures unconstitutional. For example, in 1923, the Supreme Court held that a federal minimum wage was unconstitutional. *Adkins v. Children's Hosp. of the D.C.* (1923). In 1935, the Court declared that a federal law regulating the poultry industry was unconstitutional. *A.L.A. Schechter Poultry Corp. v. U.S.*, 295 U.S. 495 (1935). However, two years later, the Court changed its position, or rather one Justice changed his.

The case that signaled the change was *West Coast Hotel v. Parrish* (1937). *West Coast Hotel* overruled *Adkins* and accepted a very broad understanding of federal authority. *West Coast Hotel* was a 5-4 decision, but the change in doctrine resulted from the switch in judicial philosophy of Justice Owen Roberts. Roberts, who joined the Court in 1930, usually voted with the four conservative members of the Court to limit federal power, and, as late as 1936, had voted to strike down a minimum wage law. However, he tended to be a swing vote, not a

---

[11] The 13th Amendment, which abolished slavery, rendered this clause void.

Owen Roberts

strong conservative. Thus, it seems that in light of Franklin Roosevelt's landslide reelection in 1936 and the accomplishments of the New Deal, he chose not to vote with the Court's conservative justices but, this time, to uphold the minimum wage, a decision for which the dissent criticized him.

West Coast Hotel was followed a few years later by *Wickard v. Filburn* (1942), the case in which the federal government fined Filburn for growing too much wheat for his own private use. The Court said that Congress could regulate any activity that in the aggregate substantially affected interstate commerce. *Federalism appeared to be dead.* The powers of the federal government were virtually without limit.

Federal power further expanded during the Civil Rights Movement. In 1964, Congress, basing its authority in part on the interstate commerce clause, enacted the Civil Rights Act which forbade racial discrimination by private business in any "public accommodation." Heart of Atlanta Motel brought suit against the Act. The motel had a policy of only renting rooms to Whites. The motel argued that renting motel rooms was not commerce as "commerce" meant buying and selling goods.

Nevertheless, the Supreme Court held that the Act was a valid exercise of power under the interstate commerce clause. While renting motel rooms was not commerce, the Court said that if even a single local motel refused service to Blacks, Black truck drivers might avoid Atlanta altogether. If Black truck drivers avoided Atlanta, that would affect "commerce among the states." This reasoning took *Filburn* to a new level. *Filburn* reasoned that wheat is a fungible commodity that easily crosses state lines. Wheat consumed in Ohio could easily be consumed somewhere else. Lodging in Atlanta is not fungible. It can only be utilized in Atlanta.

Accordingly, *Heart of Atlanta Motel v. United States* (1964) took the scope of the interstate commerce clause to a new level. The few people who dared to criticize the Court's decision were immediately branded racists. Today, many scholars criticize *Filburn*, but few have the courage to criticize *Heart of Atlanta*.

FEDERALISM REVIVED

For several decades, there appeared to be little opposition to an expansive central government. This began changing in the late 1960s when the federal government began to expand into social policy. In 1980, Ronald Reagan ran for president pledging to reduce the size and scope of the federal government. Reagan promised to appoint federal judges who would apply the constitution as written.

Just when federalism seemed dead, the Supreme Court decided a series of Tenth Amendment cases that resurrected federalism.

The first case was *New York v. United States* (1992). In 1985, Congress passed the Low-Level Radioactive Waste Management Act directing how states must dispose of radioactive waste within their borders. The Act generated little attention as it related to a fairly obscure issue that did not affect many people. Nevertheless, New York argued that the federal government could not tell a state how to dispose of its garbage. The Supreme Court, in a decision that shocked just about everyone, sided with New York. The Court began by noting that:

The Federal Government undertakes activities today that would have been unimaginable to the Framers in two senses; first, because the Framers would not have conceived that any government would conduct such activities; and second, because the Framers would not have believed that the Federal Government, rather than the States, would assume such responsibilities.

After acknowledging this growth in federal power, the Court explained, "*While Congress has substantial powers to govern the Nation directly, including in areas of intimate concern to the States, the Constitution has never been understood to confer upon Congress the ability to require the States to govern according to Congress' instructions.*" The Court said that one of the most important reasons for this was that it prevents political accountability: *[W]here the Federal Government directs the States to regulate, it may be state officials who will bear the brunt of public disapproval, while the federal officials who devised the regulatory program may remain insulated from the electoral ramifications of their decision. Accountability is thus diminished when, due to federal coercion, elected state officials cannot regulate in accordance with the views of the local electorate[.]*

In other words, when there is a problem, voters need to know who to blame. When Congress dictates to state and local officials what those officials must do, then the people will blame the local officials rather than the federal officials who are truly responsible.

The Opinion concluded:

[T]he Constitution protects us from our own best intentions: It divides power among sovereigns and among branches of government precisely so that we may resist the temptation to concentrate power in one location as an expedient solution to the crisis of the day. … States are not mere political subdivisions of the United States. … The Constitution instead "leaves to the several States a residuary and inviolable sovereignty," The Federalist No. 39, reserved explicitly to the States by the Tenth Amendment.

Whatever the outer limits of that sovereignty may be, one thing is clear: The Federal Government may not compel the States to enact or administer a federal regulatory program.

This was the first case in decades that took the Tenth Amendment seriously. People were even more shocked two years later when the Court took up a challenge to the Gun Free School Zones Act. At oral argument, Justice O'Connor, who authored *New York v. United States*, immediately interrupted the federal government's attorney and asked, "*If this is covered, what's left of enumerated powers? What is there that Congress could not do, under this rubric, if you are correct?*" The government lawyer gave a confusing response that seemed to say there were no limitations on what Congress could do. The argument continued with several justices asking him to give the Court a single example of some theoretical legislation that would be beyond the powers of Congress, and he could not provide one. Justice Thomas asked, "What would be an example of a case which you couldn't reach?" The government attorney responded "Well, Your Honor, I'm not prepared to speculate…" This was too much.

Chief Justice Rehnquist, writing for a five-justice majority, began by reminding everyone: "*The Constitution creates a Federal Government of*

Chief Justice Rehnquist

enumerated powers. See Art. I, § 8. As James Madison wrote: "'The powers delegated by the proposed Constitution to the federal government are few and defined.'" If the Court accepted the administration's view, then the federal government was not limited at all. Although Justice Thomas wanted to overrule *Wickard* and return to the original understanding of interstate commerce, the majority refused to go that far. The Court noted that "... *Wickard, which is perhaps the most far reaching example of Commerce Clause authority over intrastate activity, involved economic activity in a way that the possession of a gun in a school zone does not.* (The Gun Law) *is a criminal statute that by its terms has nothing to do with "commerce" or any sort of economic enterprise, however broadly one might define those terms.*" Although the Court drew a line at "non-economic activity," it did not overturn any of its earlier precedents.

A few years later the Court heard a case in which the federal government ordered local sheriffs to conduct background checks for citizens who wished to purchase a firearm. The *New York* case involving radioactive waste said that the federal government could not force states to enforce a federal program. *Printz v. United States* (1997) held that the same rule applied to local officials, and for the same reason: *It is an essential attribute of the States' retained sovereignty that they remain independent and autonomous within their proper sphere of authority.... We held in New York that Congress cannot compel the States to enact or enforce a federal regulatory program. Today we hold that Congress cannot circumvent that prohibition by conscripting the States' officers directly.*

The same year as *Printz*, the Supreme Court decided another hugely important federalism case. In 1993, Congress passed the Religious Freedom Restoration Act (RFRA). Under RFRA, Congress authorized religious organizations to sue state and local governments even for incidental restrictions on the free exercise of religion—even restrictions that did not violate the Constitution. In other words, RFRA demanded that state and local governments go beyond what was Constitutionally required to accommodate religious organizations.

The Catholic church in Boerne, Texas wanted to expand its church building but was denied a permit. The church sued, arguing that the denial violated RFRA. It was undisputed that the Constitution did not forbid state or local governments from enforcing building regulations that happened to affect churches or religious groups. Of course, if the City denied the permit *because* it was a church, that would clearly violate freedom of religion. This was an instance where a general regulation just happened to affect a church.

However, RFRA said that cities and towns had to provide special privileges for religious organizations. In other words, the building permit process that applied to everyone else could not be applied to religious organizations. The Court held that RFRA was unconstitutional because the Tenth Amendment does not allow Congress to impose restrictions on state or local government beyond what the Constitution itself imposes. *City of Boerne v. Flores* (1997). The Court said that Congress has no power to create new Constitutional rights, nor expand existing Constitutional rights beyond what the Constitution sets.

During the 1960s and 1970s, the Supreme Court created new rights out of thin air or re-defined old rights to mean something entirely new. *City of Boerne* held that Congress may no more create new Constitutional rights than could the Court. Fundamental rights applicable to the States are only those firmly rooted in the Anglo-American tradition. In recent years, abortion advocates have suggested that Congress pass a statute saying that no state may restrict abortion. That is exactly what *City of Boerne* prevents. The Tenth Amendment says States are free to enact policies so long as those policies are not specifically forbidden by the Constitution. The Tenth Amendment would be meaningless if Congress could simply declare new Constitutional rights applicable to the states.

The final case in this line of Tenth Amendment decisions was *United States v. Morrison* (2000). In 1994, Congress passed a law called the Violence Against Women Act. As part of this statute Congress declared, "All persons within the United States shall have the right to be free from crimes of violence motivated by gender." To enforce that new right, the Act permitted alleged victims to sue alleged attackers in federal court. Prior to this, neither Congress nor the federal courts had ever recognized any sort of general right to be "free from crime." If Congress could federalize crimes of violence motivated by gender, then what would stop the federal government from federalizing all crime? In fact, Congress claimed it had authority to pass this law as both a regulation of commerce and a protection of the right to be free from violent crime under the 14th Amendment guarantee that no state shall deny any person equal protection. The Supreme Court rejected both rationales.

First, the Court said "violence" was not a commercial activity in any conceivable sense. If person A slaps person B, this is not any sort of commercial transaction. The government argued that crime, "in the aggregate," substantially affects interstate commerce; therefore, all criminal law could be federalized. The Court noted this argument "would effectually obliterate the distinction between what is national and what is local and create a completely centralized government."

As to the "right to be free from crime" argument, the Court applied the reasoning from *City of Boerne* and noted that Congress cannot create new Constitutional rights out of thin air and then purport to enforce those rights. The Court noted that the Fourteenth Amendment's guarantee of "equal protection of the laws" had never been understood to federalize all state civil and criminal law. The Court held that "[t]hese limitations are necessary to prevent the Fourteenth Amendment from obliterating the Framers' carefully crafted balance of power between the States and the National Government." Since the adoption of the 14th Amendment it has always been understood that criminal laws such as murder, assault, etc., remain a local issue.

Observers of the Court thought that additional federal statutes would be found unconstitutional; but, the new-found support for federalism stopped there. From 1992 to 2000, a five-justice majority on the court (Rehnquist, O'Connor, Scalia, Kennedy, and Thomas) repeatedly backed a narrow reading of the commerce clause and a strong reading of the Tenth Amendment. Justice Thomas apparently drove this new position. Thomas became a member of the Court in late 1991 and his influence on the Court was immediate. While the majority never went as far as Thomas wished, for example, overruling *Wickard v. Filburn*, his consistent espousal of a logically coherent understanding of the commerce clause forced the Court to re-evaluate its case law.

THE HIGH-WATER MARK OF FEDERALISM

The decision in *Morrison* proved to be the high-water mark for Tenth Amendment jurisprudence. In fact, during the 1990s, federalism reached a new pinnacle of strength. Two famous incidents in the early 1990s inspired this renaissance of federalism. In 1992, in Ruby Ridge, Idaho, federal agents shot several civilians, including Vicki Weaver, who an FBI sniper shot in the head while she held her 10-month-old baby. The chief of the FBI's violent crimes section was convicted of obstruction of justice for trying to cover up the incident.

The FBI sniper who killed Vicki Weaver was charged with manslaughter by the local prosecutor. A federal district judge initially dismissed the criminal charges under the theory that all federal employees are immune from prosecution for acts committed in their capacity as federal employees. However, the Ninth Circuit Court of Appeals overturned the district court and held that local governments could prosecute federal employees when they committed crimes. This case represents one of the most important precedents on the power of local government to protect their citizens from violence by federal agents. After the Ninth Circuit decision, a new prosecutor opted not to pursue a conviction, but the precedent stands.

In 1993, a federal raid on a cult compound in Waco, Texas resulted in the deaths of 86 people, including 28 children. Many people were asking why the heavy hand of the federal government was involved in seemingly trivial, non-violent offenses. In both cases, the origin of federal involvement was suspicion that the people involved might have illegal firearms. This distrust in federal law enforcement was reflected in opinion polls. In 1994, polls showed that trust in the federal government had reached an all-time low. Only 19% of Americans expressed confidence in the federal government.[12]

---

[12] https://www.pewresearch.org/politics/2020/09/14/americans-views-of-government-low-trust-but-some-positive-performance-ratings/

The 1990s interest in federalism was also largely due to the end of the Cold War. During the Cold War, patriotic Americans believed that to oppose the Soviet Union they needed to support a strong central government and a standing army. The FBI had been the agency responsible for protecting against communist infiltration and spying. When the Soviet Union ceased to exist on Christmas Day 1991, many Americans wanted to go back to the historic norm of a somewhat weak central government.

Thus, in the 1990s, the voters, the Supreme Court, even the Congress and the executive branch, suddenly supported local sovereignty. Then, on September 11, 2001, terrorists attacked the World Trade Center and the Pentagon. Overnight, the federalism revolution stopped. Trust and confidence in the federal government skyrocketed from about 30% before the attacks to 54% immediately afterwards. The Supreme Court mirrored the nationalistic mood of the country and halted any further application of its federalism cases. In 2005, the Supreme Court heard a case to decide whether the federal government could criminalize marijuana possession as a regulation of commerce. It held that drug use in the aggregate substantially affects interstate commerce and therefore could be regulated.

In 2022, the Supreme Court seemed to take yet another turn. In *Dobbs*, the Court held that abortion was not a constitutional right, and disputes over abortion must be determined at the state or local level. Justice Thomas suggested that this principle should be applied more broadly to a whole group of "rights" created by the courts in the last fifty years. To date, it is too early to tell whether the *Dobbs* reasoning will be applied in other contexts.

United States Supreme Court Building

UNFUNDED MANDATES

Although the Court has determined that the Tenth Amendment generally protects the states from federal force, there is an important series of cases dealing with mandates placed on the states. While the federal government can never compel a local government or local officials to enforce federal regulatory programs, since the 1960s, the federal government has taken a subtler approach whereby it "persuades" local officials to do something by paying them to do it. This notion, often referred to as **coercive federalism**, involves a "carrot and stick" approach by the federal government in which it incentivizes state and local governments to comply with federal orders either by granting federal funds (the carrot) or withholding federal funds (the stick). The Supreme Court addressed coercive federalism in *South Dakota v. Dole* (1987).

Dole involved road construction. Prior to 1956, road construction was almost entirely a matter for state and local governments. In 1956,

I-55 under construction in Mississippi, May 1972

the Eisenhower Administration announced that national security required an interstate highway system. To fund the interstate highway system, Congress enacted a national gas tax whose funds were supposed to go into a special trust fund to be used for road construction. In 2023, the federal government collected about $45 billion in gas tax. Unfortunately, the highway trust fund soon morphed into something more than the interstate highway system. Aside from funding the interstate highway system, the gas tax and highway trust fund began to be used for anything remotely connected to "transportation," including bicycle facilities, recreational trails, and vegetation management.[13]

Moreover, this gas tax money is mostly returned to the states to build roads, walking paths and trails, etc. To receive the federal highway money, that is, *their own money back*, the States must agree to do certain things. Years ago, these federal conditions were pretty straightforward. For example, states had to agree to use the federal highway money for highway improvement. In the 1980s, Congress added new requirements to this highway money.

In 1984, Congress passed a law that *withheld* a portion of federal highway money to any state that had a drinking age below 21-years of age. The Supreme Court said that Congress could condition funds on anything that was generally related to the purpose of the federal program. Practically speaking, those who argued that the condition was unconstitutional had to demonstrate that the condition was *totally unrelated* to the purpose of the federal program. In *Dole*, the Court held that a 21-year-old drinking age was sufficiently related to highway safety to make the mandate constitutional. The Court also said that only *Congress* can impose such conditions. In other words, the president cannot add conditions to federal money that are not specifically set forth in an actual law passed by Congress.

Finally, the Court in *Dole* held that the States had to have real choice. This means that if the money at issue was so substantial that a state has no choice but to do what Congress demands, then this changes an incentive into an order. Congress

---

[13] https://www.fhwa.dot.gov/fastact/factsheets/transportationalternativesfs.cfm

can never order the states to do anything not already required by the Constitution.

The *Dole* decision proved quite controversial. After *Dole*, Congress kept adding new mandates to receive federal funds. In 1995, Congress passed the *Unfunded Mandates Reform Act*, but it only required Congress to estimate how much a mandate would cost the states.

Recently, the Court has suggested that *Dole* is ready to be overturned. In 2010, Congress passed a form of national health care called the Affordable Care Act (ACA) or ObamaCare. To implement the program, Congress demanded that the States enforce certain parts of the program, or lose federal funding for *Medicaid*, medical coverage for the poor which the states and the federal government jointly fund. In 2012, the Supreme Court reviewed the ACA and held some parts constitutional and other parts unconstitutional. Among the unconstitutional parts was the requirement that states enforce ObamaCare or lose federal funds. The four conservative Justices criticized *Dole*, arguing that the whole idea "present[s] a grave threat to the system of federalism created by our Constitution."

Today, "funded mandates" remain one of the most important ways that the federal government controls the states. It is hard for states to turn down federal grants. Many of these grants represent a significant part of state and local budgets. Of course, if state and local governments are to be truly independent they must be financially independent of the federal government—as they were for most of American history.

THE ECONOMIC INCENTIVE TO CENTRALIZE SPENDING

A gallup poll conducted in October 2023 asked people how much confidence they had in various government entities. By a wide margin, Americans placed their trust in state and local government:

	Trust
Your local government	67
Your state government	59
The Presidency	41
Federal government: International problems	44
Federal government: Domestic problems	37

This poll is consistent with earlier polls. For decades, Americans have said they trust the local government more than the federal government. By a two-to-one margin Americans prefer local governments to handle "domestic problems" rather than the federal government. It is generally agreed that this preference is based on the greater access the average citizen has to local officials. Each congressman represents about a million people, and most senators represent millions of constituents. Most state representatives represent about 5,000 to 10,000 constituents, and a city councilman often represents just a few hundred constituents. This means that local and state representatives are much more accessible and accountable to the ordinary citizen. There is an old expression "You can't fight city hall," but it is actually much easier to fight city hall than the federal bureaucracy. Polls show that a large majority of Americans agree.

So why is local government so weak compared to the central government? After all, a) local government is the most just, b) local government was the American tradition for the first 150 years, c) decentralization is constitutionally mandated, and d) the people overwhelmingly prefer local control. Yet, somehow local control is the exception rather than the rule. How is this possible? The simple answer is that very powerful interests support centralization, or, to put it more bluntly, *follow the money*.

CENTRALIZATION BREEDS WASTE AND CORRUPTION

In *Centesimus Annus* John Paul II wrote, "the Social Assistance State leads to a loss of human energies and an inordinate increase of public agencies … which are accompanied by an enormous increase in spending." While wasting money may seem relatively unimportant compared to the destruction of the family, government agents have a solemn duty to utilize public funds for the common good. Public officials have an obligation to use funds effectively, not wastefully, and certainly not to reward their friends. Moreover, insofar as taxes take money from poor families, who can scarcely afford it, to give it to the rich is a grave injustice.

The federal budget for 2024 is about $6.5 trillion. Everyone acknowledges there is massive waste in a $6.5 trillion budget, but it gets worse each year. Aristotle first identified what modern economists call **The Free Rider Problem**.[14] The Free Rider Problem essentially says when people are able to consume as much resources as they wish, at no cost to themselves, then they are incentivized to consume more and more.

The Free Rider Problem can be exemplified as follows. You and three close friends go to a restaurant and agree to split the check equally four ways. You would be unlikely to "splurge" and order some lavishly expensive meal because you will end up paying 25% of the cost anyway, and you do not want your friends to resent you making them pay for your extravagance. However, consider what happens if you are splitting the check, not with three close friends, but with one hundred million anonymous strangers. There is no incentive to be frugal. No matter how much you spend, it only affects 1/100,000,000 of the total amount. There is anonymity in large numbers, so there is no social price to pay. You may as well order the most expensive meal you can. In fact, it would be foolish not to, because everyone else is. So, why not get on *the gravy train*? This is also called a **moral hazard**. When people are protected from the consequences of their actions they are tempted to do things, and take risks, they would never do otherwise.

This example shows just how hard it is to turn down federal money, the problem of coercive federalism! Almost every state and local official will say, "Of course, we would prefer not to take federal money, but until they change the rules we have to play the game." With trillions of dollars sloshing around in federal revenue sharing, it is simply too difficult to turn down federal grants.

Moreover, much of this money breeds corruption and creates a "vicious circle." To obtain the money, local governments hire lobbyists who are often retired Congressmen or retired senior staff to Congressmen. Additionally, the lobbying groups usually make contributions to the re-election campaigns of Congressmen and Senators. In other words, Congress votes money for a local project and some of this money goes to a lobbying group, and ultimately, makes its way back to the Congressmen who voted for the project.

This is not a new problem. Plato suggested that rulers should not be allowed to own property, or even have families, to avoid the temptation for rulers to enrich themselves or their families. Preventing politicians from enriching themselves, rather than acting for the common good, is always a problem. Of course, when the budget is $6.5 trillion there is an enormous amount of opportunity – and temptation—for this sort of thing. Thus, despite the popularity of reducing the federal bureaucracy and returning control to local communities, there are too many powerful people who have a vested interest in maintaining the status quo. This is why John Paul II wrote that public agencies too often "are dominated more by bureaucratic ways of thinking than by concern for serving their client."

As previously noted, lobbying is not *per se* immoral, but with a $6.5 trillion budget, the potential for waste, fraud, and abuse are enormous. Too much money is diverted away from the common good. Moreover, virtually the entire class of political elites is "on the payroll" and these people have strong personal incentive to maintain the status quo. So, centralization deepens, despite its obvious inefficiencies, popular support for more local control, and even "lip service" given to local control by most politicians. Even concerned politicians, who appear to be genuinely committed to local control, find it impossible to change the system.

---

[14] *Politics*, book 2

SUBSIDIARITY IN CONTEMPORARY SOCIETY

UNIFORMITY ENFORCED FROM ABOVE IS NOT JUST WASTEFUL BUT UNJUST

In the 1990s, the federal government mandated "low flow" toilets due to concerns about water shortages in some areas of the country. Prior to the federal law, while some states had mandated low flow toilets, most had not. Of course, there are arid locations in North America where conserving water is conducive to the common good; however, many people wondered why communities next to the Great Lakes (the second largest basin of freshwater on Earth) are forced to use toilets that do not function as well as other toilets. Forcing people to use a mechanism they neither want nor need, serves no useful purpose and makes no sense.

The low-flow-toilet mandate created a minor inconvenience, but it illustrates an important point: problems like water shortages are usually handled better on the local level. This issue occurs countless times in a nation the size of the United States. For example, under federal law, all public accommodations must be wheelchair accessible. Creating opportunities for people with disabilities is a laudable goal. Yet, the Americans with Disabilities Act demands that an outhouse on the top of a mountain next to a hiking trail must be wheelchair accessible, even though a person in a wheelchair likely could never get to the top of the mountain. When the Americans with Disabilities Act was passed in 1990, many state and local parks removed outhouses because it was too expensive to make them wheelchair accessible. Sadly, many other conveniences were removed making life more difficult for people who were able to walk. Instead of making life better for those in wheelchairs, it made life worse for those not wheelchair bound.

This "one-size-fits-all" rule often does not help anyone, and can hurt just about everyone. Indeed, one-size-fits-all rules often result in reducing standards to the least common denominator. A "standard" that everyone can achieve will need to be a low standard.

RELIGION, THE COMMON GOOD, AND UNIFORMITY

The Church has long taught that the common good requires the state to encourage the practice of religion. *The Compendium of the Social Doctrine of the Church* proclaims (section 170), "*God is the ultimate end of his creatures and for no reason may the common good be deprived of its transcendent dimension, which moves beyond the historical dimension while at the same time fulfilling it.*" In section 397, the *Compendium* declares, "Authority must recognize, respect and promote essential human and moral values." In a country where there is a great diversity of religion, this presents certain issues.

In his *Treatise on Law*, St. Thomas explains that laws must encourage virtue but laws must be suitable to the people ruled. St. Thomas writes that human law "does not lay upon the multitude of imperfect men the burdens of those who are already virtuous." If the legislature tried to impose laws that are too strict or unacceptable to a large part of the population then these "… *imperfect people, being unable to bear such precepts, would break out into yet greater evils … if new wine, that is the perfect life, is put into old bottles, that is into imperfect men, the bottles break and the wine runneth out, that is the precepts are despised, and those men from contempt [of the law] break into evils worse still.*" Optimally, law would reflect all the principles of Christian morality, but St. Thomas recognizes that is not always possible. The best that a just legislator can do is gradually try to bring society closer to the standards of perfect justice.

In the last hundred years or so, a theory of secularism has argued that because the United State is religiously diverse that government and religion must be entirely separated. Some versions of this theory maintain that government and *morality* must be entirely separated. Many secularists openly encourage non-Christians to come to the United States specifically so that it will no longer be a Christian country. Most American Founders emphasized the importance of government supporting virtue and morality. In 21st century America, any sort of morality on the national level is probably impossible, as there is no longer agreement on even the most basic moral principles. This makes it more imperative that local government at least reflect the morality of local communities.

St. Thomas does not think it is a good idea for Christians forcibly to impose all of Christian morality on those not ready for it; but, pagans and secularists have no such scruples. Pagans and secularists, largely insist on imposing their perverse view of "morality" on everyone. Today, a small Christian community that tries to place the least restriction on immoral practices will be attacked as intolerant and evil. The clearest example of this has been the attack on those who defend the traditional Natural Law view of marriage, the family, and human sexuality. In *Obergefell v. Hodges* (2015) the Supreme Court rejected the ancient concept of marriage and announced something new called "same sex marriage." As the dissent correctly pointed out, the new definition of marriage "will be used to vilify Americans who are unwilling to assent to the new orthodoxy."

In 2022, the Supreme Court returned the power to legislate abortion to local levels. Since then, the handful of states that have placed any significant restrictions on killing preborn humans have been demonized and attacked. The Biden Administration has actively tried to undermine state laws against abortion by openly announcing that it will not enforce federal laws that prohibit mailing abortifacients and suggesting that abortions might be performed on military bases in states that protect human life at all stages.

Paul Weyrich

As a practical matter, there are great obstacles to establishing justice even on the local level. Nevertheless, many Christian leaders in the United States have emphasized local self-government as the best hope for preserving small pockets of Christian civilization. One of the most influential Catholic political thinkers of the 20th century was Paul Weyrich, who coined the term "Moral Majority." In 1999, Weyrich wrote a "Letter to Conservatives" in which he explained, "*I no longer believe that there is a moral majority. I do not believe that a majority of Americans actually shares our values. … [W]e need to drop out of this culture, and find places, even if it is where we physically are right now, where we can live godly, righteous and sober lives.*" Weyrich's letter held up homeschoolers as an example: "*[T]here were times when those who had our beliefs were definitely in the minority and it was a band of hardy monks who preserved the culture while the surrounding society disintegrated. What I mean by separation is, for example, what the homeschoolers have done.*"

Weyrich was advocating a return to the traditional American paradigm of local control and the traditional Catholic paradigm of subsidiarity. If local communities could reflect local values there might be hope of one day reaching another "moral majority."

St. Augustine defined a community as a group of people united by a common purpose, a common understanding of the goals of the community, and in a political community, a common conception of justice. Under this understanding of community, 330 million people who share little in common is no community at all. This is why the social teachings of the Church have repeatedly emphasized that centralization undermines all community.

In the 1830s, Alexis de Tocqueville was impressed at how often Americans formed voluntary associations to address social problems. Today, government bureaucracies have too often replaced private voluntary associations. Many of the community services once performed by neighbors have been replaced by a check from the federal government.

Secularists have done their best to chase the Church out of public life and even try to stop the Church from doing charity work. In 2018, Catholic Social Services in Philadelphia was told they would not be permitted to facilitate adoptions because the Church refused to place children with unmarried couples which was said to be illegal discrimination. This policy was only reversed when the Supreme Court intervened and held that this treatment of the Church violated freedom of religion. *Fulton v. City of Philadelphia* (2021). So the Church's traditional charitable activities, such as operating hospitals and orphanages, is under attack.

Of course, the most fundamental and most essential intermediate association is the family. In recent years, some people have sought to redefine the whole concept of marriage and the family. For example, many people in the past two decades have denied that marriage is between a man and woman, and have denied that procreation of children is part of marriage. This was the holding of *Obergefell v. Hodges*. The majority in *Obergefell* purported to redefine marriage. According to the majority, marriage is not a natural institution at all. The concept of marriage is purely artificial. Thus, the Court can define or redefine marriage to mean whatever they want it to mean. The Court said that the new concept of marriage is nothing more than a pairing of autonomous individuals seeking their own subjective desires. Chief Justice John Roberts pointed out the fallacy of this position in his dissent:

> The fundamental right to marry does not include a right to make a State change its definition of marriage. And a State's decision to maintain the meaning of marriage that has persisted in every culture throughout human history can hardly be called irrational. … [T]he Court invalidates the marriage laws of more than half the States and orders the transformation of a social institution that has formed the basis of human society for millennia, for the Kalahari Bushmen and the Han Chinese, the Carthaginians and the Aztecs. Just who do we think we are?

Chief Justice John Roberts

As of 2024, a majority of Supreme Court Justices have criticized *Obergefell*, and it may be overturned. If that happens, states will be legally allowed to define marriage as they wish. Some states might adopt the *Obergefell* idea, but many will not. As the Church has always emphasized, "As the family goes, so goes the nation;" a principle which the vast majority of Americans accept. A 2022 Rasmussen survey found that 84% of those polled believe a strong family is crucial to the well-being of the country and that parents should be responsible for raising their own children.

Subsidiarity demands that the state support and protect the family. The modern state does not simply fail to support and protect the family, it defines it out of existence and undermines it. A Pew Research Study conducted in 2019 concluded that the United States has far and away the largest percentage of fatherless homes: 23% of children have no father figure in the home, such as a foster father, or grand-father. More alarmingly, 37% of children in the United States do not live with their biological father.

FEDERALISM: WHO OWES WHAT TO WHOM

The system of Federalism found in the Constitution creates two relationships. The first is the relationship between the states and the federal government and the second is among the states themselves. The Constitution defines these relationships, which, essentially, are *obligations* that each party owes to the other.

THE FEDERAL GOVERNMENT'S OBLIGATION TO STATES

As this and previous chapters have discussed, the vast majority of Constitutional issues that arise, deal with the relationship of the states with the federal government. In most cases, they involve questions of who should wield the power, the state or the federal government. However, there are certain issues in which the federal government clearly possesses the ultimate power, and in which it owes the states a serious obligation.

Some of the obligations the federal government owes to the States are set forth in Article 4, Section 4 (The Guarantee Clause): *The United States shall guarantee to every State in this Union a Republican Form of Government, and shall protect each of them against Invasion; and on Application of the Legislature, or of the Executive (when the Legislature cannot be convened) against domestic Violence.* The Guarantee Clause creates three obligations, on the part of the federal government. First, it guarantees each state a republican form of government. Although "Republican Form of Government" has never been definitively addressed, the debates at the constitutional convention were explicit that this guarantee only meant that the central government would not allow a state government to be overthrown by violence. Thus, a state cannot have some form of tyrannical or despotic government. The inclusion of the two specific cases of invasion and domestic violence also shows this. Protection from external invasion and internal revolts, i.e. domestic violence, are the other two obligations the Clause creates.

As noted, Article 4, Section 3 obligates the federal government to protect the territorial integrity of the states. Under Clause 1, the "Admissions Clause," new states cannot be formed within the territory of another State; nor can a state be formed by joining two or more States, or from the parts of a state. A new state can only be formed from part of an existing state if the existing state's legislature and Congress agree to form the new state. This has occurred a few times in American history. In December 1789, Virginia agreed to the formation of the state of Kentucky from its western territory. Kentucky was admitted as a state in 1792. In 1819, Maine was formed from Massachusetts with the consent of its legislature, and admitted as a state as part of the Missouri Compromise. The most controversial creation of a new state from an existing one occurred in June 1863, when West Virginia was carved out of Virginia during the Civil War. Technically, the pro-Union "Restored Government of Virginia," Virginia's Civil War legislature, agreed to form West Virginia.

Finally, the federal government is obligated to ensure that every state has two Senators to represent it in the Senate.

THE OBLIGATIONS OF THE STATES TO EACH OTHER

Article 4, Sections 1 and 2 create three duties that each state owes its fellow states. Section 1 creates the Full Faith and Credit Clause. Section 2 creates the Privileges and Immunities Clause and the Extradition Clause. These three clauses form the fundamental obligations of one state to another.

FULL FAITH AND CREDIT

Article 4, Section 1 declares that *"Full Faith and Credit shall be given in each State to the public Acts, Records, and judicial Proceedings of every other State."* Known as the "Full Faith and Credit Clause," it means that states must uphold the laws and court decisions of other states. In most cases, this is not an issue, as laws have tended to be somewhat uniform until relatively recently. Generally, it has meant upholding laws and cases that involve contracts or property rights. More recently, as some states have recognized certain rights that other states have not, the Full Faith and Credit Clause has become more problematic.

Historically, the Supreme Court has never insisted that states follow a policy regarding marriage that violates strong state public policy. Thus, while marriages in one state are generally recognized as legal in all states, there are exceptions. For example, until *Obergefell*, most states refused to recognize a marriage that was not between a man and a woman. They had a two-hundred-year history of only recognizing marriages between one man and one woman. Thus, polygamous marriages were not recognized. States have also not recognized certain divorces in which the parties obtained state citizenship only long enough to obtain the divorce. Given the Court's recent holdings regarding marriage, there are probably no longer any viable strong state public policy exceptions.

PRIVILEGES AND IMMUNITIES

Section 2, Clause 1 reads, *"The Citizens of each State shall be entitled to all Privileges and Immunities of Citizens in the several States."* The Privileges and Immunities clause basically means that no state may unfairly discriminate against a citizen of another state who is either traveling through the state or temporarily residing in the state. For example, imagine a resident of Virginia is traveling to Ohio to visit relatives. The police in Pennsylvania, noticing the Virginia license plates, cannot treat the Virginia driver any differently than Pennsylvania drivers.

On the other hand, unfair treatment does not mean "equal" treatment. For example, state colleges and universities often offer "instate" tuition, which is a lower amount, to residents of their states. States often provide other benefits to their residents because they are paying state taxes. Also, a person must be a resident of the state to vote in that state's elections.

The privileges and immunities clause was more relevant in the 18th and 19th century when travel was more difficult and people viewed themselves as "Virginians" and "Ohioans" to a greater extent than people do today.

EXTRADITION

Finally, Section 2, Clause 2 states that *"A Person charged in any State with Treason, Felony, or other Crime, who shall flee from Justice, and be found in another State, shall on demand of the executive Authority of the State from which he fled, be delivered up, to be removed to the State having Jurisdiction of the Crime."* Known as the **extradition clause**, it essentially means that accused criminals must be returned to the state from which they fled if the state governor demands it. Although the clause speaks of treason and other felonies, the courts have broadened the rule to include misdemeanors.

Under the extradition clause, the governor of one state is obligated to return the accused, or the convicted, to the requesting governor. Historically, governors respected the wishes of their fellow governors and did so. Most governors felt they had a moral obligation under the Constitution to uphold federalism. In fact, the Supreme Court in *Kentucky v. Dennison*, (65 U.S. 66 (1861)), held that Congress could not force a governor to extradite someone, the governor only had a moral obligation to do so. In the *Dennison* case, the governor of Ohio refused to extradite a freed Black man to Kentucky, a slave state.

The *Dennison* case is somewhat unusual as governors tended to respect their fellow governors and extradite fugitives. However, in 1987, the Court overruled *Dennison* and declared that the federal courts could require governors to extradite fugitives.

CONCLUSION

The United States was founded on the principle of local self-government and the preference for families and voluntary associations to address social problems. These policies reflected the basic principle of justice called *subsidiarity*. Until the 1960s, these principles were almost universally accepted, and even today they remain overwhelmingly popular. Unfortunately, there are powerful financial interests and political ideologies that support centralization of power. Since the 1960s, these forces have actively undermined families, churches, voluntary associations, and local government.

Today, many people wonder if Federalism even exists and if the states have become an anachronism, something useful in the 19th century, but now hopelessly outdated and obstacles to progress. Yet, the Constitution created a federal system which balances power between the states and the federal government. Is the Constitution also an anachronism which is hopelessly outdated and an obstacle to progress? Certainly, there are those who believe it is. Others believe it created a great nation that has done great things. But in the end, it is only "parchment." Perhaps Ronald Reagan said it best: "*Checks and balances, limited government—the genius of our constitutional system is its recognition that no one branch of government alone could be relied on to preserve our freedoms. The great safeguard of our liberty is the totality of the constitutional system, with no one part getting the upper hand....*" Or in the words of John Adams, "*Our Constitution was made only for a moral and religious People. It is wholly inadequate to the government of any other.*"

REVIEW QUESTIONS

1. What document declared that "all sovereignty resides essentially in the nation?"

2. What are some arguments in favor of decentralization?

3. What is the principle of non-aggression?

4. Who wrote, "Our Constitution was made only for a moral and religious People. It is wholly inadequate to the government of any other."?

5. Who wrote, *"[O]nly a virtuous people are capable of freedom. As nations become corrupt and vicious, they have more need of masters."*?

6. Who wrote, *"Government is not reason, it is not eloquence—it is force! Like fire it is a dangerous servant and a fearful master[.]"*?

7. What European philosopher heavily influenced Hamilton and Madison?

8. Why did Maine separate from Massachusetts and become an independent state in 1819?

9. Who were some of the notable attendees at the Hartford Convention of 1814?

10. What was the final declaration of Hartford Convention?

11. What did the Virginia Resolution of 1798 say about interposition?

12. Who wrote Democracy in America?

13. Who developed the doctrine of Nullification in 1828?

14. What was the basic holding of *Heart of Atlanta Motel v. United States* (1964)?

15. How did the creation of a federal income tax impact government revenue?

16. Why was the holding in *Adkins v. Children's Hospital* (1923) significant?

17. Why was *New York v. United States* (1992), involving the disposal of radioactive waste, important?

18. Why was *Lopez v. United States* (1994) important?

19. What is the "moral majority?"

20. What is the full faith and credit clause?

21. What is extradition?

22. Why are "Intermediate Institutions" important?

23. What is the privileges and immunities clause?

24. Under the Guarantee Clause, what are the three obligations the federal government owes the states?

25. Which clause says that new states cannot be formed within the territory of another State; nor can a state be formed by joining two or more States, or from the parts of a state unless the existing state's legislature and Congress agree to form the new state?

26. What is Federalism?

27. What is the doctrine of Interposition?

28. When was the doctrine of interposition first explicitly stated?

29. What was the first opportunity for states to assert the doctrine of interposition?

30. What is "coercive federalism?"

CHAPTER NINE
STATE AND LOCAL GOVERNMENT

"Local government is the foundation of democracy, if it fails, democracy will fail."[1]

On the federal level, there are 537 elected people: the President, Vice President, 100 senators, and 435 representatives. There are about 7,500 elected state office holders: legislators, judges, and executive branch officials. It is estimated there are about half a million locally elected officials. There are still a few small towns where every citizen participates in direct democracy. In the United States, there are 3,000 counties, more than 19,000 cities and towns, and 13,500 school districts. Needless to say, local government varies from place to place, but most state and local governments share many of the same general functions, duties, and operations.

Historically, local self-government, where ordinary citizens had a meaningful say in how their communities functioned, was hugely important to early Americans. Today, state and local governments struggle to remain independent and avoid being reduced to a cog in an enormous nationwide bureaucracy. This threatens the very nature of democracy, because, as the quote at the head of the chapter rightly proclaims, *"Local government is the foundation of democracy, if it fails, democracy will fail."*

THE STATE CONSTITUTION

Every state has a constitution which sets forth the structure and function of that state's government. Under Article 4 of the U.S. Constitution, every state is guaranteed a "republican form of government," which has been understood to mean a type of representative government. So long as a state provides a representative form of government, the people of the state can choose the system of government which works best for them. The state constitution is the supreme law of the state. It supersedes all other state and local laws; however, it is legally inferior to the U.S. Constitution and federal law.

In general, state constitutions mirror the federal Constitution. Like the federal Constitution, they create the state government and explain how it will work. State constitutions create governments with three branches: the executive branch headed by the governor and his assistants; the legislative branch consisting of two Houses which may be called a Senate and a House of Representatives or perhaps the General Assembly; and the judicial branch with a supreme court and various lower courts. The state constitution also contains various checks and balances that each branch has over the others. Finally, the constitution contains a bill of rights.

While state constitutions share certain commonalities with the federal Constitution, they are also quite dissimilar in some respects. First, the federal Constitution is actually rather short (4,543

---

[1] Robert W. Flack

Detail of the official handwritten copy of the Preamble

words). Every state constitution is longer, and some are much, much longer! Second, while the federal Constitution is somewhat general in its explanation of government, state constitutions tend to be very specific, which accounts for their length. Finally, the federal Constitution is difficult to amend, and has been amended only seventeen times since the Bill of Rights was ratified. On the other hand, state constitutions are easy to amend and often are. In fact, in January 1987, Rhode Island ratified an entirely new constitution.

Historically, two colonies kept their charters; the other eleven wrote new constitutions after independence. The Massachusetts Constitution (45,283 words), written mainly by **John Adams** (as well as his cousin Samuel Adams and James Bowdoin) and ratified on October 25, 1780, is the oldest written constitution still in effect anywhere in the world. The Massachusetts Constitution delineates the nature of the state's government and contains an extensive bill of rights. The constitution is also unique in that it was approved by popularly elected representatives and then presented to the people for ratification; as opposed to the more common method of ratification by state legislatures or ratification conventions.

The Massachusetts Constitution has served as a model for numerous constitutions. Following its example, most constitutions begin with a **Preamble**, which explains why the document is being written.

In the words of John Adams' Preamble:

> The end of the institution, maintenance, and administration of government, is to secure the existence of the body politic, to protect it, and to furnish the individuals who compose it with the power of enjoying in safety and tranquility their natural rights, and the blessings of life: and whenever these great objects are not obtained, the people have a right to alter the government, and to take measures necessary for their safety, prosperity and happiness.

Next comes a **Bill of Rights**, or, in the case of Massachusetts, *A Declaration of the Rights of the Inhabitants of the Commonwealth of Massachusetts*. Like the federal Constitution, it lists the rights of the state's citizens. John Adams listed thirty specific rights starting with Article I:

> All men are born free and equal, and have certain natural, essential, and unalienable rights; among which may be reckoned the right of enjoying and defending their lives and liberties; that of acquiring, possessing, and protecting property; in fine, that of seeking and obtaining their safety and happiness.

Article II

> It is the right as well as the duty of all men in society, publicly, and at stated seasons to worship the Supreme Being, the great Creator

and Preserver of the universe. And no subject shall be hurt, molested, or restrained, in his person, liberty, or estate, for worshipping God in the manner and season most agreeable to the dictates of his own conscience; or for his religious profession or sentiments; provided he doth not disturb the public peace, or obstruct others in their religious worship.

State constitutions next describe the state government with its three branches and the various state officers, or as Adams calls it, "The Frame of the Government." New state constitutions often contain provisions delineating local government and its various subdivisions. Next, the constitution contains various "general provisions," which address everything from taxation to education. For example, Adams includes a section dealing with "The University at Cambridge (Harvard), and Encouragement of Literature, etc." Finally, state constitutions contain detailed procedures for amendments.[2]

STATE GOVERNORS AND THE EXECUTIVE BRANCH

Every state has a popularly elected **governor** who serves as the chief executive. Compared to the President of the United States, the powers of governors are much more limited. The president is the head of a unified administration and members of his cabinet work for him. In contrast, every state has a number of elected state officials who do not work directly for the governor and who the governor cannot fire. For example, forty-three states have a popularly elected **Attorney General**. The Attorney General is the chief law enforcement officer and chief legal officer in a state. The Attorney General can determine the criminal and civil priorities of the state without the governor's permission. Thirty-five states have a **Secretary of State** who is popularly elected and not answerable to the governor. The duties of the Secretary of State vary widely, but essentially, the Secretary of State is the state's chief administrative officer and, in most states, also supervises elections. Thirty-eight states have a popularly elected state **Treasurer**. In seventeen states, the **lieutenant governor**, similar to the vice president of the United States, is popularly elected separately from the governor. Lieutenant governors tend to have much more power than the vice president. For example, in a few states, the lieutenant governor must approve certain important decisions. Most states have a few other elected officials who are part of the executive branch. This was a deliberate choice of the citizens of the states: they did not want to see a great amount of power concentrated in the hands of one person.

One area where governors have more power than the president is the **line item veto**. Forty-four states allow the governor to veto specific spending provisions. Moreover, in about a dozen states, the governor can either veto a budget item or reduce it. **Reduction veto power** is the power of a governor to *reduce* the amount of a specific spending provision. These measures help prevent the kind of wasteful spending that is common on the federal level. Additionally, almost every state is required to have a balanced budget each year, so states cannot run a deficit as the federal government does.

Most states require a 2/3 majority vote to override a governor's veto (the same as for the federal government). Several states require the legislature to repass the measure by a mere majority. There are also some exceptions regarding what a governor may veto.

Every state has an administrative code which the executive branch promulgates. However, many regulations can be promulgated by the state attorney general or secretary of state without the governor's approval. Moreover, fifteen states have a **legislative veto**. In these states, the legislature can overrule a regulation by a simple majority vote that is not subject to the governor's veto. On the federal level, the Supreme Court has held that the legislative veto is unconstitutional.

Not all governors have absolute pardon power. In many states, the governor must obtain the approval of a commission or other state officers, such as the lieutenant governor or attorney general, to pardon a criminal. In twenty states where the governor has pardon power, the governor must send a report to the state legislature explaining the reasons for the pardon.

---

[2] The Massachusetts Constitution is one of the greatest documents in American history, yet very few Americans have read it. It is rather long, ten times longer than the U.S. Constitution. Although not required, we encourage students to at least browse it. It reflects the remarkable genius of John Adams, one of the greatest of the Founding Fathers.

About two-thirds of the states reject the doctrine of executive privilege. This means that a governor's advisors can be required to testify before state legislatures and explain what advice they gave a governor.

Overall, most states were distrustful about concentrating too much power in the hand of the governor and thus placed more checks on the governor than the U.S. Constitution places on the president. This was based on the understanding that states possessed a general police power so it was more necessary to limit the powers of a governor then the president.

ATTORNEYS GENERAL AND SUITS AGAINST THE FEDERAL GOVERNMENT

As the power of the federal government has grown, the role of state attorneys general has become more important in defense of federalism. Typically, disputes between federal and state authority are often adjudicated in the federal courts. In these cases, the state attorney general is almost always the individual who decides to sue the federal government. States are one of the few entities with the resources to stand up to the federal government.

For example, in recent years, Texas has repeatedly sued the federal government over federal policies. In 2023, the Fifth Circuit Court of Appeals held that the federal government could not require that all members of the Texas National Guard take the COVID-19 vaccine. *Abbott v. Biden*. In 2024, Texas obtained a ruling from the federal district court that the "Pregnant Workers Fairness Act" was unconstitutional as applied to Texas. *Texas v. Garland*. One of the most controversial aspects of the "Pregnant Workers Fairness Act" is that it mandated state and private employers give pregnant women time off to obtain an abortion. Although *Texas v. Garland* is only a district court case, if the Fifth Circuit affirms it, it could be a very important precedent.

Most famously, Texas has repeatedly challenged the federal government over immigration. Texas

Texas State Capitol

has asserted that President Biden's failure to comply with federal immigration law is harming Texas and if the federal government will not enforce the law then Texas will take measures of its own. In 2023, Texas passed a law making it a state crime to enter Texas from Mexico when crossing the border was also illegal under federal law. In March 2024, the Supreme Court *preliminarily* allowed the Texas law to be enforced; although, the case is not yet final and still pending in federal court.

For important federalism cases, even when the state is not directly involved, attorneys general routinely band together to file *friend of the court* (amicus curiae) briefs with the Supreme Court.

One of the most important occasions for this occurs when the Supreme Court is asked to review cases. Because the Court hears fewer than 80 appeals a year, if 30 or 40 states ask the Court to hear an appeal, it can carry a lot of weight.

Finally, state attorneys general often comment on proposed federal regulations or urge companies to change their policies. For example, in May 2023, Virginia Attorney General Jason Miyares joined eighteen other attorneys general and sent a letter to giant banking company JPMorgan Chase & Co. urging it to stop discriminating against customers because of their religious beliefs or political affiliations.

STATE LEGISLATURES

Every state but Nebraska has a **bi-cameral legislature** composed of an upper house, known as the Senate, and a lower house, known variously as the "House of Representatives," the "House of Delegates," or the "General Assembly."[3] In every state the Senate is smaller than the House. Interestingly, the size of the state does not impact the size of the legislature. For example, California, which has one of the largest populations, has a rather typical legislature: the Senate has forty members and the Assembly has eighty. On the other hand, Vermont, which has a fraction of California's population, has thirty Senators and 150 representatives, making its state legislature one of the largest!

Most states give senators four-year terms; only four use two-year terms, and a few (e.g., Texas, New Jersey) have mixed cycles. Members of the lower house serve two-year terms. Historically, state senators' districts were based on geography rather than on population, exactly like the U.S. Senate. For example, prior to the 1960s, most states had one state senator from each county, or, in states with many counties, one senator for every two counties. This benefited rural areas, and meant that a state's house and senate looked very different. Rural areas always tend to be more religious and closer to nature than urban areas. In the 1960s, the U.S. Supreme Court mandated "one-person-one-vote" and declared every state senate in the country to be unconstitutional. This was a huge shift of power away from smaller, religious communities.

Moreover, this shift to "one-man-one-vote" undermined the whole purpose of a senate. Because state senators and state representatives are elected by the same people, the house and senate almost always look exactly the same. Accordingly, many people think a bi-cameral legislature no longer serves any useful purpose. In the U.S. Congress, the House and Senate often have very different membership and it is common for one chamber to refuse to pass a bill passed by the other chamber. This rarely happens on the state level.

Structurally, nearly every state legislature resembles the federal Congress. The lower house has a speaker. In about thirty states, the lieutenant governor acts as president of the Senate and senators elect one of their own members to act as president pro temp. In the other twenty states, the senators elect their own president. Like the federal Congress, state legislatures have a number of committees. For example, in Virginia, the committees include Commerce & Labor, Courts of Justice, Education & Health, Finance, Rules, and Transportation. Often states have **joint committees** composed of senators and representatives who try and work together to improve government efficiency.

State legislatures enact laws in a manner similar to the federal process. Bills are introduced by a legislator or the governor then go to the committee in charge of the particular topic. For example, a bill to raise the pay of public school teachers would go to the Education & Health committee in Virginia.

---

[3] Nebraska has had a unicameral legislature since 1934

Colorado state capitol, Denver

The bill either works its way out of committee or dies in committee. Once out of committee, the bill is debated, amended, and eventually voted on by the first house and then by the second. Once enacted by the legislature, it goes to the governor who may sign or veto it. If vetoed, the legislature can attempt an override which usually requires a 2/3 majority in most states, although a few states only require a majority.

Unlike the U.S. Congress, most state legislatures are not in session year-round, and being a state legislator is not considered a full-time job. In fact, most state legislators receive low pay and are expected to support themselves. In New Hampshire, state legislators have an annual salary of $100 plus mileage. In New Mexico, state legislators receive no annual salary but can be reimbursed for expenses up to $59 per day when in session.

Only nine states have legislatures that are in session year-round and pay a full time salary. A handful of state legislatures only meet every other year. Most state legislatures meet for a few months and then members return home to their regular jobs. The paradigm in these states is that legislators should be ordinary people not professional politicians. This is another reason that people prefer state legislators to U.S. Congressmen: distrust of professional politicians who enrich themselves at the public's expense.

The Founders almost universally embraced the idea of the "citizen legislator." In *Federalist* 52 through 57, Hamilton and Madison repeatedly emphasized that while Senators might be more elite, members of the House of Representatives should be ordinary citizens. John Adams, George Mason, and Edmond Randolph echoed this preference. Moreover, throughout the 19th century, most U.S. representatives served a single term and the average congressman served just three years.[4] Today, professional politicians, determined to spend as long as possible in office, dominate Congress. Also, because of the enormous cost of political campaigns, Congressmen spend about half their time fundraising.

Corruption can happen at any level of government, but because state representatives are

---

[4] Congressional Research Service, "Congressional Careers: Service Tenure and Patterns of Member Service, 1789-2023."

usually not professional politicians they do not spend so much time and energy raising money from donors. It also helps that state budgets are tiny compared to the $6.5 trillion federal budget. Thirty-eight states have a total state budget under $50 billion; twenty-three have a budget under $25 billion; and nine have a budget under $10 billion. These figures include money received from the federal government, which typically amounts to about a third of the state budget.

As on the federal level, approving the state budget and new taxes is the most crucial role of the state legislature. Another significant function of the state legislature is overseeing the executive and judicial branches. In this regard, it is important to remember that the legislative branch is not only composed of elected representatives. Legislatures have permanent employees, or "staffers," who remain on the job even when the legislature is not in session. Of course, the less time that elected representatives spend doing the job the greater reliance they must place on professional staff. This is a potential drawback of the part-time "citizen legislator."

STATE COURTS AND JUDICIAL ACTIVISM

As of 2024, there are about 30,000 state judges who hear cases involving everything from disputes over small amounts of money to trials where a person might be sentenced to death. In comparison, there are about 1,770 federal judges, about half of whom are Article 3 judges appointed by the president and who serve for life. There are almost twenty times more state judges as federal judges, because state court judges hear almost ninety percent of all cases. Just as federal judges interpret federal laws, state judges interpret state and local laws.

Most states have three judicial levels: general district courts, appellate courts, and a supreme court. The **general district court**, sometimes called a **circuit** or **superior** court, is usually the state's main trial court. Every state is divided into a certain number of districts and the general court hears cases from that district. For example, Virginia is divided into thirty-two districts. Because district courts are trial courts, they are **courts of record**, which means that a record or transcript is kept of the proceedings. Trial courts hear both civil cases involving monetary controversies, usually up to $25,000, and *criminal* cases for traffic violations, misdemeanor offenses, and felonies. They are also courts of original jurisdiction.

A judge normally presides over the trial, whether civil or criminal and most cases are tried before a jury. As noted in an earlier chapter, the judge rules on the law. Most cases are decided by juries that decide on the facts; although, most states allow the parties to waive a jury trial and let the judge decide the facts. In addition to the judge, there are usually various other officials at a trial including a **clerk** who keeps the record and a **bailiff**, an official who ensures everyone behaves properly, especially any prisoners.

The next level of state courts is the **appellate court**. These courts hear appeals from the trial courts. As in the federal appellate courts, state appellate judges do not hear new facts, but issues of law that the losing side feels the trial judge incorrectly decided. For example, in Virginia, the Court of Appeals reviews decisions of the trial courts in domestic relations cases, traffic violations, criminal cases, and appeals from administrative agencies.

U.S. Supreme Court Chamber

The highest level of the state judiciary is the **state supreme court**. The state supreme court usually has between five or seven justices, although a few states have as many as nine. The governor appoints the members of the supreme court in about half the states while the people elect the members in the others. Like the U.S. Supreme Court, a state supreme court hears appeals from the appellate court and also may determine whether a state statute violates the state constitution. Of course, depending upon whether a federal law is involved, decisions from a state supreme court can be appealed to the U.S. Supreme Court.

The most important difference between state and federal judges is that state judges generally are elected by the people. In twenty-five states judges are popularly elected. In another fifteen states, judges are initially appointed but then must stand for re-election, or "retention," by the people. A few states have a combination of appointment and election. For example, in New York, all of the trial court judges are elected by the people in the local area they serve; but appellate judges are appointed by the governor with the consent of the state senate. In South Carolina and Virginia, the state legislature chooses judges and does not require the governor's approval.

Unlike federal judges, only Rhode Island grants state judges life tenure; all other states limit terms or impose a retirement age. While federal judges must be impeached to be removed from office, in most states where judges do not already need to stand for retention, they can be removed by a simple majority vote of the state legislature. This is called a **bill of address**.

These limits on state judges make them more accountable to the citizens of the states. State judges who try to impose a radical agenda on a state can be removed fairly easily. Accordingly, state court judges are much less likely to be "out of step" with the citizens and impose an agenda that the people do not support. Although state courts do issue controversial decisions, it occurs far less frequently than in the federal courts.

For example, in 2022, after the U.S. Supreme Court declared that abortion was a state issue, supporters of abortion attempted to have state courts declare abortion to be a right under the state constitutions. Almost every state court

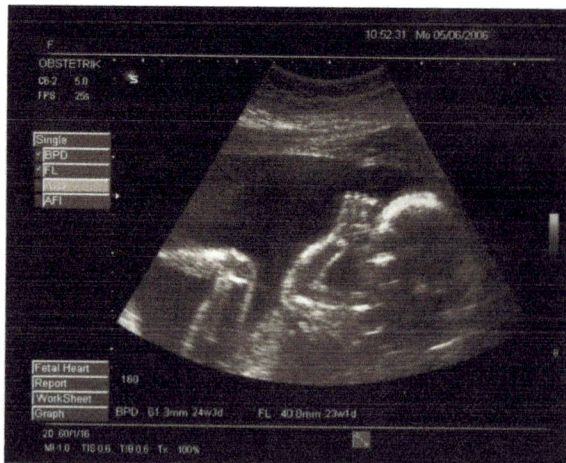

Ultrasound of a baby in the womb

rejected this approach. However, in January 2023, the Supreme Court of South Carolina, by a 3 to 2 vote, declared abortion to be a right under the South Carolina constitution. The court declared that South Carolina's *Fetal Heartbeat and Protection from Abortion Act* violated the "right to privacy." However, that did not end the story.

The term of office for the author of the majority decision expired at the end of 2022. That justice was replaced by a new justice appointed by the state legislature. In May 2023, the South Carolina legislature overwhelmingly re-adopted **The Fetal Heartbeat and Protection from Abortion Act** which governor Henry McMaster immediately signed into law. The 2021 version of the law prohibited abortion after the first eight weeks of fetal life, while the new law protects life after twelve weeks.

In August 2023, the South Carolina Supreme Court held that the twelve-week ban *was* constitutional. The majority opinion was written by Justice John Kittredge who wrote a scathing dissent in the earlier case. The Court unambiguously declared that "there is no fundamental constitutional right to abortion." This South Carolina case demonstrates the huge disparity between how the South Carolina legislature handled the state abortion decision and how Congress handled *Roe v. Wade* in 1973. Arguably, Congress could have done much more to oppose Roe at the time. Nevertheless, the structure of most state court systems makes judicial activism very difficult.

Of course, there needs to be a balance. Judicial decisions, whether at the federal or the state level, need to be grounded in the law. No one thinks judges should base their rulings on what is (currently) popular. However, when courts act outrageously and create a right to murder the most innocent and defenseless humans in society, there needs to be a mechanism for changing it.

COUNTY GOVERNMENT

As discussed in Chapter Two, shires, later called counties, have been a crucial part of self-government in the Anglo-Saxon tradition since time immemorial. The word "sheriff" is a modernization of "shire reeve." "Reeve" was a generic term meaning "officer." In addition to shire reeves, there were town reeves, port reeves, and manor reeves. The shire reeve was an important officer but was not necessarily a noble and the title was not hereditary. Reeves appears to have been commoners, although knights could be sheriffs. In many areas, the local reeve was elected, but the king or local lord could veto the popular selection. Today in England, the position of sheriff has become mostly ceremonial, but in the United States, sheriffs continue to play an important function as the chief law enforcement officer of the county.[5]

Every American state is divided into smaller regions called **counties**, except that these divisions are called "parishes" in Louisiana and "boroughs" in Alaska. Although Connecticut and Rhode Island have counties on the map, the counties no longer function as units of government. Other than Connecticut and Rhode Island, states are large enough that it makes sense to have an intermediate level of government between the town and the state government. The city where the county government is located is known as the **county seat**.

In the last few decades, counties have become somewhat controversial. Some people have advocated abolishing counties. They argue that it would be more efficient for county functions to be performed by the state. For example, county sheriffs would cease to

---

[5] Fans of Robin Hood may appreciate that there is still a High Sheriff of Nottinghamshire, an office that has existed for a thousand years, but is now entirely ceremonial.

exist and state police would handle law enforcement outside of cities and towns. On the other hand, supporters of counties want to see power taken from state government and given to counties. These people argue that state government has become too distant and bureaucratic. They claim that state police are far less responsive to citizens than locally-elected sheriffs. In large states like California or Texas it especially makes sense to have an intermediate level of government. In fact, in large western states, county government tends to play a much larger role than it does in eastern states. This intermediate level of government accords with the principle of subsidiarity. There may be issues beyond the ability of a town to resolve by itself, but these can be addressed at something below the state level.

In western states, some counties are very large. America's largest county is San Bernardino County, California. San Bernardino County is 20,052 square miles—slightly larger than Vermont and New Hampshire combined. However, counties come in all sizes. Counties tend to be small in the eastern United States and larger in the west.

County officials perform two different functions. First, counties enact and enforce their own policies. County laws are usually called county **ordinances** to distinguish them from state laws. In addition to enacting and enforcing county policies, many county officials are responsible for enforcing various state laws. Even though many laws are enacted at the state level, the local community can choose who will enforce these laws. Because these county officials are elected by the community and responsible to their local constituents, these officials are able to exercise more discretion without fear the governor or attorney general might fire them.

Most counties in the United States have a single executive officer. This official is usually called the "county executive," but in some states this officer is known as the "mayor" of the county. However, in many states there is not a single executive officer, instead a county commission or county board of supervisors exercises the executive powers. In places where there is a county commission, the commission acts as both the legislative and executive authority. In places where there is a county executive, the county council exercises legislative power. All of these positions are elected. About ten percent of the counties in the United

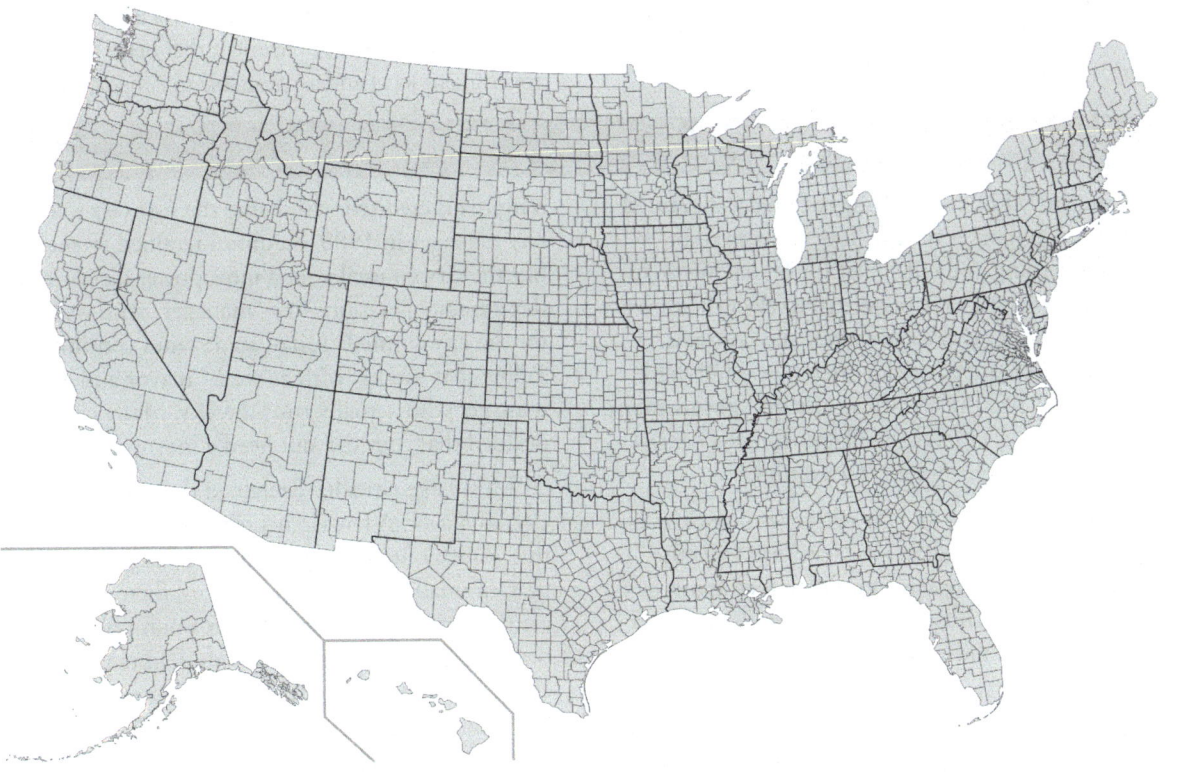

A map showing the borders of the counties across the United States

States have a "county manager," who is not elected but appointed by the county council. Some people believe that having an unelected professional in charge of the county or city results in more efficient administration.

Counties perform a wide variety of tasks including building roads, performing health inspections, enforcing zoning regulations, operating courthouses and jails, and many others. The main advantage of the county performing these tasks, rather than the state, is that local citizens have a greater say in county government than in state government. Thus, hopefully, county government will be more responsive to its citizens. For example, California's population is about forty million, so an individual citizen has difficulty influencing decisions on the state level. However, many rural California counties have very small populations. Alpine County, California, has a population of only 1,100 people. Six other California counties have populations less than 20,000 citizens.

Almost every county in the country has a popularly elected **Sheriff**. The Sheriff is the primary official who enforces state criminal law in the county. Sheriffs have a bit of discretion in the enforcement of criminal law, so they can sometimes moderate the application of state criminal law when strict enforcement might be unjust.

Forty-six states have locally-elected **county prosecutors** who are responsible for prosecuting state criminal offenses, but are accountable to local voters. This forms a kind "check and balance." While criminal laws are mostly made on the state level, locally-elected prosecutors are tasked with deciding who will be prosecuted.

Just over half of the counties in the United States have an elected **coroner**. The coroner investigates any time a person dies to ensure that the death did not result from illegal activity. In many states, the coroner is someone who has been appointed rather than elected. This person is usually called a **medical examiner**.

There are a variety of other elected county officials that vary from state to state. In many states the county **tax assessor** is elected. The tax assessor estimates the value of real estate for tax purposes. Another position that is often elected is the **county clerk**. The county clerk's office performs a variety of functions, including issuing licenses. One county clerk in Kentucky, Kim Davis, made national news when she refused to issue "same sex" marriage licenses. A federal judge sentenced her to jail for five days for "contempt." A number of other county clerks resigned rather than issue these licenses.

County governments provide a crucial link in the federal system of government that helps keep government local and accountable to America's citizens.

MUNICIPAL GOVERNMENT

In the Middle Ages, Kings of England granted charters to market towns allowing them to be self-governing and outside of the feudal hierarchy. Medieval towns were permitted to elect their own mayors, along with town reeves, and coroners. A council of elders, or aldermen, governed these towns. So, like the county, **municipal government**, that is, towns, cities, and villages, forms a central part of the Anglo-American tradition.

There are about 20,000 self-governing cities and towns in the United States. New York City, the nation's largest city, has a population of about 8 million people and a yearly budget of $100 billion — larger than most states and countries.

About half the cities in the United States have a chief executive called a **mayor**. The other half are led by a **city manager** appointed by the city council. The city manager idea is fairly recent. Staunton, Virginia is credited with being the first city to hire a city manager in 1908. Staunton retained its mayor, but the city council vested most power for the city's day-to-day operations in a "manager" who worked for the city council. Today, some cities continue to follow that model, with a "weak" mayor and a city manager who actually runs the city. Many cities decided that they did not need a mayor at all.

Most large cities have retained the traditional elected mayor. A few factors seem to account for this. First, politics is more divisive in larger cities than in small towns. In small towns, there often are not serious policy disputes, so a non-political manager is more acceptable. Second, in many large cities, the elected mayor comes from one party that has a monopoly on power and that party does not want to relinquish its power. For example, there has not been a Republican mayor of Chicago since

1931, nor of Boston since 1930. Atlanta has not had a Republican mayor since 1879. New Orleans has never elected a Republican mayor. Baltimore, Denver, Detroit, Louisville, Milwaukee, Minneapolis/St. Paul, Philadelphia, Pittsburgh, Seattle, and St. Louis have not had a Republican mayor in over 50 years. In fact, the "Democratic machine" dominates most of America's one hundred most populous cities. This presents one of the most serious criticisms of city government. In theory, local government should be most responsive to voters; unfortunately, in big cities, voters too often have no *meaningful* choice.

A mayor's powers differ considerably from place to place. In some cities, the mayor is like the president with the power to veto city ordinances as well as hire and fire city employees. In New York City, Chicago, and Los Angeles the mayor has veto power and a great deal of control.

A city council makes local laws. The size of the city council varies. Generally, large cities have large city councils. New York City elects fifty-one city councilmen from fifty-one local districts. However, Los Angeles has just fifteen city councilmen each elected by a local district. About 20% of American cities also have some "at large" districts where city councilmen are elected by the entire city, in addition to members from the local district. Philadelphia and Washington, D.C. use this mixed system.

Some small cities elect all city councilmen from "at large" districts. Some people argue that having "at large" districts minimizes competition between neighborhoods. However, "at large" elections also dilute the importance of individual voters and may make councilmen less responsive to constituents.

Some cities have a few other local elected officials. Sometimes the chief financial officer or tax assessor is elected. In some places, the zoning commission is elected. **Zoning** is the power to restrict how certain land will be used or what sort of building can be constructed upon it. For example, in an area zoned "agricultural" a person cannot build a factory, which is an "industrial" structure. In places where local government has few powers, zoning is one of its most important tasks.

STATE AND LOCAL TAXES

Like the federal government, states, cities, and towns need to raise money to finance their operations. Like the federal government, they primarily raise money through taxes. States have two main taxes: income tax and sales tax. A handful of states still charge inheritance tax. Municipal governments rely primarily on property taxes.

INCOME TAX

With a few exceptions like Alaska, Florida, Texas, and Nevada, forty-one states have a state **income tax**. Federal and state income tax is the main source of government revenue and accounts for about 45% of all government revenue. Like the federal income tax, the rates are **progressive**, which means that people who make more money pay more income tax and are taxed at a higher rate. Many people feel that such a tax is fundamentally unfair. Someone who makes $1,000,000 might pay as much as 50% in state and federal income tax compared to someone who makes $100,000 but pays 30% income tax.

However, the person paying $500,000 usually does not receive better police and fire department service than the person paying $30,000.

A progressive tax aims to redistribute wealth. Proponents argue it helps the poor. Opponents argue the money goes to wasteful government spending. They argue the money belongs to the taxpayer not the government. Progressive taxes also destroy initiative and creativity. People are disincentivized to become entrepreneurs and risk their savings when they know that if they are successful the government will confiscate their wealth. Since its inception, the Church has always taught that private charities and voluntary associations are best suited to aiding the poor.[6] This is why the Catholic Church has always been one of the largest private charitable organizations in the world.

There is another form of income taxation known as a **regressive tax** which *uniformly*, or equally, taxes a person or family regardless of their income. Regressive taxes place an undue burden on

---

[6] See for example 1 John 3:17-18: If someone who has worldly means sees a brother in need and refuses him compassion, how can the love of God remain in him? Children, let us love not in word or speech but in deed and truth.

poorer people as these taxes take a larger percentage of a person's income. For example, assume that everyone is required to pay $5,000 in income tax. Someone making $50,000 pays 10% of their income as tax; however, someone earning $500,000 pays only 1% of their income as tax although they both pay the same amount. Thus, *with a regressive tax, the tax burden decreases as income rises while with a progressive tax, the tax burden increases as income rises.*

Because both of these forms of taxation are unfair to someone, a third form of taxation known as a **flat tax** has been proposed. A flat tax is a system in which *everyone pays the same tax rate regardless of their income.* For example, assume everyone pays a 10% tax on their income. In the above example, the person making $50,000 pays $5,000 while the person making $500,000 pays $50,000. In a sense, everyone is treated equally because they pay the same rate, although not the same amount. Proponents of a flat tax argue that, besides the fairness issue, it creates a stronger economy and is easier for everyone to understand. People can literally fill out their tax returns on a postcard because all they need to list is their income and their taxes. Currently, the U.S. Tax Code with all its accompanying regulations and official IRS tax guidelines comprises 75,000 pages! Opponents of the flat tax argue that it does not redistribute wealth, a goal of the current code. As of 2023, about thirteen states have a flat income tax.

SALES TAX

For states, **sales tax** is the next most important source of revenue. Forty-five states charge a general sales tax which represents between one-third and one-half of all the income the state generates. Sales taxes are collected when a person purchases a commodity, such as a television, computer, and in some cases even food. Generally, certain items, like medicine and staple foods, are not taxed. On the other hand, a necessity like gasoline is heavily taxed. The government also imposes what used to be called "sin taxes" on certain commodities the government seeks to discourage such as alcohol and tobacco products. Today, these higher taxes also include marijuana. Technically, all these items are considered **selective sales taxes** as they are taxed at a higher rate than the general sales tax rate. Whether general or selective, retailers collect the tax at the time of sale and periodically send the money into the state.

Because everyone pays the same amount of tax for an item, sales taxes are *regressive*. Although poor people can do without certain luxury items, nearly every American owns a car which requires gasoline. The gas tax is one of the most punishing taxes the government inflicts on American consumers. While wealthy Americans can bear the burden of high gas prices, it is very unfair to the poor and middle class.

INHERITANCE TAX

Although *inheritance tax*, sometimes called the "death tax," which is a tax paid on what a person inherits, is a significant source of federal revenue, it plays a smaller part in state revenue. As of 2023, only seventeen states and the District of Columbia impose some form of inheritance tax. Most states have begun to abolish the inheritance tax. First, many people argue that it is fundamentally unfair to *re-tax* money that has already been taxed. Remember that the government has already taxed all the money a person leaves in an inheritance. They are now double taxing. Many family fortunes have been nearly obliterated by this incessant government generational taxation. Second, because of this never-ending taxation, wealthy individuals have moved out of these states. The reasons are clear: the taxes disincentivize investment thereby hurting the general economy. States have begun to realize this and are phasing out inheritance taxes. For example, Iowa will abolish its tax in 2025.

PROPERTY TAX

Today, *property taxes* are the major source of revenue for local governments, comprising just over 70% of all revenue collected, and all states impose property taxes – although at different rates. On the other hand, while these taxes were once the primary source of state income, they now comprise less than 2% of state revenue. Property taxes are used to support nearly all aspects of local government including funding public schools, police and fire departments, as well as road construction and repairs.

Property falls into two categories: real and personal. **Real property** is land, buildings, and any improvements made to the land and buildings. Thus, a home or a factory and the land they sit upon are real property. **Personal property** are the *possessions* a person owns like a car, furniture, or computers. Personal property is usually divided into **tangible** property, which are things a person can easily see and hold like a car or a computer, and **intangible** property which is not so easy to see or hold like a bank account. Property tax on real property is usually called "real estate tax" or "property tax," while tax on personal property is called "personal property" tax.

Property taxes are generally a fair way to tax people as the rates are a flat amount based on the value of the property. Thus, a more expensive home is taxed at the same rate as a less expensive home, but the owner of a luxury home pays more in taxes. In every locality, a local tax assessor does an assessment to determine the value of the property, whether a home or a commercial property. Based on the assessed value, the owner pays a tax. Whether a home is assessed at $500,000 or $5,000,000 the homeowners pay the same rate.

Some people have argued that property taxes are regressive and place an undue burden on the poor. They suggest that as property taxes have increased, some form of progressive tax system should be implemented in which more expensive homes are taxed at a higher rate. One should note that this often happens organically as certain counties charge higher tax rates. For example, Fairfax county, Virginia, one of the nation's wealthiest counties which is located in suburban Washington D.C. and where the average home costs $550,000, charges an effective tax rate of 1.03%. Fauquier, a rural county thirty miles west of Fairfax, where homes average $384,000, charges .84% property taxes. Fairfax is noted for possessing one of the finest public school systems in the nation. That, along with its proximity to the nation's capital, make it a desirable location. In general, wealthy people tend to live in Fairfax to a greater extent than in Fauquier.

Historically, assessors value homes at less than their fair market value. Often, assessments are as much as 60% below the market price. Also, owners can challenge assessments they believe are too high and have their property re-assessed.

OTHER SOURCES OF REVENUE

In addition to these "major" taxes, localities raise revenue through innumerable "minor" taxes. These include various licenses such as business licenses and marriage licenses. Nearly every business from doctors to hairdressers is required to have a license to operate. States also raise a great deal of money from drivers licenses and license plates.

Cities and towns also raise money through "non-tax" revenue such as charging for trash removal. Other cities operate local transportation systems such as bus lines. One of the greatest, and most controversial, sources of income in the past decades is the state operation of multi-million-dollar lotteries. Since Nevada and New Jersey have seen increased revenues from casinos and gambling, numerous other states have also legalized gambling whether in casinos, on racetracks, or a combination of both.

SCHOOL BOARDS, SCHOOL DISTRICTS, AND LOCAL CONTROL

Another part of local government is the school district, which is usually run by a board of elected officials. Unlike city and county government, **school boards** are a relatively recent development. In the 19th century, when public schools became more widespread, school districts were to be composed of elected officials who focused solely on education and were accountable to parents.[7]

The Catholic Church has always taught that parents are the primary and natural educators of their children. Parents possess a natural impulse to care for their children and know their children far better than anyone else. Parents have a personal incentive to see their children succeed. Even bad parents want to see their children succeed, if only to help themselves. This desire of parents, who have given their children life, who cherish and know them more deeply and intensely than anyone else could, to see their children receive a good education which will aid them in their adult life, has long been recognized in the United States and in English Common Law. William Blackstone's 1755 "Commentaries on the Laws of England" notes that under English law, fathers had almost total authority to direct the education of their children.[8]

In 1817, Thomas Jefferson supported a plan to fund elementary schools. However, he adamantly opposed requiring parents to send their children to school. Jefferson wrote:

It is better to tolerate the rare instance of a parent refusing to let his child be educated, than to shock the common feelings and ideas by the forcible transportation and education of the infant against the will of the father.

Early Americans almost universally accepted Jefferson's view. They found it unthinkable that the state would interfere with parents' educational decisions for their children. This idea was closely connected to freedom of religion. In the 19th century, Americans understood that education was intimately related to the formation of character and teaching religious values.

Government support for schools was common in the 18th century, especially in New England. Schools were rarely tuition free, but education was subsidized. In New England, schools were supported by the town government, often in association with the established church which received support from the government.

In the 1790s, the New York legislature authorized the creation of school districts run by an elected school board with authority to raise money by taxation. This was a radically new idea at the time. Schools would be independent of state, county, or town government, and be directly accountable to local voters.

At the same time that New York was experimenting with this new government-run educational system, the first Catholic school in New York City was opened in 1800. Four years earlier, St. Peter's Church opened in Manhattan. Irish and German immigrants founded St. Peter's School which had about one hundred students when it began offering classes. St. Peter's School offered free Catholic education to all children. In March 1805, Elizabeth Ann Seton was received into the Catholic

St. Peter's, Barclay Street, 1785

---

[7] Although called "public schools" today, in the 19th century government-run schools were usually called "common schools."
[8] One unfortunate exception is that English Penal Laws forbad teaching the Catholic faith to children in Britain and Ireland.

Church at St. Peter's. St. Elizabeth Ann Seton later founded the Sisters of Charity and established more free schools to educate Catholic children.

This dual system of "public schools" funded by taxes and a parallel system of Catholic schools began a controversy that continues to this day. Since the mid-nineteenth century, Catholics have argued that Catholic families who pay for their own education should not be forced to pay school taxes as well. It is an unjust form of "double taxation."

Historically, many states placed restrictions on who could vote for school board members. For example, in New York, only citizens who paid school taxes or had children enrolled in the public school could vote in school district elections. However, in 1969, the Supreme Court held that it violated equal protection for states to limit the vote in such a way. *Kramer v. Union Free School District* (1969). Today, all states permit all eligible voters to vote for the school board. In some ways, this reduces the power of parents with children in the schools by potentially diluting their ability to impact how the school system is run. Of course, it is also true that what the public schools teach is important to all citizens.

Eventually, every state adopted the New York style school district; although, in some places school boards do not have taxing authority. In a few states, school boards are no longer elected but appointed. Today, local school boards are much less independent than they once were, as they are required to follow a host of federal and state directives.

In the first decade of the 1800s, Massachusetts towns began dividing into multiple school districts. In 1807, the small town of Dover, with a population of about 500, was divided into three separate school districts. Larger cities like Boston were divided into dozens of school districts. Previously, the town had directed education in Massachusetts, but evidently local parents wanted small districts with more control. This design was copied across the country as cities were typically divided into many different school districts.

It must be noted that in almost every state, public schools were **racially segregated**, that is, Black students were required to attend their own schools. Remarkably, in the 1840s and 1850s there

St. Elizabeth Ann Seton

were cases in which Blacks students sued the local board arguing that such discrimination violated the state constitution.[9] Racial segregation plagued public schools for more than a century. Until the mid-20th century, every state and federal court that addressed the issue ruled that local school boards *could* segregate schools.

In the early 19th century, most rural schools were independent. Of course, home schooling was very common, but children who attended school almost always walked. Because students walked to school, hundreds of thousands of small schools sprung up within "walking distance" of the students they served. The vast majority of schools were "one-room schoolhouses" with a small number of students and a single teacher. Circumstances varied across the country, but

---

[9] *Roberts v. Boston*, (Mass. 1849); *Jacobs v. School Dir. of Frederick Township, Pa* (Pa. 1859).

typically these one-room schoolhouses received little or no government support, but were subject to little or no government *control*. In most western states, students attended private "subscription schools," so-called because parents typically paid $1 a month per child, like a subscription to a monthly magazine.

The one-room schoolhouse came under criticism in the late 19th century. However, it gave parents maximum control to oversee their children's education. It was also highly flexible. Students often attended school part-time and were able to spend part of each day working on the family farm or in the family shop.

In the 1870s and 1880s, public schools and school districts spread to the western states. Most historians agree that rural parents preferred subscription schools to public schools. One history of this period says "rural dwellers often intensely resisted the common (public) school concept" and only the promise of "local control" of schools convinced parents to drop their opposition.[10]

School boards in the 19th century tended to be very large. In many places, the school board had more than twenty members and were mostly composed of ordinary parents. By this time school boards also began hiring **superintendents**, on both the state and district level.

On the state level, the state superintendent serves as the chief officer for the State Department of Education, the agency which oversees the management of the state's public school system. Thirty-eight states have appointed superintendents, with the governor appointing half and the state Board of Education the other half. Twelve states have a popularly elected superintendent.

District superintendents manage the public schools in their districts. The various school principals in the district report to the district superintendent. Technically, the local school board hires district superintendents and can fire them as well. However, superintendents have grown extremely powerful in the past few decades.

Originally, state and district superintendents dealt primarily with educational issues and were not "professional" educators. For example, William Henry Ruffner, who is credited with creating Virginia's public school system after the Civil War, was a Presbyterian minister and farmer. However, by the early 20th century, a new professional class of superintendents began to emerge. Colleges began offering classes on managing schools. Less emphasis was placed on educational content and more on financial management.

One unusual aspect of late 19th century school districts involved women's suffrage. Many states allowed women to vote in school board elections and be elected to school boards at a time when women were otherwise ineligible to vote in elections. It is not entirely clear why women were allowed to vote in school board elections, but it seems people thought mothers should be involved in their children's education.

By the end of the 19th century, there were over 200,000 school districts in the United States. It seems indisputable that such a huge number existed because parents wanted to monitor their children's education as closely as possible.

Another, less admirable, reason for the proliferation of school districts was **racial gerrymandering**. Racial segregation was almost universal in the late 19th century, but New Jersey and Ohio had laws prohibiting local schools from discriminating on the basis of race. In those states, and others as well, school districts were "gerrymandered" around Black neighborhoods. In effect, small groups of Black families had their own school district. Sadly, there were not only Black school districts. Many ethnic minorities including Asians, Native Americans, Mexicans, and certain European ethnicities, especially Irish, Italians, and Germans, had their own schools. Although not precisely accurate, school segregation was not so much about Black versus White, but White-Anglo-Saxon-Protestant versus everyone else. Unfortunately, these Black and ethnic neighborhoods were often poor and had few resources for the school.

In the 19th and early 20th century, school districts were mostly self-supporting, and received little support from the state. This led to arguments about "inequality," as some school districts were much poorer than others. However, until

---

[10] Paul and Briana Theobald, "Education in a Rural Context" in The Routledge History of Rural America, Pamela Riney-Kehrberg, ed., p. 167-8.

James Blaine

the late 20th century, most people accepted these inequalities as inevitable in a system that maximized local control.

Then and now, racial gerrymandering was a controversial issue. Most Americans think the government should be *colorblind*, so there should be no districts based on race. However, a few Black leaders supported Blacks having their own schools rather than being integrated into "white" education. On the other hand, imagine if a state gerrymandered Catholics into a Catholic school district where parents could teach the Catholic faith in "government" schools. Most Catholics would welcome this if they really could control the curriculum without government interference. Many of these racially gerrymandered school districts continued into the 1960s, but no longer exist.

The example of the Catholic school district is, unfortunately, hypothetical. In fact, in the late 19th century, one exception to local control was that most states explicitly forbad aid to Catholic schools. Most states adopted "Blaine Amendments." In 1875, **Congressman James Blaine** proposed an amendment to the U.S. Constitution that would have prohibited any state aid to religious schools. This federal amendment was never ratified; however, all but ten states adopted similar provisions. Unfortunately, in the 1880s, many public school districts became increasingly anti-Catholic.

To oppose this growing anti-Catholicism in public schools, in 1884, at the Third Plenary Council of Baltimore, America's Catholic bishops decreed that every parish church should have a parish, or *parochial*, school. The Council of Baltimore further decreed that Catholic parents have a profound moral obligation to send their children to a Catholic school or to educate them in the Faith at home.

The Blaine Amendments formed part of a larger anti-Catholic trend. In the second half of the 19th century, immigration from non-British parts of Europe increased. The period from 1850 to 1920 is often called the Age of Mass Migration as about twenty million people immigrated to the United States. People who feared this would change America for the worse opposed this mass migration. This opposition was partly racial, but partly, if not largely, anti-Catholic. Immigrants from Ireland, southern Germany, Poland, and Italy were Catholic.

Critics of immigration suggested using public education as means of "Americanizing" these immigrants and forcing immigrant children to adopt the dominant Anglo-Saxon Protestant culture. One example of this involved Edward Bellamy who composed the Pledge of Allegiance in 1892. Bellamy advocated forcing all school children to pledge allegiance to the American flag to secure their loyalty, even if parents objected. Bellamy also promoted national school standards. Needless to say, local control proved a major hindrance to using the public school systems to create a common set of values. Even today, this remains highly controversial, as Catholics and Christian resist these "common values," insofar as they are secular and anti-Christian; thus, an attack upon the Faith.

To Americanize immigrants, most states mandated that all students say the Pledge of Allegiance. Some states even attempted to ban private education and require that all children attend government schools. In *Pierce v. Society of the Sisters of the Holy Names of Jesus and Mary* (1925), the Supreme Court held that an

Oregon law banning all private education was unconstitutional. The Supreme Court declared:

> [We] think it entirely plain that the (Oregon) Act … unreasonably interferes with the liberty of parents and guardians to direct the upbringing and education of children under their control. … The child is not the mere creature of the state; those who nurture him and direct his destiny have the right, coupled with the high duty, to recognize and prepare him for additional obligations.

The Court correctly expressed a principle of natural justice: parental control of education was so firmly rooted in the Anglo-American tradition that it was implicit in the Constitution.

In 1900, there were approximately 210,000 school districts in the United States. Since then, the number has steadily declined. Small schools and small school districts were consolidated into larger schools and larger districts. Despite serving many more students, the size of school boards was reduced. Today, the average school board has just six members, and they are far more likely to be self-described "professionals" rather than average parents. Most modern school boards consider their most important function to be hiring the district superintendent.

One of the most significant innovations in public education was the introduction of the school bus in the 1920s. Children no longer had to walk to school, so they began to be transported miles away, especially in rural areas. Many small rural schools were consolidated into big regional schools. Proponents promised education would be better and less expensive. State educational bureaucracies also promised state funding in exchange for consolidation and state control. Public education has certainly not become less expensive. In 2024, more than half of all public school employees are non-teachers. Many people today doubt that schools are better than in the 19th century.

SCHOOL DESEGREGATION AND COURT-ORDERED BUSSING

One of the most painful and controversial moments in American history involved the controversy over school desegregation. The Fourteenth Amendment guaranteed that no state could deny any person equal protection of the law. Between the adoption of the 14th Amendment in 1868 and 1950, the Supreme Court repeatedly held that *segregation was not a denial of equal protection*—most famously in *Plessy v. Ferguson* (1896). *Plessy* held that a state could require train companies to operate segregated train cars for Black passengers as long as accommodations were "equal" to the accommodations given to other (White) passengers. Over the following decades, minorities often claimed these separate accommodations were inferior, not equal. In the dozens of cases that state and federal courts heard involving the issue of school segregation, they all held that segregated schools did not violate "equal protection."

By 1954, it was "settled law" that "separate but equal" was permissible. Black schools invariably had fewer resources than other schools. This was greatly complicated by the wide diversity of school districts. In 1950, there were 83,642 school districts in the United States, about 40% of the number that existed in 1900, but still a large number. Many people argued that disparities between districts were inevitable. Others pointed out that states had become more involved in education, including funding local schools, so the disparity was *intentional* not *accidental*.

In 1954, in the landmark case of *Brown v. Board of Education of Topeka, Kansas*, the U.S. Supreme Court shocked everyone by reversing fifty-eight years of settled law, and announcing that all state-sponsored racial discrimination was a violation of equal protection. The Court might have decided that segregated schools were not equal in material terms. However, the court declared that even *assuming* Black schools were the equivalent to white schools by every tangible measure, nevertheless:

> [T]he policy of separating the races is usually interpreted as denoting the inferiority of the negro group. A sense of inferiority affects the motivation of a child to learn. … Separate educational facilities are inherently unequal.

Later cases would propose a more definitive idea: government should be colorblind and dividing people based on their race is presumptively unconstitutional. While this is a much more compelling argument, it was not set forth in *Brown*.

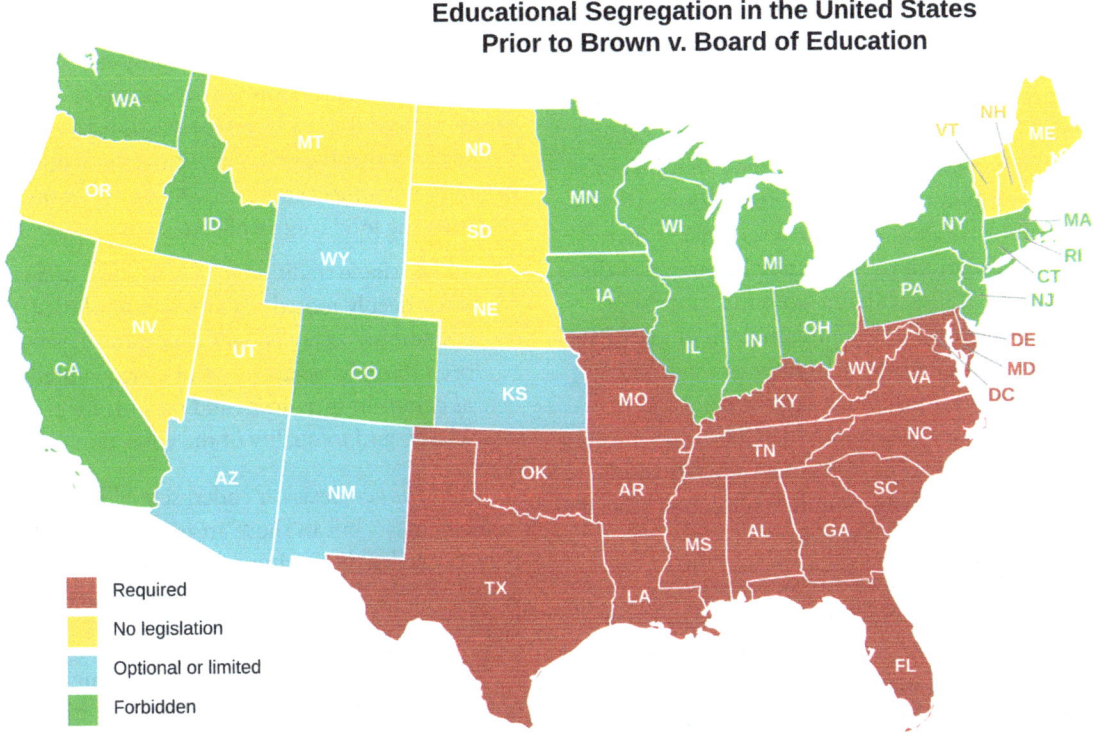

Brown assumed that "[a] sense of inferiority affects the motivation of a child to learn." Many Black leaders found it insulting that nine White justices said Black children had "a sense of inferiority" to Whites. In 1995, Justice Thomas, who is Black, criticized *Brown* for this reason, explaining:

> [T]he [district] court has read our cases to support the theory that black students suffer an unspecified psychological harm from segregation that retards their mental and educational development. This approach not only relies upon questionable social science research rather than constitutional principle, but it also rests on an assumption of black inferiority. …
> [I]f separation itself is a harm, and if integration therefore is the only way that blacks can receive a proper education, then there must be something inferior about blacks.
>
> …
>
> Psychological injury or benefit is irrelevant to the question whether state actors have engaged in intentional discrimination — the critical inquiry for ascertaining violations of the Equal Protection Clause. … Regardless of the relative quality of the schools, segregation violated the Constitution because the State classified students based on their race.

MISSOURI V. JENKINS (1995) (JUSTICE THOMAS CONCURRING).

If a policy is immoral, it should be halted no matter how long it has been occurring. A good example is the so-called right to abortion announced in *Roe v. Wade*. In 1971, Pope Paul VI expressed the Catholic position on racial discrimination when he wrote, "*Men rightly consider unjustifiable and reject as inadmissible the tendency to maintain or introduce legislation or behavior systematically inspired by racialist prejudice.*" Octogesima Adveniens, #16. Nevertheless, one reason for following precedents is that people make long-term decisions for their families based on precedents that are settled law. Families often will buy a house because it is located in a quality school district or near a quality school. This is why the next step the federal courts took was so unpopular. Federal courts did not simply order local schools to stop discriminating, which had broad support; federal courts ordered school districts to take active measures to eliminate even the vestiges of discrimination, or eliminate racial imbalances that had **not** been the result of deliberate discrimination.

In the 1960s, federal courts ordered schools across the country to "integrate" by bussing children from all over an area to try to achieve racial balance in individual schools. In many large cities, Blacks tended to live in the inner city while Whites lived in the suburbs. Thus, federal courts ordered that Black children from the inner city be bussed to the suburbs and White children from the suburbs be bussed to the inner city. Children from kindergarten to high school often spent an hour or more each way on the bus. Most of the large urban areas in the United States had court-ordered bussing in the 1960s and 1970s. Even cities like Cleveland and Columbus had bussing, although Ohio had officially *prohibited* racial discrimination.

Forced bussing proved hugely unpopular. Polls consistently found that the vast majority of Americans *from every ethnic group* opposed forced bussing. It proved so unpopular that in 1974 Congress passed a law which forbad any federal funds to be used to pay for court-ordered bussing. One of the many urban areas that had court-ordered bussing was Wilmington, Delaware. Delaware Senator Joseph Biden repeatedly called for an end to bussing and backed legislation to limit federal court jurisdiction over the issue.

Finally, in 1974, the Supreme Court backed off and held that lower federal courts could not order bussing to achieve racial balance unless the district had previously practiced deliberate and overt discrimination. *Milliken v. Bradley* (1974). In *Milliken*, the federal district court ordered eighty-five school districts in Detroit to consolidate, and ordered students bussed around the city to achieve racial balance. The Court noted that federal courts across the country had begun to micromanage public schools, but at the cost of destroying local control of education:

> No single tradition in public education is more deeply rooted than local control over the operation of schools; local autonomy has long been thought essential both to the maintenance of community concern and support for public schools and to quality of the educational process.

The *Milliken* decision ended school bussing in many areas, but in those areas where there had been overt discrimination court-ordered bussing continued for decades. Court-ordered bussing in Boston only ended in 2013.

In 1964, Reverend Martin Luther King, Jr, in one of the greatest speeches in American history, proclaimed:

> *I have a dream that my four little children will one day live in a nation where they will not be judged by the color of their skin but by the content of their character.*

School bussing seemed to violate Dr. King's noble goal of a colorblind society. Millions of children were forced to ride a bus for hours each day based on the color of their skin. Many families had sacrificed to buy a home in a quality school district where they could have their children walk to school in a safe neighborhood. Moreover, property values were often tied to the school district because people would pay a premium to live in those school districts, e.g. Fairfax, Virginia. At one stroke, forced bussing hit many families with a "triple whammy." First, their children were forcibly removed from a local quality school and bussed across town where they received an inferior education. Second, the value of their home, which usually constituted the family's life savings, dropped. Third, parents who complained were often branded as racists.

In some areas of the country, federal courts took almost total control of schools. As Justice Thomas noted in his important discussion in *Jenkins*:

> In this case, not only did the District Court exercise the legislative power to tax,

Integrated bussing in Charlotte, North Carolina

it also engaged in budgeting, staffing, and educational decisions, in judgments about the location and esthetic quality of the schools, and in administrative oversight and monitoring. ... When district courts seize complete control over the schools, they strip state and local governments of one of their most important governmental responsibilities, and thus deny their existence as independent governmental entities.

The desire to create *multi-racial* districts strengthened the trend towards consolidating school districts. For example, in 1976, the U.S. District Court for Delaware ordered that eleven school districts in Wilmington consolidate into a single district governed by the New Castle County Board of Education. By 1980, the number of school boards in the United States had declined to 18,000. As of 2022, there were 12,546 school districts in the United States—a decline of about 90% since the historic high.

Another aspect of local control was the reliance on local taxes. Until the 20th century, local school districts relied almost entirely on local school taxes with an occasional state grant. In the last half of the 20th century, the desire to eliminate inequalities between school districts led to centralization of school funding. As of 2022, school funding in the United States was 13.6% federal, 43.7% state, and 42.7% from local sources. With state and federal funding come conditions about how the money can be used.

To add insult to injury, during the 1970s and 1980s, federal judges sometimes raised taxes to pay for court-ordered changes in schools. In 1990, the Supreme Court held that federal district court judges *could order* local taxes to be raised. As Justice Thomas pointed out in the *Jenkins* case, this was a remarkable departure from 800 years of Anglo-American tradition that said the people or their representatives had to approve new taxes. In the 17th century, when Charles I tried to raise taxes without the consent of parliament, he was overthrown.

In the late 19th and early 20th centuries, the school board was the most local and most democratic form of government in the United States. Local school boards were highly accountable to parents who tended to form the bulk of the school board anyway.

As of 2024, school boards often take an adversarial position towards parents. Parents who attend school board meetings to complain about anti-Christian ideology are often threatened with arrest. In October 2021, Attorney General Merrick Garland issued an infamous memo proclaiming the need to use federal law enforcement to protect school board meetings from "threats" and "intimidation" by concerned parents. Unfortunately, today, most school board members are more concerned with pleasing state and federal education bureaucrats than in serving the people who elect them. Historically, school boards had broad power to determine school budgets and school curriculum, but today that local control has been largely sacrificed to state and federal bureaucrats.

SCHOOL CHOICE AND CHARTER SCHOOLS

Since about 1990, there has been a growing movement of people seeking alternatives to traditional school districts, that is, the system where everyone living in the geographic district went to that district's schools.[11] As of 2024, about thirty states offer some form of **school choice**. Plans vary considerably from state to state. Some states offer **vouchers** to pay for education while other states offer **tax credits** for money paid for tuition. Some states only permit assistance to *traditional* schools, but some states aid with home schooling as well.

Most early school choice plans refused to pay for Catholic schools due to the state Blaine Amendments. In 2020, this changed. In *Espinoza v. Montana Department of Revenue* (2020) the Court held that states could not discriminate against churches by allowing tax credits for secular education but denying tax credits for religious schools. Two years later, in *Carson v. Makin*, the Court held that states could not give tuition assistance to secular private schools but deny such assistance to parents who send children to religious schools. These new policies addressed the criticism Catholics had for two centuries: Catholics are doubly taxed by paying both school taxes and private tuition for their children. However, many people are concerned that if Catholic schools accept government aid, it may result in unacceptable state control over Catholic schools. As the old saying goes, "he who pays the piper calls the tune."

---

[11] In 1991, Minnesota became the first state to legalize charter schools.

Another form of school choice is known as **open enrollment**. In some states, parents can enroll their children in any public school, sometimes even schools outside of their district. Open enrollment is often used in conjunction with **charter schools** or **magnet schools**. Charter schools are independent of the school district so often have greater flexibility and usually higher academic standards. Magnet schools take the charter school a step farther with high academic standards and usually a specific educational focus, such as science or classical languages.

These public and private options allow parents greater flexibility to educate their children than even the old subscription schools. Although local communities have lost much of the control over education they once had, some of these new trends have re-empowered parents to direct the education of their children.

POPULISM, INITIATIVE, AND HOME RULE

Twenty-four states have a process known as a **ballot initiative**, by which citizens can enact laws by popular vote. If citizens collect a certain number of signatures on a petition, then all the citizens of the state vote on the measure. Many cities also have ballot initiatives that operate the same way.

About twenty states follow the principle of **home rule**. Home rule is similar to the Tenth Amendment but on the state level. In home rule jurisdictions the state constitution vests primary authority in local governments.

The rise of the ballot initiative and home rule were largely a result of the populist movement of the early 20th century. **Populism** is a theory of government that advocates giving power to ordinary people while taking power away from political elites or "the establishment." Populism has been an important strand of American politics for more than a century and remains so today.

Historically, populism arose for many of the same reasons as the Progressive Movement (1890-1917). During the Gilded Age (1870-1890) there was a massive increase in wealth and the number of very wealthy individuals. Progressivism was a reaction to this, but so was Populism. Progressivism and Populism are distinct movements but not mutually exclusive. In the early 20th century, Progressives and Populists often worked together.

Populism is typically divided into "right wing" and "left wing" populism. Unfortunately, the terms "left" and "right" often are used quite loosely. Today, left and right often refer to the size of government people want. "Leftists" favor bigger government because they feel government can solve society's problems, while "right wingers" advocate smaller government because they feel that government is often the cause of society's problems, or as Ronald Reagan so succinctly said, "The nine most terrifying words in the English language are: I'm from the Government, and I'm here to help."

Progressives tend to be leftist because they want to expand the power of government to address perceived problems. Historically, they believed the government was best suited to fix the problems caused by the Industrial Revolution, such as unsafe working conditions. Many Progressives were, and remain, anti-populist. Many Progressives supported the creation of a professional bureaucracy run by experts. Populists oppose any professional bureaucracy and want ordinary people to make decisions and correct society's problems. They note that the Industrial Revolution created problems, but it also created more wealth than any other movement to that point in history. Populists believed that the Church, private charitable associations, and small local government run by ordinary people were best suited to solve these problems.

Progressives and populists agreed in some areas, such as the secret ballot and direct election of senators. Many populists saw direct election of senators as a way of returning power to the people, even though it also resulted in a shift of power away from the states and towards the federal government. Everyone agreed that secret ballots lessened corruption by eliminating coercion and monetary inducements (bribes) from political machines. Another area of agreement was the **referendum**, an election in which the people vote directly on a proposed law. The referendum, so-called because the matter at issue is *referred* directly to the people, along with the initiative and direct election of Senators, formed some of the most important new political advances during the Progressive Era as it allowed for more direct self-government.

Direct citizen control of American government has its roots in the 18th century New England town meeting. In 1778, Massachusetts became the first state to hold a statewide legislative referendum when her citizens ratified the state constitution. Despite this tradition, by the late 19th century, elected representatives made all laws. In 1898, South Dakota amended their constitution to allow a statewide initiative and popular referendum; thus, becoming the first state to permit citizens to make laws instead of the elected representatives in the state legislature. The person most responsible for the adoption of the referendum in South Dakota was a Catholic priest, Father Robert Haire. Haire studied theology at the University of Louvain in Belgium and was ordained a priest in 1874. Father Haire became a missionary to the Dakota Territory in 1879. In the 1880s, Father Haire became president of the Dakota Knights of Labor, the Catholic labor organization. He became the intellectual leader of the People's Party, later renamed the Populist Party. Father Haire was critical of professional politicians who tended to promote their own narrow interests over the common good.

In the 1890s, there was a strong feeling in the western states that the two main parties, Democrats and Republicans, were dominated by an Eastern Elite who did not represent the common people, especially westerners. In 1892, the Populist Party met for its first national convention in Omaha, Nebraska and adopted The Omaha Platform. Among other ideas, **the Omaha Platform** called for direct election of senators and the popular initiative. Populists also sought universal male suffrage and opposed poll taxes. The Platform also demanded that the federal government give away public lands in the West so that as many people as possible could have their own homesteads.

For a time, it appeared the Populist Party might mount a challenge to the two dominant parties. In 1896, the Democrat Party nominated William Jennings Bryan, who the Populist Party also endorsed. Over the next decade, the Democrat Party co-opted much of the populist message. By 1910, the Populist Party ceased to exist, but populism has continued as a part of American politics. Prior to Franklin Roosevelt's administration, the Democrat Party was the party of small government and local control. As late as 1932, the Democrat Party advocated "*drastic reduction of governmental expenditures by abolishing useless commissions and offices, consolidating departments and bureaus, and eliminating extravagance to accomplish a saving of not less than twenty-five per cent in the cost of the Federal Government.*"

Today, any candidate calling for reduction of the federal budget by 25% would be a radical. With the Roosevelt administration's abandonment of populist

People's Party nominating convention held at Columbus, Nebraska, July 15, 1890

issues, populism ceased to be a major force nationally. This began to change with extremely unpopular judicial rulings by the Warren Court involving decisions on school prayer, bussing, and abortion. There was a "populist" strain to this criticism as many people saw Supreme Court justices as "ivory tower elitists" who thought they knew what was best for everyone. In the 1970s, westerners complained about "eastern elites" who ran the government in Washington. In the 1970s and 1980s, this western movement was known as the **Sagebrush Rebellion**. Westerners objected to legislation like the federal *Endangered Species Act* (1973) that disproportionately affected western states whose economy depended on mining and logging.

Ronald Reagan tapped into this renewal of populism. Reagan promised to appoint judges who would interpret the law and not rewrite it. Reagan, who had been governor of California, also promised to return control to local communities and roll back some of the environmental regulations that westerners found objectionable. Reagan often emphasized his humble background. He used to say, "We didn't live on the wrong side of the tracks, but we lived close enough that we could hear the whistles." Finally, Reagan repeatedly claimed to be the heir to the older populist strain of the Democrat Party. Reagan often said, "I didn't leave the Democratic Party, the party left me." He repeated this statement throughout his career asking "populist" Democrats to follow him.

When Reagan's vice president, George Bush, ran for president in 1988, much of the Reagan coalition backed Bush, but Bush was no populist. A graduate of Yale, one of the most elite eastern universities, Bush was a consummate Washington insider. In 1992, much of the Reagan coalition, led by prominent Catholic Patrick Buchanan, abandoned Bush. Buchanan styled himself a populist, often comparing his followers to "peasants with pitchforks"

Newt Gingrich and the "Contract with America" tapped into the populist spirit, but some populists were disappointed. George W. Bush was elected in 2000 and then Barack Obama in 2008, but both men seemed to be typical party insiders. From 2009 to 2016, "The Tea-Party Movement" was quite popular. The Tea Party Movement argued that elites dominated both parties and that power should be returned to the people. In

Ronald Reagan

2016, much of the Tea Party Movement supported Donald Trump, who was seen as a political outsider. On the Democrat side, many left-populists supported socialist Bernie Sanders as an alternative to the ultimate insider Hillary Clinton.

Trump successfully ran as an outsider against the establishment and was elected president in 2016. Like the Populists who opposed the Spanish-American War in 1898, many populists who supported Trump were critical of what they called "forever wars" in Afghanistan, Iraq, and Syria. In 2016, candidate Trump pledged to stop these wars and focus on protecting America's own border.

As of 2024, many people, both Trump's supporters and opponents, consider him to be a populist. Much of the political elite hate Trump because "he's not one of us." Nevertheless, Trump's popularity shows the continued importance of populist feeling in American politics.

The Catholic position has always been that ordinary people sometimes require guidance from experts, but elitism carries dangers. In 1520, in *Open Letter to the Christian Nobility*, Martin Luther famously declared "every man a priest." This quickly morphed into "every man a pope," with each individual protestant becoming infallible on matters of faith and morals. In *Veritatis Splendor* (1993) Pope St. John Paul II condemned the idea that "each individual will independently make his or her decisions and life choices" without guidance from the Church. St. Thomas often explained the need for expertise in matters of theology, morality, and science. While some issues of morality are obvious to everyone with a conscience, others require study and wisdom. St. Thomas points out that human progress in many areas relies on experts who have aptitude, inclination, and time to devote long years to studying a specific subject.[12]

So, experts or "elites," are important, but elites and common people must work together. As Leo XIII wrote in *Rerum Novarum*, "capital cannot do without labor, nor labor without capital." Our Lord himself warned his Apostles in Matthew 20:25-26: "*You know that the rulers of the Gentiles lord it over them, and their great ones are tyrants over them. It will not be so among you; but whoever wishes to be great among you must be your servant.*"

No one can be an expert on everything. People rely on the expertise of others for a wide range of things, from translation of Scripture to treatment of illness. Scripture teaches that it is too easy for "experts" to become "full of themselves." Some forms of populism go too far and seek to reject any sort of elite as illegitimate. Populism accords with Catholic teaching insofar as it rejects elitism when these experts lose their humility and want to "lord it over" the common people.

RECALL OF ELECTED OFFICIALS

Recall is the procedure by which citizens are able to remove an official from office before the term of office is complete. Generally, citizens are required to obtain a certain number of signatures to back a recall election. Then, the "recalled" official must stand for re-election. Recall allows citizens to remove an unpopular official without waiting for his term to expire. As of 2024, nineteen states have recall for elected state officials and twenty more have recall only on the local level. The requirements for recall vary; but, in most places, proponents of a recall election must collect signatures on a recall petition equal to 25% of the voters in the last election.

Recall of elected officials is an ancient idea, but uncommon in the United States until the first decade of the 20th century. In the early 20th century, populists in many states enacted recall, often in conjunction with popular referendums. In most states, the recall election is a simple up or down vote on whether the incumbent will remain in office. In about a third of states, the recall election is a multi-candidate election, where the incumbent must run against other candidates. The winner serves out the remainder of the term.

Recall of officials rarely succeeds. Many voters think that if an official's term will expire in a year or two anyway, that a recall is a waste of time. One of the most famous recall elections in American history involved the 2003 California governor recall. Democrat Gray Davis faced recall and Republican movie actor Arnold Schwarzenegger defeated him. While successful recalls are rare, some people think the mere threat of a recall helps keep politicians under control.

Arnold Schwarzenegger

---

12   See, Commentary on De Trinitate of Boetheus, Question 3

THE SECRET BALLOT

Another plank of the Populist Platform was the secret ballot, also called the **Australian Ballot** as it was the first nation to employ it. This was an issue on which both Progressives and Populists agreed. In 1888, Massachusetts became the first state to adopt a secret ballot, but almost every other state quickly accepted the practice over the next decade. For centuries, Englishmen had voted in large public meetings. However, during the Gilded Age, with the rise of powerful political machines and city "bosses," people were being bribed or pressured into voting a certain way. If the way a person voted could not be confirmed then bribery and coercion would be discouraged. A person might take money to vote one way, but then go into the voting booth and vote for someone else.

Note that the secret ballot applies to general elections. In many places, primaries occur in public caucuses or mass meetings.

HOME RULE

In home rule states, the state constitution vests primary authority in local government. This means that local government can take any action which the state constitution does not explicitly prohibit. In non-home rule states, local government only exercises those powers permitted by the state legislature. There are a number of variations to this division. In a few states, the home rule principle applies to larger cities but not to small towns. Other times, there are specific exceptions to home rule, such as the power to raise local taxes. Like the referendum, home rule resulted from the populist revolution of the early 20th century. Many of the same people who enacted referendums in the state constitution passed home rule for the same reasons.

In home rule jurisdictions, local governments must follow the state and federal constitutions; however, home rule allows local government to reflect the values of the community. For example, in Texas, the state "Fetal Heartbeat Law" makes it a crime to kill an unborn child after a heartbeat can be detected, which normally occurs around the fifth week of life. However, local Texas jurisdictions can restrict abortion earlier, or ban abortions entirely, within their jurisdiction. For instance, in Lubbock, Texas, human life is protected from the moment of conception. Allowing local communities to enact such measures, that might be impossible to pass on the state level, avoids the problem of laws being reduced to "the least common denominator."

Home rule can sometimes be confusing. Ohio is a home rule state where local governments have broad regulatory authority. As a result, Ohio has a very diverse set of local ordinances regarding weapons' possession. For example, Bowie Knives are illegal in Warrensville Heights and in Euclid, Ohio, but legal in the rest of the state. Obscure local laws like this can lead people to "run afoul of the law" for innocent conduct. However, simply because local control can sometimes be misused, does not negate the importance of communities trying to set their own local priorities.

In home rule jurisdictions, the division between local and state governments often creates debate and litigation. As with disputes between state and federal government, the state constitution sometimes does not clearly define what is a state power and what is a local power. For example, Ohio's Home Rule Amendment, which voters ratified in 1912, provides that "municipalities shall have authority to exercise all powers of local self-government and to adopt and enforce within their limits such local police, sanitary and other similar regulations, as are *not in conflict with general laws*." The language, "not in conflict with general laws" creates a potentially big exception which Ohio courts have struggled to interpret. Many advocates of local control have complained that the courts tend not to give enough control to localities. In Ohio, all judges are elected, so they are more accountable to the people than federal judges.

PROHIBITION: THE 18TH AND 21ST AMENDMENTS

Despite its short duration, Prohibition offers valuable insights into understanding the changes in local government and federalism. Progressives championed laws restricting the sale of alcoholic beverages. In fact, it was one of their main goals. They saw banning alcohol as a good way to use the power of government to improve society.

In the early 1900s, Progressives enacted legislation banning, or at least severely restricting, alcohol in almost half the states. Because alcoholic beverages were so easy to transport, advocates demanded a nationwide ban on alcohol. In the early 1900s, no one imagined that Congress could simply ban a commodity. Accordingly, in December 1917, Congress approved what would become the 18th Amendment, with Republicans overwhelmingly in favor but Democrats voting overwhelmingly against the amendment. Three-fourths of the states ratified the amendment in just thirteen months. The 18th Amendment reads:

> After one year from the ratification of this article the manufacture, sale, or transportation of intoxicating liquors within, the importation thereof into, or the exportation thereof from the United States and all territory subject to the jurisdiction thereof for beverage purposes is hereby prohibited.
>
> The Congress and the several States shall have concurrent power to enforce this article by appropriate legislation.

Many people who supported the Amendment thought the term "intoxicating liquors" only meant distilled liquor, not beer or wine. When Congress approved the Volstead Act, which implemented Prohibition, beer and wine were included. However, as previously noted, there were many exceptions.

Today, it is somewhat difficult to understand how radical this amendment was. These days, the *Interstate Commerce Clause* has been so expanded that Congress bans all manner of things. However, in 1919, the idea that the federal government could ban the intra-state sale of something was a huge and unprecedented expansion of federal power.

Prohibition agents destroying barrels of alcohol in 1921.

U.S. Government for Catholic Students

Additionally, for the first time in American history, the federal government began taking a serious role in law enforcement.

In 1908, the U.S Department of Justice created a "Bureau of Investigation," but it was quite small. In 1924, J. Edgar Hoover became head of the "Bureau of Investigation," which changed its name to the Federal Bureau of Investigation (FBI) in 1935. As soon as Prohibition began, the Bureau became the main federal agency that enforced it, and it expanded greatly in the next few years. In the first six months of Prohibition, the Bureau arrested 269 people for violating the Volstead Act. While this seems like a small number today, in 1920, it represented a huge expansion of federal police activity. By the time Prohibition ceased in 1933, the Bureau had over 1000 law enforcement agents—something unimaginable in 1900. However, when Prohibition ended, the Bureau agents were not fired. Hoover convinced the Attorney General that Bureau agents could be used for other law enforcement purposes, and they were. In the early 1930s, Bureau agents shifted from combatting bootlegging to combatting new federal crimes such as bank robbery.

Many of the Bureau's exploits against bootleggers and bank robbers were well publicized and became almost legendary.[13] In October 1933, the first radio dramatization of a Bureau case was broadcast on national radio. Over the next twenty years, Hoover carefully fed stories of FBI cases to radio, movie, and TV producers to craft a public image of the FBI as the greatest crime fighters in the world. Nevertheless, it was Prohibition that launched the idea of federal law enforcement and gained public acceptance because there was an Amendment that permitted the federal government to become involved in what had always been a state and local issue.

By 1932, Prohibition was accepted as a failure. The liquor laws were widely ignored which led to a general loss of respect for law. Democrats had long opposed Prohibition and in 1932 they promised to repeal the 18th Amendment as soon as possible. The Republicans were divided, and did not take a position on repeal, but insisted that the 18th Amendment be strictly enforced until it was repealed. Republicans accused state officials who refused to cooperate in the enforcement of Prohibition as engaging in "nullification." In 1932,

J. Edgar Hoover

Democrats won the White House and Congress in a landslide. Prohibition was one of the biggest issues, but the ongoing Depression was another. The Democrat Congress passed what became the 21st Amendment, which three/fourths of the states approved before the end of the year. It repealed the 18th Amendment and ended Prohibition.

Section 2 of the 21st Amendment allowed the federal government to support state laws banning liquor, but seems implicitly to acknowledge that the federal government had no authority to prevent the transportation of liquor between states. It was widely accepted in 1933 that the interstate commerce clause did not allow the federal government to ban the interstate transportation of liquor or anything else. Today, the generally accepted view of the interstate commerce clause is very different. However, the 21st Amendment can be said to stand for the principle that the federal government should support state criminal law, not supplant it.

---

[13] In the 1920s and 1930s, the FBI investigated such famous criminals as Al Capone, John Dillinger, Willy Sutton, "Baby Face Nelson," "Pretty Boy Floyd," and "Bonny and Clyde."

DUTIES OF CITIZENS TOWARDS THEIR GOVERNMENT

On the last day of the Constitutional Convention, as Benjamin Franklin left the Hall, Elizabeth Willing Powel approached him and asked, "Well Doctor, what have we got, a republic or a monarchy?" "A republic," the eighty-one-year-old Franklin replied, "if you can keep it." The majority of this book has addressed the rights individuals possess and the duties which the government owes to them. As this book concludes, it seems appropriate to address the duties that citizens owe to the government. In other words, what do individuals need to do to "keep it."

In a republic, citizens are not involved in the day-to-day operations of government. However, citizens should try to be aware of what transpires in their government at all levels, especially the federal level. The 21st century is the "Information Age" and information has never been more readily available and in greater amounts to average people than it is today.

People should know at least their national representatives, that is, their Senators and Representatives. Where do they stand on the important moral issues of the day? What are their positions on economic and other issues?

Citizens should be familiar with the key issues confronting the nation. Find news outlets that are trustworthy for unbiased reports. Also, there are numerous blogs and podcasts from reliable, and Catholic/Christian, sources. Be aware that almost all news programs have an agenda—often one that is contrary to Catholic social teachings.

People, especially young energetic people, need to become active in the legislative/political process to whatever degree is possible. For some individuals, this means becoming a politician and running for office. For others, it means simply voting in the elections. Most people try to become involved in those issues that directly impact their lives, such as economic issues; or ones about which they feel deeply, such as pro-life issues, religious freedom issues, or issues involving parental rights and home education. In these instances, it is important to contact your representatives at the state or federal level and let them know how you feel about the issue. Whenever you contact an elected official, be courteous, informed, and appreciative. Often, a politician may not even know about a bill under consideration. Remember there are hundreds of bills presented every year and, unfortunately, many are not read. A friendly call from a constituent often does more good than a person might imagine. Finally, do not discount the power of prayer. Say a rosary, then call!

CONCLUSION

The United States has always had a healthy tradition of local government. If local government was important in the 19th century, when the population was much smaller and more homogenous than today, then contemporary local government is even more vital. This tradition of strong local government also fully accords with Catholic social teaching, particularly the doctrine of subsidiarity. St. Augustine, St. Thomas, and other Church Doctors have consistently expressed their preference for government on a human scale. The bigger a society and a government become, the more the government must become impersonal and bureaucratic. In *The City of God*, St. Augustine criticized Rome for becoming an empire. All their great empire brought Rome a thousand years of violence and strife. Rome would have been much better off remaining a simple city at peace with its neighbors.

In his landmark book, *After Virtue: A Study in Moral Theory* (1981), the great Catholic, Thomistic philosopher Alasdair MacIntyre famously described modern politics as "civil war carried on by other means." MacIntyre says many modern states have become so large and diverse that the population shares little in common. As a result, politics becomes purely the use of force in which one group imposes its will on the rest of the population. MacIntyre argues that in nations the size of the United States, dialogue and understanding are impossible. Large modern nation-states are not real communities; rather, the modern nation-state is a dangerous parody of a true community. Consequently, politics becomes more and more polarized. While he acknowledges that the nation-state has a role in protecting local communities from invasion or attack; he asserts that the common good is only truly found in "*some form of local community within which the activities of families, workplaces, schools, clinics, clubs dedicated to debate and clubs dedicated to games and sports, and religious congregations may all find a place.*"[14] Early Americans would have agreed.

The trend for the last hundred years has been away from local government and towards centralization. Powerful interests support centralization; but, there is also a powerful human attraction to genuine community. This being so, we can expect a constant tug-of-war between the local and the national.

As American citizens on the verge of obtaining the right to vote, readers of this textbook will soon be able to play a vital role in this on-going tug-of-war. Whether you marry or remain single, have a religious vocation or join the military, you are going to become part of the great American political experiment. As Benjamin Franklin said on the bright September day in 1787, responding not only to Mrs. Powel but to every generation that followed, "A republic – if you can keep it."

---

14   MacIntyre, Dependent Rational Animals (1999) chapter 11.

REVIEW QUESTIONS

1. What is the oldest existing Constitution still in effect in 2024?

2. What powers does the president of the United States possess but which most state governors do not?

3. What powers do most governors have but the president of the United States does not?

4. Who was J. Edgar Hoover?

5. What is the only state that does not have a bi-cameral legislature?

6. Where do county administration and officials primarily work and have their offices?

7. What term is typically used to describe the power to restrict how land can be used?

8. Who is the person who manages a school district?

9. What Congressman advocated a Constitutional amendment that would have forbidden any public funds from being used to pay for Catholic education?

10. What was the name of the now infamous Supreme Court case which declared that racial discrimination was not contrary to the U.S. Constitution?

11. What is the purpose of the Preamble in a constitution?

12. What powers have federal district courts claimed to deal with racial imbalance in schools?

13. What is the Initiative?

14. Who famously said that people should not be judged by the color of their skin but by the content of their character?

15. Who famously said, "We didn't live on the wrong side of the tracks, but we lived close enough that we could hear the whistles."?

16. What is the referendum?

17. What is the purpose of the state constitution?

18. What are the three levels of a state's judiciary?

19. What is the main source of state revenue?

20. What is the main source of revenue for local government?

21. In what case did the U.S. Supreme Court declare that all state-sponsored racial discrimination was a violation of equal protection?

22. What does a city manager do?

23. What are some examples of school choice?

24. What is Recall?

25. Who told Elizabeth Willing Powel that America had "A Republic, if you can keep it"?

26. Who primarily wrote the Massachusetts state constitution?

27. In state government, the lieutenant governor's duties mostly closely resemble which federal official?

28. What is the difference between a progressive and a regressive tax? Regressive tax

29. What were some of the main parts of the Progressive Agenda during the late 19th and early 20th century?

30. What is inheritance tax?

IMAGE ATTRIBUTIONS

Chapter 1

Saint Thomas Aquinas: Public Domain: Wikimedia, Carlo Crivelli
Grimani Breviary: The Month of September: Public Domain: Wikimedia
Aristotle: Public Domain: Wikimedia, Lysippos
St. Augustine: CC BY-SA 4.0: Wikimedia, Syrio
Bears in a field: Copyright: Adobe Stock, WildMedia
Perugino Marriage virgin: Public Domain: Wikimedia,
Scene of family farming: Public Domain: Wikimedia, Adolf Müller-Grantzow
Rose window of the Cathédrale Notre-Dame de Paris: CC BY-SA 4.0: Wikimedia, Krzysztof Mizera
Judge striking a gavel: Copyright: Adobe Stock, Sebastian Duda
James Madison: Public Domain: Wikimedia, John Vanderlyn
Antigone is arrested: CC BY-SA 3.0: Wikimedia, VladoubidoOo
Portrait of Hammurabi by Thomas Hudson Jones: Public Domain: Wikimedia, Architect of the Capitol
Pope St. John Paul II: CC BY-SA 4.0: Wikimedia, Kotyłło art.mal
The symbol of Communism: CC BY-SA 3.0: Wikimedia, Carlosbenitez26
Chair of St. Peter: Copyright: Adobe Stock, e55evu
King David: Copyright: Adobe Stock, thauwald-pictures
Charlemagne is crowned by Pope Leo III: Public Domain: Wikimedia, Chroniques de France ou de Saint-Denis
St. Robert Bellarmine: Public Domain: Wikimedia
Thomas Hobbes: Public Domain: Wikimedia, David Beck
James II and Family: Public Domain: Wikimedia, Pierre Mignard I

Chapter 2

Appius Claudius Caecus replies to Cineas to leave Italy first and then negotiate peace: Public Domain: Wikimedia, Giuseppe Sciuti
Portrait of Alfred the Great: Public Domain: Wikimedia, Samuel Woodforde
Modern trial by jury: Copyright: Adobe Stock, Heidi Patricola
Emperor Justinian: CC BY-SA 3.0: Wikimedia, Roger Culos
Presentation of the Pandects to the Emperor Justinian: Public Domain: Wikimedia, Hermann Knackfuß
Battle of Stamford Bridge: Public Domain: Wikimedia, Matthew Paris
St. Thomas Becket: CC BY-SA 4.0: Wikimedia, Fallaner
Copy of the Magna Carta: Public Domain: Wikimedia, Earthsound
Archbishop Stephen Langton by John Thomas: CC BY-SA 4.0: Wikimedia, Storye book
King John: Public Domain: Wikimedia
King John reluctantly signs the Magna Carta: Public Domain: Wikimedia, Arthur C. Michael
King Edward I presiding over Parliament: Public Domain: Wikimedia
Portrait of Sir John Fortesque: Public Domain: Wikimedia, William Faithorne
Portrait of Sir Thomas More: Public Domain: Wikimedia, Hans Holbein the Younger
Portrait of Henry VIII: Public Domain: Wikiemedia, Hans Holbein the Younger
Pilgrimage of Grace: Public Domain: Wikimedia, John Cassell
Portrait of Mary I: Public Domain: Wikimedia, Master John
Queen Elizabeth I: Public Domain: Wikimedia, William Segar and George Gower
The Battle of Marston Moor: Public Domain: Wikimedia, John Barker
Portrait of James II of England: Public Domain: Wikemedia, Peter Lely
The Battle of the Boyne: Public Domain: Wikimedia, Jan Hoynk van Papendrecht
The Lords and Commons presenting the crown to William of Orange and Mary Stuart: Public Domain: Wikimedia, Edward Matthew Ward
A "pine tree shilling,": CC BY-SA 2.0: Wikimedia, The Portable Antiquities Scheme/ The Trustees of the British Museum
Re-creation of a settler's house in Jamestown: Copyright: Adobe Stock: spiritofamerica
The Mayflower on Her Arrival in Plymouth Harbor: Public Domain: William Halsall
The Mayflower Compact: Public Domain: Wikimedia, Jean Leon Gerome Ferris
Seal of the Massachusetts Bay Colony: Public Domain: Wikimedia
The founding of Maryland and the first Mass celebrated in English America: Public Domain: Wikimedia, Emmanuel Leutze
East and West New Jersey: Public Domain: Wikimedia, Worlidge, John; Thornton, John
Major George Washington at the Battle of the Monongahela: Public Domain: Wikimedia, Junius Brutus Stearns
Parliament Stamp Act: Public Domain: Wikimedia, British Parliment 1765
An engraving of the Boston Massacre: Public Domain: Wikimedia, Engrav'd Printed & Sold by Paul Revere Boston
The first Continental Congress, 1774: Public Domain: Wikimedia, USCapitol

Chapter 3

Stand Your Ground: Public Domain: Wikimedia, Don Troiani
Patrick Henry: Public Domain: Wikimedia, George Bagby Matthews, after Thomas Sully
The Signing of the Declaration of Independence: Publid Domain: Wikimedia, Charles Édouard Armand-Dumaresq
Thomas Jefferson: Public Domain: Wikimedia, Rembrandt Peale
United States Declaration of Independence: Public Domain: Wikimedia
John Adams: Public Domain: Wikimedia, Gilbert Stuart
Martin Luther King admired the Declaration of Independence: Public Domain: Wikipedia, Rowland Scherman
Benjamin Franklin: Public Domain: Wikimedia, Joseph-Siffred Duplessis
The first page of the Articles of Confederation: Public Domain: Wikimedia
The Northwest Territory: CC BY-SA 4.0: Wikimedia, Isochrone
A Continental thirty dollar bill: Public Domain: Wikimedia, University of Notre Dame
Scene at the Signing of the Constitution of the United States: Public Domain: Wikimedia, Howard Chandler Christy
George Washington: Public Domain: Wikimedia, Gilbert Stuart
Alexander Hamilton: Public Domain: Wikimedia, John Trumbull
The modern-day Capitol building: Copyright: Adobe Stock, baiyi126
Portrait of George Mason: Public Domain: Wikimedia, Boudet Dominic W. after John Hesselius
Portrait of John Jay: Public Domain: Wikimedia, Gilbert Stuart
James Madison: Public Domain: Wikimedia, John Vanderlyn

Chapter 4

Capitol building ,Washington DC: Copyright: Adobe Stock, Frédéric Prochasson
Graph of congressmen: Seton Staff
The Gerry-Mander edit: Public Domain: Wikimedia, Elkanah Tisdale
Graph of senators and their terms: Seton Staff
The symbols for the modern-day parties: Copyright: Adobe Stock, Li Artis
Leadership positions in congress: Seton Staff
English fox hunter holding a whip: Copyright: Adobe Stock, cheekylorns
How a Bill Becomes Law: Seton Staff
Coin stack by the congress building: Copyright: Adobe Stock, sangkribo
Postal Inspectorbadge: Public Domain: Wikimedia, United States Postal Inspection Service
John Marshall: Public Domain: Wikimedia, Henry Inman
New York harbor: Copyright: Adobe Stock, Mark Hunter
Bankruptcy Law Books: Copyright: Adobe Stock, Lane Erickson
Application for Naturalization: Copyright: Adobe Stock, mehaniq41
Printing money dollar bills: Copyright: Adobe Stock, Maksym Yemelyanov
US military ships and planes: Copyright: Adobe Stock, Adrian
Nixon's involvement in Cambodia: Public Domain: Wikimedia, Jack E. Kightlinger
Massachusetts Militia: Public Domain: Wikimedia, Charles M. Lefferts
U.S. Army National Guard Seal: Public Domain: Wikimedia, U.S. Army
Texas National Guard: Public Domain: Wikimedia, 1st Lt. Alicia Lacy
The District of Columbia: Copyright: Adobe Stock, vichie81
Federal public land surface & subsurface: Public Domain: Wikimedia, Bureau of Land Management
John D. Rockefeller: Public Domain: Wikimedia
Portrait of Pope Leo XIII: Public Domain: Wikimedia, Fabio Cipolla
Franklin Roosevelt's New Deal: Public Domain: Wikimedia, Social Security Online

Chapter 5

Mount Rushmore: Copyright: Adobe Stock, checubus
The Peacemakers: Public Domain: Wikimedia, George Peter Alexander Healy
U.S. 2024 presidential election: Copyright: Adobe Stock, Dimitrios
A campaign poster for Rutherford B. Hayes: Public Domain: Wikimedia, Currier & Ives.
Cincinnatus receives ambassadors calling him to lead Rome against her enemies: Public Domain: Wikimedia, Alexandre Cabanel
Executive Branch: Seton staff
Washington and His Cabinet: Public Domain: Wikimedia, Cornell University Library
President Lyndon B. Johnson with the Joint Chiefs of Staff: Public Domain: Wikimedia, Yoichi Okamoto
Federal reserve system symbol on hundred dollar bill: Copyright: Adobe Stock, AlexGo
Andrew Jackson: Public Domain: Wikimedia, Ralph Eleaser Whiteside Earl
The Bosses of the Senate: Public Domain: Wikimedia, Joseph Keppler
President Reagan delivers his Farewell Address from the Oval Office: Public Domain: Wikimedia,
President Clinton vetoing line items for a bill: Public Domain: Wikimedia, Ralph Alswang, White House
President Truman signs the North Atlantic Treaty: Public Domain: Wikimedia, Abbie Rowe
President Carter meets with the leaders of Israel and Egypt at Camp David: Public Domain: Wikimedia
U.S. Department of State official seal: Public Domain: Wikimedia, United States Department of State
Satellite viewing cars: Copyright: Adobe Stock, Tomasz Zajda
Cuban soldiers in the failed Bay of Pigs invasion: Public Domain: Wikimedia
First Reading of the Emancipation Proclamation by President Lincoln: Public Domain: Wikimedia, Francis Bicknell Carpenter
President Biden signs an executive order: Public Domain: Wikimedia, The White House
Student Vietnam War protesters: CC BY 2.0: Wikimedia, uwdigitalcollections
Court of law and justice trial: Copyright: Wikimedia, Gorodenkoff
President Nixon holding transcripts of the Oval Office tapes: Public Domain: Wikimedia, Jack Kightlinger

Chapter 6

Portrait of John Jay: Public Domain: Wikimedia, Gilbert Stuart
Court of Justice and Law Trial: Copyright: Adobe Stock, Gorodenkoff
The Jury: Public Domain: Wikimedia, John Morgan
Lawyer showing documents to jury in court: Copyright: Adobe Stock, KOTO
US Court of Appeals and District Court map: CC BY-SA 2.5: Wikimedia, Tintazul
The Warren Court: Public Domain: Wikimedia, Leffler, Warren K.
The first photograph of the U.S. Supreme Court: Public Domain: Wikimedia, Alexander Gardner
Sir Edward Hales, Baronet, of Hales Place, Hackington, Kent: Public Domain: Wikimedia, Philippe Mercier
St. Thomas Aquinas: Copyright: Adobe Stock, Adam Ján Figeľ
Trails of Tears: Public Domain: Wikimedia, Nikater
Samuel Chase: Public Domain: Wikimedia, John Wesley Jarvis
John Marshall: Public Domain: Wikimedia, Henry Inman
Dred Scott: Public Domain: Wikimedia, Schultze, Louis
Balanced gold scale: Copyright: Adobe Stock, Sashkin
Hugo Black: Public Domain: Wikimedia, Harris & Ewing
Antonin Scalia: Public Domain: Wikimedia, Collection of the Supreme Court of the United States
John Rutledge Statue: CC BY-SA 4.0: Wikimedia, Nicholemacgregor
Gerald Ford: Public Domain: Wikimedia, David Hume Kennerly
Jimmy Carter: Public Domain: Wikimedia, Department of Defense. Department of the Navy. Naval Photographic Center
Sandra Day O'Connor: Public Domain: Wikimedia, Library of Congress Transferred by Sven Manguard
Robert Bork with President Ronald Reagan: Public Domain: Wikimedia, White House Photographic Collection
The Supreme Court (2025): Public Domain: Wikimedia, Fred Schilling

Chapter 7

James Madison: Public Domain: Wikimedia, Gilbert Stuart
First page of the original Bill of Rights: Public Domain: Wikimedia, 1st United States Congress
Alexander Hamilton making the first draft of the Constitution: Public Domain: Wikimedia, Hamilton Buggy Company
Bennett Baltimore from Federal Hill: Public Domain: Wikmedia, Bennett, W. J.
Old Salem County Courthouse: Public Domain: Wikimedia, Smallbones
Scene at the Signing of the Constitution of the United States: Public Domain: Wikimedia, Howard Chandler Christy
A bishop holding a Monstrance: Copyright: Adobe Stock, jorisvo
Church ceiling dome image: Image by Armin Forster from Pixabay:
Oliver Wendell Holmes, Jr: Public Domain: Wikimedia, Harris & Ewing Collection
Newsprint image : Image by kalhh from Pixabay
The First Muster: Public Domain: Wikimedia, Don Troiani
Edward Coke: Public Domain: Wikimedia, Gilbert Jackson
policemen are standing in front of the building: Copyright: Adobe Stock: Photographee.eu
Policeman searching a thief: Copyright: Adobe Stock, Robert Kneschke
Police car on the street: Photo by Matt Popovich on Unsplash
A police officer reading the Miranda warning: Public Domain: Wikimedia, Gerald L. Nino, CBP, U.S. Dept. of Homeland Security
Sir Walter Raleigh: Public Domain: Wikimedia, William Segar
King James I of England: Public Domain: Wikimedia, John de Critz
New York Court of Appeals hearing oral arguments: CC BY-SA 2.0: Wikimedia, tracy collins, edited by Daniel Case
A courtroom at the Cherokee County Courthouse: CC BY 4.0: Wikimedia, Harrison Keely
Death penalty in the United States: CC BY-SA 4.0: Wikimedia, Atakuzier
Pope St. Paul VI: CC0 1.0: Wikimedia, BastienM
The Supreme Court Building: Copyright: Adobe Stock, nadl2022

Chapter 8

Charles-Louis de Secondat, Baron de Montesquieu: Public Domain: Wikimedia, After Jacques-Antoine Dassier
Portrait of Pope Pius XI: Public Domain: Wikimedia, Philip de László
Pope John Paul II: CC BY-SA 3.0: Wikimedia, Gregorini Demetrio
Saint Augustine: Public Domain: wikimedia, Philippe de Champaigne
Saint Isidor of Sevilla: Public Domain: Wikimedia, Bartolomé Esteban Murillo
Russell Kirk: Public Domain: wikimedia
George Cabot: Seton Press Public Domain, based on sketch
John C. Calhoun: Public Domain: Wikimedia, George Peter Alexander Healy
Alexis de Tocqueville: Public Domain: Wikimedia, Théodore Chassériau
Owen Roberts: Public Domain: Wikimedia, Harris & Ewing, photographer
Chief Justice Rehnquist: Public Domain: Wikimedia
United States Supreme Court Building: Public Domain: Wikimedia, Joe Ravi
I-55 under construction in Mississippi: Public Domain: Wikimedia, William C. Shrout
Wheelchair on a handicap ramp: Copyright: Adobe Stock, RioPatuca Images
Paul Weyrich: CC BY-SA 3.0: Wikimedia, Birdgram
Chief Justice John Roberts: Public Domain: Wikimedia, Steve Petteway

Chapter 9

Constitution We the People: Public Domain: Wikimedia
Texas State Capitol: Copyright: Adobe Stock, jdross75
Colorado state capitol, Denver: CC BY-SA 3.0: Wikimedia, Onetwo1
Judge listening to prosecutor: Copyright: Adobe Stock, LIGHTFIELD STUDIOS
U.S. Supreme Court Chamber: Copyright: Adobe Stock, Clinton
Ultrasound of a baby in the womb: Copyright: Adobe Stock, Mikael Damkier
A map showing the borders of the counties across the United States: Public Domain: Wikimedia
Individual income tax return form: Copyright: Adobe Stock, devrim_pinar
St. Peter's, Barclay Street: Public Domain: Wikimedia
St. Elizabeth Ann Seton: Public Domain: Wikimedia, Amabilia Filicchi
James Blaine: Public Domain: Wikimedia, Mathew Benjamin Brady, Levin Corbin Handy
Educational separation in the US prior to *Brown v. Board of Education* Map: CC BY-SA 3.0: Wikimedia, King_of_Hearts
Integrated busing: Public Domain: Wikimedia, Warren K. Leffler, U.S. News & World Report Magazine
People's Party nominating convention held at Columbus: Public Domain: Wikimedia, Solomon D. Butcher
Ronald Reagan: Public Domain: Wikimedia, Michael Evans
Arnold Schwarzenegger: Public Domain: Wikimedia, State of California
Prohibition agents destroying barrels of alcohol in 1921: Public Domain: Wikimedia
J. Edgar Hoover: Public Domain: Wikimedia, Marion S. Trikosko
Foundation of the American Government: Public Domain: Wikimedia, Henry Hintermeister

INDEX

A

Abbott, Greg, 218, 241
Abortion, 1, 102, 107, 159, 164, 170-173, 181, 185, 201, 204, 232, 246, 259, 262
Absolute Monarchy, 35
Act for Church Liberties (1638), 43-44
Act for the Liberties of the People (Maryland, 1638), 43
Act of Settlement (1701), 36
Acton, Lord, 11
Adams, John, 33, 49, 56, 58, 60, 62, 68, 85-86, 119, 121, 126, 129, 131, 138, 149, 163, 214, 239, 266
Adams, John Quincy, 59, 120, 137
Adams, Samuel, 49, 68, 239
Adkins v. Children's Hospital (1923), 222
Administrative law, 140
Administrative Procedures Act (APA), 80, 113-114, 138
Administrative state, 111, 113-114
Admiralty Courts, 48
Admissions Clause, 234
Adoption, 6, 233
Adultery, 129
Advisory opinion, 165
Advocate, 41, 122, 222, 260
Affordable Care Act (ACA), 229
Afghanistan, 137, 262
African-Americans, 173, 201
Age of Mass Migration, 255
Agencies, independent, 124-126, 149, 154
Agricultural Adjustment Act (1938), 98
Agriculture, Department of, 124
Alaska, 81, 85, 119, 246, 249
Alaskan Natives, See Native Americans
Aldermen, 248
Alien Act (1798), 100
Alien and Sedition Acts, 100, 105, 163, 179, 217
Alito, Samuel, 157, 174
Allegheny v. Am. Civ. Liberties Union Greater Pittsburgh Chapter (1989), 159
Alliances, 61, 63, 74, 103, 129, 133
Amendments (to U.S. Constitution)
  First, 33, 163, 179, 181-183, 185, 187-189
  Second, 189-190
  Third, 191
  Fourth, 191-194
  Fifth, 33, 180, 195-196, 198
  Sixth, 180, 197-198
  Seventh, 151, 181, 199
  Eighth, 28, 196, 199-202
  Ninth, 177, 203
  Tenth, 63, 75, 100, 203, 211, 217, 222-226, 228
  Eleventh, 153, 168, 205
  Twelfth, 119, 121, 205, 208
  Thirteenth, 166, 206, 222
  Fourteenth, 99, 181-182, 185, 188, 190, 192, 203, 206, 256-257, 260
  Fifteenth, 166, 203, 206
  Sixteenth, 207, 222
  Seventeenth, 72, 81, 84, 207, 222
  Eighteenth, 207, 265-266
  Nineteenth, 203, 207
  Twentieth, 89, 207
  Twenty-First, 207-208, 265-266
  Twenty-Second, 121-122, 208
  Twenty-Third, 119, 208
  Twenty-Fourth, 208
  Twenty-Fifth, 131, 209
  Twenty-Sixth, 85, 209
  Twenty-Seventh, 89, 179, 209
American Indians, See Native Americans
Americans with Disabilities Act (1990), 231
Amicus curiae, 156, 242
Anabaptists, 31, 39
Anarchy, 10, 15, 20-21, 67, 177
Angels, 2-3
Anglican Church, 31, 39, 44, 74
Anglo-Saxons, 23-26, 28, 30, 246, 255
Annapolis Convention (1786), 66, 69
Anne, Queen of Great Britain, 37
Anti-Catholicism, 255, 259
Anti-Christian sentiment, 59, 172, 232, 259
Anti-Federalists, 68, 72-73, 75, 77, 92, 94, 100, 105, 160, 163, 167-168, 178, 181, 189
Antigone, 10-11
Appeal to Caesar, 22
Appellate courts, 148, 154-155, 158, 164, 191, 244-245
Appellate jurisdiction, 155, 162, 164, 167
Apportionment, 82, 101, 206-207
Appropriations Committee, 88
Aquinas, St. Thomas, 1-2, 4-9, 11-13, 15-16, 18, 22, 25, 28, 56, 114, 122, 137, 141-142, 161, 184, 190, 202, 212, 215, 231, 233, 263, 267
Arbitrary agreement, 18
Aristocracy, 15-16, 61, 81
Aristotle, 2, 4-9, 13-14, 16, 213, 230
Arizona, 120
Arkansas, 83
Arrest, 31, 34, 101, 144, 150, 180, 194-195, 197, 259
  warrantless, 194
Articles of Confederation, 58, 61-69, 71, 73, 81, 89, 94, 101, 109, 122, 160, 222
Artisans, 7-8
Asia, 258
Assault, 94, 101, 141, 153
Assembly, right to, 50, 183
Asser, Bishop of Sherborne, 23-24
Asset forfeiture, 200
Atheism, 4, 60, 172, 234
Atlanta, Georgia, 60, 223, 249
Atwater v. City of Lago Vista (2001), 194-195
Augustine of Canterbury, St., 23
Augustine of Hippo, St., 4, 10-11, 22, 213, 233, 267
Australian Ballot, 264
Authority
  civil, 8, 10, 55, 213
  delegated, 62-63, 75, 94, 100, 161, 166, 211, 218, 220, 222
  ecclesiastical, 138
  executive, 38, 42-43, 63, 71, 80, 85, 103, 113, 122, 125-126, 138, 143, 160, 162, 183, 207, 235, 240-241
  federal, 75, 93, 97-100, 102, 138, 141, 153, 162, 165, 179, 183, 217-218, 220, 222, 226-227, 229, 235, 241, 248-249, 251, 259, 262, 264-266
  judicial, 148, 153, 165, 206, 238
  legislative, 24, 29-30, 36-37, 39-43, 45-46, 48-50, 52-54, 71-73, 75, 80-81, 85, 87, 89-90, 92-95, 97-103, 105-107, 109-114, 121-123, 125-127, 129-135, 137-144, 148-150,

INDEX

152-174, 177-193, 195-203, 206-209, 211-212, 215-236, 238-267
  local, 41, 43, 48, 66, 73-74, 105, 109-110, 141, 147, 157, 182-183, 185, 211-213, 216, 221-222, 224-225, 227-233, 236, 238, 240-243, 245-267
  of Parliament, 29, 32, 36, 41-42, 48-50, 103, 112, 122, 161-163, 179, 183, 189, 196, 216, 220, 240, 259
  of Pope, 39
  paternal, 8-9, 213
  political, 2, 16-17, 19, 21, 31, 39, 57, 59, 86-88, 110, 124, 126, 146, 160, 173, 212, 219, 222, 224, 227-230, 232-233, 236, 240, 243-267
  presidential, See Authority, executive
  state, 43, 48, 72, 75, 94, 100, 109-110, 217-236, 238-267
Autocracy, 15, 21
Automobile exception (to search warrant), 194
Autonomy, 19, 50, 58, 62, 126, 214, 224
  moral, 19
Aztecs, 74, 233

B

Bail, 36, 41, 150, 178, 180, 199-200, 205
  excessive, 36, 199, 205
Bailiff, 244
Baker, 11, 157
Baltimore, Maryland, 42, 180, 249, 255
Bank of the United States, 94-95
Bankruptcy, 99
Baptism, 14
Barret, Amy Coney, 174
Barron v. Baltimore (1833), 180
Battle of Bunker Hill (1775), 53
Battle of Hastings (1066), 26
Battle of Lexington and Concord (1775), 52
Battle of Marston Moor (1644), 33
Battle of Stamford Bridge (1066), 26
Battle of the Boyne (1690), 31, 35
Bay of Pigs Invasion (1961), 137
Becket, St. Thomas, 27
Bellarmine, St. Robert, 16-17, 21, 57, 59
Bellamy, Edward, 255
Berkeley, Lord John, 44
Berkshire, 24
Bibb v. Navajo Freight Lines (1959), 98

Biden, Joseph R., Jr., 90, 108, 131, 139, 173, 232, 241, 262
Bigelow, Timothy, 219
Bill of attainder, 169, 178
Bill of address, 245
Bill of Rights (English, 1689), 36, 90, 200-201
Bill of Rights (U.S.), 36, 63, 77, 100, 107, 148, 171, 176-182, 190, 192-193, 203, 205
Bills (legislative), 86-87, 90-91, 93, 267
Bipartisan system, 86, 105
Bishops, 23-27, 29, 40, 128, 172, 213, 255
Black, Hugo, 169
Blackstone, William, 252
Blaine Amendments, 255, 259
Blaine, James, 255
Blasphemy, 187
Blessed Virgin Mary, 6, 43
Body of Liberties (Massachusetts, 1641), 41
Boerne, Texas, 225-226
Bohemia, 128
Bork, Robert, 173
Boston Massacre (1770), 49, 58
Boston Tea Party (1773), 49
Boston, Massachusetts, 23, 40, 48-49, 52-53, 58, 65, 106, 172, 249, 257-258
Bowie Knives, 264
Bribery, 15, 30-31, 85, 141, 157, 264
Brown v. Board of Education of Topeka, Kansas (1954), 204, 256-257
Brownson, Orestes, 20-21
Brutus (Anti-Federalist writer), 73, 105, 160
Bryan, William Jennings, 261
Buchanan, Patrick, 262
Budget, federal, 92, 125, 130, 230, 243, 261
Budget, state, 240, 243-244, 259
Bully pulpit, 129
Bureaucracy, 111, 113-114, 125, 127, 212, 229, 233, 247, 253-254, 259, 267
Burger, Warren, 173
Burr, Aaron, 119, 144
Bushel, Edward, 45
Bushel's Case (1670), 45
Bush, George H.W., 124, 173, 262
Bush, George W., 120-121, 262
Bussing, school, 257-258, 262
Butler, U.S. v. (1936), 93

C

Cabinet, presidential, 86, 123-124, 132, 138
Cabot, George, 219

Caesar, Julius, 22
Calhoun, John C., 220
California, 81, 108, 119-120, 158, 188, 242, 248, 262
Callender, James Thompson, 163
Calvert, George (Lord Baltimore), 42-43
Calvert, Leonard, 43
Calvinists, 31
Cambodia, 104
Cambridge University, 25
Camp David Accords (1978), 134
Canada, 46-47, 157-158
Canals, 93, 96
Canon Law, 25, 27
Cantwell v. Connecticut (1940), 184
Cape Cod, Massachusetts, 40
Capital punishment, 41, 57, 64, 201-202
Capitol (U.S.), 11, 54, 70, 109, 251
Capone, Al, 266
Carolina, 46, 51 (See also North Carolina; South Carolina)
Carroll, Charles, of Carrollton, 59
Carroll, Daniel, 68
Carroll, Fr. John, 69
Carson v. Makin (2022), 259
Carter, Jimmy, 122, 133-134, 137, 140, 172
Carteret, Sir George, 44
Carthaginians, 233
Case-Zablocki Act (1972), 135
Casey, Planned Parenthood of Southeastern Pennsylvania v. (1992), 170
Castro, Fidel, 137
Catechism of the Catholic Church, 2, 8, 10, 12, 59
Catherine of Aragon, 31
Catholic Church, 1-2, 13-14, 17, 28, 31, 35, 39, 42-43, 57, 59, 85, 128, 172, 174, 185, 190, 202, 211-216, 232-233, 236, 249, 252-253, 255, 259, 261, 263, 267
  social teaching of, 1, 12, 114, 212, 214, 231, 233, 263, 267
Catholics, 1, 11, 19-20, 23, 31-35, 39, 41-44, 59-60, 68-69, 85, 163, 172, 174, 185, 196, 201-202, 216, 222, 232, 242, 249, 253, 255, 259, 261-262
Cato (Anti-Federalist writer), 73
Cattle, 13, 151
Caucus, 88, 264
Cause of action, 150, 153-154, 168
Celts, 22
Censure, 89
Census, 82-83, 101, 125, 207
Census Office, 125
Central Intelligence Agency (CIA),

INDEX

125-126, 136-137
Centralization of power, 26, 58-59, 62-63, 66, 68, 71, 73-75, 114, 177, 212, 214, 216-217, 221-233, 236, 240-241, 243-267
Ceremonial functions (of president), 129
Certiorari, petition for, 155
Charlemagne, 17
Charles I, King of England, 32-33, 39-40, 42, 259
Charles II, King of England, 32-34, 36, 45-46
Charter of Liberties (1100), 26-27, 51
Charter of Liberties and Privileges (New York, 1683), 45
Charter schools, 259
Charters, colonial, 37-42, 44-46, 50, 54, 56, 58, 64, 66, 178, 216, 252
Chase, Samuel, 163
Checks and balances, 11, 74-75, 80, 161, 171, 177, 218, 238, 240
Cherokee Indians, 161
Chicago, Illinois, 190, 249
Chief Executive (President), 117, 140
Chief Justice, 34, 45, 95, 149, 155-157, 161, 164-165, 171, 173, 224, 233
Chief Legislator (President), 117
Child labor, 98
Children, 4-6, 32-33, 37, 39, 42, 111, 147, 169-170, 185, 204, 214, 227, 231, 234, 252-259
China, 74, 100, 133-134, 151, 212, 233
Chisholm, Alexander, 168
Christianity/Christians, 23, 25, 37-38, 40-43, 45, 59, 85, 148, 172, 185-186, 231-232, 255, 259, 267
Chrysostom, St. John, 3
Church, The, 1, 14, 17, 23, 25-28, 31, 33, 39, 41-45, 59-60, 114, 128, 148, 172, 185-186, 202, 204, 211-215, 221, 230, 232-233, 236, 249, 252-253, 255, 259, 263
  and state, separation of, 59, 148, 185-186
Cicero, 14, 22
Cincinnatus, 121-122
Circuit courts, See Appellate courts
Citizen legislator, 243
Citizenship, 5, 12, 22, 29, 32, 38, 41, 44-45, 48, 50, 57, 63, 77, 81, 83-84, 90, 95, 99-100, 105-107, 109, 117-120, 122, 128, 136, 140-142, 145, 147, 150-151, 153, 160-161, 168, 170-171, 177, 181, 189, 192-195, 201, 203, 205-209, 211, 213, 215-219, 221, 223, 225-227, 229, 235, 238-239, 241, 243, 245, 247-

250, 252-255, 257-264, 267
City manager, 247-248
City of Boerne v. Flores (1997), 225-226
City of God (St. Augustine), 10-11, 22, 267
Civil law, 24-25, 28, 30, 34, 41, 55, 85, 97, 135, 141-142, 149-151, 156, 167, 177, 180, 199, 206, 226, 244
Civil rights, 60, 143, 168, 185, 223
Civil Rights Act (1964), 223
Civil Rights Movement, 223
Civil servants, 125-127
Civil Service Commission, 127
Civil War, American (1861-1865), 33, 101, 111, 117, 180, 214, 222, 234, 243, 254
Civil War, English (1642-1649), 20, 31, 33, 43
Clarendon, Assize of (1166), 34
Clarendon, Constitutions of (1164), 27
Clark, U.S. v. (1878), See *Wilkerson v. Utah*
Classical languages, 260
Cleveland, Grover, 121
Cleveland, Ohio, 258
Climate change, 135
Clinton, Bill, 90, 118, 122, 131, 140, 262
Clinton, Hillary, 83, 121, 262
Clinton v. City of New York (1998), 131
Cloture, 84
Coast Guard, U.S., 136
Code of Federal Regulations, 80
Code of Hammurabi, 11
Codex (Roman Law), 25
Coercion, 8, 212-213, 215, 224, 228, 264
Coercive federalism, 228, 230
Coke, Edward, 192
Cold War, 227
Colonial charters, See Charters, colonial
Colorado, 185, 243
Columbus, Ohio, 258
Commander-in-Chief (President), 103, 117, 138
Commerce, 22, 37, 45-46, 61, 63, 66-67, 71, 93-99, 130, 133, 142-143, 181, 204, 222-223, 225-227, 242, 249
Commerce Clause, 96-99, 223, 225-226, 266
  dormant/negative, 98
Commerce, Department of, 124
Commissions, federal, 126-127, 163-164, 261

Committees, Congressional, 86-88, 90-91, 129, 137, 143, 173-174, 177
  Appropriations, 88
  Conference, 90
  Intelligence, 88, 137
  Judiciary, 88, 173-174, 177
  Rules, 88, 90
Common good, 8-10, 12-15, 19, 21, 57, 61, 76, 114, 120, 212, 214, 230-231, 261
Common law, 23, 26, 40, 43, 45, 51, 55, 60, 65, 152, 157, 187-188, 195-198, 200, 252
Communism, 13, 21, 59, 104-105, 133, 136-137, 151, 181, 212, 227
Community, 2-3, 7-10, 12, 14-20, 22-24, 39, 41, 46, 57, 59-60, 66, 76-77, 105, 108, 114, 122, 125, 136, 160, 200, 212-213, 216, 221, 232-233, 236, 243, 247-248, 258, 260, 262-264, 267
Compendium of the Social Doctrine of the Church, 212-214, 231
Compromise
  Connecticut (Great Compromise), 69
  Missouri (1820), 165-166, 234
  Three-Fifths, 70
Comstock Act (1873), 102, 141-142
Concord, Massachusetts, 52
Concordat of London (1107), 27
Confederacy (Confederate States of America), 138
Confederation, 58, 61-62, 64, 66, 68, 71, 73, 94, 103, 109, 148, 160, 167, 216
Conference committee (Congressional), 90-91
Confession (Sacrament of), 143
Confiscation of property, 10, 16, 27, 31, 200, 214
Confrontation clause, 198
Congress (U.S.), 28-29, 32-38, 40-43, 45-50, 52-55, 58-59, 61-77, 79-90, 92-114, 117, 119, 121-123, 125-126, 128-145, 148-149, 152-153, 155-158, 160-174, 177-190, 193, 200-209, 211, 217-220, 222-230, 234, 238, 240-243, 245, 251, 258-259, 261, 265-267
  First Continental (1774), 49-52
  Second Continental (1775-1781), 52-55
  Stamp Act (1765), 47-49, 51
Congressional districts, 82-83, 258-259
Congressional Record, 88-89
Connecticut, 41, 44, 65, 69, 97, 169, 200, 246

U.S. Government for Catholic Students 273

Conscience, freedom of, 35, 46, 57-58, 179, 183, 240
Consent of the governed, 17-18, 50, 57, 59-60, 106, 144, 168, 194, 217, 234, 240, 245, 259
Constitution (English), 48, 50
Constitution (U.S.), 1, 28, 34, 36, 42, 48, 50, 53, 57-59, 61-77, 79-90, 92-97, 99-103, 105, 108-111, 113-114, 117-118, 121-123, 125-126, 128-132, 134-135, 138-146, 148-174, 176-209, 211, 214-222, 224-229, 233-236, 238-242, 245-253, 255-264, 267
Constitutional Convention (1787), 54, 61, 68-69, 72-73, 100, 105, 117-119, 129, 141, 148, 152, 178, 211, 234, 238-239, 267
Constitutional courts, 148
Consuls, 84, 132, 153, 164
Continental currency, 66-67
Contraception, 102, 141, 169
Contracts, 8, 22, 112, 150, 153, 178, 235
Contract with America, 262
Conventions, ratifying, 74, 100, 105, 163, 179, 183, 208, 239
Cooper, Thomas, 163
Copley, Sir Lionel, 46
Coroner, 248
Corporal punishment, 5
Corporate theory of government, 16
Corruption, 11, 90, 128, 140, 149, 212, 214, 230, 243, 260, 264
Cotton, 74
Council of Arles (314), 23
Counterfeiting, 67, 101, 160
Counties, 24, 26, 29, 51, 168, 217, 238, 245-248, 251, 253
County clerk, 248
County executive, 247
County ordinances, 247
County seat, 246
Court packing, 101, 155, 171-172
Court of Appeals, See Appellate courts
Court of King's Bench, 34-36
Court of Military Appeals, 149
Court of Veterans Appeals, 149
Covert actions, 88, 136-137
COVID-19 pandemic, 75, 139, 241
Creativity, 10, 130, 249
Crime/Criminals, 7, 11-13, 21, 24-26, 28, 30, 41, 45, 56, 58, 65, 67, 80, 85, 89-90, 94, 97, 101-102, 106-107, 112, 114, 135, 140-142, 145, 148-151, 156, 160, 163, 165, 168, 179-180, 184, 187-189, 192, 194-202, 206, 213, 220, 222-223, 225-226, 232, 235, 239-242, 244, 246-248, 254, 262, 264-266
Crimes Act (1790), 141, 148
Criminal law, 24-25, 28, 34, 48, 97, 140-142, 145, 147, 149-151, 156, 160, 163, 180-181, 183, 192, 195-197, 199-200, 202, 206, 213, 226, 235, 241, 244, 247-248, 266
Cromwell, Oliver, 33
Cross examination, 22, 180, 198
Cruel and unusual punishment, 36, 41, 64, 199, 201, 205
Cuba, 137
Culture, 4, 74, 221, 232-233, 255
Currency, 47, 61, 66-67, 96, 101
Cushing, Cardinal Richard, 172
Customs (traditions), 8-9, 16, 18, 20, 22-26, 28-30, 39, 43-44, 58, 101, 152, 215-216, 238
Cyberwarfare, 125

D

Dakota Territory, 261
Danes, 23, 26
Danbury Baptist Church, 185
David, King of Israel, 15
Davis, Gray, 263
Davis, Kim, 248
Day of Prayer and Thanksgiving, 129, 138, 165
Dean, John, 144
Death penalty, See Capital punishment
Debasement of currency, See Counterfeiting
Debt, national, 66-67, 92-93, 95, 99, 101, 206, 249-250
Declaration of Independence (U.S.), 36, 50-51, 55-61, 68, 163, 171
Declaration of Right (English, 1689), 35-36, 51
Declaration of Rights (Massachusetts, 1780), 178
Declaration of Rights (Stamp Act Congress, 1765), 48-49
Declaration of Rights (Virginia, 1776), 178-179, 184
Declaration of the Causes and Necessity of Taking Up Arms (1775), 53, 78
Declaration of the Rights of Man and Citizen (French, 1789), 211
Declaratory Act (1766), 48
Deep state, 127
Defamation, 187-188
Defense Department, See Department of Defense
Defense Intelligence Agency, 136
Delaware, 40, 44-45, 55, 66, 82, 119, 258, 261
Demagogues, 15

Democracy, 15-16, 21, 57, 60-61, 71, 73, 77, 81, 171, 211-212, 221, 238, 260
Democratic Party, 83, 86, 149, 163, 172-174, 249, 261-262, 266
Democratic-Republican Party, 86, 163, 244
Demonstrative evidence, 152
Dennison, Kentucky v. (1861), 235
Department of Agriculture, 124
Department of Commerce, 124
Department of Defense, 123, 136
Department of Education, 124, 214, 254
Department of Energy, 124, 136
Department of Health & Human Services (HHS), 124, 142
Department of Homeland Security, 124, 132
Department of Housing and Urban Development, 124
Department of Interior, 124
Department of Justice, 106, 123, 125, 147, 179, 266
Department of Labor, 124
Department of State, 123, 133, 135-136, 163-164
Department of Transportation, 124
Department of Treasury, 25, 93-94, 112, 123, 126, 136
Department of Veterans Affairs, 124
Department of War, See Department of Defense
Deportation, 100
Despotism, 59, 218, 234
Detroit, Michigan, 249, 258
Deukmejian, George, 108
Dickinson, John, 111
Dictatorship, 15, 21, 121-122, 131
Digest (Roman Law), 25
Dignitas Infinita, 204
Dillinger, John, 266
Dinwiddie, Robert, 47
Diplomacy/Diplomats, 84, 117, 125, 132-135, 144, 153, 162, 164
Direct evidence, 152
Director of National Intelligence, 136
Disability, 206-207, 209, 231
Discharge petition, 86
Discovery (legal), 150
Discrimination, 41, 66, 97, 126, 143, 147, 152, 181, 184-186, 204, 233, 235, 242, 253, 256-258
  racial, 143, 147, 152, 185, 204, 253, 256-258
  religious, 126, 143, 185, 204, 259
District courts (federal), 148-149, 154-155, 158, 167, 224, 227, 241, 258
District courts (state), 244

District of Columbia, 45, 109-110, 119, 124, 155, 163, 169, 173, 190, 200, 208, 249
District of Columbia v. Heller (2008), 158, 190
Divine Law, 14
Divine Right of Kings, 32
Divorce, 235
Dobbs v. Jackson Women's Health Organization (2022), 227
Dockyards, 109-110
Dole, South Dakota v. (1987), 228-229
Domestic violence, 234
Donnelly, Lynch v. (1984), 159
Double jeopardy, 195-196
Dover, Massachusetts, 253
Draft, military, 57, 67, 85, 106, 108, 140, 201
Dred Scott v. Sandford (1856), 165-166, 171-172, 222
Drug Enforcement Administration (DEA), 136
Drugs, illegal, 193-194, 200, 202, 227
Drunk driving, 90
Due process, 22, 57, 95, 141, 177, 180-182, 188, 195, 197, 203, 206
Duke of Brunswick (King George I), 37
Duke of York (King James II), 44-45
Dulles, Trop v. (1958), 201
Dutch, 37, 44-45, 47

E

East Jersey, 44
Ecclesiastical courts, 27
Economic boycott, 50
Economy, 10, 46, 66-67, 74, 99, 101, 111, 123, 125, 137, 200, 212, 249-250, 262
Education, 6, 14, 22, 42, 65, 124, 186, 214, 231, 239-240, 242, 249, 251-260, 267
    Catholic, 42, 252-253, 255, 259
    Department of, See Department of Education
    public, 148, 172, 204, 214, 239, 243, 251-260
Edward I, King of England, 24, 26, 29
Edward III, King of England, 29
Edward VI, King of England, 24, 26, 31
Edward the Confessor, King of England, 26
Egbert, King of Wessex, 23
Egypt, 134
Eisenhower, Dwight D., 118, 129, 137, 228

Elections, 15, 29, 38-39, 42-43, 48, 55, 59-60, 62, 66, 70-72, 77, 81-87, 89, 100, 118-122, 130-131, 149, 160, 163, 172-173, 205-209, 223-224, 235, 238-240, 242-243, 245-249, 252-254, 257, 259-264, 267
Electoral College, 71, 118-122
Elizabeth I, Queen of England, 32
Ellsberg, Daniel, 189
Ellsworth, Oliver, 141
Emancipation Proclamation (1863), 138
Eminent domain, 197
Engel v. Vitale (1962), 148, 172, 185
England/English, 7, 13, 19-20, 22-56, 58, 60, 65-67, 71, 74, 78, 81-82, 88-90, 92, 101, 103, 106, 111-112, 117, 133, 135, 151-152, 157, 160, 163, 171, 178, 180, 187, 189-190, 192, 196, 200-201, 216, 235, 246, 248, 252, 255, 260, 264
Enclave Clause, 109-111
Endangered Species Act (1973), 262
Energy, Department of, See Department of Energy
Enumerated powers (of Congress), 66, 73, 75, 78-80, 92-96, 99, 102, 109-111, 149, 211, 225
Environmental Protection Agency (EPA), 125
Episcopalian Church, 174
Equal footing doctrine, 64-65
Equal Protection Clause, 181, 203-204, 226, 253, 256-257
Equality, 12, 56, 59-62, 118, 203-204, 215, 221, 254
Espionage, See Spying
Espionage Act (1917), 187
Espinoza v. Montana Dept. of Revenue (2020), 186, 259
Establishment Clause, 183, 185-186
Ethnic minorities, 85, 254
Euclid, Ohio, 264
Euthanasia, 159
Evangelium Vitae (Pope John Paul II), 12-13
Everett, Edward, 220
Evidence, 4, 14, 22, 33, 64, 150-152, 154, 181, 185, 192-193, 196
Ex post facto law, 28, 169, 178
Exclusionary Rule, 152, 192-193
Exclusion Controversy/Crisis (England), 33-34, 45
Executive agreements, 132, 134-135
Executive branch (federal), 62-63, 69, 71, 73, 75, 80, 85, 90, 103, 112-113, 116-174, 177-178, 180-181, 183-185, 187, 195, 206-209, 224, 227-236, 238-267

Executive branch (state), 238, 240-241, 244
Executive committee (under Articles of Confederation), 62-63, 71, 122
Executive Office of the President (EOP), 124-125
Executive orders, 117, 137-139, 183
Executive privilege, 143-145, 241
Exigent circumstances (exception to search warrant), 194
Explosives Act (1917), 189
Exports, 29, 48, 67, 71, 74, 97, 207
Extradition, 63, 235
Extradition Clause, 235

F

Family, 3-6, 7-8, 10, 14, 118, 152, 190, 214-216, 218, 221, 233-234, 254, 258, 268
Federal Bureau of Investigation (FBI), 136, 226, 266
Federal court jurisdiction, 153
Federal Courts, 95, 149, 152-154, 157-159, 161-164, 166-168, 170, 173, 178, 181, 184, 186-187, 193-194, 198-199, 201, 203-204, 219-220, 223, 225-230, 232-234, 241-246, 248, 250, 253, 258-259, 261, 263
Federal districts, 154, 158
Federal Election Commission, 126
Federal government, 1, 8, 61-77, 80-83, 86, 88, 92-115, 117-118, 122, 124-128, 130-146, 147-174, 178-195, 197, 199, 201-204, 206, 208, 211-236, 238, 240-244, 246-267
Federal judicial districts, 154
Federal judiciary, 148-149, 154, 163
Federal question jurisdiction, 153
Federal regulations, 80, 110
Federal Reserve Board ("the Fed"), 126
Federalism, 73, 211-212, 217, 221-224, 226-232, 234-236, 241-243, 245
Federalist Papers, The, 1, 69, 73-77, 81, 84, 86, 88, 92-94, 96-97, 103-107, 110, 114, 128, 133, 143, 148, 152, 156-157, 160, 162, 164-167, 171-172, 176, 178-188, 191-197, 208, 215-218, 220-236, 238-239, 241-242, 245, 247, 252, 256, 259-263, 265-270, 272-273
Federalists, 69, 73-75, 77, 86, 92, 94, 97, 99-100, 105, 107, 163, 167-168, 176, 178-179, 181-183, 185, 187, 216-236, 238-239, 241-243, 245, 247, 252, 256, 259-263, 265-270, 272-273
Felony, 30, 63, 68, 89, 102, 141, 191,

196, 201, 235
Fetal Heartbeat and Protection from Abortion Act (South Carolina), 246, 264
Fifth Amendment, 28, 180, 184, 195-197, 201
Filibuster, 84
Filburn, Roscoe, 98, 223, 226
Fines, 12, 28, 33, 84, 89, 98, 142, 184, 197, 199-201, 205, 215, 244, 249
First Amendment, 28, 75, 102, 163, 177, 179, 181-194, 197-198, 200-206, 208, 210-215, 221, 233, 237, 249, 255-256, 259-272
First Continental Congress, 49-52, 215
FitzSimons, Thomas, 69
Flat tax, 250
Florida, 46, 67, 120-121, 125, 210, 232, 249
Food and Drug Administration (FDA), 125, 142, 146
Ford, Gerald, 172
Foreign policy, 117, 123, 129, 132-134, 136-137, 140
Fortesque, Sir John, 30-31, 51
Fourteenth Amendment, 99, 170, 174, 181-182, 185-186, 188-191, 194, 203-204, 206, 210, 226, 230, 258, 261
Fourth Amendment, 184, 191-195
France, 34, 37, 46-47, 50, 53, 96, 100, 103, 111, 137, 163, 211, 215, 219, 221
Franchise, 38, 43
Franklin, Benjamin, 61, 66, 68-71, 73, 124, 215, 218, 267, 272
Free exercise clause (First Amendment), 183, 185-186, 190
Free Rider Problem, 230
Freedom of conscience, 46, 57-58, 179, 181, 183-184
Freedom of contract, 178
Freedom of opinion, 183, 221
Freedom of religion, 26, 32, 38, 40-46, 59, 64, 176, 178-179, 181-186, 190, 208, 225, 233
Freedom of speech, 75, 92, 159, 176, 178-179, 181-183, 186-188, 191-192, 208
Freedom of the press, 75, 178-179, 183, 189
French and Indian War, 47, 50
French Revolution, 100, 211, 215, 219
Fugitive Slave Act, 222
Fugitive Slave Clause (Art. IV, Sec. 2, Cl. 3), 222
Full Faith and Credit Clause (Art. IV, Sec. 1), 63, 235, 241
Fundamental Orders of Connecticut (1639), 41
Fundamental rights, 59, 159, 181-182, 186, 191, 200-201, 204, 225
Fundamental Constitutions of Carolina, The, 46, 51

G

Garland, Merrick, 246, 259
Gas tax, 232, 250
General Assembly (Virginia), 38-39
General Welfare Clause (Art. I, Sec. 8, Cl. 1), 61, 92-95
George I (King of England), 37
George II (King of England), 37
George III (King of England), 37, 47, 49, 53
Georgia, 46, 51, 53-54, 67, 73, 84-85, 161, 168, 210, 215, 217, 220, 226, 232, 244, 263, 267
Germanic tribes, 23
Gerry, Elbridge, 83
Gerrymander, 83, 254, 259
Gettysburg Address, 59, 129
Gingrich, Newt, 262
Ginsberg, Ruth Bader, 174
Gitlow v. New York (1925), 181, 188
Glorious Revolution (1688), 34, 37, 44
Godden v. Hales (1686), 34-35, 51, 159
Golden Rule, 56
Goldwater v. Carter (1979), 134
Gorsuch, Neil, 174
Governors, 30, 37-41, 43-44, 46-47, 68, 84, 118, 120, 126, 129, 161, 172, 210, 220, 223-224, 234-235, 238, 240-248, 250, 252, 254, 258-264, 267
Grand jury, 151, 196
Grant, Ulysses S., 118, 122
Gratian, 25
Great Depression, 98, 113
Great Lakes, 47, 64, 231
Greene, Thomas, 43
Griswold v. Connecticut (1965), 169, 173, 203
Groff v. DeJoy (2023), 185
Guarantee Clause (Art. IV, Sec. 4), 234
Gun Control Act (1968), 189
Gun Free School Zones Act, 224

H

Habeas corpus, 34, 41, 51, 64, 178
Habeas Corpus Act (1679), 34
Haire, Father Robert, 261
Hales, Sir Edward, 34-36, 51, 159
Hamilton, Alexander, 3, 9, 61, 66, 68-69, 71, 73-77, 80-81, 84, 86, 88, 92-97, 99-100, 103-108, 110, 112, 114, 117-126, 128-153, 156-157, 160-168, 171-173, 176, 178-179, 181-188, 191-197, 203, 208, 213, 215-218, 220-236, 238-239, 241-248, 252, 256, 259-263, 265-270, 272-273
Hammurabi, Code of, 11
Hancock, John, 66, 68, 210
Hardrada, Harald, 26
Harris, Kamala, 86
Harrison, Benjamin, 121
Harrison, William Henry, 118, 131
Hartford Convention (1814), 219, 241
Hayek, Friedrich von, 213
Hayes, Rutherford B., 120
Haynsworth, Clement, 146
Head of State, 117, 129, 133
Health and Human Services, U.S. Department of (HHS), 124, 142
Heart of Atlanta Motel v. United States (1964), 223, 241
Heller v. District of Columbia (2008), 158, 190
Helvidius (James Madison pen name), 103
Henry I (King of England), 20
Henry II (King of England), 27
Henry III (King of England), 29
Henry V (King of England), 30
Henry VIII (King of England), 30-31
Henry, Patrick, 54, 68, 105, 179
Heresy, 187, 220, 222
HHS, See Health and Human Services, U.S. Department of
High seas, 63, 102, 141
Hobbes, Thomas, 18-19, 215
Hobbs Act, 97, 141
Holmes, Jr., Oliver Wendell, 187
Home rule, 260, 264
Homeland Security, U.S. Department of, 124, 132
Hoover, J. Edgar, 266, 273
House of Commons (English Parliament), 29, 81, 122
House of Lords (English Parliament), 29, 81
House of Representatives (U.S. Congress)
　Bills for raising revenue, 90
　Committees, 86, 88
　Creation of, 69, 80-81
　Election of president by, 118-119
　Eligibility requirements, 83
　Impeachment power, 85
　Leadership positions (Speaker, Majority/Minority Leaders, Whips), 85-87

INDEX

Number of members/apportionment, 62, 81-82, 206
Role in treaty approval, 72, 133, 143-144
Term length, 81-82, 205
Hull, Cordell, 135
Hull, William, 128
Hull-Lothian Agreement (1940), 135
Human nature, 3-4, 7, 12, 16, 18, 211-212
Hume, David, 19

I

Iceland, 9
Illinois, 83, 98, 119-120, 166, 192
Immigration, 99-101, 241, 255
Immunity
  Congressional, 89
  Diplomatic, 134-135, 141
  Presidential, 145
  Sovereign (Eleventh Amendment), 153, 167-169
Impeachment, 85, 89, 131, 140, 145-146, 149, 171
Imperial Presidency, 146
Implied powers, 63, 94
Income tax, 222, 249-250
Incorporation doctrine (Bill of Rights), 181-182, 185-186, 188-192, 194, 199, 203-204
Indiana, 65, 119-120, 200, 205, 228
Indians, See Native Americans
Indictment, 66, 151, 196
Industrial Revolution, 30, 111-112, 260
Ineligibility Clause (Art. I, Sec. 6, Cl. 2), 90
Inheritance tax, 249-250, 273
Initiative (ballot), 260-261, 273
Innocent X (Pope), 166
Institutes (Justinian), 25, 51
Insurrection, 60, 77, 102, 105-107, 140, 206, 210, 217
Intelligence Committee (Congressional), 88
Intermediate institutions, 215, 219, 233, 241
Internal improvements, 93
International law, 68, 134
Internet, 89
Interposition, doctrine of, 217-222, 241
Interstate commerce, 96-99, 101, 141, 143, 204, 223, 227, 265-266
Intolerable Acts (1774), 49-53, 191, 216
Investiture Controversy, 27
Iowa, 250
Ireland, 33, 35, 112, 124, 170, 188, 194, 212, 217, 220-222, 252, 254-255, 258, 266, 268
Irish, 19, 22, 252, 255, 258
Israel, 15, 89, 129, 134, 137
Italians, 254
Italy, 255

J

Jackson, Andrew, 118, 120, 127, 161
Jackson, Ketanji Brown, 155, 174
Jamestown, 31, 38-40, 42
Jay, John, 69, 74, 81, 117-118, 123, 149, 152, 171
Jay Treaty (1794), 143, 162, 171
Jefferson, Thomas, 55-57, 59-62, 64, 66, 68, 86, 93, 99-100, 103-105, 111, 113, 117-119, 121, 123-124, 126-127, 129, 133, 137, 144-145, 149, 152, 163-164, 167-169, 179, 185, 187, 215, 218-220, 222, 242-243, 249, 252-254, 256, 258-259, 261-264, 266-272
Jehovah's Witnesses, 184
Jenkins, Missouri v. (1995), 257, 259
Jesuits, 43
Jesus Christ, 40-41, 45-46, 213
Jews, 11, 41, 60, 85, 174, 190
John (King of England), 27-28
John XXIII (Pope), 3
John Paul II (Pope), 12-13, 21, 59, 212, 214, 230, 263
Johnson, Andrew, 145
Johnson, Lyndon B., 125, 130
Johnson, Samuel (Dr. Johnson), 96
Joint Chiefs of Staff, 124-125
Jones Law, The, 160
Joshua (Biblical figure), 11, 136
Judges
  Appointment/Confirmation, 27, 34, 45, 49, 69, 71-73, 77, 84-85, 88, 95, 100-101, 104-105, 110, 113, 117, 120-121, 123-127, 129, 131-146, 148-174, 176-177, 179, 182-206, 208, 210-215, 217-230, 232-253, 256, 258-273
  Federal, 71-72, 77, 85, 88, 95, 100, 141, 146, 148-174, 176, 178-179, 182-208, 210-215, 217-230, 232-253, 256, 258-273
  Role in trials, 22-24, 26-28, 30-32, 34, 41-46, 48, 50-52, 56, 58, 62, 64, 68, 85, 88, 95, 100, 102, 104, 106-107, 111-112, 114, 120, 123, 125, 127-128, 131-146, 148-173, 176-215, 217-230, 232-253, 256, 258-273
  State, 148, 152-173, 176-177, 179, 181-208, 210-215, 217-230, 232-253, 256, 258-273
Judicial activism, 170, 246
Judicial Branch (U.S. Government), 127, 148, 198
Judicial review, 35, 162-167, 171
Judiciary Act of 1789, 106, 125, 148, 152, 164, 167-168, 176, 198
Judiciary Committee (Congressional), 88, 172-174, 177
Jurisdiction
  Appellate, 154-155, 159, 162, 164-165, 167, 169, 262
  Diversity, 153-154
  Federal court, 153-154, 167, 169
  Original, 154-156, 164-165, 167-169, 244
Jury trial, right to, 24, 28, 30, 41, 45, 50, 56, 58, 62, 151, 176-177, 179, 197-198, 203
Justice, 5, 9-10, 12-14, 16, 18, 23, 26, 29-31, 34, 41, 43, 49, 53, 58, 62, 67, 72, 74, 85-86, 88, 93, 95, 97, 99-102, 105-106, 110, 113-114, 123-126, 130-146, 149-174, 176-177, 179-208, 210-273
Justice, U.S. Department of, 100, 123, 125, 142-143, 179
Justices of the Peace, 75, 163
Justinian (Emperor), 25

K

Kennedy, Anthony, 173
Kennedy, John F., 118, 131
Kennedy, Joseph (football coach), 185
Kentucky Resolution, 100, 179, 218, 220
King, Martin Luther, Jr., 60, 258
Kirk, Russell, 216
Kleptocracy, 15
Knights of Labor, 112, 261
Knox, Henry, 123
Kramer v. Union Free School District (1969), 253

L

Lamont v. Postmaster General of the United States (1964), 181, 188
Land and Naval Forces Rules (Clause 14), 102
Langton, Stephen, 27, 51
Law
  Anglo-Saxon, 23-24
  Canon, 25
  Common, 9, 13, 22, 26, 43, 55, 65, 152, 187, 196, 252
  Divine Positive, 14
  Moral, 4
  Natural, 4-5, 8-10, 13-14, 25, 55, 59, 174, 190, 213

U.S. Government for Catholic Students

INDEX

Roman, 22, 24-25, 198
Law of Nations, 26, 100, 102
Lawrence v. Texas (2003), 170
Lee, Henry, 116, 140
Legal Voluntarism, 9, 21
Legislative Branch, 80-115
Legislative Courts, 149
Legislature
    Bi-cameral, 69, 242
    Unicameral, 242
Legitimacy (of government), 8, 16-20, 57, 59, 109, 161, 166, 233, 262
Leo XIII, Pope, 13, 112, 263
Letters of Marque and Reprisal, 102
Lexington and Concord, Battles of, 52, 78
Libel, 187
Liberalism, Political, 10, 12, 21, 214
Liberties
    Charter of (1100), 26-27, 51
    Massachusetts Body of, 41
Liberty, 10, 56-58, 60, 62, 64, 73, 75, 77, 80, 105, 122, 130, 160, 170, 174, 179, 181, 183-184, 192, 203, 215, 218, 234
Libido Dominandi, 11
Life, Right to, 56-58, 169, 203, 232, 237
Lincoln, Abraham, 59, 83, 117, 131, 138, 171
Line Item Veto, 131, 240
Lobbying/Lobbyists, 127-128, 230
Locke, John, 18-19, 46, 51
Long Parliament, 32
Lord Acton, 11
Louisiana Purchase, 111
Low-Level Radioactive Waste Management Act, 223
Lyman, Daniel, 219
Lynch v. Donnelly (1984), 159

M

MacIntyre, Alasdair, 267-268
Madison, James
    Alien and Sedition Acts, response to, 100, 179, 187, 217
    Articles of Confederation, 61, 66, 73, 218
    Bill of Rights, 107, 177-179, 183
    Checks and balances, 75, 218
    Commerce Clause, 93, 96-97, 101
    Constitutional Convention, 68-73, 152
    Declaration of Independence, 56-58, 60, 171
    Factions, 76-77
    Federalist Papers, author of, 10, 68, 73-77, 92-94, 97, 103-105, 107, 110-111, 152, 160, 178, 183, 216, 218, 220, 224
    Federalism, 75, 216, 218, 220
    General Welfare Clause, 92-93
    Interposition, doctrine of, 217-218, 220
    Judicial review, 152, 160, 166
    Justice, 10
    Militia, 105-107
    National Bank, opposition to, 95
    Necessary and Proper Clause, 94
    Nullification, 220
    Pardon power, 139
    Religious freedom, 179, 183
    Representation, 69-70, 82, 243
    Separation of powers, 104, 122-123
    Standing armies, 105
    Supremacy Clause, 71, 76, 218
    Term limits, opposition to, 121
    War powers, 103-104, 123
Madsen v. Women's Health Center (1994), 188
Magna Carta, 27-29, 31, 34, 39, 41, 51, 56, 60, 178, 200
Magnet Schools, 260
Mapp v. Ohio (1961), 192
Marbury v. Madison (1803), 1, 153, 163-167
Maritime Crimes (Clause 10), 102
Marriage, 4, 6, 174, 233, 235, 249
Marshall, John, 95, 161, 163-165, 170
Martial Law, 38, 49
Martin, Luther, 72, 95
Mary, Queen of England, 31-32
Maryland
    Catholic settlement, 20, 42-43, 59, 63, 68, 110, 216
    Charter, 42-43, 46
    Declaration of Rights, 184
    Ratification of Articles of Confederation, 63
    Revolution of 1689, 44
Mason, George, 68, 72-73, 105-107, 196, 243
Massachusetts
Body of Liberties, 41
Charter, 40
Circular Letter of 1768, 49
Constitution, 179, 184, 239-240
Gerrymandering, 83
Government Act (Intolerable Acts), 49
Militia, 52, 105, 107, 190
Secret Ballot, 264
Masterpiece Cakeshop v. Colorado Civil Rights Commission (2018), 185
Mayflower Compact, 40
Mayor, 215, 248-249
McCord, James W., 144

McCulloch v. Maryland (1819), 95
McDonald v. City of Chicago (2010), 190
McIntyre, Cardinal, 172
Media, 124, 131, 137, 189, 267
Merit Systems Protection Board, 127
Miyares, Jason, 242
Military
    Draft, 85, 139-140
    Industrial Complex, 129
    Militia, 23, 42-43, 65, 75, 102, 105-108, 140, 189, 219, 241, 246
    National Guard, 107-108, 241
    Standing Army, 36, 50, 105-106, 227
Miller v. California (1973), 188
Miller v. United States (1939), 189
Milliken v. Bradley (1974), 258
Ministerial Exception, 185
Minority Leader, 87-88
Miranda v. Arizona (1966), 196, 198
Miranda Warning, 196-197, 210
Missouri Compromise, 165, 238
Molasses Act (1733), 47
Monarchy, 15, 21, 33, 35, 40-41, 60, 81, 105, 133, 137, 267
Money
    Coining of, 8, 37, 63, 67, 101
    Counterfeiting, 101, 160
    Printing of, 66, 101, 115
Monroe Doctrine, 130
Monroe, James, 130, 135, 152
Montesquieu, Charles-Louis de Secondat, Baron de, 211, 213, 217, 221
Montgomery Amendment, 108
Moot (shire, people's, volk), 24, 26-29, 51
Moral Majority, 232, 237
Moral Subjectivism, 18, 21, 214
More, St. Thomas, 30-31, 149
Morris, Gouverneur, 268
Morrison v. United States (2000), 153, 226
Morrissey-Berru, Agnes, 185
Murphy v. National Collegiate Athletic Association (2018), 222

N

National Aeronautics and Space Administration (NASA), 125
National Bank, 94-95, 126
National Firearms Act (1934), 189
National Guard, 107-108, 241, 246
National Security Agency (NSA), 136
National Security Council (NSC), 124-125
National Security Act of 1947, 136-137

Native Americans, 38, 40, 43, 49, 53, 67, 70, 96, 107, 161, 206, 254
Natural Law, 4-5, 8-10, 13-14, 25, 55, 59, 174, 190, 213
    and human nature, 4
    and justice, 5
    and Moral Law, 4
    precepts of, 5, 14, 21
Naturalization, 99-101
Naturalization Clause, 99-101
Navigation Acts, 46-47, 51
Navy (Clause 13), 102
Necessary and Proper Clause (Clause 18), 92, 94-96, 98, 115
Negative Commerce Clause, 98
Negligence, 150, 154
New Deal, 113, 117, 121, 155
New Hampshire Constitution, 57, 61, 78
New Jersey
    Charter or Fundamental Laws of West New Jersey, 44
    Concessions and Agreements of the Proprietors of East Jersey, 44
    Constitution, 55
    Ratification of Constitution, 73
New York
    Charter of Liberties and Privileges, 45
    Constitution, 184
    Declaration of Independence, 55, 78
    Ratification of Constitution, 73-74
    Restraining Act, 48-49
New York v. United States (1992), 223-224
Nicholas, George, 100, 179
Nieves v. Bartlett (2019), 195
Nineteenth Amendment, 203, 207
Ninth Amendment, 177, 181, 203, 208
Nixon, Richard, 104, 135, 144-146, 152
Non-Aggression Principle, 212-214
Non-Delegation Doctrine, 113, 115
Norman Conquest, 26, 30
North Atlantic Treaty Organization (NATO), 103, 132
Northwest Ordinance, 64-65, 78, 111, 184
Northwest Territory, 64-65, 78, 111
Nullification, 217, 219-220, 266

O

Obama, Barack, 105, 118, 262
Obergefell v. Hodges (2015), 232-233, 235
Obscenity, 102, 187-188
O'Connor, Sandra Day, 172-173, 226
Office of Management and Budget (OMB), 124-125
Oligarchy, 15
Olive Branch Petition, 53, 78
Omaha Platform, 261
Onís, Luis de, 133
Open Enrollment (schools), 260
Organic Theory of Government, 16, 18, 21
Original Jurisdiction, 153-155, 162, 164-165, 167-168
Osgood, Samuel, 122, 124
Our Lady of Guadalupe School v. Morrissey-Berru (2020), 185

P

Pacem in Terris, 3, 13
Paine, Thomas, 35
Papendrecht, Jan Hoynck van, 35
Pardon Power, 139-140
Parker, John, 52
Parliament (English)
    Alien and Sedition Acts and, 100
    American colonies and, 46-47, 49-50, 53-54
    Checks on power of, 30
    Civil wars and, 31-33
    Colonial charters and, 178
    Declaration of Right and, 36
    Described, 29
    First Continental Congress and, 50
    Glorious Revolution and, 35
    Gun control and, 190
    Habeas Corpus Act and, 34
    Investiture Controversy and, 27
    Judicial review and, 160
    King Charles I and, 32-33
    King James II and, 35
    Magna Carta and, 28-29
    Maryland Assembly and, 43
    Origins of, 29
    Quebec Act and, 49-50
    Self-incrimination and, 196
    Separation of powers and, 122
    Speech or Debate Clause and, 90
    Stamp Act and, 47-48
    Supremacy of, 36-37, 50, 218
    Taxation and, 29, 32, 48-49
    Third Amendment and, 191
    Townshend Acts and, 48-49
    Unfunded mandates and, 229
Parochial schools, 255
Paschal II, Pope, 27
Patriarchy, 6
Paul VI, Pope St., 204, 257
Paul, St. (Apostle)
    Authority of government, 59
    Marriage and, 6
    Organic theory of government and, 16
    Roman Law and, 22
Paulet, William, 31
Peace, as common good, 12
Penn, William, 45
Pennsylvania
    Annapolis Convention and, 66
    Constitutional Convention (1787) and, 68, 73
    Described, 45
    Hartford Convention and, 219
    Quebec Act and, 50
    State legislature, 243
Pentagon Papers, 189
People's Party (Populist Party), 261
Perpich, Rudy, 108
Perpich v. Department of Defense (1990), 108
Perugino, Pietro, 6
Peter, St. (Apostle), 25
Petition, right to, 36, 41, 50, 182-183
Philadelphia, 50, 54, 66, 68-69, 233, 249
Pickering, Timothy, 219
Pierce v. Society of the Sisters of the Holy Names of Jesus and Mary (1925), 255-256
Pilgrimage of Grace, 31
Pinckney, Charles, 72
Pinker, Steven, 4
Pitt the Younger (William Pitt), 117
Pius IX, Pope Bl., 13
Pius XI, Pope, 212
Plain view doctrine, 193
Planned Parenthood of Southeastern Pennsylvania v. Casey (1992), 170
Plato
    Government purpose and, 9-10
    Interposition and, 230
    Natural Law and, 14
    Organic theory of government and, 16
Plessy v. Ferguson (1896), 171, 256
Plymouth, 39-40
Pocket veto, 90
Police power, 73, 213
Political liberalism, 10, 12
Political parties, 33, 86-87, 119
Pollock, Sir Frederick, 24, 26
Polls/Public opinion, 226-227, 229, 258
Polygamy, 184
Pope (Papacy)
    Authority of, 21, 26, 31, 40, 44, 100-273
    Church establishment and, 25, 185
    Legitimacy of rulers and, 17-18
Populism, 260-263

Posner, Richard, 141
Posse Comitatus, 106-107
Postal Department/Post Office/Postal Service, 94, 101, 110, 123-124, 141
Postmaster General, 101, 124, 181, 188
Powel, Elizabeth Willing, 267-268
Prayer in school, 148, 172, 262
Preamble (U.S. Constitution), 239
Precedent (legal concept), 154-155, 157-159, 191, 202, 204, 224, 227
President (U.S.)
   Administrative Procedures Act and, 113, 138
   Appointment power, 71, 84, 123, 125-126, 132, 140, 149, 153, 226, 240, 248, 254
   Budget and, 125, 130
   Cabinet, 123-124, 129, 132
   Checks on power of, 71, 122, 130
   Chief Diplomat, 117, 132-134, 136
   Chief Executive, 71, 117, 140, 146
   Chief Legislator, 117, 146
   Commander-in-Chief, 103, 117, 138, 146
   Congress and, 80, 84, 89, 103-105, 113, 118, 122-123, 125-126, 129-146, 148-273
   Covert actions and, 136-137
   Election of, 71, 118-121, 205
   Executive Agreements, 134-135
   Executive Orders, 137-139
   Executive Privilege, 143-145
   Faithful execution of laws, 80, 123, 140-142
   Foreign policy and, 103, 123, 129, 132-135, 140
   Head of State, 117, 129-130, 133
   Immunity, 145
   Impeachment of, 85, 140, 145-146, 149, 153, 171
   "Imperial" Presidency, 146
   Line of succession, 86, 131-132, 209
   Pardon power, 71, 139-140
   Qualifications for, 117-118
   Regulations and, 80, 95, 110, 113, 118, 138, 142, 228, 240
   Spying and, 136
   State of the Union Address, 130-131
   Term of office, 121-122, 208
   Veto power, 30, 63, 69, 71, 80, 90, 130-131, 240, 243
   War powers, 102-105
President pro tempore (Senate), 85-87, 132, 209

Press, freedom of the, 179, 182-183, 187, 189
Prime Minister (British), 37, 62, 117, 122
Printz v. United States (1997), 225
Privacy, right to, 169-170, 185, 191, 203
Private property
   Common good and, 13
   Fifth Amendment and, 180, 195
   Protection of, 12-13, 54, 180
   Privileges and Immunities Clause
   Articles of Confederation, 63
   Described, 235
   Fourteenth Amendment, 181
Probable cause, 192, 194, 200
Procedural rights, 181
Progressive Era/Progressivism, 98, 111-113, 222, 260, 265, 269
Prohibition (of alcohol), 207, 265-266
Property Clause (Article IV, Sec. 3), 109-111
Property qualifications (voting/office), 29, 64, 250
Property rights, 12-13, 41, 54, 57, 180, 191, 195, 235
Property tax, 249-251
Proportional representation, 29, 62, 64, 87, 118-119
Providence Agreement, The (1637), 40-41
Public defender, 150, 198
Public good, 13, 146
Publius (pen name), 74
Puritans, 32-33, 39-41, 43, 45, 73

Q

Quadragesimo Anno, 212
Quakers (Society of Friends), 45
Quartering Act (1765/1774), 48-49, 58, 191
Quebec Act (1774), 49-50
Qui Pluribus, 13
Quorum, 89, 205-206

R

Racial discrimination/segregation, 56, 146, 152-153, 170-172, 204, 243, 253, 256-259
Raleigh, Walter, 198
Randolph, Edmund, 68, 73, 105, 123-124, 179, 243
Ranked choice voting, 85
Rawls, John, 118
Reagan, Ronald
   Appointments by, 173, 226
   Bureaucracy and, 111, 125, 260
   Covert actions and, 137
   Farewell Address, 130

   Federalism and, 223
   Populism and, 262
   Treaties and, 134
Recall (of elected officials), 263
Recess (Congressional), 89
Redistricting, 83, 258
Referendum, 260-261, 264
Regulations (federal)
   Administrative Procedures Act and, 113, 138, 142
   Bureaucracy and, 112-113, 142, 229-230
   Congress vs. Executive, 80, 110, 112-113, 138, 142, 146
   Described, 80
   Environmental, 231, 262
   Judicial review of, 241
   Number of, 80
   State attorneys general and, 242
Rehnquist, William, 224, 226
Religion, freedom of
   Bill of Rights and, 179-186
   Catholic Church and, 233
   Colonial charters and, 38, 41-46, 178, 183, 216
   Compelling interest test, 183, 185
   Establishment Clause, 183, 185-186
   Free Exercise Clause, 183-186
   Government support for religion and, 12, 59, 129, 172, 186, 231-232, 259
   Limits on, 184
   Ministerial Exception, 185
   Northwest Ordinance and, 64, 184
   Prayer in school and, 148, 172, 262
   Separation of Church and State, 59, 148, 185-186
Religious Freedom Restoration Act (RFRA), 225
Republic (form of government)
   American system as, 15, 54, 77, 163, 212, 238, 267
   Distinguished from democracy, 15, 77, 212
   Guarantee Clause and, 234
Republic, The (Plato), 10, 16
Republican Party, 83, 86-87, 101, 131, 172-174, 249, 261-262, 265
Rerum Novarum, 13, 112, 263
Reserved powers (Tenth Amendment), 62, 67, 75, 187, 203, 211, 218, 222, 225-226
Revenue Act of 1767, 48
Revere, Paul, 49
Revolving door (lobbying), 128
Reynolds, George, 184
Reynolds v. U.S. (1878), 184

Rhode Island
  Colonial government, 41
  Constitutional Convention (1787) and, 68
  Counties in, 246
  Declaration of Independence and, 54
  Judicial tenure in, 245
  Ratification of Constitution and, 217
  State constitution, 239
Right to Counsel, 180, 195, 198
Roads/Highways, 22, 93, 101, 228, 247, 250
Roberts, John (Chief Justice), 155, 174, 233
Roberts, Owen, 222-223
Robespierre, Maximilien, 35
Robinson v. California (1962), 201
Rockefeller, John D., 111-112
Roe v. Wade (1973), 169, 171-173, 256
Roman Law
  American law and, 22
  Anglo-Saxon law and, 24-26
  Canon Law and, 25
  Confrontation Clause and, 198
Roosevelt, Franklin D.
  Administrative state and, 113, 233
  Court packing plan, 155, 171
  Executive agreements and, 135
  Executive Orders by, 138
  Executive Office of the President, 124
  Populism and, 261-262
  Term of office, 122
  Vice President Truman and, 131
Roosevelt, Theodore
  "Bully pulpit" and, 129
  Executive Orders by, 138
  Judicial review and, 171
  Militia/National Guard and, 108
  Presidential qualifications and, 118
  Term of office, 122
Rotten boroughs, 30, 65
Rousseau, Jean-Jacques, 18
Ruby Ridge, Idaho, 226
Ruffner, William Henry, 254
Rules Committee (House/Senate), 88, 90
Run-off elections, 85
Rutledge, John, 146, 171

S

Sedition Act (1798), 100, 163, 179, 182, 187
Sales tax, 249-250
Sanders, Bernie, 262
Sanford, John, 166

Scalia, Antonin
  Appointment of, 173-174
  Bill of Rights and, 177
  Judicial activism and, 170
  Second Amendment and, 190
  Tenth Amendment and, 226
Schenck v. United States (1919), 178, 187
Scheidler v. National Organization for Women (2006), 97
Schilb v. Kuebel (1971), 199
School choice, 259-260
School districts/boards, 238, 252-254, 256-259
School prayer, 148, 172, 262
Schwarzenegger, Arnold, 263
Scott, Dred, 165-166, 171
Search and seizure (Fourth Amendment), 180, 191-195
Search incident to arrest, 194
Search warrant, 149, 191-194
Second Amendment, 183, 189-191
Second Continental Congress, 52-55
Secret ballot, 260, 264
Secretary of State (U.S.), 123, 132-133, 163-164, 219
Secretary of State (state official), 240
Secretary of the Treasury (U.S.), 93-94, 123, 126
Secularism, 232
Self-defense, right to, 189-191
Self-government
  American tradition of, 20, 38, 46, 50, 53-54, 58, 66, 75, 211, 216, 234, 238, 243, 260, 267
  Colonial, 38, 42, 46, 50, 53-54, 58, 66, 75, 178, 216
Self-incrimination, privilege against (Fifth Amendment), 195-197
Semayne's Case (1604), 192
Senate (U.S.)
  Advice and Consent, 71, 84, 132-133, 144, 146, 148-150, 153-154, 160, 171-174, 177, 240, 245-246
  Composition and election, 69, 71-72, 80-81, 84, 153, 207, 234
  Filibuster and cloture, 84, 269
  Impeachment trials, 85
  Leadership (President of, President pro tempore), 85-87, 131-132, 207, 209
  Powers of, 69, 72, 84-85, 133-135, 144, 146, 148-150, 153-154, 160, 171-174, 177, 240, 245-246
  Qualifications for, 84, 117
  Treaty ratification, 72, 84-85, 132-135, 144
Separation of Church and State, 59, 148, 185-186
Separation of powers, 104, 122-123, 145, 160
Seton, St. Elizabeth Ann, 252-253
Seventh Amendment, 151, 181, 199
Seven Years' War (French and Indian War), 47, 50
Shays, Daniel, 66, 139
Shays' Rebellion, 66, 99, 139
Sheriff, 24, 49, 106, 213, 225, 246, 248
Sherman Anti-Trust Act (1890), 112
Shire, 24, 26, 106, 246
Shire moot, 24, 26
"Shot Heard Round the World", 52-53
Simony, 18
Sixth Amendment, 151, 180, 195, 197-198
Slavery
  Abolition of, 59, 65, 206, 222, 226
  Catholic Church and, 1
  Compromises at Constitutional Convention, 70-71
  Declaration of Independence and, 56, 59
  Dred Scott case and, 165-166, 171, 222
  English common law and, 65
  Fugitive Slave Clause/Act, 65, 222
  Northwest Ordinance and, 65
  Republican Party and, 86
Smith, Adam, 35
Social contract theory, 18-20, 54
Social Security Administration (SSA), 125
Social teachings (Catholic), 1, 12, 212, 233, 267, 272
Sons of Liberty, 48-49
Sophocles, 10
Sotomayor, Sonia, 174
Souter, David, 124, 173
South Carolina
  Calhoun and Nullification Crisis, 220
  Chisholm v. Georgia and, 168
  Colonial government (Carolina), 46
  Constitutional Convention (1787) and, 72
  Judicial selection, 245
  State constitution, 184
  State Supreme Court and abortion, 246
  Taxation and, 67
South Dakota, 119, 261
Sovereignty
  Colonial, 38, 42, 45-46, 50, 54-55, 62, 66-67, 71, 75, 211,

216-217, 222-273
   Defined, 18, 71, 211
   Of states, 20, 50, 54-55, 58, 62-63, 66-68, 71-73, 75-76, 167, 217-222, 224, 226-227
   Popular, 54, 60, 62
Sowell, Thomas, 128
Spain/Spanish, 31, 46-47, 59, 67, 129, 133, 233, 262
Speaker of the House, 85-88, 90, 132, 209, 219
Speech, freedom of
   Bill of Rights and, 178-179, 181-183, 187-188
   Compelling interest test, 182, 188
   Content-based restrictions, 188
   Expressive conduct, 188
   Limits on (obscenity, defamation, true threats, incitement), 187-188
   Sedition Act and, 100, 163, 179, 182, 187
   Taxing power and, 92
   Time, place, and manner restrictions, 188
Speedy trial, right to, 41, 180, 197-198
Spellman, Cardinal, 172
Spoils System, 127
Spying, 88, 136-137, 227
Stamp Act (1765), 47-48, 58, 92, 182, 198
Stamp Act Congress (1765), 48
Standard Oil, 111
Standing army, 36, 41, 50, 105-107, 227
Stare decisis, 158-159
State constitutions, 54-55, 61, 64, 167, 181, 183-184, 186, 203-204, 210, 238-240, 246, 249, 260-261, 264
State Department (U.S.), 123, 135-136
State of the Union Address, 130-131
States' rights, 217-218, 222
Statutory rights, 177
Stevens, John Paul, 172
Stewart, Charles, 65
Stewart, Jimmy, 84
Stewart, Potter, 173
Strict scrutiny test, 182, 185, 191, 204
Suárez, Francisco, 20
Subpoena, 88, 143-144
Subsidiarity
   Catholic teaching on, 10, 212-213, 217, 231, 234, 236, 247
   Defined, 10, 212
   Federalism and, 212, 216-217, 231, 234, 236, 247

Local government and, 217, 231, 234, 236, 247
Substantive due process/rights, 181
Sugar Act (1764), 47
Summa Theologica (Aquinas), 9, 11-13, 16, 18-19, 22, 28, 61, 114, 161, 165, 170, 184, 190, 202, 215, 231, 233, 263
Sununu, John, 124
Supremacy Act (English, 1534), 31, 34
Supremacy Clause (U.S. Constitution)
   Described, 71, 76, 114, 152
   Federalist Papers on, 76, 114
Supreme Court (U.S.)
   Abortion and, 146, 159, 169-174, 203, 227, 232-233, 246, 256
   Appeals to, 149, 152, 155-156, 167-168, 201, 242, 245
   Appointment of Justices, 84, 124, 126, 146, 149, 153, 155, 159, 171-174
   Bill of Rights and, 180-273
   Checks on, 161-162
   Commerce Clause and, 93, 95-99, 101-104, 204, 223-273
   Creation of, 148
   Federalism and, 223-273
   General Welfare Clause and, 93, 95
   Judicial activism/restraint, 170-171
   Judicial review, 35, 101, 162-167, 171, 182, 222
   Justices (number of, current members), 146, 149, 155-157, 171-174
   "Least dangerous branch" (Federalist 78), 159-162
   Necessary and Proper Clause and, 94-96, 98, 101
   Operation of (conferences, opinions, oral arguments), 156-157
   Original jurisdiction, 153, 155, 162, 164-165, 167-168
   Political nature of, 171-174
   Precedent and stare decisis, 155, 157-159
   School desegregation and, 256-259
   State sovereignty/Eleventh Amendment and, 153, 167-169

T

Taiwan (Republic of China), 133-134
Taiwan Relations Act, 134
Tariff Act of 1890, 112

Tariffs, 65, 71, 97, 101, 112, 220
Taxation
   Colonial protests against, 48-49, 58, 182
   Enumerated power of Congress, 92-95, 101
   Federal income tax, 222, 249
   Generally, 249-251
   Inheritance tax, 249-250
   Internal improvements and, 93
   Judicial power over, 226, 259
   Line item veto and, 131, 240
   Local government and, 244, 248-249, 251, 253, 259
   National Firearms Act and, 189
   Parliament and, 29, 32, 48-49
   Property tax, 249-251
   Sales tax, 249-250
   School funding and, 253, 255, 259
   Stamp Act, 47-48, 58, 92, 182, 198
   State income tax, 249-250
   Three-Fifths Compromise and, 70
Tea Act, 58
Tea Party Movement, 262
Tenth Amendment
   Described, 63, 75, 181, 183, 203, 211, 222-226, 228
   Federalism and, 217, 222-226, 228
Term limits, 121-122, 171, 208
Terry Search/Terry Stop, 193
Terry v. Ohio (1968), 193
Texas
   Attorney General of, 241-242
   Counties in, 247
   Electoral votes, 119
   Home rule in, 264
   National Guard, 108
   State legislature, 242
Texas v. Brown (1983), 193
Texas v. Garland (2024), 241
Thanksgiving Proclamation, 129, 138, 165
Theocracy, 15
Thirteenth Amendment, 166, 206, 222
Thomas, Clarence
   Appointment and confirmation, 173-174
   Clerkship and, 157
   Federalism and, 225-227
   Judicial philosophy, 174, 225-227
   School desegregation and, 257, 259
   Second Amendment and, 190
Thurmond, Strom, 84
Tilden, Samuel, 120
Timbs v. Indiana (2019), 200-201

INDEX

Tlaib, Rashida, 89
Tocqueville, Alexis de, 221, 233
Toleration Act (Maryland, 1649), 43-44
Tories, 33
Torture, 32, 196, 201
Town meeting, 41, 261
Town reeve, 246
Towns/Townships, 29, 41, 46, 66, 72, 168, 217, 225, 238, 240, 246-253
Townshend, Charles, 48
Townshend Acts (1767), 48-49
Trade Representative (U.S.), 125
Tragedy of the commons, 13, 21
Trail of Tears, 161
Treason, 33, 85, 90, 141, 144, 199, 201, 235
Treasury Department (U.S.), 112, 123, 126, 136
Treaties
    Checks and balances and, 72, 84-85, 132-135, 144
    Executive agreements vs., 134-135
    Federal court jurisdiction and, 153, 161-162
    Jay Treaty, 143, 162, 171
    Judicial review of, 161
    Presidential power regarding, 63, 103-104, 132-135, 143-144
    Supremacy of, 71, 76, 134
Trial by jury
    Anglo-Saxon law, 24
    Bill of Rights and, 180-181, 183
    Colonial charters and, 41, 43
    Described, 151
    Fifth Amendment and, 195-197
    Fortesque on, 30
    Magna Carta and, 28, 56
    Northwest Ordinance and, 64
    Right to, 48, 50, 56, 151, 180-181, 183, 195, 197-199, 244
    Seventh Amendment, 151, 181, 199
    Sixth Amendment, 151, 197-198
    State courts and, 244
Trinity Lutheran Church v. Comer (2017), 185-186
Troiani, Don, 53
Trop, Albert, 201
Trop v. Dulles (1958), 201
True threats (as unprotected speech), 188
Truman, Harry S., 122, 131, 138-139
Trump, Donald
    Appointments by, 174
    Electoral College and, 121
    Executive Orders by, 139
    Populism and, 262
    Presidential qualifications and, 118
    Prosecution of, 142
    Spying on, 136
    State of the Union Address and, 131
Trust (economic), 111-112, 228
Tyler, John, 131
Tyranny/Tyrant, 10-12, 15-17, 20, 57, 59, 71, 234, 263

U

Unalienable Rights, 56, 203
Unfunded Mandates Reform Act, 229
Uniform Clause, 99
Union (American), 58, 61, 63, 77, 105, 217, 219, 222
Union Jack, 54
United Colonies of North America, 54, 61
United States Constitution, 1, 28, 36, 42, 45, 50, 59, 61-64, 67-81, 83, 89-90, 92-97, 99-100, 103-107, 109, 113-114, 117-119, 121-123, 126, 128-129, 131-132, 135, 138, 140, 143, 145-146, 148-149, 152-153, 155, 157-174, 176-189, 191-195, 197-209, 211, 215-222, 224-226, 228-229, 233-236, 238-246, 248, 251-252, 255-256, 258-259, 263-264, 267
    Amendments, 1, 57, 63, 69, 72, 75, 77, 81, 85, 89, 100, 107, 131, 151, 153, 163, 166, 171, 176-209, 217, 222, 226, 229, 239, 249, 255, 258, 260, 265
    First Amendment, 28, 177, 179, 181-189
    Second Amendment, 189-191
    Third Amendment, 191
    Fourth Amendment, 191-195
    Fifth Amendment, 28, 151, 180, 195-197
    Sixth Amendment, 151, 176, 197-198
    Seventh Amendment, 151, 181, 199
    Eighth Amendment, 28, 36, 196, 199-202
    Ninth Amendment, 177, 203
    Tenth Amendment, 63, 75, 203, 211, 217, 222, 224-226, 228
    Eleventh Amendment, 153, 168, 172, 205
    Twelfth Amendment, 119, 205-206, 208
    Thirteenth Amendment, 166, 206, 222
    Fourteenth Amendment, 99, 180-182, 188, 190, 203-204, 206, 226, 258
    Fifteenth Amendment, 166, 203, 206
    Sixteenth Amendment, 207, 222
    Seventeenth Amendment, 72, 81, 84, 207, 222
    Eighteenth Amendment, 207, 212, 265-266
    Nineteenth Amendment, 171, 203, 207
    Twentieth Amendment, 89, 207-208
    Twenty-First Amendment, 207-208, 265-266
    Twenty-Second Amendment, 122, 171, 208
    Twenty-Third Amendment, 119, 208
    Twenty-Fourth Amendment, 208-209
    Twenty-Fifth Amendment, 131-132, 209
    Twenty-Sixth Amendment, 85, 209
    Twenty-Seventh Amendment, 89, 179, 209
United States Conference of Catholic Bishops (USCCB), 128, 156, 213
United States v. Butler, 93
United States v. Morrison, 153, 225-226
United States v. Pink, 135
Universalism, 60
Unwritten Law/Traditions, 24, 26-27, 159
Usurpation(s), 20, 58, 72, 75-76, 79, 106, 114, 123, 138, 159, 179, 218-219
Utilitarianism, 5, 12, 21, 214

V

Veto, 30, 33, 37, 39, 41, 45, 71, 80, 90-91, 104, 130-131, 229, 240, 243, 248
Vice President, 34, 55, 86, 119, 121, 131-132, 140, 144, 205-209, 238, 240
Vietnam War, 85, 104, 140, 189
Violence Against Women Act, 225
Virginia, 20, 37-39, 40, 42, 46-47, 50, 54, 62, 68, 73, 95, 100, 105, 129, 178-179, 184, 187, 196, 217-218, 220, 222, 234, 239, 242, 245-246, 248, 251, 254, 258, 262
    Declaration of Rights, 178, 184
    General Assembly, 38-39
    Ratifying Convention, 100, 105-106, 179, 183, 196
Virginia Resolutions, 100, 187, 217-218, 220, 222
Virtue, 8-11, 21, 67, 116-118, 143, 214, 218, 232

INDEX

Volksmote (people's moot), 24, 26
Volstead Act, 265-266
Voluntarism (legal), 9-10, 21
Voting/Suffrage, 19-20, 24, 29, 38, 40-41, 46, 54-56, 59, 61-64, 70-72, 81, 83-85, 87-88, 90, 117-122, 126, 128, 131, 140, 145, 155-157, 159, 171-174, 181, 203, 205-207, 209, 227, 233, 235, 239-240, 242-243, 245, 248-249, 253-256, 258-264, 267

W

Waco, Texas, 226
Walpole, Robert, 37
War of 1812, 100, 180, 219
War on Poverty, 130
War Powers, 100, 102-108, 111
War Powers Act (1973), 103-105
Warrants (arrest, search), 149-150, 191-194
Warren Court, 155, 170, 262
Warren, Earl, 170
Washington, George, 10, 37, 47, 50, 53-54, 68-69, 85-86, 93, 100, 103, 116-117, 121-124, 126, 129, 137-140, 143-144, 149, 171, 173, 215, 217, 219-220, 266, 268
    Farewell Address, 129, 137
Watergate Scandal, 124, 144-145
Wealth, redistribution of, 16, 249
Weights and Measures, regulation of, 61, 101
Welfare, 61, 64, 73-74, 92-95, 130, 212
West Coast Hotel v. Parrish, 222
West Virginia, 234
Weyrich, Paul, 232
Whigs, 33, 37
Whip (Congressional), 87-88
Whiskey Rebellion, 139-140
White House, 124-125, 144, 149, 172, 240, 249, 266
    Office, 124
Wickard v. Filburn, 98, 223, 226
Wilkerson v. Utah, 201
William of Orange (King William III), 35, 37
William the Conqueror, 26
Williams, Roger, 40-41
Wilson, James, 71-72
Wilson, Woodrow, 132, 187
Winner take all (elections), 85, 87, 121
Witchcraft, Salem trials
Witnesses, 22, 80, 143, 151-152, 176, 195-198
Wollstonecraft, Mary
Women's suffrage/right to vote, 19, 56, 59, 85, 117, 121, 171, 203, 207, 254
World War I, 108, 132
World War II, 101, 135-136, 171, 214
Worship (religious), 14, 21, 37-38, 40-41, 43, 45, 49-50, 64, 184, 203, 239
Writs, 26, 34, 54, 64, 164, 178, 207
    of assistance
    of certiorari, 155
    of mandamus, 164
Wulfred, Archbishop, 24
Wyoming, 81-82, 119, 151

X

(No index entries for X)

Y

Yaocomico (Native American Tribe), 43
Yates, Robert, 73, 105
Yeardley, George, 38
Yorkshire, 24, 31
Youngstown Sheet & Tube Co. v. Sawyer, 139
Yugoslavia, 105

Z

Zablocki, Clement, 135
Zenger, John Peter
Zoning, 247, 249